S0-BUG-093

The Financial Services Handbook

EDITORIAL ADVISORY BOARD

The editors received valuable advice on the organization of *The Financial Services Handbook: Executive Insights and Solutions*, and on the selection of its contributors. This list of distinguished editorial consultants includes representatives from private industry and the academic community:

The Financial Services Handbook

EXECUTIVE INSIGHTS AND SOLUTIONS

Edited by:
EILEEN M. FRIARS
ROBERT N. GOGEL

A WILEY-INTERSCIENCE PUBLICATION
JOHN WILEY & SONS
New York · Chichester · Brisbane · Toronto · Singapore

This publication is designed to provide accurate and
authoritative information in regard to the subject
matter covered. It is sold with the understanding that
the publisher is not engaged in rendering legal, accounting,
or other professional service. If legal advice or other
expert assistance is required, the services of a competent
professional person should be sought. *From a Declaration
of Principles jointly adopted by a Committee of the
American Bar Association and a Committee of Publishers.*

Library of Congress Cataloging in Publication Data:

The Financial services handbook.

(Wiley professional banking and finance series,
ISSN 0733-8945)
"A Wiley-Interscience publication."
Bibliography: p.
Includes index.
1. Financial institutions—Management. 2. Finance.
I. Friars, Eileen M. II. Gogel, Robert N. III. Series.
HG175.F55 1987 332.1'068 86-23415
ISBN 0-471-82267-1

Printed in the United States of America
10 9 8 7 6 5 4 3 2 1

Series Preface

The worlds of banking and finance have changed dramatically during the past few years, and no doubt this turbulence will continue through the 1980s. We have established the Wiley Professional Banking and Finance Series to aid in characterizing this dynamic environment and to further the understanding of the emerging structures, issues, and content for the professional financial community.

We envision three types of book in this series. First, we are commissioning distinguished experts in a broad range of fields to assemble a number of authorities to write specific primers on related topics. For example, some of the early handbook-type volumes in the series concentrate on the Stock Market, Investment Banking, and Financial Depository Institutions. A second type of book attempts to combine text material with appropriate empirical and case studies written by practitioners in relevant fields. An early example is a forthcoming volume on The Management of Cash and Other Short-Term Assets. Finally, we are encouraging definitive, authoritative works on specialized subjects for practitioners and theorists.

It is a distinct pleasure and honor for me to assist John Wiley & Sons, Inc. in this important endeavor. In addition to banking and financial practitioners, we think business students and faculty will benefit from this series. Most of all, though, we hope this series will become a primary source in the 1980s for the members of the professional financial community to refer to theories and data and to integrate important aspects of the central changes in our financial world.

EDWARD I. ALTMAN

Professor of Finance
New York University,
School of Business

Preface

When we set out to assemble a book that would capture the latest management thinking about the apparent consolidation of the financial services industry, we envisioned a collection that would be of special value to readers in two regards. First, the authors would be attempting to look across industry segments rather than remain within the familiar but dissolving confines of a single, traditional segment such as banking or insurance. Second, the great bulk of the chapters would be written *by* executives *for* executives. Discussions would center on the authors' real-time observations about problems commonly encountered in their fields, and about some of the solutions that they had either personally witnessed or foresaw evolving.

Bringing a book to print that met these criteria has turned out to be an even bigger challenge than we expected. But we learned some valuable lessons in the process and believe that readers can also benefit from hearing what we discovered. To begin with, we were impressed with the variety of perspectives and approaches that are espoused—almost too many to catalog. Some of these perspectives, if not exactly contradictory, are so different that they could never be applied simultaneously in one firm. What is interesting, though, is that the diversity of these approaches does not signal mass confusion within the industry. Far from it. Often two approaches, while different, are both highly successful.

What we are seeing is not disorientation within the industry, but independence and the willingness to bet on nontraditional methods to succeed in a less and less traditional world. The corollary observation is this: No single approach can be right for all firms. Each institution needs to examine the particulars of its situation and choose an approach of its own.

In recruiting our authorities, we also encountered concern among some potential authors about their ability to include suggestions that would apply to all industry segments. Most authors did, perhaps courageously, adopt a cross-industry perspective. However, bankers were reluctant to speak about insurance, brokers declined to make statements about banking, and so on. Hard-won as their expertise may have been during long careers in one field, our colleagues were uncertain whether their experience might be equally valid in other areas of financial services. We ascribe much of this attitude to a commendable sense of professional modesty. Still, such widespread concern must be genuine and cannot be ignored.

At present, then, bankers remain bankers at heart, brokers remain brokers, and insurance executives remain insurance executives. In few cases do they see themselves in any broader sense as financial services managers. And remember, these are the very people who are directing the amalgamation of diverse financial services. Plainly, the movement towards a single, overarching industry will be more gradual than many of the seers outside financial services would lead us to believe.

Moreover, what strikes us is that for a long time to come financial services will be characterized, not by its homogenization, but by its subtle differences in flavors. A bank that adds brokerage to its business will offer its clientele very different advantages than its opposite, a brokerage house that extends its field of operation into banking. The reasons for this, we emphasize, are far from exclusively managerial. The economic dynamics of, say, insurance are so different from those of banking or brokerage, that achieving any kind of workable convergence is bound to be hard. Similarly, the dominant marketing approaches and technological capabilities have taken different shapes in each industry segment. Reaching easy consolidation of operation and outlook between industries is therefore difficult to imagine. Only time and novel approaches are going to create the fundamental unities required to fuse these disparate enclaves into one community.

Finally, compiling this book has given us the experience to deny the validity of one generalization that we often heard expressed. Much has been said about the stultification of managerial skills that decades of regulation ostensibly permitted. We are justifiably proud of our collaborators on *The Financial Services Handbook: Executive Insights and Solutions*. In reading the excellent chapters submitted for this book, we feel we have chosen the very best. But these are only a sample of the thinking that is going on now. The authors, we think, are representative of the many outstanding people to be found in the financial services industry. With this kind of talent, the industry is indeed an interesting place to work.

* * *

The creation of *The Financial Services Handbook: Executive Insights and Solutions* has been an extraordinary and exciting challenge for both of us. With the proliferation of business literature about various industry segments, and the consequence of a flurry of mergers, collapses, and government interventions, the task of compiling a handbook for managers that was both unique and practical became all the more difficult. However, with the assistance of a distinguished editorial advisory board and a superb list of contributing authors, we feel that the task has been accomplished.

The publication of this *Handbook* has taken the countless and tireless efforts of many people. The MAC Group, an international general management consulting firm, has been most generous to both of us in allowing us to devote a significant part of our consulting time over the past two years to this effort. We would like to thank all of our colleagues who contributed their input and assistance. We would also like to acknowledge Ed Altman, the editor of this series for John Wiley & Sons, for having originally contacted us to produce this *Handbook*.

The editorial advisory board provided both conceptual guidance in the formulation of the original outline as well as valuable assistance to the authors in reviewing drafts. We want to thank all members of the board for their patience and support throughout the duration of the project.

We would especially like to acknowledge the extraordinary organizational efforts of Linda Brady, who kept both of us on track throughout this effort, and Steve Farwell, who devoted himself to the difficult task of helping us edit such a diverse group of chapters.

Finally, we would like to thank Stephen Kippur and Nettie Bleich of John Wiley & Sons—Stephen for his enthusiasm and encouragement in undertaking this effort, and Nettie for managing the production and promotion of this *Handbook* over the past year.

We look forward to the opportunity to update this *Handbook* as the transition continues, and we would very much like to hear from our readers with comments or ideas for additional chapters.

EILEEN M. FRIARS
ROBERT N. GOGEL

Chicago, Illinois
December 1986

Contents

PART 2 MANAGING FOR SUCCESS

Contributors

SUSAN B. BASSIN is Senior Vice-President and Principal in King-Casey, Inc., a strategic marketing and design consulting firm in New Canaan, Connecticut. Clients in financial services include Merrill Lynch, Citibank, Goldome, and Citytrust. Beginning her career at McKinsey & Company, Ms. Bassin spent 10 years with ITT in New York and Europe, and was Vice-President of Marketing at the Singer Company prior to joining King-Casey. She holds an A.B. degree from Smith College and an M.B.A. from Harvard.

ROBERT N. BECK is Executive Vice-President of Bank of America's Human Resource Division in San Francisco, assuming this position in 1982 after serving as IBM Director of Benefits and Personnel Services for the previous four years. Mr. Beck is a member of various key committees within the Bank and also serves as a board member and advisor on a large number of professional, educational, and business organizations and foundations. He frequently lectures at leading universities across the United States and has been actively involved for several years in the fields of health care and aging. He has published numerous articles, coauthored two books, and is the recipient of the 1985 ASPA Personnel Executive of the Year award. He earned his bachelor's degree in business administration, and his master's degree in behavioral science and industrial relations at San Diego State University.

DAVID J. BLACKWELL is Executive Vice-President and Chief Administrative Officer of Massachusetts Mutual Life Insurance Co., with responsibility for Corporate Strategic Planning as well as the Information Systems Division and the Management Systems Division. He serves on the Corporate Management Committee of the Company, and is a Director in the MML Bay State Life Insurance Company, the MML Pension Insurance Company, and the Mass Life Insurance Company of New York, subsidiaries of Mass Mutual. He has over 20 years of experience in the insurance industry.

DAVID C. CATES is President of Cates Consulting Analysts, Inc., in New York City. Prior to forming his own firm in 1969, he worked as a bank stock analyst for M.A. Shapiro & Co., Salomon Brothers, and Shearson Loeb Rhoades. He is a member of the New York Society of Security Analysts, the Bank and Financial Analysts Association, and the Bank Industry Subcommittee of the Financial Analysts Federation. Mr. Cates and his associates consult with large and small banks on corporate strategy, financial planning, mergers, and investor relations.

Mr. Cates also publishes analytic reports on all banks, on subscribing trust departments in cooperation with the ABA Trust Division, on retail banking, on all S&Ls, and on all bank mergers. Mr. Cates is a graduate of Harvard College and the University of Chicago.

STANLEY M. DAVIS is a business advisor and writer about the management and organization of large corporations. He has worked with the senior management of many global companies on matters of strategy implementation, organization design, corporate vision and values, and management development. His clients have included Bank of America, Chase Manhattan, and Citicorp. Dr. Davis is the author of five books, including *Matrix*, *Managing and Organizing Multinational Corporations*, and *Managing Corporate Culture*. He is currently completing his sixth book, *2001: Management*, an exploration of management in the future. Dr. Davis was on the faculty of the Harvard Business School for eleven years, Columbia University's Graduate School of Business for two years, and has been Research Professor at Boston University's School of Management for seven years. He is the President of Stanley M. Davis Associates of Boston, on the Board of Directors of the MAC Group, Inc., and a member of the Board of Trustees of the Boston Ballet.

WYLIE R. DOUGHERTY is Executive Vice-President of CUNA (Credit Union National Association)/CSG for planning and development. He assumed his current post in January, 1983, after serving as President of the Arizona Credit Union League from 1977 through 1982. From 1971 to 1976 he was President of ICU Services Corporation. He was also one of the founders of U.S. Central Credit Union, and served as its first President from 1974 to 1976. Mr. Dougherty previously was Assistant Managing Director of the New Mexico Credit Union League and Manager of New Mexico Central Credit Union. He is a former member of the Association of Credit Union League Executives (ACULE), having served as First Vice-Chairman, and is currently a member of the American Society of Association Executives and American Management Associations. Mr. Dougherty attended New Mexico State University.

LAWRENCE K. FISH is Executive Vice-President of the First National Bank of Boston. He has been with the Bank of Boston since 1970, working in Brazil, Tokyo, Hong Kong, and, finally, Boston. He serves as a Board Member on a variety of civic and political organizations. Mr. Fish received his B.A. from Drake University and his M.B.A. from Harvard University.

EILEEN M. FRIARS is a Senior Vice-President and head of the Chicago office of the MAC Group, a general management consulting firm. As Co-Director of the firm's Financial Services Industry Group, she has concentrated her practice on helping banks, thrifts, finance companies, insurers, and securities firms manage strategic and organizational change as well as develop sound marketing plans. Ms. Friars has written for many business publications, including the "Corporate Planning 100 Review" of *Business Week*, *Bankers' Monthly*, and *The American Banker*. She holds an M.B.A. from Harvard University and a B.A. in Economics from Simmons College.

ROBERT N. GOGEL is a Vice-President in the MAC Group's Paris office, where he directs assignments in strategy formulation, market and financial analysis, organization and culture diagnosis. His clients have included the full range of international, regional, and money center financial institutions. He was an active contributor to Ballinger Press's *Managing Corporate Culture* and *Implementing Strategy: Making It Happen*, as well as the Bank Marketing Association's study, "The Consumer Market for Financial Services—Before and After Deregulation." Mr. Gogel holds an M.B.A. from the University of Chicago, an A.B. from Harvard University, and an applied economics degree from the Université de Louvain, Belgium.

IRA B. GREGERMAN is a Senior Productivity Management Officer at State Street Bank in Boston, and has over 25 years' experience in the field of productivity improvement. He has held management positions in the financial services industry as well as the consulting, aerospace, metalworking, and aviation industries. He has authored several articles on productivity improvement and two earlier books, *Knowledge Worker Productivity* and *Productivity Improvement: A Guide for Small Business*. He has served on the graduate school adjunct faculty of several colleges and designed and taught courses in productivity management concepts and strategies. As part of an executive loan program, Mr. Gregerman was selected as an Associate of the American Productivity Center. He is also a co-founder and past director of the American Productivity Management Association. He holds B.S.M.E. and M.S.M.E. degrees from the Polytechnic Institute of New York and an M.B.A. from Worcester Polytechnic Institute.

WILLIAM T. GREGOR is a Senior Vice-President and the co-director of the Financial Services Industry Committee of the MAC Group, a general management consulting firm which has headquarters in Cambridge, Massachusetts. He is administratively responsible for management and development of the Cambridge office of 70 professionals. His primary consulting experience has been in the areas of marketing, strategy, and organization for private and public, domestic and international clients. He has consulted to money center banks, regional banks, securities companies, insurance companies, financial exchanges, industry associations, and other financial services firms. He is author of numerous articles in the areas of strategy, marketing, and organization, as well as co-author of a book on international capital markets. Mr. Gregor holds an M.B.A. and a B.A. from Harvard University.

LAURA GROSS is an Associate Editor for *American Banker*. She first joined the *American Banker* reporting staff in 1974. In her 12-year career with *American Banker*, Ms. Gross has covered foreign, legislative, and regulatory news. She represents the newspaper periodically, speaking about consumer financial services on the Cable News Network and before conventions and conferences. She has also appeared as a guest on the CBS Morning News. She was honored as a recipient of one of the first Honorable Mentions to be awarded in the 1984 Pannell Kerr Forster Awards for Excellence in Financial Journalism for her reporting on *American Banker*'s first national consumer attitudes survey and received

Boston University's Young Alumni Achievement Award in October 1975. Ms. Gross, who also developed the *Marketing to the Affluent Directory*, received her Master of Arts degree in communications from Columbia University and a Bachelor of Arts in psychology with honors from Boston University.

PAUL HINES is Executive Vice-President of E.F. Hutton Group's Development and Finance Division, Chairman of E.F. Hutton Insurance Group, and Director of Hutton Venture Investment Partners. Mr. Hines' major responsibilities for E.F. Hutton & Company include the Corporate Development Group, the Control Department, the Treasury Department, and the Executive Development function. Prior to joining E.F. Hutton in 1970, Mr. Hines spent seven years as a consultant, first for Arthur Young & Company in 1963 and then with the MAC Group in 1966. He is the author of numerous articles and chapters, including "Relations with Professional Resources," and "Controlling Service Organizations." Mr. Hines was an initial member and one of the founders of the SIA Industry and Analysis Group. He holds an A.B. in Economics and an M.B.A. from Harvard University.

MAX D. HOPPER was named Senior Vice-President, Information Systems for American Airlines in November 1985, rejoining the airline after serving since 1982 as Executive Vice-President and head of BankAmerica Systems Engineering. At BankAmerica, Mr. Hopper was responsible for managing and applying technology as a strategic resource and an integral part of their business. He also had functional responsibility for management of application development. He began his professional career with Shell Oil Company in 1953. He served in their Exploration and Production research laboratory and their Management Information Services Department. For three years he served as Project Manager and consultant for Electronic Data Systems in Dallas and Chicago before moving to United Airlines as Director of Computer Services. Mr. Hopper is also a member of the University of California, Berkeley Computer Science Advisory Board; IBM Information Systems Customer Advisory Board; and Infomart Board of Directors. He holds a Bachelor of Science in Mathematics and an M.S. in operations research from the University of Houston.

MARK D. JOHNSON is a Senior Associate in the Chicago office of the MAC Group, a general management consulting firm. Since joining the firm, Mr. Johnson has focused on the role of distribution in creating competitive advantage. In 1984, Johnson worked with the MAC Group's Financial Services Committee to produce "Distribution: A Competitive Weapon" and in 1985, with the Marketing Development Committee, on "Channels of Distribution: Gaining a Competitive Edge." Mr. Johnson earned his B.S. in finance at Arizona State University and his M.B.A. at Harvard University.

RALPH C. KIMBALL is a Senior Associate on the Financial Services Industry Committee at the MAC Group, an international general management consulting firm. Dr. Kimball holds a B.A. degree in economics from Claremont McKenna College and the M.A. and Ph.D. degrees in economics from the University of California, Berkeley. From 1974 to 1981, he was Assistant Vice-President and

Economist at the Federal Reserve Bank of Boston, where he published numerous articles on financial institutions in the *New England Economic Review*.

MATTHEW M. LIND is a Senior Vice-President for Diversification and Corporate Development Operations at MONY Financial Services in New York. In addition to his responsibilities for MONY's Canadian, reinsurance, and securities brokerage operations, he is responsible for corporate strategic planning, development, and diversification, including acquisitions, divestitures, new business start-ups, and major cross-cutting internal development activities. Prior to joining MONY, Dr. Lind held similar responsibilities at The Travelers Corporation as Vice-President of Corporate Planning and Research. At Travelers, he was responsible for the company's diversification into securities brokerage and mortgage banking, the development of Travelers' successful business and individual cash management account programs, and major diversification efforts involving new distribution channels for the Travelers' wide range of financial services. Dr. Lind joined Travelers in 1979 from the Pension Benefit Guaranty Corporation, the Federal Government's private pension insurance agency, where he served as Executive Director during the administrations of Presidents Ford and Carter. He holds undergraduate and graduate degrees in Electrical Engineering from M.I.T. and a Ph.D. in Applied Mathematics from Harvard.

CHRISTOPHER H. LOVELOCK is a leading authority on management in the service sector. Formerly a professor at the Harvard Business School, he taught for 11 years in the school's master's, doctoral, and executive programs. He has also taught at Stanford and the University of California. Professor Lovelock has consulted to a variety of service companies in different industries, is a frequent speaker at professional associations, corporations, and nonprofit groups, and has developed and taught executive seminars to various noteworthy associations and industry organizations. Professor Lovelock's business experience includes two years in advertising with the London office of J. Walter Thompson Co. and another two years in market analysis and corporate planning with the Montreal headquarters of Canadian Industries Limited. He is author or co-author of nine books, including *Services Marketing, Marketing for Public and Nonprofit Managers*, and *Marketing Challenges: Cases and Exercises*. His articles have appeared in the *Harvard Business Review, Business Horizons, Journal of Marketing Research, Sloan Management Review, Wall Street Journal, Financial Times* of London, and other publications. In 1984, he received the Alpha Kappa Psi Foundation's award for the article in the previous year's *Journal of Marketing* that made the most significant contribution to the practice of marketing. A native of Great Britain, Professor Lovelock graduated from the University of Edinburgh with an M.A. in economics and a B.Com. degree. He is one of the few individuals to hold advanced degrees from both the Harvard and Stanford Business Schools, having obtained his M.B.A. from Harvard and his Ph.D. from Stanford.

ROWLAND T. MORIARTY is an Assistant Professor of Business Administration at Harvard University. He currently teaches Industrial Marketing and Procurement, a second year course in the M.B.A. Program. In the past, he has taught the first year Marketing course and the Creative Marketing Strategy course. He received his D.B.A. in Marketing from Harvard Business School. Prior to entering the doctoral program, he held a variety of marketing and sales management positions for Xerox Corporation and IBM Corporation. He also holds an M.B.A. in Marketing from the Wharton School and a B.A. in Biological Sciences from Rutgers University. Mr. Moriarty's research focuses on industrial and service marketing. Recent publications on these topics include a book entitled *Industrial Buying Behavior, Concepts, Issues and Applications*, and articles appearing in the *Journal of Marketing Research*, *Journal of Business Research*, and *The Sloan Management Review*. He is a consultant to a number of companies and has taught in several executive programs.

NEIL B. MURPHY is currently Professor of Finance and Director, Center for Research and Development in Financial Services, Department of Finance, School of Business Administration, University of Connecticut. Professor Murphy has completed assignments in the Federal bank regulatory agencies, the private sector, and the academic community. He started his professional career on the research staff of the Federal Reserve Bank of Boston and was also Chief, Economic Research Unit, Federal Deposit Insurance Corporation. In addition, he served as Staff Economist on the President's Commission on Financial Structure and Regulation (Hunt Commission). He was Principal Economist, Leasco Systems and Research Corporation, and Senior Vice-President, Payment Systems, Inc., then a research and consulting subsidiary of the American Express Company. His academic assignments include service on the faculties of the Universities of Maine and Oklahoma, and visiting professorships at the Amos Tuck School of Business Administration, Dartmouth College, and the Leon Recanati Graduate School of Business Administration, Tel-Aviv University. He has published extensively in the professional journals and the trade press. Professor Murphy has been on the editorial boards of the *Journal of Finance*, the *Journal of Bank Research*, and the *Journal of Retail Banking*. He has a B.S. and M.S. from Bucknell University and a Ph.D. in Economics from the University of Illinois.

JUDY A. NILSON is currently Assistant Director, Center for Research and Development in Financial Services, Department of Finance, University of Connecticut. She participates in the preparation and delivery of all the research programs of the Center. Ms. Nilson has taught courses in Financial Management in the Department of Finance. She has both a B.S. and an M.B.A. from the University of Connecticut.

R. ALAN PLATOW is Senior Vice-President, Finance and Planning, for CIGNA Worldwide. In this position, he directs the strategic and business planning functions as well as international budget, treasury, accounting and financial reporting for operations in over 85 countries. Dr. Platow has over 15 years of international experience in the financial services field including merchant banking and insurance. He holds a J.D. from the Albany Law School of Union University, and a B.A. from the University of Vermont.

M. LUCILE REID is a Vice-President in the MAC Group's Cambridge office. She joined the MAC Group in 1981 after 10 years working in the public and private sectors in both line and staff positions. Her consulting has been concentrated in the financial services industry and includes experience with banks, credit unions, life and property casualty firms, and brokerage firms. Ms. Reid has worked on the MAC Group's Financial Services Committee's annual research efforts, particularly "Money Merchandising" (1982) and "Distribution: A Competitive Weapon" (1984), and is especially knowledgeable about trust, pension, and life insurance products. Ms. Reid earned a B.A. from Smith College and an M.B.A. from Boston University.

RICHARD A. RIZZOLO is a Vice-President and Group Head of the General Services Group at Chemical Bank, where he has been employed since 1971. Mr. Rizzolo has been in Chemical's Operations Division for the last seven years, where he has also had responsibility for the Commercial Deposit and Loan Services Group as well as the division's controllership. Previous to his operations assignments, he was Controller/Treasurer of Chemical Realty Corporation, Chemical N.Y. Corporation's commercial real estate lending subsidiary. Mr. Rizzolo has an M.B.A. in finance from the Graduate School of Business Administration at New York University and an A.B. in math from Holy Cross College.

D. WILLIAM SCHREMPF is President of Teledyne's Property and Casualty Insurance Group, a position which he assumed in 1985. Prior to that he was President of CIGNA Worldwide, a $2 billion international insurer with subsidiaries and branches in more than 80 jurisdictions worldwide. Prior to his involvement in insurance, Schrempf managed medical electronics, medical imaging, and appliance businesses. He was a White House Fellow in 1972-1973. Mr. Schrempf holds an M.B.A. and an A.B. in Economics from Stanford.

RICHARD J. SHIMA is Executive Vice-President and Chief Investment Officer at The Travelers Companies with responsibility for the Real Estate Investment Department; Securities Department; Travelers Investment Management Company (TIMCO); Keystone Massachusetts Group, Inc.; Securities Settlement Corp. (SSC); and Travelers Asset Management International Corporation (TAMIC). He joined the companies in 1961 and served in various actuarial, accounting, and planning positions for both life and casualty-property operations. He was elected Senior Vice-President in 1976, and Executive Vice-President in charge of all casualty-property business including claim services in 1980. He was appointed Executive Vice-President and Chief Investment Officer in February, 1985. A cum laude graduate of Harvard University, Mr. Shima is an Associate of the Society of Actuaries and a member of the American Academy of Actuaries. He is a trustee of The Hartford Graduate Center and the Connecticut Public Expenditure Council, and a corporator of the Institute of Living as well as a Director of Hartford Hospital.

JAMES J. SMITH, JR. is a Department Manager and head of Wholesale Marketing Services for Marine Midland Bank in New York City. Smith began his professional career with J. Walter Thompson Co. (JWT) in August, 1959, with initial assignments in international and domestic marketing research. He then became an Account Supervisor, providing marketing and advertising services to a variety of major consumer, industrial, and institutional clients. In 1972, Mr. Smith served as Vice-President and head of Trust Marketing at First Chicago, and thereafter was promoted to Vice-President and Manager of Corporate Marketing. He joined Marine Midland in 1982, where he is responsible for providing marketing planning, research, and market communications support for Marine's Asset-Based Finance, Corporate Banking, International Banking, and Capital Markets businesses. Mr. Smith is presently on the Board of Directors of the Bank Marketing Association. He holds a B.S. in Marketing from the University of Notre Dame and an M.B.A. in Marketing from Michigan State University.

JOHN L. STEFFENS is President of Merrill Lynch Consumer Markets, the sector which provides investment as well as residential real estate services to individuals, partnerships, and small corporations through its nationwide network of offices. He is also an Executive Vice-President of Merrill Lynch & Co., the parent company. Mr. Steffens joined Merrill Lynch in 1963 as a member of its Junior Executive Training Program. Upon completion of the program, he became an account executive in the Merrill Lynch Cleveland office, serving there until 1970, when he attended the firm's Management Training Program, returning to Cleveland as Sales Manager of the office. In 1973, Mr. Steffens became Manager of the Birmingham, Michigan office of Merrill Lynch. He came to New York in 1975 as Manager of the Operations Planning Department. The following year, he was named Assistant Division Director of the Operations Division, and in 1978 became Division Director of Investor Products and Services. He was appointed Director of Marketing for Merrill Lynch Individual Sales in 1981. He was elected a Vice-President in 1974, a Senior Vice-President and Director of National Sales for the Consumer Markets sector and member of its Board of Directors in 1981, and Executive Vice-President of the parent company in 1985. He graduated from Dartmouth College in 1963 with a B.A. in Economics. He attended the Harvard Advanced Management Program of the Harvard Business School in 1979.

BENJAMIN V. STRICKLAND is Group Managing Director, Operations of Schroders PLC, the publicly quoted holding company for the international merchant banking and financial services group. This responsibility has included group strategy since 1982. Prior to this, he was Chairman and Chief Executive of Schroder's Australian operations, and before that a director of the London merchant bank handling mergers, acquisitions, and new issues in the Corporate Finance Division.

A. CHARLENE SULLIVAN is an Associate Professor of Management, Krannert Graduate School of Management, and Associate Director, Credit Research Center, Purdue University, where she is engaged in research in consumer credit, studying factors associated with consumer choice of adjustable- versus fixed-rate loans and time series models of loan delinquency. Dr. Sullivan has authored numerous publications dealing with consumer bankruptcy and the effects of restrictive loan rate ceilings on consumer credit markets. Dr. Sullivan received M.S.M. and Ph.D. degrees in management from Purdue University.

WILLIAM V. WHITE is Senior Vice-President and head of the Consumer Banking Division of The National Bank of Washington in the District of Columbia. His division's activities include branch banking, consumer lending, small business lending, personal trust, and marketing. He is the author of *Strategic Planning for Bankers*, published in 1984 by the American Bankers Association, and co-authored *Bank Branch Location: A Handbook of Effective Technique and Practice*, published by the Bank Marketing Association in 1973. He has authored a number of articles on financial services and has served on the faculty of two graduate banking programs. Mr. White holds a Master of Economics Degree from North Carolina State University, with a minor in business administration from the University of North Carolina at Chapel Hill. He holds Bachelor of Arts and Bachelor of Sciences degrees from North Carolina State University.

PHILLIP WILSON is a Senior Vice-President and Head of the Marketing Group at Bankers Trust Company. He began his professional career with Bankers Trust Company in their Executive Training Program from 1966 to 1968. From there he was assigned to the Europe Group, beginning as an Account Officer in 1968, Vice-President of North Europe Section in 1971, Vice-President of Europe Banking Group in 1973, Vice-President and Deputy Head of the Europe Division in 1974, and Senior Vice-President and Head of the North America Division in 1975. With over 17 years of experience in business development and management of domestic and international operations, his responsibilities have included strategic and market-level planning, including formulation of programs, implementation and evaluation criteria; management of credit and noncredit product areas; financial management of budgets, forecasts, P&L, etc.; and designing effective organizational structures. In addition to his position at Bankers Trust, he is currently working as a financial marketing consultant to the International Finance Corporation, an affiliate of the World Bank in Washington, D.C. Mr. Wilson received his B.A. in Economics with honors from Trinity College.

The Financial Services Handbook

Introduction

The Financial Services Handbook: Executive Insights and Solutions is primarily intended for managers at all levels who are active participants in the financial services industry or are affiliated with the industry in such capacities as corporate CFO, treasurer, investment analyst, and so on. The authors were asked to write their chapters from a perspective that would enable these readers to more readily identify common issues or concerns within their own organizations.

The Handbook can either be read cover to cover for a broad perspective on the financial services industry, or it can be used as a traditional handbook that provides a reference and starting point for deeper research into particular subject areas. To that end, we have divided the Handbook into two major parts.

"The Changing Industry Structure" (Part 1) is intended to provide a number of perspectives to assist readers in their own analyses of the evolving industry structure. We thought that two major themes were important to that analysis, and they are reflected in our selection of authors.

The first theme, elaborated in Section 1, is the impact of deregulation and other environmental forces on types of products offered, fundamental cost structures within the industry, the nature of competition, and customers. The second theme, explored in Section 2, pertains to the characteristic ways in which economic models are changing in each of the industry's segments. The following seven segments are covered: banks, securities firms, insurance, thrifts/savings and loans, credit unions, investment managers, and finance companies. These segments are intentionally divided along traditional industry lines—a system of organization used only in this section of the book. This decision reflects our belief that executives must first understand how they make money in their core businesses today before they embark on new ventures. An important assumption is that how money will be made in the future is apt to be quite different from the way it is made now. Further, we believe the choices executives make will necessarily differ according to the economic characteristics of their present businesses. For those readers already beginning to pursue opportunities to expand into businesses unfamiliar to them, these chapters will also be useful in fostering an understanding of how potential competitors view their own economic models.

"Managing for Success" (Part 2) looks at three key areas that can help executives to manage their institutions more effectively through the current transition period and beyond. It is our belief that the institutions which survive and prosper will require superior skills in marketing, technology, and strategy implementation. The authors in Section 3 stress the importance of choosing the right customer segments and getting close to them. In Section 4, the authors describe the key leverage points in the management of technology and operations within financial institutions. In Section 5, the authors explain the elements of managing an institution through a major strategic change.

For the benefit of readers who are thinking through plans of action for their own organizations, the editors have supplied a brief introduction to each section. The introductions highlight key issues and suggest how the chapters complement each other.

PART 1 THE CHANGING INDUSTRY STRUCTURE

SECTION 1 THE IMPACT OF DEREGULATION AND ENVIRONMENTAL FORCES

The transition from a clearly defined and stable industry structure to a redefined structure is among the toughest issues facing senior management in the financial services industry. Moreover, the prospect that the transition will continue over the next decade is very real, as various players attempt to determine a set of ground rules that will be acceptable to all interested parties, including regulators, competitors, stockholders, employees, and perhaps most importantly, customers.

Therefore, as executives continue to manage their institutions throughout this transition period, it is imperative that they analyze where their respective institutions stand within the industry structure and establish a reference point against which future strategies can be evaluated. This section is intended to facilitate that analysis.

Establishing this benchmark analysis requires a systematic self-diagnosis on the part of an institution of its competitive strengths and weaknesses, as well as of the resources available to capitalize on those strengths and attend to those weaknesses. The analysis must also examine environmental trends and regulatory activities to see how these forces are affecting current and future courses of action. Lastly, it requires an understanding of the key levers in an institution's economic model, a topic discussed in Section 2.

Surprisingly, however, many financial institutions have failed to take a realistic view of their current position before striking out into new territory. Managements often have difficulty in objectively answering such questions as:

1. Where is our firm positioned in the total financial services industry?
2. How is it positioned against:
   Competitors within our segment of the industry?
   Competitors within other segments of the industry?
   New entrants?
3. What perspectives and blind spots are influencing competitors' strategic moves? Similarly, what is influencing *our* strategies?
4. What strategic options are truly realistic for our firm?

In fact, while most institutions have gone through some formal strategic planning efforts over the past decade, and many have identified the structural shifts within the industry, few have defined the necessary actions to be taken and most have tended to underestimate the competition significantly.

In many such cases, inaction has been a result of information overload. There is so much information available covering developments in the financial services industry that many executives find themselves tuning it out completely. They need some kind of framework to sort through all of the information and make knowledgeable decisions. In other cases, executives feel that much of the information is speculative. Risk aversion, though a cultural holdover from the past, is nevertheless real. Executives prefer to wait until the future is upon them or until a competitor makes the first move before acting. Waiting to see what will happen is understandable as an impulse, but it certainly does nothing to improve management of activities through this transition period. A simple yet comprehensive process must be put in place to keep the management team informed of what is going on in the industry on an ongoing basis, and to alert them to how those developments may affect the strategic position of the institution. Management need not be, and rarely is, 100 percent accurate in predicting the outcome or direction of the industry shifts around it; rather, management needs to be concerned with developing enough flexibility within the institution to respond to various scenarios, whichever might occur.

The purpose of this first section is to describe how the financial services industry got to be where it is today and what it may look like in the future. As a result of changing regulatory structure, customer sophistication, and the growth of technology, the industry has found itself faced with a new and continually changing set of rules. It is likely that for the next several years, most institutions will have to live with some ambiguity and adapt themselves to a new environment. This section provides several important perspectives on how managers can do that, by examining the factors that will continue to influence industry change.

In Chapter 1, Matthew Lind discusses the nature of competition that is evolving across the industry. Matt, who has unusually broad experience in financial services, currently directs diversification development activities at MONY Financial Services. As industry change unfolds, he believes competitive analysis will be a cornerstone in successful strategies.

Similarly, customers cannot be ignored, as they will ultimately determine what will be bought and from whom. Laura Gross, a veteran financial reporter at *American Banker,* takes the consumers' perspective, describes their reactions to recent changes, and suggests how institutions might best respond to customer concerns. Chapter 3 is written by Neil Murphy and Judy Nilson, who head the University of Connecticut's Center for Research and Development in Financial Services. From a rigorous historical perspective, the chapter describes how the nature of product and service offerings has evolved as a result of major regulatory and environmental changes. Neil was personally involved in much of the regulatory activity, both as a staff economist for the Hunt Commission and later in an executive capacity in private industry. Finally, in Chapter 4 Benjamin Strickland reviews how the globalization of financial services has added yet another level of pressure to industry executives who must now take on a much broader perspective in managing their businesses. Ben is group managing director, operations, of Schroders PLC, the British-based international merchant banking firm.

The ambiguity of the future will not lessen over the next few years, but we hope the insights in these chapters can provide a useful guide for senior executives who are trying to gauge the changes likely to occur and the directions that their institutions should take.

1 The Impact of Deregulation and Environmental Forces: Competition

MATTHEW M. LIND

In a letter written not long ago to his senior management, George Dixon, president and CEO of First Bank System, Inc. of Minneapolis, compared deregulation of financial services to paddling a canoe along a smooth, placid river and then suddenly entering a long stretch of boiling, rushing, churning white water filled with rocks—some seen and some unseen.[1] In Dixon's words: "Competition in the banking industry today is like a white-water river: once in it, the only choice is to get through without swamping. There's no turning back."

I think this "white water" metaphor is apropos for just about every one of us in financial services. Probably nothing dominates the thoughts of top financial services executives more than the prospects and consequences of deregulation. In fact, some measure of deregulation has already arrived on a de facto basis, and we are moving irresistibly toward a more competitive industry.

As recently as early 1984, many of us believed that broad-scale deregulation was a good possibility by 1985 or 1986. At that time, there were several bills in Congress that would have substantially expanded the permissible geographic and business scope of financial firms, especially banks. Since then, a number of events and forces have conspired to slow the advance of deregulation. Concerns over foreign loans, the debacles of Continental Illinois and Financial Corporation of America, and the growing number of banks and S and Ls on various federal "watch lists" have added a semblance of credibility to those who would have banks "stick to their knitting." Election-year politics was also clearly at play, tending to work in favor of the status quo rather than major change.

Certain observers see these and other developments as signaling a long-term slowdown in deregulation; others see them merely as temporary setbacks. The outlook for financial services deregulation, however, is probably less important than the actual fact of "*deregulated thinking*" which is found today in the industry. In fact, legal or formal deregulation may turn out to be a nonevent, merely ratifying what has already taken place in the market.

In the last decade, and especially in the last five years, innovative companies have overcome or gotten around many perceived regulatory restrictions and barriers. They have achieved this "de facto deregulation" by exploiting available technology; by reinterpreting and testing the limits of existing laws; and by entering into creative product, service, and distribution combinations with other firms having complementary capabilities.

To understand this point, note the chart (Exhibit 1.1, adapted from data by Citicorp) illustrating "who does what" in financial services. A quick look shows banks selling securities services; big insurance companies and financial service conglomerates doing pretty much everything; and a number of nontraditional competitors such as Kroger and K-Mart offering a fairly diversified range of consumer services. Moreover, although not illustrated, credit subsidiaries of such major manufacturers as General Electric, General Motors, Ford Motor Company and IBM have significantly expanded both their consumer and commercial lending activities. Although started primarily for the purpose of financing product sales and dealer inventories, these companies are now moving to use their asset-based lending expertise, their data processing capabilities, and their appetite for tax credits and depreciation as leverage into the areas of consumer and commercial lending.

While government can put the brakes on deregulation in some areas and possibly call a halt in others, it will not materially arrest de facto deregulation. In effect and without any really major legislative reform, innovative companies have rewritten the law. For when companies start thinking "customer" instead of product—when they begin to really appreciate the importance of technology and getting their costs down; and when consumers continue to demonstrate growing sophistication in price, performance, and supplier alternatives—then only the strictest "*re*regulation" can stem the drive towards a more competitive industry. And given current "white water" conditions, there seems to be little possibility of that happening!

Thus, while various industry participants and interest groups may continue to work at removing, perpetuating, or adding to regulatory imbalances, successful competitors will need to think and plan as if deregulation were here.

It is within this context of "de facto" deregulation that this chapter has been organized. In the section immediately following, the key developments flowing from deregulation in the various industries are reviewed. Against this backdrop, the next section explores the broad competitive structure emerging in financial services. The final substantive section examines the more specific business strategies and tactics that will likely be pursued by successful financial services competitors.

Exhibit 1.1 Who Does What

Product/Service	*Commercial Bank*	*American Express*	*Merrill Lynch*	*Prudential*	*Sears*	*Kroger*	*K–Mart*	*Control Data*
Take $/Pay Int.	■	■	■	■	■	■	■	■
Check Writing	■	■	■	■	■	■		■
Loan	■	■	■	■	■			■
Mortgage	■	■	■	■	■			■
Credit Card	■	■	■	■	■			■
Interstate Branches		■	■	■	■	■	■	■
Money Market	■	■	■	■	■	■		
Securities	■	■	■	■	■	■		■
Life Insurance		■	■	■	■	■	■	■
Property Insurance		■	■	■	■	■	■	■
Casualty Insurance		■	■	■	■	■	■	■
Mortgage Insurance		■	■	■	■			■
Real Estate		■	■	■	■			■
Cash Management Acct.	■	■	■	■	■			

THE NEW ENVIRONMENT

A few years ago, McKinsey & Company undertook a study[2] of the deregulation experience in the following five industries: securities brokerage, airlines, trucking, railroads, and business communications terminal equipment. Their main objective was to provide some useful insights and lessons to companies in industries on the threshold of deregulation. In all of the industries studied, deregulation was followed by three key and related industry developments.

The elimination of competitive restraints quickly brought about a much greater variety of product/service offerings and price/service tradeoffs for customers. In the airline industry, for example, the number of fare structures almost tripled during the four-year period following deregulation in 1977. In banking, the phase-out of interest rate ceilings on deposits brought about a virtual explosion in fee structure, interest rate, and service level combinations available to depositors.

The second key development was the rapid entry of new low-cost producers. In most cases, these new players focused their efforts on price-sensitive market segments, discount brokerage firms and "no frills" airline carriers being obvious examples. The new players generally achieved lower costs by avoiding significant industry-wide structural costs which had typically built up over the years. These include generous labor contracts, high commission levels, executive perquisites, and lavish facilities, to name just a few.

More generally, the entry of new low-cost competitors that target price-sensitive customers is likely to intensify indirectly the competition in other customer segments as well. Unable to compete effectively for price-sensitive customers, many firms will redouble their efforts to woo more quality- and service-conscious customers. In financial services, for example, most banks and life insurance companies are planning significant increases in the resources they allocate to serving the currently more profitable affluent client. Eventually, of course, this stampede to the affluent will drive down prices and erode profitability. Thus, the obvious result of new low-cost capacity in one major customer segment is eventually to drive prices down in almost all segments, thereby putting tremendous pressure on the margins of established competitors.

Shrinking margins result in the third key development: the intensified introduction of new technology and drastic cost-reduction programs. Following trucking deregulation, for example, layoffs by local and national transport carriers amounted to 20 percent of teamster union members; in the airlines, over 2000 pilots belonging to the Air Line Pilots Association (ALPA) were laid off within one year of deregulation as major carriers sought to get costs in line with new low-cost entrants. This drop of more than 5 percent followed decades of sustained growth in employment.

In financial services, it's the same story. Just about any annual report of a significant financial services company these days shows a healthy amount of copy devoted to cost-reduction efforts. Whereas product and service improvements might have dominated the stage in the recent past, today's watchwords are "cost-reduction" and "productivity." And for financial services, technology is, of course, a key weapon in the cost-reduction arsenal.

But it is very much more than a cost reducer, for much of the technology from which our industry expects to realize productivity improvements can simultaneously improve and add to both product offerings and service levels. Transaction services via video text or home computers can not only lower costs, but can also significantly add to customer convenience. By lowering the cost of expert advice, artificial intelligence software has the potential to bring meaningful financial advice within the price range of middle-income households, not just the affluent. And the continuing price/performance improvements in data processing hardware, software, and communication, augurs not only greater back-office productivity, but far greater opportunities to package products and services in ways that afford still greater convenience and helpfulness for customers.

Finally, the application of data processing, information, and communications technology can significantly alter the power relationships and dependencies that have traditionally existed among manufacturers, distributors, and customers in various key market sectors of financial services.[3] In fact, the application of technology for such purposes is a major, if not the key, element of business strategy for many companies.

For weaker firms, these three developments create a vicious circle. To meet intensified competition, most firms in an industry must invest heavily to acquire new technology, new product capabilities, or new distribution channels. In the case of weaker firms, this need to invest comes at the same time that access to capital markets is becoming more difficult to obtain as a result of declining profitability. These firms are obliged to forego necessary investments, thus further weakening their competitive position. And eventually, many such firms may have no choice but to go out of business or sell out to a stronger competitor.

THE EMERGING COMPETITIVE STRUCTURE

Four Strategies

In the industries they studied, McKinsey found that following deregulation, firms that are emerging successfully have pursued one of the four basic strategies, delineated in Exhibit 1.2.

- Firms pursuing a national distribution strategy and typically serving a broad geographic range of customers who typically buy a full line of attractively priced products and services.
- Low-cost producers—usually new entrants to an industry—that generally provide a narrower line of products targeted on customers willing to accept lower service levels in return for a low price.
- Specialty or "niche" firms that operate in still more narrowly defined markets, leveraging specialized skills or customer relationships into high value-added services that make entry of new competitors difficult.
- Finally, firms pursuing a "community" or local area strategy. By operating in smaller, relatively isolated areas, established community firms have been

Exhibit 1.2 Strategies to Prosperity

Strategies	Brokerage	Airlines	Trucking	Railroads	Business Terminal Equipment
National Distribution Company	Merrill Lynch	Delta Airlines	Consolidated Freightways	Burlington Northern	Western Electric
Low-Cost Producer	Charles Schwab	Midway Air	Overnite Transportation	None	Oki
Specialty Firm	Goldman Sachs	Frontier Airlines	Ryder Systems	Illinois Central	Northern Telecom
Community/ Regional Firm	A.G. Edwards	Ransome Airlines	None	El Dorado and Wesson	None

Strategies for prosperity in deregulated industries.

largely protected from outside competition owing to the disproportionately high distribution costs a new competitor would likely incur to enter their market. Lacking intense competition, successful community firms typically offer a fairly full line of products to a broad range of customers within their geographic scope.

Both by tradition and regulation, most financial service firms have typically operated in one or perhaps two of the industry's three major segments: banking, insurance, or investment services. But many barriers have fallen—de facto deregulation again—and will likely disappear entirely as formal deregulation progresses.

Thus, the possibilities facing firms are many. They involve numerous choices as to customers, geographic presence, product scope, service level, and distribution. But by applying the lessons of other industries, we can reasonably project the broad pattern of competition for financial services. In fact, we can already see its outlines.

Competitive Patterns

The first key competitive pattern will be "conglomeration" (see Exhibit 1.3). General conglomerates will be firms seeking to provide, largely in-house, a full range of services to diverse customer groups on a nationwide basis. Citicorp, Bank America, Merrill Lynch, and American Express fall into this category.

Specialized conglomerates are firms that limit themselves to a major market area (see Exhibit 1.4). Sears, for example, is seeking to provide banking, insurance, and investment services to a broad cross-section of consumers. And for

Exhibit 1.3 Conglomerate Strategies

Major Industry Segments

Strategies	*Business* Banking	*Business* Insurance	*Business* Inv. Services	*Consumers* Banking	*Consumers* Insurance	*Consumers* Inv. Services
National Distribution	• Citicorp	• Bank of America		• Merrill Lynch	• American Express	
Low-Cost Production						
Specialization						
Local Distribution						

Companies positioning themselves as financial service conglomerates.

Exhibit 1.4 Specialized Conglomerate Strategies

Major Industry Segments

Strategies	*Business* Banking	*Business* Insurance	*Business* Inv. Services	*Consumers* Banking	*Consumers* Insurance	*Consumers* Inv. Services
National Distribution	• Bankers Trust	• CIGNA			• Sears	
Low-Cost Production						
Specialization						
Local Distribution						

Companies positioning themselves as more specialized financial service conglomerates now at least, Sears is showing no significant appetite for the corporate or business market. CIGNA, on the other hand, is emphasizing broad insurance services to business, while Bankers Trust is focusing on banking services, again targeted on businesses.

"Mass marketing" will be another key competitive pattern (see Exhibit 1.5). In this category, we will primarily find low-cost firms emphasizing no-frills financial services to consumer segments. In investment services, for example, low-cost direct response marketing skills have enabled Fidelity Management Company to establish a strong position among those affluent investors not desiring or willing to pay for a high degree of personal service. Kroger Stores, on the other hand, is focusing on distributing financial services to middle-income consumers. Kroger emphasizes basic insurance, investment, and payment services, conveniently delivered. Other consumer goods retailers, like K mart and Zayre, are moving in a similar direction, executing strategies that emphasize low-cost distribution of financial products sourced from outside suppliers.

As in other industries, financial services will have its "specializers" or "niche" players—firms that bring a high degree of value-added services to a relatively narrow customer base (see Exhibit 1.6). Donaldson, Lufkin and Jenrette, recently acquired by the Equitable Life Assurance Society, has, for example, established a strong "niche" position in institutional trading and money management. In insurance, General Reinsurance has been immensely successful in providing reinsurance, primarily to other carriers. This company has chosen a relatively narrow field within insurance and focused on being very, very good at

Exhibit 1.5 Mass-Marketing Strategies

Major Industry Segments

	Business			*Consumers*		
Strategies	Banking	Insurance	Inv. Services	Banking	Insurance	Inv. Services
National Distribution						
Low-Cost Production					• Kroger	• Fidelity
Specialization						
Local Distribution						

Financial service companies pursuing mass-marketing strategies.

Exhibit 1.6 Specialization Strategies

Major Industry Segments

Strategies	Business			Consumers		
	Banking	Insurance	Inv. Services	Banking	Insurance	Inv. Services
National Distribution						
Low-Cost Production						
Specialization		• GEN-RE	• DLJ	• US Trust		
Local Distribution						

Financial service companies pursuing "niche" or specialization strategies.

it. And U.S. Trust Company, after flirting with extending its banking and trust services to a more broad-based affluent clientele, has returned to its roots of targeting only the very affluent with highly personalized service.

The final key competitive pattern of the industry will be "networking." One of the key elements of strategy for community firms is linking up with a major service provider for services that are either too expensive or too difficult for them to provide on their own. Many short-haul or "feeder" airlines, for example, have established agreements with a major carrier for ground personnel and marketing support. In financial services, new low-cost delivery technologies, in particular, will pose a threat to community firms by lowering or eliminating the economic barriers that have long sheltered such firms from outside competition. Telemarketing, ATMs, video-text, and in-home computer banking services are clear examples of such new distribution technology.

While community firms can look to customer loyalty and stress personal services as part of their defense, they will be under unprecedented pressures to broaden their services, price more competitively, cut their costs, and, more generally, improve productivity. To accomplish this they will have to go outside to source many of the new products, services, and technology they need.

Thus, it might not be uncommon for a community bank to sell insurance and investment products produced and franchised by a financial conglomerate. For the bank, such an arrangement might be an effective means to improve both its survivability and its profitability; for the conglomerate, it may be a low-cost and effective means to broaden distribution. This situation is illustrated in Exhibit 1.7. The dark areas denote those products and services offered by the bank which are

Exhibit 1.7 Networking Strategies

Major Industry Segments

Strategies	*Business*			*Consumers*		
	Banking	Insurance	Inv. Services	Banking	Insurance	Inv. Services
National Distribution	Conglomerate					
Low–Cost Production						
Specialty Firm						
Local Distribution		Small Community Bank				

A networking strategy being pursued by a community bank with a conglomerate.

sourced from the conglomerate; the shaded areas, those products and services provided in-house.

The concept of networking is of course nothing new. After all, supplier-distributor relationships have existed for years. What is new here is the emerging scale, scope, and structure of such relationships and the increasing interdependencies involved.

New competitive necessities—coupled with needs to get to market quickly, to expand distribution rapidly and economically, to find scarce capital to undertake in-house development efforts, or to keep costs both competitive and variable—are bringing new players together under generally tighter relationships. These relationships often involve longer-term commitments, more explicit sharing of costs and profits, and frequently greater joint visibility to customers.

THE BASIS OF COMPETITION: BUSINESS STRATEGY AND TACTICS

The position of a particular financial services firm within this macro competitive structure will largely result from the specific or micro business strategies adopted.

Elements of Winning Business Strategies

In virtually all industries, successful business strategies typically exhibit a strong market focus characterized by a well-defined customer segmentation, and a combination of products, services, and distribution methods that not only respond to customer needs but also clearly target competitor vulnerabilities. Whether the emphasis is on low-cost, quality, customer service, innovation, or leveraging some important corporate strengths (such as an established image and customer base)—successful business strategies seek a decisive, significant edge, and these strategies must be *capable of being executed.*

This last point cannot be overstressed. Too often these days the idea of being "market oriented" or "market driven" is confused with being merely "customer oriented." No doubt, a successful market-driven company will both understand and respond to customers. But it will also be expert at selecting those market opportunities at which *it* can succeed, and at which *it* can develop sustainable competitive advantages. To do this, it will know the strengths, weaknesses, and strategies of key competitors in relation to its own capabilities and market position. Thus, it will know which strategies it can execute, and which it cannot.

Large Company Strategy: Broad Markets

Against this backdrop, the business strategies of most large financial service companies are likely to emphasize large market segments; that is, market segments which by virtue of the customers, products, and services involved have large-scale revenue and profit potential.

Typically, these scale considerations will push large companies towards strategies incorporating nationwide distribution of a wide range of products and services to relatively broad customer groups. Business strategies that are more focused, and consequently smaller in scale, are not likely to receive support in large organizations. More often than not, they will be perceived as just not worth the management time and attention involved. In the space program during the 1960s, for example, NASA found it almost impossible to get large aerospace companies to exploit the commercial potential of much of the new technology developed as part of the Apollo and other major space exploration programs. Instead, this "commercialization" breach was filled by smaller firms, frequently created by entrepreneurial engineers leaving the aerospace giants.

Thus, while large financial services companies will continue to speak about not being all things to all people, many of them will leave themselves vulnerable to smaller competitors who can chip away at their customer base by tailoring products, service levels, and distribution methods to specific customer subsegments. In this regard, it is probable that the top-tier large competitors of the future will be those companies that can bring more focused customer segmentation to their business strategies and that organize accordingly. Accomplishing this, however, will not be easy. It will require an unusual blend of "loose" and "tight" management style—loose in its encouragement and support of new ideas, risk-taking, and experimentation; and tight in its insistence on customer focus, the pursuit of competitive advantage, and the integration of various business strategies across the company from the standpoint of financial objectives, technology, duplicative resources, and strategy consistency.

Small Company Strategy: Niching and Networking

At the other end of the spectrum, smaller financial services firms will, in most cases, gravitate towards niche or networking strategies. They will simply not be able to execute business strategies calling for significant in-house financial, technological, and human resources; hence, they will need to focus their efforts sharply, and seek to reduce personnel requirements and both investment and operating costs by means of relationships with other firms having complementary capabilities and compatible objectives.

Whether networking will result in long-term survivability for smaller firms is a subject of hot debate. To some extent, survivability will depend upon the market segments involved. Generally, where smaller firms have positioned themselves to participate in noncommodity market segments, networking can help them to compete effectively over the long term. For example, a small securities broker-dealer serving affluent clients and stressing a high degree of professional competence and personal service can compete with the Merrill Lynches of the world if it can have access to comparable research, products, back-office services, and other support from suppliers. On the other hand, in commodity-type markets, where price is highly important, it may be more difficult for a smaller firm to develop networking relationships that deliver services at the same low cost and with the convenience that a diversified, fully integrated and nationally recognized competitor offers.

What makes this issue problematic is that scale economies in many financial services occur at relatively low volumes. Moreover, there is a growing number of firms that are positioning themselves as wholesalers of both products and technology support services to other firms. The Travelers, for example, has widely stated its objective to become a leading wholesaler of a broad range of financial products and support services to independent relationship-oriented distributors serving affluent households and small businesses. Automated Data Processing, Inc. (ADP), for years a leading supplier of back-office data processing services to banks, brokerage firms, and credit unions, has extended its services to include ATM networks, cash management accounts and, shortly, in-house banking for the customers of the financial institutions it supports.

But despite all the alternatives available to smaller competitors, many will conclude that there are no really attractive options for going it alone. The lucky or smart ones may reach this decision early and be able to sell out at attractive prices. Others, however, will wait too long, and will be forced to sell under distressed circumstances. In any event, we are likely to witness substantial consolidation in many industry sectors, especially banking and insurance. The consolidation of independent insurance agencies into a smaller number of larger agencies has been underway for years; and the recent Supreme Court decision approving regional interstate banking pacts can be expected to precipitate a spate of regional bank mergers and acquisitions motivated by desires to capture customers, eliminate duplicative resources, improve scale economies, and leverage developmental investments into a more profitable enterprise.

Key Competitive Themes

The specific business strategies and tactics adopted by various firms will be as varied as the firms themselves, reflecting their size, traditions, capabilities, and current market positions. Nevertheless, three major recurring and related themes will be perceived in all this variety: first, customer segmentation is becoming more focused and is taking some nontraditional approaches; second, the expansion and control of distribution channels is being more strongly emphasized; and, finally, technology is being aggressively applied, not only to lower costs, but also to redefine products and services and gain greater access to and control over both end customers and distributors.

Customer Focus

Many examples of these themes are currently visible in financial services. In banking, for example, the intense competition for the business of large corporations by major money center and regional banks that occurred in the 1970s has given way to a new focus on smaller corporations, emphasizing personal relationships and relationship-based selling of a variety of fee-generating products and services.[4]

As the large corporate markets have become increasingly price competitive and commodity-like, most commercial banks have had to redirect their efforts to those customer segments where they have the potential to differentiate themselves on the basis of value-added services. Similarly, many community banks, which have traditionally positioned themselves to serve relatively undifferentiated local consumer and small business segments, are beginning to focus their efforts towards small business owner-managers. In addition to offering broader products and personal advisory services, some of the more innovative of these smaller banks are experimenting with conducting their small business banking services out of small business centers or specialized branches.

In fact, as these trends evolve, we may eventually see many formerly retail-oriented bank branches transformed into small business centers, with retail customers largely served via automated "kiosk" type branches supplemented by a few traditional "bricks-and-mortar" facilities.

Particularly significant in all of this is that for perhaps the first time, many banks are not just talking about being customer-oriented, but are actually developing and experimenting with business strategies that incorporate customer-differentiated products, services, distribution, delivery, and promotional approaches. In addition, they are organizing themselves around these market-oriented business thrusts. While many of these efforts may not succeed competitively—because of poor execution, inability to build a lasting competitive edge, and so on—they nonetheless underscore the growing trend toward more focused customer segmentation as the foundation of business strategy.

Packaged Services: One-Stop Shopping

Among consumer segments, most emerging business strategies are emphasizing a combination of new distribution channels, delivery methods, and advanced technology. So-called "one stop" or "one source" shopping strategies are prime examples of this. Firms pursuing this type of strategy—most notably Sears—are seeking to become the primary, if not the single, source of their customers' key financial services. By using advanced back-office transaction and record-keeping systems capable of integrating diverse product relationships on a customer account basis, firms offering one-source shopping not only can make various products more convenient to use (e.g., check access to credit lines, automatic fund transfers among accounts, integrated statements) but have the potential to substantially lower overall administrative expenses and efficiently implement joint pricing programs as part of cross-selling efforts.

Such technology therefore positions these firms to build upon almost any initial financial service relationship, especially if the relationship allows them regular and convenient customer contact for purposes of product sales and promotion. In this latter regard, retailers such as Sears, Kroger, Penney, and K-Mart hope to parlay direct response marketing techniques and the heavy retail traffic in their stores into multiple financial service relationships with both existing and new customers.

Although the concept of one-source shopping largely grew out of Merrill Lynch's milestone development of the cash management account (CMA) for its affluent brokerage customers, its greatest potential seems to lie among middle-income groups. These customers typically have relatively basic financial needs and are relatively price sensitive and convenience oriented. The nature of their needs does not require the customized products, the service levels, or the advice-giving skills sought by the affluent. Packaging of the basic commodity-type services most needed by middle-income groups into a single bundle will have real attraction for them (although the services need not be bought on a bundled basis at the same time). While certain retailers may be able to pursue such "financial supermarket" approaches successfully, commercial banks, thrift institutions, and credit unions may be in even stronger positions because of their relatively high degree of public trust and existing consumer financial relationships.

Although the convenience and price advantages of one-source shopping would also be attractive to higher income groups, the high service levels, sophisticated advice, and product tailoring required will likely make this strategy a very difficult one for almost any firm to pursue. High-income households can therefore be expected to continue to maintain multiple relationships with more specialized providers.

But the rewards of bringing these relationships together remain high. The need is there, and many firms are currently trying to respond. Private banking services, financial planning practices, and groups of affiliated financial service specialists practicing out of a common facility are all examples of efforts to serve affluent customers on a "holistic," total relationship basis.

Control of Distribution Channels

For large institutions, such affluent consumer-oriented strategies may be especially difficult. In addition to the expenses involved in attracting, training, and retaining capable people, large institutions will constantly face the loss or turnover of customers who follow departing employees (either cannibalized by other firms or going out on their own) unless they can shift customer ties away from their customer or sales representatives and onto the firm or institution itself. In fact, one of the supposedly unspoken objectives of Merrill Lynch's CMA account has been to tie customers more closely with Merrill, thereby shifting power away from the firm's registered sales representatives (RRs), and eventually permitting Merrill to reduce broker commissions. Similarly, one of the objectives of Travelers' Capital T cash management account (provided on a wholesale basis through correspondent broker-dealers of Travelers' clearing and execution services subsidiary, Securities Settlement Corporation) was to make it more difficult for correspondents to shift to other back-office firms because of the complexities of untying their customers from the Travelers' cash management service.

Both of these examples illustrate technological approaches to "co-opting" independent distributors (even Merrill's company-employed sales force can be viewed, in actuality, as independent contractors) by gaining greater control over end customers. More generally, many firms, through a variety of tactics and strategies, are seeking to gain greater control over their distribution channels. First Interstate Bancorp, for example, is attempting to leverage its name and many of its back-office, product, and service capabilities via franchising arrangements with regional banks. Moreover, this unique restructuring of traditional "wholesale" banking relationships positions First Interstate for nationwide interstate banking if and when that occurs.

In insurance, a few independent and career agency companies are beginning to develop or expand their mass marketing approaches to both consumer and small business markets, using a combination of association sponsorship and direct response marketing techniques. Through such methods, they are hoping to develop large numbers of quality customer leads, thereby giving them greater leverage in their share of an agent's business; increased ability to reduce agent commissions to more competitive levels; and a better opportunity to go direct, if necessary.

Expansion of Distribution Channels

In addition to strategies that seek to "co-opt" or restructure existing distributors, many financial service firms are simultaneously seeking to expand their distribution channels as well; and much of this distribution diversification flows out of nontraditional ways of segmenting customers.

A number of firms, for example, have targeted home buyers as a key consumer segment, and are executing strategies involving bundling home buyer services (e.g., mortgages, insurance, moving services, home furnishing discounts, etc.)

distributed via direct marketing (Prudential), realtors (Merrill Lynch), financial supermarkets (Sears, K-Mart), or some combination thereof. Underlying all of these efforts is the recognition that for most consumers, most of their financial purchases and relationships arise or change in the context of buying a home. Thus, by simply looking at customers in this way, these firms have opened up a whole range of new and powerful business strategies.

Other firms are beginning to focus their distribution diversification efforts on the workplace, emphasizing convenient delivery of basic financial services to credit union members or middle-income employees of large corporations, and using payroll deduction. Especially for large multiline insurance companies—those having both substantial employee benefits and individual financial services businesses—workplace distribution is a way to both lower distribution costs and finesse agent distribution problems.

SUMMARY

Against this broad backdrop of emerging competition, it is not surprising that most financial services firms—large and small—are today busily trying to figure out their strategies, conceive appropriate actions, and take farsighted positioning steps.

The stakes are high. For many firms it is a matter of survival. But the surviving firms—the "winners"—will be those that can effectively choose from among the many strategy options available. While they will vary as to size, market focus, and business strategy, these winning firms will share certain attributes: they will know customers, they will know competitors and—perhaps most important—they will know their own capabilities, all of which augurs well for the customers for whose benefit these firms exist.

NOTES

1. Bleeke, J. A., *The McKinsey Quarterly* (Summer 1983).
2. Ibid.
3. Light, D., and G. Warfel, Jr., "Distribution Strategies for Services," *SRI Business Intelligence Program Research Report No. 698* (Winter 1983–1984).
4. Masson, P. A., "Trends in Corporate Financial Services," *SRI Business Intelligence Program Research Report No. 696* (Winter 1983–1984).

2 The Impact of Deregulation and Environmental Forces: Customers

LAURA GROSS

One hundred years from now historians will look back at today's America to judge deregulation's success. Will they picture a financial services system awash in volatility and uncertainty? Or will they see one thriving on the freedom to create new products and distribution alternatives, one where prices are competitive and everyone is served through the constant tension in the free market? There is no way of telling at this point since financial services today are in the midst of the transition into that as yet indiscernible world. This chapter will leave these determinations to the historians. Instead, it will explore the customer's reaction, as seen today, to both deregulation and the other forces that have begun shaping the new worldwide financial system up to mid-1985.

The myriad changes which have been occurring in the financial services world are the result of many forces, perhaps the most important of which achieved prominence when the economic expansion of the 1960s, the boom years, collided with the harsher economic realities of inflation prevalent throughout most of the 1970s. For financial institutions, the birth of a new kind of economic scenario promising high and volatile market interest rates began a series of events which has led to the complete upheaval of banking and financial services as it was once known in America and around the world.

In addition to the increased cost of funds, inflationary pressures have caused operating costs to skyrocket, producing a new emphasis on the automation and technology which financial intermediaries thought could help balance the new volatility. Vanishing spreads have led to a cry for diversification as financial intermediaries concentrate on driving as many products through their existing distribution systems as possible. New, more automated forms of distribution have also been created in an effort to deliver products to customers anywhere and anytime.

The old boundaries marking off what is a bank from what is a stockbroker, insurance company, mutual fund firm, finance company, thrift institution, or retailer are vanishing in a world whose principal imperative is the need to maintain profitability. Although deregulation has evolved as a way to create what has been called a "level playing field," giving all financial intermediaries a fighting chance in the new economy, the other forces shaping this economy have also contributed to the political debate in the 1980s. Financial services deregulation follows the deregulation of other American industries and is part of a general transition from a manufacturing-oriented to an information- and service-oriented society.

DEREGULATION IN AMERICA

By 1986 the term "deregulation" has become as familiar as "apple pie" or "inflation." First it was the oil companies and railroads, then the airlines, and, most recently, the break-up of Ma Bell which captured headlines and attention. Most people by now have experienced first-hand the effects of deregulation on at least one of these industries and accordingly have developed a set of conceptions and expectations about the process. In these already-deregulated industries, deregulation has substantially increased competition and lowered prices, creating more alternatives. This evolution of new options has both negative and positive consequences.

On the negative side, increased choice has brought with it increased complexity: There are people who are still struggling to understand their new, seven-page telephone bills more than a year after the break-up of Ma Bell; even airline representatives have difficulty comprehending the restrictions on new, lower airfares; cars hesitate at service station entrances as drivers debate whether to spend a few extra pennies being served as opposed to doing it themselves. On the positive side, buyers are no longer trapped into doing business with only a few, usually high-priced service providers.

Proponents of deregulation argue that greater complexity is a small price to pay for lowering costs and increasing the availability of services. The price, in fact, is fair only so long as people risk nothing they did not risk before, or so long as they take actions that put them at risk only with full awareness of the potential consequences. Ask them to take new risks implicitly—without explaining to them the new rules—and it is a safe bet that most people will get angry.

That is one reason for what can be seen today as a consumerist backlash to financial services deregulation. Most consumers as yet understand deregulation as nothing more than receiving market rates of interest on their deposits and paying market rates on their loans. They do not even understand that paying a fair market rate for a loan causes them to share the interest rate risk with the financial services provider making the loan.

No one ever asked consumers if they wanted to share that risk. Yet, without fully comprehending, people are confronted by two facts: that retail and corporate customers have lost money in the failure of banks and thrifts, and that securities firms plagued by 24-hour trading schedules and increased competition have bitten the dust, taking the potential profits of corporate traders along with them. They read newspaper stories that say deregulation of the securities business has produced new, grey areas of activity. Money brokering, they hear, has been questioned for its possible role in contributing to these failures. Branches of banks and thrifts have closed, leaving communities without banking services. Fees have increased dramatically for services that once were free. Adjustable rate mortgages and variable rate business loans do not promote a sense of security in a world where uncertainty about the future of interest rates has become commonplace.

Yet deregulation also provides opportunities for financial institutions to diversify, a step that can reduce risk if done wisely. Charles S. Sanford Jr., president of Bankers Trust Co., N.Y., explained it succinctly in a 1984 speech delivered at the Robert Morris Associates annual fall conference: "There may not be much that economists agree upon, but one of them is this: diversification reduces risk. . . . In other words, the business enterprise which diversifies is more likely to be a profitable and safe enterprise."

William M. Isaac, former chairman of the Federal Deposit Insurance Corp., agreed with that diagnosis when he said that the rescue of Continental Illinois National Bank & Trust Co. might have been prevented if the company had been involved in more than a wholesale banking business. Mr. Isaac's desire to set deposit insurance premiums based on the riskiness of investments is in line with his sense that it is the marketplace which, by example, ought to be educating people as to the pitfalls of deregulation in the financial services world. The collapse of state-chartered thrift institution insurance funds in Ohio and Maryland are additional methods by which people are receiving an education at the hands of the marketplace. But in some cases it is a difficult education, acquired by waiting weeks (and in one case even months) to get at funds on deposit.

Both consumers and corporate customers are affected by these changes. However, since the greatest impact to date has been on consumers, they will be given most emphasis in the remainder of this chapter.

HISTORICAL PERSPECTIVE

In the financial services sector the characteristically American trend toward less government regulation and more private sector initiative began in the mid-1970s with the lifting of required commission schedules for stockbrokers, a move that created a whole new industry: discount brokerage. Despite the birth of this industry, the consolidation of securities dealers is continuing and the cost of full-service stock brokerage is growing. The increasing concentration results not from deregulation per se, but from the need to diversify. It can be seen in the creation of conglomerates, such as Shearson Lehman American Express (one of whose affiliates is Fireman's Fund Insurance) and Prudential-Bache Securities, and in Sears Roebuck's acquisition of Dean Witter Reynolds. There is great conglomeration occurring in the banking, thrift, and insurance industries as well. In the insurance industry, it is the profit squeeze caused by a downturn in the long property/casualty business cycle that has stimulated concentration.

When restrictions on bank and thrift deposit and loan rates were lifted in the early 1980s, these institutions were allowed to expand geographically and offer new products and services. But Congress's failure to create simultaneously a national interstate banking policy has caused a rash of new state laws that permit broader expansion of banks and thrifts than the federal government sanctions. Congress only allowed merger and acquisition of troubled financial institutions across state lines. New regional interstate banking compacts have sprung up to supplement these federal rules, permitting pacts between healthy institutions.

By 1990, according to a recent survey by Arthur Andersen & Co. and Bank Administration Institute, the number of banks in the nation is expected to decline by almost one-third from about 15,000 to 9600.[1] The number of thrift institutions has also shrunk markedly from a recent high of near 5200 in 1978 to about 3500 at year end 1985. In 1960, prior to economic pressures on their business there were 6835. In part the decline will be due to the impact of inflation on banks' bottom lines, the increased cost of funds, and higher operating expenses. A McKinsey study in 1981 showed these forces could produce a profit gap of as much as $44 billion by 1986, unless banks reduced the gap by charging more for loans, tripling service fees, and reducing operating expenses.[2] Despite these predictions, there is evidence that an end to restrictions on interstate banking would not cause excessive concentration of the U.S. banking system. In five other countries with some form of nationwide banking, high concentration has resulted from geographic restrictions, a liberal merger policy, product line restrictions, and a payments system controlled by only a few firms.[3]

Thrifts, among the first beneficiaries of deregulatory relief, were released from their inability to broker real estate, securities, and insurance. Many immediately diversified their services in response. Some began by installing booths in their lobbies to sell what were for them new products. Empire of America Federal Savings Bank (Buffalo, New York) found its own branch-booth experiment, Moneyflex, so successful that it decided to make a deal with Montgomery Ward stores to put booths in some Ward stores. These booths are an attempt to increase the value of the branch system, as well as to increase profitability through multiple forms of distribution and the sale of more services. The ability of the nonbanks such as insurers, stockbrokers, finance companies, retailers, and other companies that are not chartered as banks or savings associations to enter what once was exclusively the domain of insured depository institutions, has added yet another dimension to financial services deregulation and substantially increased competition in the marketplace.

Deposits

The need for Congress to authorize new deposit products for insured banks and thrifts was intensified in the late 1970s and early 1980s when money market mutual funds siphoned some $240 billion out of them. Congress's creation of the SuperNow and money market deposit accounts recognized the need to protect the insured depositories, and also acknowledged the consumer's right to be paid a market rate of interest on deposits.

Beginning in 1972 with the invention of the negotiable order of withdrawal account by a Massachusetts banker, the marketplace showed its ability to expand around existing laws and through loopholes in them. The creation of the "loophole certificate" later in the 1970s further enabled banks and thrifts to offer higher interest rates to people without the $10,000 necessary to qualify for a six-month money market certificate. Although these innovations occurred without coordinated responses from Congress, which was still grappling with broader public policy concerns, consumers responded in droves. Finally, with the authorization of nationwide negotiable order of withdrawal accounts—essentially interest-bearing checking accounts—Congress began a long process of abdicating control over the establishment of deposit interest rates, their province since the 1930s. The Depository Institutions Deregulation Committee was established in 1980 to oversee the phaseout of all deposit interest rate limits.

Paying interest on funds that previously had cost nothing increased operating costs for banks and thrifts. These new costs forced them to look around for additional sources of revenue and new ways of marketing and distributing products that created economies of scale. Relationship banking, financial planning, and asset management-type accounts that link many financial services under one umbrella were among the possibilities.

On the asset side, new products such as home equity lines of credit became commonplace, offered by banks, thrifts, stockbrokers, insurers, and finance companies. Consumers have perceived this trend as positive, as it means higher interest rates on their savings and a wide array of products to choose from. Corporate customers have been less affected by these changes since interest rates are not allowed on corporate deposits. Nonetheless, institutions are experiencing some impact.

One-Stop Shopping for Corporations and Consumers

Corporations. The at one time near-universal emphasis on relationship banking, or relationship financial servicing, was meant to encourage customers to expand the number of products or services they purchased through a single institution. It first made its appearance on the corporate side of the business, where accounts were often combined for analysis, and loan pricing was fixed according to the overall profitability of the other services.

However, with the disappearance of corporate deposits into the commercial paper and government securities markets, banks increased service fees markedly on the corporate side and each product was priced to make a profit on its own. A recent study of corporate banking by the MAC Group showed that there are two significant segments of commercial bank customers: relationship buyers and performance buyers. Relationship buyers value willingness to lend, personal attention, and account officer caliber and continuity. Performance buyers value service flexibility, operations capability, international services, and cash management capabilities. While it seems like coming full circle, the move to relationship pricing with more explicit knowledge of the profit or loss of individual services is actually a new development. Importantly, the study found that "despite the fact that customers are increasingly looking at performance as the main criterion, many firms are increasing their emphasis on relationship management."[4] This desire for performance is stimulating a trend toward use of multiple suppliers.

Consumers. The same sort of trend could be at work on the retail side of the business as well. While the theory is the same on the consumer side, the evolution of relationship pricing has been slower in retail financial services. On both the wholesale and the retail sides there has been what at first glance seems a contradictory emphasis on stand-alone pricing. In fact it is not contradictory. Prior to the arrival of explicit pricing, many services were offered free and without any awareness of the real costs—to say nothing of the opportunity costs—incurred.

In the late 1970s SRI International, formerly Stanford Research Institute, released a survey of consumer money management practices that in essence took a snapshot of the birth of a new movement in financial services marketing. Although the survey showed that affluent households bought about 38 financial services a year from 20 different vendors, while nonaffluent households bought 20 products or services a year from 12 vendors, it also found that 85 percent of U.S. households saw some advantage to one-stop financial services shopping. Financial services executives, bankers in particular, began to perceive a way to lock up customer relationships and increase profitability. They could cross-sell new products to their existing consumers while touting multi-faceted offerings to noncustomers.

According to leading marketing experts, there are at least three consumer orientations that are important to financial services marketers. They are: the "get my money's worth" orientation, which produces value-conscious shoppers; the "time buying" orientation, associated with people who believe they have a dearth of time and respond to opportunities to preserve what little they have; and the "I am an individual" orientation, found in consumers who frequently assess service quality by the level of personalization involved. Relationship banking is a strategy that can appeal to consumers with all three of these orientations. But if a bank puts together a strategy called relationship banking that is really something else, it risks adding costs and limiting effectiveness, especially with "get my money's worth" consumers.[5]

Despite the potential for failure and the trend toward using multiple suppliers, relationship financial servicing has been touted as *the* financial services strategy of the 1980s and 1990s. Its attraction is its potential for tying consumers and corporations into an institution via multiple products. The theory is that the more products someone buys from a supplier, the harder it will be for the customer to leave. Financial services companies that practice this strategy say convenience-oriented consumers like the idea because it makes obtaining financial services more efficient for them. But some industry observers question whether or not one-stop shopping is really what customers are after, especially in a world where each service is priced to make a profit and relationship pricing is yet to become a reality. It may be, in fact, that relationship pricing, not one-stop shopping, holds the greatest benefits. Nonetheless, retail and corporate customers may be willing to forgo relationship pricing if it means giving up their ability to comparison shop.

Today's financial services customers, retail and wholesale, are far more sophisticated than yesterday's. Inflation, if nothing else, has educated them to seek high rates of return on their funds. At the same time, the relative stability of noninsured repositories such as money market mutual funds has broadened their risk orientations. Consumers today are more educated, earn more, and are more interested than their predecessors in leveraging both their financial resources and their own personal time and effort to achieve the greatest return. With the maturation of the baby boom generation has come a boom in two-career families, working women, and more affluent households. People are also more self-reliant with respect to financial advice than ever before. Still, they are willing to trade off more money for a convenient, functional product. Frank Partel, formerly of American Express and now an executive with Chase Manhattan Bank, warns, "To those creating financial products I say woe to you if it doesn't work right the first time." Consumers, he suggests, need more than high interest on deposits and low interest on loans: "They need to be dealt with as individuals, to be identified as unique beings, to feel they belong, are supported, helped, and respected. And they need to feel that they can meet their cultural expectations for success." Mr. Partel says people are more interested today than ever before in planning for the future.[6]

That is why financial planning, a strategy similar to one-stop shopping and relationshipping, is being utilized today as an umbrella structure through which to introduce consumers and small businesses to many products and services. Here the customer deals with one contact person who recommends a course of action predicated on each individual's particular financial needs and goals. Once the customer has invested time and money in a relationship with an investment advisor or financial planner, he or she is likely to buy many financial services from that advisor. At least, this is the rationale behind IDS/American Express's thrust to be seen as "financial planners" and Prudential-Bache Securities' advertising campaign announcing "total financial planning" and inviting the public to "bring us your future."

When the Financial Institutions Marketing Association, an affiliate of the U.S. League of Savings Associations, queried 1200 households nationwide about financial planning in a study released in 1985, it found that only 4 percent had used a planning service in the prior 12 months, but 36 percent said they would be extremely or very likely to use such a service if it offered record-keeping, budget planning, retirement planning, and investment counseling. Banks and thrifts have a good leg up in competing to offer these services, the study found, with 4 percent of households saying they would prefer assistance with their financial planning from their bank or savings and loan association. The more affluent households, earning over $50,000 a year, expressed the least desire for financial planning assistance. The greatest market appears to be households earning $25,000–$50,000. Those individuals, however, would most likely pay less than $50 for such a service, while households whose occupants earned $50,000 or more showed willingness to pay upwards of $100.

Another survey, by Market Facts, Inc., showed that 8 percent of all households are interested in personal financial planning and that this interest is highest in four unrelated market segments: young families just starting out, preretirees aged 50–69, affluent people earning $40,000 or more, and people living in the Middle Atlantic states. This study found that people who are interested in personal financial planning would switch banks or thrifts to get it. What is more, they would take the rest of their financial business with them.

Also on the financial planning bandwagon is Sears Roebuck, which is offering a $25 financial plan, a sort of do-it-yourself version of the more sophisticated models. Numerous insurance companies also foster a planning focus among their agents, whose bread and butter has always been a shoot-from-the-hip kind of financial planning. Many independent agents are chartered life underwriters and certified financial planners as well.

It remains to be seen whether financial institutions offering financial planning and one-stop shopping can keep their recommendations free from the biases they naturally have toward pushing their own products.

Another outgrowth of the popularity of one-stop shopping is the boom in asset management-type products such as Dean Witter's Active Assets account, Prudential-Bache's Command account, Citibank's FOCUS account, Fleet National Bank's Westminister account, and Chase Manhattan's Universal account. These are all variations on the theme of tying together checking, savings, lending, and investing products in one package. Other banks, stockbrokers and even insurers have created products like this. All of these "cash management clones," as they are called by Edward Furash, a bank consultant, are modeled on Merrill Lynch's Cash Management Account. CMA was the first and, as far as limited research reveals, is still the only measurably profitable one-stop financial services product on the market. The level of Merrill's success is widely attributed to the fact that for many years CMA was the only such game in town.[7]

Another facet of one-stop shopping is the evolution of in-store or in-lobby financial services booths that combine securities, insurance, real estate, and other offerings to consumers. Perhaps the most famous are Sears Roebuck's in-store facilities that sell Dean Witter securities, All-State insurance, and Coldwell Banker real estate services. But Kroger stores also have a deal with Capitol Holdings Corp. to sell insurance, mutual funds, and annuity products. First Nationwide, the giant national thrift institution, has a similar deal going with K mart stores. Many banks are slowly building to these levels of activity as laws and economies permit. They share branches with insurers, stockbrokers, tax preparers, their own or other discount brokers, and with investment advisors. As more financial services are permitted to be offered by more providers, it is likely that these arrangements will expand the types of services offered and increase in frequency among providers of financial services.

Service Fees

In addition to pushing consumers to concentrate their deposits and lending business in one place, financial institutions have also begun to emphasize pricing as a way to help their sagging bottom lines and insure profitability in the consumer arena. Prior to deregulation of deposit interest rates, many banks and thrifts offered free checking services or checking services with very low minimum balance requirements, and minimal fees. They concentrated most on interest income, not seeing noninterest income, or fees, as a viable revenue-generator.

But increasing competition and the steadily rising cost of funds mandated by the Depository Institutions Deregulation Committee's scheduled phaseout of limits on deposit interest rates changed all that. Fee income became the industry's salvation in the 1980s. All over the country banks and thrifts began charging money for what historically had been free or low-cost services: checking accounts and related services, such as items returned for insufficient funds, stop payment orders, and the like. Cashing checks, maintaining savings accounts, and processing withdrawals all became revenue-producing activities.

A study released in 1985 by the House Banking Committee showed that the cost of banking services to average American households had more than doubled in the previous four years and that fees were still on their way up in 1985. In agreement was a telephone survey of 1000 consumers by Reichman Research Inc. for the *American Banker* newspaper in the summer of 1984; 52 percent of those polled reported recent service fee increases at their principal financial institutions.[8]

Loans

Studies by reliable consultants and some financial services players[9] showed banks and thrifts that simply increasing fee income would never suffice to offset increased operating costs in the new financial services world. If they were to survive as viable competitors when everyone from Merrill Lynch to Sears Roebuck was competing for loans, banks and thrifts had to have as much flexibility as possible in the design of asset products and the amount of interest they could charge. Their response was to clamor for the ability to charge a market rate on loans matching what they would shortly pay out to consumers on deposits. Most state legislatures answered the call. While Congress increased deposit rates to match those in the marketplace, most state legislatures removed interest rate limits on the amounts banks and thrifts could charge for loans.

In order to further balance their assets and liabilities in this more volatile marketplace, banks and thrifts also began offering loans whose interest rates could be adjusted up and down depending on market conditions. Such variable or adjustable rate loans are becoming more common in consumer financial services every day. A few banks have as much as 50 percent of all consumer loans in variable rate products.[10] Credit unions, which entered the variable rate lending business in the early 1980s, say both they and their members have been pleased with the results. One of these, McCoy Federal Credit Union (Orlando, Florida), launched a variable rate loan program in 1980 when an unsecured signature loan was priced at 21 percent. The initial interest on its variable loans was set at 16.5 percent. Since then, the variable rate has fallen two points, while the fixed rate has been steady. Consequently, 97 percent of McCoy's loans are variable rate.[11]

New Products/New Powers

Driving as many new products as possible through their highly expensive distribution systems is seen as paramount to increasing profitability by all providers of financial services today. Banks have been agitating in Congress for the ability to broker real estate and insurance, to underwrite municipal revenue bonds and insurance, and to offer investment advice and trade securities. The American Bankers Association and other banking trade and lobbying groups argue that the entry of nontraditional providers of banking services into their business makes imperative the ability of banks to compete head to head in the others' businesses. They refer here not only to quasibanking services, such as money market mutual funds, and lending competition such as brokers offering home equity lines or second mortgages, but also to the creation of the nonbank bank, also called the consumer or limited service bank. These nonbank banks were created by mutual funds, and lending competition such as brokers offering home equity lines or second mortgages, but also to the creation of the nonbank bank, also called the accepts demand deposits (checking accounts). Nonbank banks do one and not both, thereby escaping the definition of a bank. Congress has yet to decide what to do about these new, specially designed institutions.

New Forms of Distribution

At the same time that they fight over allowing each other into each others' businesses, banking and nonbanking institutions are also cooperating with each other in the offering of consumer financial services. New linkages have grown up between banks and nonbanks by which the rental of bank lobby space enables insurers or stockbrokers to bring to the table their own particular strengths and capabilities. There are also third-party marketing arrangements under which a bank will offer its credit card holders, for example, an insurer's hospital protection plan, group term life insurance, or accident insurance policies. These arrangements exist because competitors recognize that offering a service with the competition is better than not offering the service at all—especially if someone else in the market *is* offering it.

Finding other ways to create new distribution systems is closely allied with the need for banks and thrifts to cut costs. To this end these institutions have been streamlining and closing branches, installing automated teller machines, joining with competing depositories to form ATM networks, shortening hours, cutting staff and, for some progressive institutions, pushing computerized home banking and other nonlabor intensive forms of service delivery. The 1984 *American Banker* survey found that 37 percent of 1000 consumers would be comfortable doing their banking business through the telephone, the mail, or an automated teller machine with a financial institution that has no branches (see Exhibit 2.1). Bankers conducting their own surveys have uncovered similar findings. Manufacturers Hanover Trust Co., for one, is attempting to capitalize on the potential acceptance of this kind of banking to create a new strategy called Bankless Banking designed to appeal to that segment of the population that would be comfortable banking in less traditional, sometimes less personal ways.[12]

Freedom of Choice

Allowing people the option of using either machinery or humans to conduct their banking business seems to work far better than taking away their freedom of choice. BankAmerica executives say that their program of discussing contem-

Exhibit 2.1 No More Branches: Will Consumers Buy It?

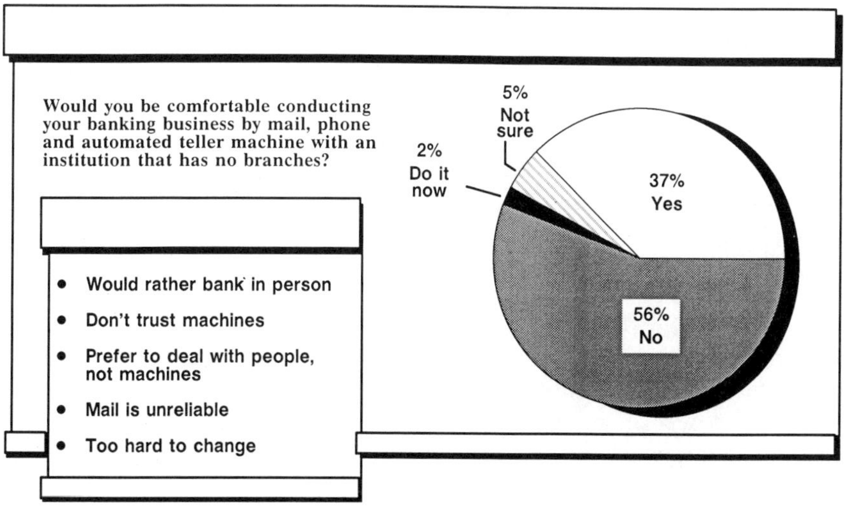

Would you be comfortable conducting your banking business by mail, phone and automated teller machine with an institution that has no branches?

- Would rather bank in person
- Don't trust machines
- Prefer to deal with people, not machines
- Mail is unreliable
- Too hard to change

5% Not sure

2% Do it now

37% Yes

56% No

plated branch closings with community activists met with much less criticism than it would have if they had failed to talk to community leaders first. In this way, the community was able to voice its reaction to the substitution of fully staffed branches with unattended automatic teller machines. By contrast, in 1984 Citibank tried to institute a policy under which any consumer with less than $5,000 on deposit at 39 of its 275 New York City branches would have to use an automated teller. People with more money on deposit could see a human teller. The policy caused such an outcry from consumers and the media that Citibank reversed itself immediately. This experience is an example of what happens when an institution attempting to streamline service delivery does not handle carefully changes in policies that consumers consider sacrosanct. A related example of a more gentle way to steer consumers toward less-costly electronic delivery systems is given by bankers who are pricing automated teller transactions differently than those performed in branches by human employees.

New Marketing

Traditionally, banks and thrifts dealt with all segments of the consumer population. Stockbrokers dealt with a more upscale, risk-oriented bunch. Most insurance companies dealt with the mass market and had special departments to handle more complex accounts and perform sophisticated financial planning. Most mutual fund firms took any purchase of at least $1,000. Finance companies were for poor people and financial planners for the rich.

But in the new financial services world, almost all suppliers have targeted the 20 percent of their customer bases that they are sure provide 80 percent of the profits. This trend is especially prevalent today in the banking industry. Banks have moved away from a quantity-oriented approach, in which market share is the winning determinant, to a quality-oriented approach, in which those individuals with the highest profit potential to the bank are the principal focus of attention. Not all banks can adopt this approach: they simply are not operating in markets with high concentrations of affluent individuals.

While financial services suppliers other than banks may be acting on these same strategies, their actions are not causing anywhere near the same reaction from consumer advocates. This is partly because the historical franchise of stockbrokers and firms such as American Express has been almost exclusively the affluent segments of the consumer market, while the franchise of banks and insurance companies has been far broader. Additionally, however, there is something in the way people perceive banks which is causing a strong reaction.

The new marketing at banks translates into banks treating higher-balance customers or major borrowers differently than they treat everyone else. Flexible credits are designed for the affluent to complement their needs and lifestyles. Deposit interest rates are being tiered in many areas of the country—the more money kept on deposit, the higher the rate paid. Keep enough on deposit, the banks say, and they will waive service fees on checking accounts and, sometimes, on other products.

Because it is less expensive for banks to cross-sell services through the mail, phone, or some form of automation, once initial contact has been made in person, streamlined branches are popping up in many parts of the country. Some bankers devote their branch lobbies and their personnel's efforts to selling services or giving personal treatment to target customers. For other institutions, automation is becoming the rule. All sorts of variations on these distribution themes are occurring. Branches exist today at which customers see no personnel at all, except by appointment. There are also branches with separate lines for individuals of different means, although the distinctions are not usually made obvious, so as to prevent nonupscale customers from becoming upset. In this, bank marketers are following the lead of the airlines.

As this new marketing has evolved in the financial services world, some executives have begun to wonder what to do about snaring tomorrow's affluent. Lately, new strategies have begun cropping up to deal with this issue. These programs recognize a practical reality: just as today's affluent were not always rich, tomorrow's are not today. The goal should therefore be to create loyalty in tomorrow's best customers, not lose them between the cracks of strategies designed only for those who are well off at present.

During 1985, financial services marketers became more intent on luring these individuals. Manufacturers Hanover Trust Co., for example, has been running an ad campaign that promises "to realize your potential." Along the same lines, Merrill Lynch has started to offer a sort of junior cash management account for individuals just starting out.

Today's bank marketers speak of a time when they will provide a menu of services to consumers, something of a Chinese restaurant approach, where individuals can create their own financial services smorgasbord by choosing one service from "Group A" and one from "Group B." Pricing would be based on the options selected. Whether marketers can get people to view money the same way they look at Chinese food remains to be seen.

Such segmented marketing approaches have been commonplace in other, nonfinancial industries, but have not until recently been used in the financial services industries. The fact that much of this change has occurred already in the form of "market segmentation without explanation"[13] has had a profound impact on how consumers view deregulation of the financial services scene.

THE NECESSITY FOR CONSISTENCY

In a financial services world where everything is constantly changing, consistency is a powerful strategic weapon. Those providers that do not recognize this truth may find themselves losing customers to more steadfast institutions that project consistent images backed by sound service. To cite an easily appreciated example, McDonald's is not successful because once in Peoria it made a decent hamburger, delivered it on a clean plate, and served it with a smile. It has thrived by doing this everywhere, all the time. Similarly, Sears Roebuck & Co. did not win its reputation for excellent service in every area of its business by projecting an image of responsiveness and delivering another reality. And when Coca-Cola's break with tradition to change its secret formula caused half of America to cry out for the old Coke, management showed its savvy by rereleasing the original favorite as "Coke Classic." Commercial bankers could take a lesson from what Coke did to protect itself against loss of market share.

Banking's Image Switch

Of all the financial services industries, it is probably fair to say that the banking industry has changed most in the way it views itself and presents itself to consumers. For years banks promoted themselves as what they were: safe, helpful places where people could go for loans, advice, or storage of whatever they had of value. Advertising campaigns were not particularly distinguishable. Banks all seemed so earnest and were FDIC insured. They did everything in their power to get a larger share of market than the competitor up the street—if it had not yet become a finance company, securities firm, Seven-Eleven store, or insurance company. Banks did such a good job of convincing people of their interchangeability and solidity that, according to one major state bankers association, about 10 years ago, 60 percent of the schoolteachers in the state thought that national banks were an arm of the federal government.

But then inflation and the banks' increased funds costs washed away all that interchangeability and consistency. Suddenly there were new fees for checking accounts, tougher minimum balance requirements, and refusal to cash checks that had not cleared. The new policies were confusing to consumers, more so in light of the placid image the banks had carefully built up in the 1950s and 1960s. The many new products, services, and competitors proved overwhelming to people. *Money* magazine's 1985 survey of 2491 consumer financial decision makers showed that only half felt they understood the words "IRA account" and "certificates of deposit" well enough to explain them to someone else. Only a quarter were comfortable describing a NOW account or municipal bond.

The Pitfalls of Inconsistency

It is dangerous for an industry with so many competitors to cause such a great deal of confusion in the public domain. American society is like a giant percolator with each person a grain of coffee in the pot. If enough people get anxious about something, or are affected by it, and nobody tries to address the issues or provide comfort, the anxiety and discomfort bubble around and eventually percolate up through state legislatures and into the U.S. Congress, not to mention the courts.

That is what is happening today. The adjustable rate mortgages, the repurchase agreements that were not insured, the foreign loans, the bank failures, the thrift crisis, the merging and acquiring, the money laundering, the violation of once-virgin state lines, the closing of branches, the raising of bank services fees, the introduction of automated teller machines, the seeming refusal to lower credit card interest rates more than a point or two while deposit rates drop 5–10 points—each new source of insecurity adds to the already substantial discomfort. The banking industry's failure to explain to consumers the reasons for these occurrences has affected how consumers think of commercial banks—and how they perceive the banking systems and the financial system in general.

That it is the banking industry which has become the principal target of consumer discontent is clear. Results of the *American Banker* telephone survey show that of the three insured depositories—savings institutions, commercial banks, and credit unions—consumers like commercial banks least. A fifth of people who identify commercial banks as their principal financial institutions say they get an excellent deal there. Almost two and a half times as many who name credit unions say the same of their principal provider.

But it is not the banking industry alone in which consumers have lost confidence. The *American Banker* survey also found that this lessening of confidence was generalized to the overall financial system. While 46 percent of those surveyed said they had as much confidence today in the banking and financial systems as they did a few years ago, 36 percent said they had less. As only 16 percent had more, that represents a net loss in confidence. Many consumers attributed their change in feeling directly to bank failures, loans to foreign countries, high interest rates, and an unstable economy.[14]

CONSUMERISM IN AMERICA: GENESIS

To add fuel to these smoldering fires, traditional consumerist issues have been exhausted, leaving financial services deregulation—particularly deregulation of the commercial banking industry—at the top of the priority list for many consumer groups.[15] This phenomenon could probably have been predicted. Meredith Fernstrom, senior vice president, Public Responsibility, for American Express, writes that "the consumer movement has been a force in the American economic and political arenas for the past century. At its peak periods the movement has had significant influence in bringing about a more equal balance between the interests of buyers and sellers. Much of that influence has gone to shape aspects of the financial services industry. . . ." Ms. Fernstrom cites the Truth in Lending Act which passed Congress in 1968 after a long struggle between consumer leaders and industry representatives. That the passage of the act, as well as others affecting the financial services industry, was markedly delayed she attributes to "the industry's opposition to most of the legislative proposals, opposition which in some cases failed to acknowledge legitimate consumer abuses and concerns."[16]

The wariness produced by these protracted battles has persisted and is combining with other forces to increase the chances that reregulation could begin. Ms. Fernstrom emphasizes that her survey found "a remarkable degree of consensus" on issues related to financial services deregulation on the part of consumer leaders from disparate groups and different geographic locations. And as Orin Kramer, president, Financial Services, Communications & Co. says, "The confusion spawned by deregulation, the reconfiguration of delivery systems, the market segmentation strategies, the exhaustion of traditional consumerist issues and the increased financial services expertise of consumer activists" have all contributed to the evolution of a new consumerism directed right at financial services deregulation.[17] In other words, the high level of consumerist interest in financial services deregulation to date is not a fluke that will disappear with time. "Serious concerns exist among consumer leaders which must be addressed responsively," Ms. Fernstrom stresses in her report on the new consumerism.[18]

The Consumerist Agenda: Access to Financial Services

According to the American Express survey, access to financial services is the issue most consumer leaders discuss first when they address their doubts about deregulation:

> Consumer leaders are clearly aware of the fact that most financial service providers have their sights set on the high-balance, multiple-account relationships customer, and that their pricing policies reflect that strategy. . . . Current pricing strategies, and those anticipated in the future, have the potential for cutting off access to routine financial services for [low income, elderly, disabled and non-English speaking consumers].[19]

Clearly, for a selective provider like American Express the problem is not nearly as profound as it is for a bank or other depository institution whose historical role has been to serve the general public. Nonetheless, the question at the root of the access issue is: Is a banking institution supposed to be a form of commercial enterprise that can pick and choose the customers it wants to do business with? Or instead, because banks are backed by federal deposit insurance and because banks are custodians of the money supply, should banks be forced to provide affordable banking services to the poor? Should they be directed to make full service available to all comers? This issue of regulating or legislating bank services fees or other proprietary policies strikes at the very heart of the role of banks and other depository institutions in this society.

But at the same time the issue begs a deeper question: Are banks businesses, or are they utilities? Results of the *American Banker's* 1984 survey are clear: two-thirds of the public regard banks to be more like businesses than utilities. But one-third disagrees, perceiving banks to be more like utilities than businesses.

In accordance with Americans' historical bent toward keeping the government out of the private sector as much as possible, a majority of the public is also opposed to government regulation of retail banking policies concerning fees and balance requirements, check holding, and the closing of branches.[20] That consensus is heartening, since it is not the government's role to regulate proprietary practices of other kinds of businesses.

Lifeline Banking

Where the banks' strategies and the public's desires part company is on the issue of affordable, bare-bones—or lifeline—banking services for low-income people and the elderly poor. Here, a majority of people favor the government's forcing banks to offer such services, and most people who feel that way want the government or the banks to subsidize the service.

The issue of lifeline banking points out how difficult it is to get people to change their perception of the financial system in midstream. Lifeline banking, like lifeline telephone, gas, or electric services, comprises those banking services provided at or below cost to individuals who can no longer afford to buy them at a market rate. Some consumer activists see lifeline as the consumer's right, not privilege. Although activists are conducting research to support this view and are vigorously lobbying legislators, their viewpoint ignores an important argument: other options are available.[21] Cash, travelers checks, money orders, check-cashing outlets, credit unions, finance companies, and other options exist to service those people who cannot afford to use a commercial bank. This argument has been raised by commercial bankers and others trying to answer the access question.

Reliable data are currently unavailable on how much of the consumer population, and which individuals, are truly disenfranchised from the commercial banking system. The Federal Reserve Board recently issued results of a survey that showed that, in 1983, 12 percent of the population did not have a checking account. That figure compares with 9 percent in 1977. The number of low-income households with checking accounts decreased from 56 percent to 44 percent between 1977 and 1983.[22] In order to head off any movement to force the offering of lifeline banking by their members, the American Bankers Association and the Consumer Bankers Association have also recently released data showing that many banks already offer low-cost or no-cost, no-frills bank accounts, primarily to senior citizens, but increasingly to other individuals.[23]

These efforts will not stop legislative initiatives unless the efforts address the issue of poor and elderly individuals being priced out of bank lobbies. Banks will have to show that no class of people is being discriminated against in the deposit area.

Branch Closings

Closely allied with the access issue in lifeline banking, branch closings also deeply concern community activists. During 1980, banks opened 1430 branches and closed 248. In 1984 they opened 1057 and closed 865, with closings outstripping openings in the Cleveland and San Francisco Federal Reserve districts.[24]

When a branch is closed and no other branch is nearby, people are made unhappy, no matter how many check-cashing outlets or money order companies there are in the community. Consumers see branch closings as a sign that a bank is abandoning their neighborhood. Nonetheless, the 1984 *American Banker* survey found that seven out of 10 people say banks are justified in closing unprofitable branches. That number dropped to five out of 10, however, when the question was rephrased to point out that some of the branches were in poorer neighborhoods having few branches to begin with. This drop implies that before taking steps to close branches, bankers need to originate a dialogue with consumer and community leaders, and with people whose interests are vested in keeping those branches open. It is possible that, together with like-minded financial institutions and community leaders, they can find a working compromise. Perhaps the answer lies in sharing automated teller machines or other streamlined facilities.

Delayed Funds Availability (Check Holding or Float)

The issue of float or delayed funds availability is one which appears to be of primary concern to individuals living in New York and California, although problems in other states have been reported. The consumer outcry in this case is over the fact that it sometimes takes three or four weeks before customers can withdraw funds that were deposited as checks. In states where the problem exists, a number of different solutions have arisen—all of them legislative. In California, New York, and Rhode Island, laws were passed during 1984 and 1985 that limit the number of days banks can hold onto checks before releasing funds to consumers. A similar measure has been pending in Massachusetts. In Connecticut a milder approach to the problem was legislated, with banks now required to notify people of how long they must wait before using funds deposited by check.

The 1984 *American Banker* survey found a great deal of confusion among bank customers about this issue. This confusion would imply that disclosure of proprietary policies will be enough to satisfy most people, as long as the policies are what consumers consider reasonable.

The Other Issues

Although access and check holding are the major issues of concern to consumer advocates, credit availability, trust-in-savings, privacy security, and error resolution are secondary issues that are never far from their minds. In her American Express survey, Ms. Fernstrom identifies the three major areas of interest to consumer leaders as access to services, consumer information, and customer service/error resolution. In June of 1984, at a conference on the consumer and the financial services revolution sponsored by the White House Office of Consumer Affairs, several bankers proposed disclosure of proprietary policies as a means of heading off more substantial, and they feared, onerous legislation at both the state and federal levels. Stephen Brobeck, president, Consumer Federation of America, remarked at the conference that much of the public supports such disclosure.

EVOLUTION OF CONSUMER–FINANCIAL INDUSTRY DIALOGUE

One thing happening now which could change the future is that bankers are beginning to follow the lead of other financial services executives in establishing a dialogue with consumer leaders. A new consumer/business coalition has come together to deal with issues of concern to both consumers and financial services executives. Individuals present at the coalition's first meeting identified as a top priority the compiling of, and perhaps even the conducting of, research that gets at some of the questions over who is benefiting from deregulation and who is not. This group grew out of two conferences, one in June of 1984 and another in January of 1985, sponsored by the White House Office of Consumer Affairs. These were a first attempt to get financial services executives and consumer leaders to begin a formal dialogue on shared concerns. The major question left up in the air at this point, however, is whether the consumerist backlash against financial services deregulation will find an outlet in Congress and state legislatures before the new communication between bankers and consumer leaders bears more voluntary fruit.

CONCLUSION

Financial services deregulation has already begun to produce the chief effect its proponents applaud: There has been a substantial increase in financial services suppliers. Sears offers financial services. So do Kroger stores, Seven-Eleven, and other retailers. The 1984 *American Banker* survey showed that 44 percent of 1000 consumers conduct financial services business with one of eight giant conglomerates such as American Express, Sears, Prudential Insurance, and Merrill Lynch.

But consumers are not yet abandoning banks for these giants, nor do they like the idea of their banks turning into financial services supermarkets. A full fourth of the 1984 *American Banker* survey sample said the reason they opposed granting banks the power to offer additional, nontraditional services like insurance and real estate, is that they did not want banks to become too diversified.

The public seems quite happy to shop in many places for financial services: The survey found that they use an average of three types of financial institutions, no matter how hard financial firms push relationship strategies.

Also, in an economic environment that some people see as unstable or risky, most consumers seem to prefer the federally insured depositories over newer nonbank competitors. Four-fifths of those who used banks but do not regard them as their principal institutions identify thrifts or credit unions as principal. That they could have chosen insurers, stockbrokers, mutual fund firms, or other nonbanks seems significant.

In general, people like being paid a market rate of interest on their deposits, but they do not like the growing disparity between market loan rates to large corporations and rates for consumers, especially where credit cards are concerned.

Arguments that financial services deregulation is only half over do not wash with consumer leaders who are looking five and 10 years ahead and wondering if there will be a financial system left to worry about. Their concerns stem from the fact that, so far, the deregulation of the financial services industry has not conformed to rules consumers have learned about deregulation from other industries: In banking there is nothing comparable to lower air fares, there are no cheaper long-distance telephone services. Interest rates may have risen on deposits, but prices for loans as well as fees and balance requirements for basic banking services, instead of dropping, have gone up and stayed up. And while there are more choices in where to get loans and put deposits and investments, risk has multiplied substantially as the government has surrendered control.

It is this issue of risk and the transferring of it that is most likely to cause a reregulatory backlash in the consumer public, if there is to be one. Consumer leaders are operating from a perspective that takes into account the fact that the failure of a deregulated Braniff, Exxon, or MCI does not have the same sweeping implications and potentially negative consequences as the failure of a bank or thrift institution. If deposit runs on several financial institutions can result from a half-baked rumor that a single institution is suffering, the damage that can be done to the stability of the American economy by widespread failure of banks and thrifts is unlimited. This is especially so, first because the system depends on confidence, and second because no one has explained to people why so many institutions are merging into each other or why others are failing.

For financial services deregulation to proceed without an educational agenda that addresses this concern is for it to proceed on a course that is destined, at the very best, for difficulty.

There has to be a way to share both risk and responsibility among all of the providers of financial services so that the stability of the financial system is insured. To pass along risk to customers, both corporate and retail, without creating provisions that ensure the safety and soundness of traditional insured institutions, is unfair both to the customers and to the system.

NOTES

1. *New Dimensions in Banking — Managing the Strategic Position*, Arthur Andersen & Co. and Bank Administration Institute, 1983, p. 14.
2. Internal study by McKinsey & Co., "Banks Warned of Huge Profit Drop in 1986 if They Fail to Act Now." *American Banker* (August 25, 1981), p. 8.
3. Mote, Larry R. and Herbert L. Baer. "The Effects of Nationwide Banking on Concentration: Evidence from Abroad." *Economic Perspectives*, the publication of the Federal Reserve Bank of Chicago (January–February 1985), pp. 13–16.
4. Friars, Eileen M. and William T. Gregor, "Corporate Financial Services: Solving The Profit Puzzle," a speech delivered at the October 1985 convention of the American Bankers Association.
5. Donnelly, James H. Jr., Leonard L. Berry and Thomas W. Thompson. *Marketing Financial Services—A Strategic Vision*. Dow-Jones Irwin, 1985, pp. 116, 117.

6. Partel, Frank. Speech delivered to the Consumer Bankers Association Conference in Atlanta, Georgia in February 1984.
7. Case Study Data on Asset Management Accounts by the Counsel on Financial Competition, the Research Counsel of Washington, September 1984: "In the context of bank activities and bank profits, asset management accounts are wholly insignificant. Our tentative conclusion is that it is highly unlikely AMAs will generate important fee income for any but the smallest banks. It is a high risk product with relatively few banks satisfied to date."
8. *American Banker* 1984 National Consumer Attitudes Survey, October 20–29, 1984.
9. Weiant, William M., managing director, First Boston Corp., and Donald C. Waite III, director, McKinsey & Co., Inc., October 1983, in speeches before the Bank Marketing Association annual convention, Atlanta.
10. Gross, Laura. "On Target." (column) *American Banker*. (January 20 and 24, 1984), p. 1.
11. Dishneau, David. "Marketing Variable Rate Loans," *Credit Union Management* (March 1985), p. 24. Published by Credit Union Executives Society.
12. 1984 *American Banker* National Consumer Attitudes Survey. (October 20–29, 1984).
13. "Market segmentation without explanation" is originally from a speech by Laura Gross before the Bank Marketing Association annual convention in New Orleans, September 1984.
14. 1984 *American Banker* National Consumer Attitudes Survey.
15. Fox, Alan, Consumer Federation of America. "Marketing Management." (column) *American Banker*. (August 7, 1985), p. 4.
16. Fernstrom, Meredith. "Consumerism: Implications and Opportunities for Financial Services," an independent study sponsored by American Express, June 1984.
17. Kramer, Orin. Internal memorandum, "Implications of Consumerism for Financial Institutions," 1984.
18. Fernstrom, "Consumerism."
19. Ibid.
20. 1984 *American Banker* National Consumer Attitudes Survey.
21. Naylor, Bartlett. "Survey Says Many in U.S. Can't Afford Banking Services." *American Banker*. (January 10, 1985), p. 1, and "The Consumer Crusade." *American Banker*. (December 9, 1985), p. 19.
22. *Bank Service Charges and Fees, their Impact on Consumers*, a 1985 study by the Federal Reserve Board of Governors, p. 91.
23. "Everyone Has a Place in Banking's Line," *American Bankers Association Banking Journal*. (April 1985).
24. "Liberty, Justice and Bank Accounts for All?" *Business Week*. (July 1, 1985).

3 The Impact of Deregulation and Environmental Forces: Products and Costs

NEIL B. MURPHY
JUDY A. NILSON

In recent years, the financial services industry has changed dramatically with new services, new service providers, blurring of institutional distinctions, and substantial deregulation of providers of financial services. This process is directly related to the environment in which the industry delivers its services. Environmental factors render old products obsolete, create an opportunity for new products, and cause regulatory regimes to become outdated and unrealistic. The purpose of this chapter is to discuss the process of environmental change that has affected the industry, led to new product developments, and caused the ensuing deregulation. The chapter opens with a brief discussion of environmental changes. Later sections describe the types of services that have evolved to respond to the new environment, and then examine those innovations that occurred directly in response to an outmoded regulatory regime.

ENVIRONMENT AND DEREGULATION

Deregulation does not occur in a vacuum. Indeed, deregulation is a *response* to environmental pressure and would not occur in its absence. Once marketplace realities have made a particular regulatory regime redundant, the ensuing deregulation creates a new equilibrium that will last until the next wave of environmental change.

The past 20 years have been ones of inflation and high, volatile interest rates.

The writing and research for this chapter were supported by the Center for Research and Development in Financial Services, University of Connecticut.

Instability in the economy—manifested as inflation followed by recession—has brought even greater instability to interest rates. Between 1966 and 1980 each bout of inflation ended in a recession, with prices rising more rapidly than was the case at the previous trough. This situation has increased risk in both financial instruments and financial institutions. The pattern of change in the prime rate, traditionally the lowest rate available to the most credit-worthy customers and a reflection of banks' costs of funds, provides a striking record of the recent volatility. From 1933 until the end of 1971, there were only 48 changes in the prime rate. From January 1972 until December 1981, the prime rate changed 261 times, from a little more than once a year to over 26 times per year. In 1980 alone the prime rate changed 39 times.

Since almost all interest rates are quoted in nominal terms, it is assumed that they contain a component that reflects expected inflation. That is, it makes a great deal of difference to the value of a return if inflation is expected to be, say, 3 percent or 7 percent or 15 percent. It also makes a difference if there is no consensus about the expected inflation in the next year. In addition, most interest rates contain a premium reflecting the term of maturing and the probability of default. When interest rates rise, the value of all previously held long-term securities declines, making it difficult to convince investors to commit funds for long periods of time, and causing corporations difficulties in issuing long-term debt. In this world, corporations are only able to borrow on the short term, and thus face the problem of continually refinancing at unknown future rates. Mortgage and other long-term lenders have recently faced the same problem, albeit from the other side. The result has been a more vulnerable financial structure.

Following this brief overview, it is time to consider specific developments that have occurred in response to these phenomena. Each of the parties in the regulatory environment (regulated providers, regulators, legislators, and customers) has a set of incentives that is affected when the external environment changes. The regulated may lose market share to unregulated competitors, the regulators may have to deal with more failures, the legislators may have to observe their constituents bear some of the cost of disruption, and the customers may find superior deliverers of their needed financial services. Clearly, the affected parties have incentives to restructure the regulatory environment to be consistent with the altered external environment. The result will be a trade-off of short- and long-run costs and benefits by each group.

RESPONSE TO INTEREST RATE RISK IN THE ENVIRONMENT: DERIVATIVE SECURITIES

In a changing environment, especially one of volatile interest rates, the marketplace needs new ways to hedge against interest rate risk. What has evolved most recently in response are so-called "derivative" securities. These are financial instruments whose returns reflect the behavior of an underlying security. The main derivative securities discussed in this section are interest rate futures, interest rate options, and interest rate swaps. These are alternatives for effectively managing interest rate risk.

The Interest Rate Futures Contract

The financial futures contract is an obligation to buy or sell a stated amount of a particular financial instrument at a future date at a price that is determined today. Thus, the price and interest rate on that designated financial instrument, which does not begin until sometime in the future, are currently locked in. All financial futures contracts are traded on an exchange and are of a standard size, type, maturity, and delivery time. The way the price is quoted is also standardized.

The typical trade is initiated when the floor brokers of the exchange, at the order of their respective clients, reach an agreement on a price for buying and selling a contract. Then the exchange's clearing house takes over the contract. It promises delivery of the underlying instrument to the buyer and also requires receipt of the instrument from the seller. A margin deposit, which acts as a good faith deposit, must be made by the member firms to the clearing house and is marked to the market at the end of each trading day. This means that if the market moves unfavorably, a margin call is made; if the market moves favorably, the trader's margin account will be credited. By the delivery date, almost every contract is closed out by an offsetting transaction—it is very rare when the actual delivery of securities is made against the contract.

Hedging and Speculating with Interest Rate Futures

There are two main reasons for using interest rate futures—hedging and speculating. In hedging, one is concerned with changes in the basis. Basis is the difference between the futures contract's yield and the yield on the cash contract. A short hedge consists of a long position in the cash market and a short position in the futures market. Short hedges are also known as "long the basis." A profit is made by the futures contract's maturity date if the cash price increases more than, or decreases less than, the future price. Long hedges are the opposite of short hedges and are correspondingly known as "short the basis." The way one hedges is dependent upon basis expectations.

An example of a short hedge occurs when a bank expects to issue one-year certificates of deposit in three months. Anticipating interest rates to rise, the bank wants to lock in today's rate on CDs. To do this, the bank could sell a futures contract on a 90-day T-bill, for example, and then cover this short position at a later date. The bank is betting that profits from the short position will at least offset the increased costs in the cash market.

It must be noted that hedging strategies do not always work. Sometimes a no-hedge position may be preferable. The hedge ratio used is dependent upon the expectations of the basis. Needless to say, it is impossible to have perfect hedges all the time. Thus, it can be said that hedges are really speculations on the basis.

Speculators are similar to hedgers but do not have an offsetting position in the cash market. Positions are taken based upon expectations of the yield curve. If yields are expected to drop, a long position is taken. If an increase in yields is anticipated, a short position is taken. Speculation also occurs on the relationship among rates, which is known as a spread. Intermonth spreads involve a sale on one contract month and purchase of a different contract month for the same underlying instrument. Interinstrument spreads involve a sale of one contract month on one instrument and purchase of the same contract month on a different instrument. When leverage opportunities and degrees of liquidity are high while transactions costs are low, interest rate futures are very appealing to speculators.

Historical Background of Interest Rate Futures

Interest rate futures were first introduced by the Chicago Board of Trade (CBT) in October 1975 in the form of Government National Mortgage Association (GNMA) certificates. Following this successful introduction, other contracts were introduced and other organizations entered the market. The International Monetary Market (IMM), a division of the Chicago Mercantile Exchange, introduced trading on 90-day treasury bills in January 1976. In August 1977, $100,000 treasury bonds were introduced by the CBT. Successfully introduced in July 1981 were three-month domestic CDs, followed in December 1981 by three-month Eurodollar time deposit futures. Over time, more financial futures have evolved. Financial futures trading takes place on foreign currencies, Eurodollars, GNMAs, U.S. treasury bills, notes, and bonds, and various exchanges. By 1982, annual trading had grown to 28,825,112 contracts. Not only has the number of these contracts increased, but the percentage of trading in all futures contracts represented by trading in financial futures has also risen. In 1980, financial instruments accounted for 13.5 percent of all futures contracts. By 1982, this amount had risen to 25.6 percent. Given such a successful start, continued growth in the popularity of financial futures contracts is to be expected.

Interest Rate Options

Continuing the innovativeness of the financial marketplace in deriving instruments to protect against volatile interest rates, the U.S. treasury bond option contract was introduced in October 1982 by the Chicago Board of Trade. Currently, interest rate options are written in U.S. treasury notes, bills, and bonds, and are traded on the American Exchange and the Chicago Board Options Exchange.

An interest rate option is a contract that gives the holder the right to buy or sell a stated amount of a security at a stated price within a certain time period. A call option is a right to purchase the security and a put option is a right to sell the security.

There are four basic market strategies—call buying, call writing, put buying, and put writing. Writers of options are interested in the immediate income from the premium. However, they are faced with the potential of a substantial loss if the underlying security is not owned and they have to fulfill their obligation either to make or take delivery. In contrast, buyers have an immediate outflow from paying the premium. They are exposed to only a limited risk, but have the potential for unlimited profits. The strategy employed is dependent upon the expected direction and magnitude of interest rate changes. Call buyers and put writers expect lower interest rates and higher prices. Put buyers and call writers expect higher interest rates and lower prices.

An example of an interest rate option, such as buying a call option, is as follows. If an investor anticipated falling interest rates, and therefore rising prices on the treasury securities, he could purchase a call option. If prices did go up, he could exercise his option and receive delivery of the security at the striking price, thus paying less than the market price. On the other hand, if the prices went down, he could let his option expire, or close it out, and purchase the security on the open market. The use of the call option in this example set a maximum price for the underlying security and acted as a hedge against interest rate movements.

Interest Rate Futures Versus Options

When interest rate futures and options are compared, some noticeable differences become obvious. First, a futures contract is an obligation requiring either delivery or acceptance of a financial instrument at some later date. The position must be reversed before expiration or else the delivery or acceptance will occur. On the other hand, an options contract gives the right to buy or sell a financial instrument during the life of the contract. It is the holder's option to act or just let the contract expire.

A second comparison: the holder of a futures contract may experience unlimited losses, whereas the holder of an options contract will not lose any more than the premium he paid. Third, with regard to cash flows, futures contracts require daily settlement, being marked to the market. That is, every day that interest rates change, additional cash will either be required or released, depending upon the direction of the change. The total cash flow is unknown. In contrast, options have just one fixed cash flow. It is the premium paid at the time of purchase.

While the above may indicate that the use of options contracts may be better than the use of futures contracts, it really depends on one's risk preference and the underlying reasons for using these derivative securities.

The Typical Interest Rate Swap

An interest rate swap is an agreement between two institutions to exchange periodic interest rate payments. In a typical swap, one party is paying a fixed rate of interest and the other is paying a variable or floating rate indexed to treasury bill rates or LIBOR (London Interbank Offer Rates). The fixed-rate payor has bought a swap and has a "long" position in swaps and a "short" position in the bond market. The variable-rate payor has sold a swap and has a "short" position in swaps and a "long" position in the bond market. Interest payments are calculated based upon what is called the "national principal" amount, which is not exchanged. The term of the contract is usually less than 15 years, and payments are made quarterly, semiannually, or annually.

For example, firm ABC uses short-term consumer deposits to fund long-term fixed rate mortgages. Firm XYZ uses long-term fixed rate debt to fund variable-rate assets. Due to the maturity mismatches, both firms are exposed to a substantial amount of risk if interest rates change. However, the asset-liability managers can substantially reduce this risk by using interest rate swaps.

Firm ABC would want to take a short position in swap in order to hedge against rate increases. ABC would make variable rate payments and receive long-term fixed payments, thus lengthening the maturity of its liabilities. Firm XYZ would want to take a long position in swaps in order to hedge against falling variable rate payments, thereby shortening the maturity of its liabilities.

In minimizing the maturity gap, it is usually preferable to alter the liabilities to better match the assets that already exist. This is what the typical or generic interest rate swap described above did. There are several variations of the standard contract, mainly due to the fact that the participants currently have a great deal of flexibility in negotiating a swap. It is hard to believe that as recently as the late 1970s such swaps were used almost exclusively by international banks and corporate counterparties. The market has developed so rapidly that almost every type of institution at the present time can use this investment/hedging vehicle.

The Benefits and Drawbacks of Using Interest Rate Swaps

Interest rate swaps provide a variety of benefits. The biggest benefit is the reduction of interest rate risk by achieving a better match between the maturities of assets and liabilities. Swaps entail a fair amount of negotiations and can therefore be designed to meet the specific needs of the participants. Corporations are given more flexibility in varying their source of funds; that is, obligations may be transformed from a fixed rate to a variable rate or from a variable rate to a fixed rate. Swaps may also enable an institution to lock in larger hedged spreads than are available with other funding techniques. Furthermore, the swap contract is very straightforward and easier to design than are futures and options contracts.

While interest rate swaps appear to be extremely beneficial for all concerned parties, there are some drawbacks that should not be ignored. One potential risk is that a party could default and not make the agreed-upon payment. However, this risk is reduced by requiring collateral or letters of credit to guarantee the payments. Furthermore, most counterparties need excellent credit ratings in order to even participate in the swap market; therefore, this credit risk is limited. A second drawback of interest rate swaps is that early cancellation may be difficult and more expensive than closing out similar contracts in other markets. The swap would have to be sold or reversed by writing an offsetting swap.

Although there are some disadvantages associated with the use of interest rate swaps, it appears that the benefits far outweigh the potential risks. They are a viable alternative for dealing with interest rate risk.

Benefits or Values of Derivative Markets

Derivative markets perform a variety of functions that have value. The first major function is related to price discovery. The market's pricing function provides information about the expected future shape of the yield curve and the level of interest rates. With prices adjusting to market conditions, more information is provided than just an individual prediction of the future. The second major function is the shifting of risk. Financial futures and options provide a mechanism for transferring risk from those who want to avoid risk (hedgers) to those who will accept risk in anticipation of profits (speculators). A third function is to increase the liquidity of the cash markets underlying the contracts. Liquidity is increased by the linkage between the derivative market and the cash market and the resulting decisions. For example, if a bank funds fixed-rate loans with variable-rate deposits, it may give more loans if it can reduce this risk in the derivative markets.

RESPONSE TO INTEREST RATE RISK IN THE ENVIRONMENT: THE SECONDARY MORTGAGE MARKET

Interest rate volatility has greatly influenced the behavior of participants in the mortgage market. The portfolios of savings and loan associations were restructured beginning in 1981. Activity in the secondary mortgage markets increased, as did the variety of mortgage-backed securities involved. These securities can be split into two major categories. First is the mortgage pass-through, which is issued as a sale of assets by the issuer. Second is the mortgage-backed bond, which is debt financing of the issuer that is collateralized by mortgages. New types of mortgages also evolved. The most successful innovations in response to the increased interest rate risk are the 15-year mortgage and the adjustable rate mortgage.

The Secondary Mortgage Market

Mortgages and mortgage-related securities are traded on the secondary mortgage market. Lending institutions sell their mortgages to a firm that either resells these mortgages or packages them as securities which it sells to investors on the secondary market. When the security is sold, the secondary market experiences an inflow of cash which it can then use to buy additional mortgages, enabling the lending institutions to make new loans and starting the process over again.

The secondary markets can erase mismatches that sometimes occur in the housing finance system. Institutional mismatches occur when different institutions specialize in different markets. Insurance companies, for example, are not set up for mortgage lending. Geographic mismatches occur when one region has a surplus of capital while another lacks sufficient capital. When the supply of funds does not match the demand, the secondary market comes into play and the flow of funds between savers and borrowers is improved.

Mortgage Pass-Through or Swaps of GNMA

The first mortgage pass-through was issued in 1970 by the Government National Mortgage Association (GNMA). The GNMA pools mortgages that are issued under the programs of the Federal Housing Authority (FHA) or the Veterans Administration (VA), and then issues pass-through certificates. Payments from the pooled mortgages are passed on to investors through issuers on a regular basis. These certificates are guaranteed by GNMA and backed by the U.S. government.

Under the GNMA-I program there is a single contract rate for the pooled mortgages, which are on one- to four-family units; and for each mortgage pool there is only one issuer. An investor in GNMA-I pools receives a separate check for each of the pools he or she is invested in. Payments are on the 15th of the month, and there is a 45-day delay on the initial payment.

Under the GNMA-II program (an improvement begun in 1983), interest rates on mortgages within the same pool may vary by 1 percent. Also, there may be more than one issuer for each pool, a feature which tends to average the fluctuations in the prepayments that occur among different geographic regions. Payments from the various pools are combined so that each investor only receives one monthly check. Payments are on the 20th of the month, and there is a 50-day delay on the initial payment.

During 1970, less than $1 billion of GNMAs were issued. This amount increased to almost $14 billion in 1976; from then through 1982, the annual issuance rarely surpassed the $20 billion mark.

In 1983, issuance of GNMAs skyrocketed to $50 billion. Interest rates had fallen and demand for housing rose along with mortgage originations and refinancings. FHA/VA financings were preferred over the conventional mortgages since they were less expensive. Another reason for the increased issuance is that home builders were beginning to issue bonds, which used GNMAs as collateral, to finance homebuyers. Furthermore, FMNA reduced their investment in FHA/VA mortgages and GNMA took up the slack.

After a stellar performance in 1983, issuance of GNMAs declined significantly in 1984. One of the biggest factors contributing to this decline was the increasing popularity of adjustable rate mortgages (discussed below). First-time homebuyers, who usually use FHA/VA financing, were turning to the lower rates offered by adjustable rate mortgages (ARMs). Thus, new originations of FHA/VA loans declined. Since GNMA only securitized these loans, issuance of GNMAs also fell. By 1985, volume of GNMA issues had begun to increase.

Mortgage Pass-Through or Swaps of FHLMC and FNMA

In 1971, a program similar to that of GNMA was introduced by the Federal Home Loan Mortgage Corporation (FHLMC). Under this program, pass-throughs were called participation certificates (PCs). The FHLMC pools are made up of conventional loans on one- to four-family units and a limited amount of multifamily mortgages (less than 5 percent of the pool's balance). The loans for the regular PC program are 30-year level payment mortgages and interest rates for the pool do not vary. Investors receive one check per month and there is a 75-day delay on the initial payment.

During 1971, less than $1 million of FHLMC PCs were issued. This amount increased to $1 billion in 1976; and from 1976 up to and including 1981, the annual issuance rarely exceeded $5 billion.

In August, 1981, FHLMC enhanced the PC with a new program, called the Guarantor Program. In November, 1981, the Federal National Mortgage Association (FNMA) began to issue mortgage-backed securities. Under these programs, seasoned mortgages were purchased mostly from thrifts and pooled by FHLMC and FNMA, respectively. These agencies would then sell guaranteed pass-throughs, based on these same pools, back to the thrifts. As a result, the thrifts' mortgage portfolios were more liquid and more marketable. By 1983, seasoned FHA/VA loans were included, as well as newly originated loans. The loans for these programs also included 15-year level payment mortgages. Furthermore, under these programs interest rates on mortgages within the pool could vary by 2 percent.

The Guarantor Program proved to be extremely successful. In 1982, approximately $24 billion of FHLMC PCs were issued, which was more than all of the PCs issued prior to 1981. Since then, at least $20 billion of PCs have been issued annually.

The FNMA mortgage-backed securities also proved to be quite successful. By 1982, FNMA had issued a total of approximately $14.5 billion of pass-throughs. Volume has remained around $14 billion per year.

Mortgage-Backed Bonds

The first mortgage-backed bond, called a collateralized mortgage obligation (CMO), was issued by the Federal Home Loan Mortgage Corporation in June 1983. Initially, the CMOs issued by the FHLMC used conventional single-family mortgages as collateral and the cash flow generated by a pool of these mortgages is used to fulfill the obligations of the issue.

The bondholders are divided into three or four different classes based upon maturity preferences with all classes receiving semiannual interest payments, which may be at different rates. The shortest maturity class receives all of the principal repayments until it is retired, and then the next maturity class will start receiving principal payments. Based upon previous prepayment experience, the FHLMC guarantees a minimum amount each time, even if the payments are less than the minimum schedule. On the other hand, if the prepayments are greater than expected, they are passed through.

CMOs are also issued privately by subsidiaries of mortgage bankers, investment bankers, and home builders. The collateral for private issue CMOs is usually GNMAs. Unlike the CMOs issued by the FHLMC, these CMOs do not have guaranteed sinking fund payments. The cash flow from the collateral pays off the debt, but there is no guarantee.

Due to the different maturity classes of CMOs that are available, a larger number of investors are able to participate. These people are not attracted to other mortgage-backed securities such as FNMAs, GNMAs, or FHLMC participation certificates. Thrifts find the shorter-term classes most appealing, whereas pension funds and insurance companies are more attracted to the longer-term classes.

The structure of CMOs offers a great deal of certainty, especially for the longer classes. Since the shorter maturity classes are paid off first, the longer maturity classes have lower prepayment risk. These investors need not worry as much about early receipt of payments, which would be subject to reinvestment risk.

15-Year Mortgages

Shorter maturity mortgages, especially the 15-year mortgage, became popular when interest rate volatility increased. Like the traditional 30-year mortgage, each monthly payment is a constant amount. Since the loan is amortized over a shorter time horizon, the monthly payment is higher. However, the interest costs associated with the 15-year mortgage are less than half of those associated with the 30-year mortgage. Such savings are extremely attractive to borrowers.

Homebuilders are also attracted to the 15-year mortgage. To help sales, interest subsidies are often offered to prospective purchasers of the homes. The builders found that buy-down financing was cheaper through a 15-year mortgage as opposed to a 30-year mortgage.

Investors also find 15-year mortgages appealing. By 1983, 15-year mortgages were incorporated into pass-through programs. With volatile interest rates, investors want to shorten the maturity of their investments in order to reduce interest rate risk exposure. Investors that were previously not able to participate in the pass-through market could now take advantage of more investment opportunities due to the inclusion of the shorter-maturity mortgage.

The Adjustable Rate Mortgage

While adjustable rate mortgages (ARMs) appear to be complex, most ARM contracts have the same underlying features. One common feature is that the contract rate is indexed to some market interest rate. The lender receives the index rate plus a margin of perhaps 200 basis points. Most contracts use a one-year U.S. treasury index. Another index that is used, but to a lesser extent, is the Federal Home Loan Bank Board's contract rate. Programs using the treasury index are more successful since they are easier to obtain and understand. Furthermore, the rate adjustments for the ARMs that are treasury indexed are determined by changes in securities with similar maturities.

Another common feature of ARMs involves the use of caps. Interest rate caps are most popular on contracts that are adjusted often. Interest caps limit how much the contract rate can be revised on the adjustment day. If market rates exceed the cap, the investor cannot recover the difference. Standard interest rate caps are 1 or 2 percent per adjustment period.

Lifetime interest rate caps also exist. These caps are fixed and do not change as the adjustment period interest rate caps do. Standard lifetime caps are 5 percent over the initial rate of the contract.

Payment caps, which limit the amount of the monthly payment, are also used. If market rates increase in such a way that the monthly payment would exceed the cap, the difference can be added on to the outstanding balance of the loan. Thus, in periods when amortization is negative, payment caps are less popular than interest rate caps. Standard payment caps are 7 to 8 percent per year.

Another common practice is to use discount or "teaser" rates to induce borrowers to use ARMs. Such plans offer an introductory rate that is below the initial rate generally being offered at that time. After the initial period is over, the rate is adjusted back to the current index plus the lender's margin. Obviously, a tremendous adjustment may occur. However, this may be partially offset by the use of caps.

ARMs were beginning to grow in popularity in late 1981/early 1982, which was when long-term mortgage rates were at all-time highs. In the first quarter of 1982, ARMs represented approximately 40 percent of the conventional mortgage originations.

RESPONSE TO CREDIT RISK IN ENVIRONMENT

Intensified volatility also led to a greater need for new ways of reducing the risk associated with financial agreements. For example, following the 1983 default of the Washington Public Power Supply System, investors in municipal securities demanded more protection. As a result, the amount of insured municipals increased tremendously. Guarantees on corporate issues also became more popular. While some types of guarantees (i.e., insurance bonds and standby letters of credit) have been available for some time, a variety of new applications has evolved.

The Financial Guarantee

There are basically two types of financial guarantees. The first type can be referred to as credit rating enhancement. As the name implies, coverage is purchased from an insurer in order to enhance the credit rating of the issuer. The insurer collateralizes the underlying credit and also requires additional collateral as a protective measure in case of a default. No loss is expected though, since only sound, high-quality issues are underwritten. Therefore, the premium charged is not based on risk exposure, but is a reflection of the benefit provided to the debt issuer for enhancing its marketability. The insurer is being paid for putting its name, and superior credit rating, on the paper. As a result, the bonds can be offered at a lower rate, providing the issuer with a substantial savings.

The second type of financial guarantee deals with economic losses. In this case, the insurer is taking on real risks while providing a guarantee that the financial obligation will be fulfilled. As with traditional insurance, losses are expected and premiums are set according to the level of risk. Since there is potential for a significant loss, investors should be certain that the insurer could survive such an event.

Some basic guidelines are used as general risk parameters of the deals that can be worked out: First, the term is usually less than 10 years. Second, the underlying credit must be fundamentally sound with at least a BBB rating from Standard & Poor or a Baa from Moody's. Third, the transaction itself must make economic sense. Finally, the value of the transaction ought to be at least $2 million—it is usually too expensive to do smaller deals.

Typical Financial Guarantees

A variety of financial guarantees has evolved in recent years. Some examples of payment guarantees are as follows: commercial paper; contractual payment obligations; corporate notes or bonds; letters of credit; limited partnership notes; municipal bonds, notes, or leases; pass-through securities; and repurchase agreements. The value of assets can also be insured by policies covering equipment or residual value. Financial guarantees also act as indemnity contracts. Policies are written on commercial or consumer credit; contract repudiation; excess FDIC, SIPC, or private deposit insurance; and retirement fund deficiency. Financial guarantees can also cover risks related to interest rates and currency, such as: basic risk; currency inconvertibility; exchange rates; futures contract guarantees; interest rates; repatriation. Fluctuations in price level indices, such as the consumer price index and the producer price index, can also be insured. Coverage can also be written on equipment performance; production levels of items such as cement, energy, or water flow; and recovery levels of resources such as oil or gas. Since the area of financial guarantees is still evolving, there will be new opportunities for more applications of the products.

Major Benefits of Financial Guarantees

One major benefit of using financial guarantees is that more financial transactions can occur. The financial strength of the insurance company is applied, thereby facilitating the closing of the transactions. Without guarantees, it may not be possible to obtain the necessary financing. Another benefit is that the AAA ratings are supported. Risk-averse investors are insured against the deterioration of the credit rating or quality of the insured issue, even if the underlying credit deteriorates. It is the guarantor's rating that is crucial to the investors.

REGULATORY RESTRUCTURING

While the new financial innovations discussed in the previous sections are largely new products not requiring substantial regulatory restructuring, it became apparent that the instability of the past 20 years rendered the regulatory environment obsolete. Most of the regulatory changes that have been made govern depository financial institutions, conferring greater freedom in pricing, most notably in establishing rates to be paid depositors and in allowing product and geographic diversification. One area that has not been reformed is the structure and pricing of federal deposit insurance, and there is some question as to the desirability of fixed-price deposit insurance for all financial institutions in a less regulated environment.

An Interim Regulatory Adaptation to an Alternative Stimulus: The NOW Account

The economic and financial environment is not the only source of external change leading to a lack of equilibrium. In our federal system of government, there is always an opportunity for a change resulting from state action.

For example, a unique situation existed in Massachusetts. Mutual savings banks in that state had to belong to a state chartered deposit insurance fund, the Mutual Savings Central Fund, which guaranteed 100 percent of customer deposits. In 1972, only eight mutual savings banks chose to belong to both the Central Fund and the Federal Deposit Insurance Corporation. Hence, for most Massachusetts savings banks, which are a major force in the state's retail banking, federal law pertaining to interest payments on demand deposits was not operative. Although interest payments on demand deposits had been prohibited on the federal level since 1933, a bank in Worcester, Massachusetts which was not insured by the FDIC could therefore decide to market an account that paid interest and allowed customers to write checks. Instead of calling it a checking account, the bank chose to call it a negotiable order of withdrawal, and the acronym NOW was born. The Commissioner of Banks denied the request of the bank, Consumer Savings Bank, to market the NOW account. Undaunted, the bank appealed to the Massachusetts Supreme Judicial Court which ruled in its favor on May 21, 1972. The bank began marketing the NOW account shortly thereafter and was followed by mutual savings banks in Massachusetts and New Hampshire.

Commercial bankers were understandably unhappy, as the previous equilibrium was upset. A legislative and lobbying battle ensued in the state legislatures and in the U.S. Congress. The choices were three: to try to prohibit the practice, a difficult task once the product reached the marketplace; to allow the savings banks to have checking accounts but pay no interest; or to allow all depository financial institutions to offer the NOW account. The latter solution was adopted, and in January 1974, all financial institutions in Massachusetts and New Hampshire were empowered to offer NOW accounts. Even though New England states are relatively small, with travel, radio and television, and regional newspapers the NOWs could not be quarantined to Massachusetts and New Hampshire. In March 1976, all of New England permitted NOWs, followed by New York in 1978. Thus, several regional financial centers, Boston and Hartford, and the world's largest financial center, New York, were included in the NOW "experiment." In 1981, after their trial run in the Northeast, NOW accounts went nationwide. Hence, disequilibrium occurred when state actions created a new product. Federal law responded such that eventually the interest-bearing checking account spread to the entire nation.

In the Hunt Commission Report of 1971 there is a curious recommendation regarding interest payments on demand deposits. After several pages of material outlining the problems associated with a ceiling of zero on demand deposit interest payments, the Commission (officially, the President's Commission on Financial Structure and Regulation) decided that for the time being the prohibition of interest payments on demand deposits should be retained. After the ceilings on savings and time deposits were removed, the Commission recommended a reconsideration of the prohibition. Given the rhetoric and the overall thrust of other recommendations, it seemed clear that the Commission also eventually wanted to see this ceiling eliminated. In this instance, the role of the states was to accelerate a financial innovation that might not otherwise have occurred. The relatively favorable experience of banks in New England in coping with the innovation also likely conditioned the various interested parties to gain confidence in the ability of the system to adapt to further change.

The Unregulated Competitor Impact: The Case of Money Market Mutual Funds

If a regulatory regime does not provide a realistic framework in which to deliver financial services, one possible response in the marketplace is the development and growth of unregulated competitors. This is what happened in the late 1970s and the early 1980s in the case of money market mutual funds, or "money market funds" (MMFs). An MMF is a mutual fund offered by stock brokers and insurance companies to the public or to institutional investors. The MMF invests totally in money market instruments, such as U.S. treasury bills, large banks' CDs, commercial paper, Eurodollar deposits, and bankers' acceptances. The mix of money market instruments varies from fund to fund, ranging from low-risk, low-yield U.S. government paper to somewhat more risky instruments. However, the credit risk is very low compared to other financial instruments. Moreover, many of the MMFs aggressively sought to compete with banks by establishing very low minimum balances, the majority between $1,000 and $5,000. Finally, the MMFs allowed the customer to gain access to funds through check writing and, in some cases, through a bank credit card. A close substitute for bank deposits with check-writing privileges, this package of services, which was limited at the time to New England NOW accounts, was attractive indeed. MMFs became especially popular as interest rates rose above the ceilings established by Regulation Q for small time deposits and savings deposits. In November 1982, the balances in money market funds peaked at $242 billion, enough to get the attention of the nation's depository financial institutions, who were still laboring under a regime of interest rate ceilings. Since the money market funds used aggressive marketing techniques, including effective deployed toll-free telephone numbers, they were able to reach many bank customers all over the nation, including the small cities and towns. To the extent that they were successful, the effect was to remove funds from the small banks and funnel them, through the purchase of CDs, to the large money center banks. In essence, the combination of MMFs and their purchase of large banks' CDs resulted in a nationwide "banking system" without large banks bothering to establish a physical presence in the many small towns and cities across the nation. This de facto entry did not escape the attention of bankers in these areas, however.

The Establishment Strikes Back: DIDMCA and Garn-St. Germain

Faced with the competition of MMFs and others, the depository financial institutions realized that it was pointless to fight with each other—which was their usual posture. Rather, the deposit interest rate ceilings that had been installed to protect them from the environment had now changed to walls hemming them in and preventing them from competing effectively. In 1980, Congress passed and the president signed into law the Depository Institutions Deregulation and Monetary Control Act (DIDMCA), which included the following:

1. A phased removal of all ceilings on time and savings deposits
2. Nationwide expansion of NOW accounts to all insured depository financial institutions
3. An expansion of powers for thrift institutions to allow them to diversify their interest rate risk
4. Access to the payments system and similar reserve requirements for all insured depository financial institutions offering transactions accounts

But the phase-out of ceilings was not stemming the outflow of funds to MMFs. For that reason the Congress, in 1982, passed the Garn-St. Germain Depository Institutions Act. That act included a provision for the establishment of two new retail deposit accounts, both to be offered with no ceilings. The most popular of the two was the money market deposit account (MMDA), which was to have a minimum balance of $2,500, no interest ceiling, no maturity (funds deposited and withdrawn at the option of the customer), and limited transactions capability (limited to a certain number of transactions per month). The other account was labelled the Super NOW account. Similar to the MMDA, it had a higher reserve requirement and permitted unlimited transactions.

The intent of this legislation was to give insured depository financial institutions the capability to survive in a volatile financial environment. The greater freedom has essentially removed the differences between commercial banks, mutual savings banks, and savings and loan associations. The MMDA was a spectacular success in terms of customer acceptance. Since their implementation, the minimum balance requirements for MMDAs and Super NOWs have been successively reduced and eliminated, and the ceilings on savings accounts have been removed.

In summary, the environment described above created various kinds of imbalances and disequilibrium in the regulatory system. Consequently, there has been a pattern of continued change. When the existing arrangements become unsatisfactory for all the parties, the response is a rearrangement in which the costs and benefits are restructured to create a new, if only temporary, equilibrium.

SUMMARY AND CONCLUSION

The economic and financial environment of the past two decades has been characterized by rapid inflation, successive bouts of prosperity and recession, and high and volatile interest rates. As a result, the financial structure of the nation has been under stress, and the riskiness of the financial marketplace has increased. One aspect of the financial system that has been affected is the regulatory structure. Regulatory regimes that help maintain an equilibrium in one environment do not necessarily serve that function in another one. The participants then reorganize the system to provide a new equilibrium, until the environment changes again. Of course, the marketplace also responds on its own with new products and services that meet needs created by a changed situation.

New products that have arisen in direct response to increased riskiness include interest rate futures, options, and swaps. The development of secondary market securities for mortgages also gives lenders the choice of making and holding a long-term loan or making the loan and selling it, effectively reducing the maturity or duration of its assets. Also, because the volatile nature of the economic environment has created more credit (or default) risk, many lenders have incorporated the increased risk into their interest rates, while banks and especially insurance companies have rapidly expanded their guarantee services.

Finally, the regulatory environment must reflect the reality of the financial marketplace. When it has not, alternative means of delivering financial services have evolved. This response has included disruptive disintermediation in wholesale money markets early in the period and the rapid growth of money market mutual funds in the latter part of the period. In both cases, the regulatory environment changed to create a more beneficial outcome. In addition, the federal nature of our regulatory system allows some role of the states. In the case of one service, the NOW account, state action upset the previous equilibrium, and the NOW account subsequently spread across the nation.

In retrospect, the financial system has shown remarkable resiliency. Even though it was severely abused, it adapted and performed its major functions. New products and services emerged to meet the needs of the participants, and the regulatory structure eventually adapted itself, although with some delay. It is likely that a period of relative stability, as the system seems to exhibit at the moment, will result in the digestion, consolidation, and refinement of the products and services that arose from the turmoil of the last two decades. The only thing that seems certain is that any changes in today's environment will bring about responses to permit participants to cope with those changes.

BIBLIOGRAPHY

Asay, Michael R. "Pricing and Analysis: Adjustable Rate Mortgages." *Mortgage Banking* (December, 1984).

Board of Governors of the Federal Reserve System. *Banking and Monetary Statistics, 1941-1970.* 1976.

Board of Governors of the Federal Reserve System. *Annual Statistical Digest.* Various issues.

Brueggeman, William B. and Leo D. Stone. *Real Estate Finance.* Illinois: Richard D. Irwin, 1981.

Center for Research and Development in Financial Services, University of Connecticut, *Credit Enhancement/Financial Guarantee Seminar*, Hartford, Connecticut, May 30, 1985.

Cholewicki, Victor. "CMOs Transform Mortgage Credit Markets." *Mortgage Banking* (February, 1985).

Clauretie, Terrence M. and Daniel Sklar. "Designing ARMs for Interest Rate Uncertainty." *Mortgage Banking* (May, 1985).

Colton, Kent W. and Michael J. Lea. "ARMs and the Secondary Markets: The Next Boom?" *Secondary Mortgage Markets* (May, 1984).

Cortes, Diane. "Everything You Always Wanted to Know About ARMs." *Mortgage Banking* (December, 1984).

Cortes, Diane L. and Adrienne W. Schuette. "Keeping in Step with ARMs." *Mortgage Banking* (December, 1984).

Dunham, Constance. "The Growth of Money Market Funds." *New England Economic Review* (September-October 1980).

Eisenbeis, Robert A. "Regulation and Financial Innovation: Implications for Financial Structure and Competition Among Depository Institutions." *Issues in Bank Regulation* (Winter 1981).

Erlanger, Richard A., Alexander & Alexander of New York Inc., *Credit Enhancement/Financial Guarantee Seminar*, Houston, Texas, March 21, 1985.

Federal Reserve Bank of Chicago, *Leveling the Playing Field*, 1983.

Federal Home Loan Bank of San Francisco, *Interest Rate Swaps for Eleventh District Member Institutions*, 1983.

Financial Security Assurance Inc., *Financial Guarantees: Are a Few Bad Apples Spoiling the Bushel?* New York, 1986.

Flick, Frederick E. "Mortgage Markets and Mortgage-Related Securities: Developments and Implications." *Mortgage Banking* (June, 1984).

Forbes, Daniel. "Financial Guarantees: Providing New Hope to the Insurers?" *Risk Management* (October, 1984).

Garcia, Gillian and Annie McMahon. "Regulatory Innovation: The New Bank Accounts." *Economic Perspectives*, Federal Reserve Bank of Chicago (March-April 1984).

Hu, Joseph. "Proliferation of Mortgage-Backed Securities." *Mortgage Banking* (September, 1985).

Hu, Joseph C. "The Revolution in 'Securitizing' Residential Mortgages." *Real Estate Review* (Summer 1984).

Kane, Edward J. "Accelerating Inflation, Technological Change, and the Decreasing Effectiveness of Bank Regulation." *Journal of Finance* (May 1981).

Kaufman, George G. "The Role of Traditional Mortgage Lenders in Future Mortgage Lending: Problems and Prospects." *Staff Memoranda*, Federal Reserve Bank of Chicago (1984).

Khoury, Sarkis J. *Speculative Markets.* New York: Macmillan, 1984.

Kopprasch, Robert, John Macfarlane, Daniel R. Ross, and Janet Showers. *The Interest Rate Swap Market: Yield Mathematics, Terminology and Conventions.* New York: Salomon Brothers, June, 1985.

Kruse, Adrian F. and James M. Zinn. "Interest Rate Swaps: An Analysis for Bankers." *The Magazine of Bank Administration* (June, 1984).

Milligan, John W. "The Insurance Industry's New Pot of Gold." *Institutional Investor* (February, 1985).

Murphy, Neil B. "Technological Change in Delivery Systems in the Evolving Structure of Financial Institutions." in *Strategic Planning for Economic and Technological Change in the Financial Services Industry*. Federal Home Loan Bank of San Francisco (1983).

Murphy, Neil B. and Lewis Mandell, *The NOW Account: Profitability, Pricing and Strategies*. Bank Administration Institute, 1980.

Murphy, Neil B. and Ronald C. Rogers. "Commercial Banking." *Handbook of Financial Markets*. Edward I. Altman, ed. New York: Wiley, 1986.

Navratil, Frank J. "Freddie Mac & Ginnie Mae Securities: How Close Is The Family Resemblance?" *Secondary Mortgage Markets* (Fall 1985).

Phillips, Almarin. "Technology and the Nature of Financial Services." *Strategic Planning for Economic and Technological Change in the Financial Services Industry*. Federal Home Loan Bank of San Francisco (1983).

Powers, Mark J. and David J. Vogel. *Inside the Financial Futures Markets*. New York: Wiley, 1981.

President's Commission on Financial Structure and Regulation (informally known as the Hunt Commission), *Report*, U.S. Government Printing Office, 1971.

Villani, Kevin E. "The Secondary Mortgage Markets: What They Are, What They Do, and How to Measure Them." *Secondary Mortgage Markets* (February, 1984).

4 Globalization of Financial Services

BENJAMIN V. STRICKLAND

There is one point, at least, on which financial commentators and industry participants would seem to agree, and that is that the globalization of financial services is an inexorable process. Beyond this, however, there is disagreement on precisely what globalization means, the pace at which it will proceed, which product areas and services will be most affected, and above all, what strategies should be adopted if organizations are to benefit from the process and avoid being overwhelmed by it.

The purpose of this chapter is therefore to examine the major forces at work, to explain and quantify the recent trends and current extent of globalization, to provide pointers on future pace and direction, and to stimulate thought on the strategic responses that might be appropriate for industry participants.

GLOBALIZATION DEFINED

Before attempting to describe and measure the impact of globalization on industry participants, customers, and the markets in which they operate, it may be useful to clear the ground by attempting a description, if not a definition, of what is meant by the term. "Globalization" has become fashionable jargon to describe, often in a rather loose way, the flow of products and provision of services by firms on a worldwide (rather than domestic or intercountry) basis. While no two observers could be expected to agree on one simple description, in its purest form globalization might be thought of as the growing homogeneity of products, services, and customer preferences. Complete globalization would be reached at the point where industry participants would be able to look at the world as a single undifferentiated marketplace.

For obvious reasons, true globalization can never be achieved. Geographical, temporal, political, cultural, regulatory, and other barriers may be diminished, but they can never be completely removed. Because of barriers remaining in some of these areas, internationalism will continue to flourish. Some products and services will always have to be tailored and priced to suit the requirements of a given country or customer. The distinction between the global and international approaches can perhaps be seen most clearly in a manufacturing context. International Business Machines, which basically markets one line of computers around the world, with only minor adjustments to suit local requirements, is a global marketer. In contrast, a Ford Motor Company now produces clearly distinct U.S. and European models to appeal to the preferences of the separate markets in which it operates.

THE FORCES DRIVING GLOBALIZATION

No one factor can be cited as the sole force behind globalization; rather a convergence of various strands can be seen, strands that have combined to drive the process onwards. This section briefly considers each of the major strands—technology, multinational clients, increasing user sophistication, world imbalances, deregulation, and disintermediation—as they affect the financial services industry.

Technology

The vital role of technology, not only as an enabler but also now as an instigator of globalization, is beyond question. Both the speed and cost of computers and communication linkages have declined so dramatically in the last 30 years that the change is not just one of format, but one of substance. In the late 1950s, Citibank's telex line between New York and London transmitted at a rate of seven characters per second—today that rate is over 150,000. Data that in 1955 took 6 minutes and over $14 to process can now be processed in 1 second for 7 cents. Consequently, the growth in the investment has been rapid in the last 15 years: From devoting less than 3 percent of total operating expenditures to technology in 1970, leading U.S. banks are now devoting closer to 15 percent, and this level is projected to rise to 20 percent by the end of the decade. Whereas in the past, the greater proportion of these expenditures (perhaps 80 to 90 percent) was devoted to 'back-office' processing for reasons of speed and cost, the trends are increasingly toward expenditure on new or improved delivery systems to customers, and toward development of decision-support systems. Technology is thus moving rapidly from the back office into the front office, creating business opportunities that never before existed. As yet, this movement remains in its formative stages.

In 1978, Dr. Daniel J. Boorstin wrote that in "the Republic of Technology [the] supreme law is convergence, the tendency for everything to become more like everything else."[1] In data processing, similarities in types of computers and the need for information transfer between organizations have created just such a convergence of methods and products. In the United Kingdom, for instance, bank statements from the major clearing banks are now remarkably similar, as are the checks with which those accounts are tapped. This tendency towards homogeneity is even more apparent when it comes to new delivery systems. Thus automated teller machines (ATMs) are being produced that impose almost identical service standards on the institutions around the world that use them, be they banks, building societies, savings and loan institutions, retailers, or other intermediaries.

Clients are not desirous of a standardized service. Other things being equal, they would prefer something to be personally tailored to their needs. The acceptable compromise must be that a standard product can score by offering a distinct price and/or quality advantage sufficient to overcome any innate shortcomings. Thus, customers are prepared to use ATMs because their transaction costs are lower (they are cheaper than human tellers), they are accessible at all hours, and they can be located more conveniently than their human equivalents.

Perhaps the greatest impact of technology in the next 10 years will be the further development of decision-support systems, particularly where these are linked to electronic distribution networks. Software linked to video switching equipment already makes it possible for instantaneous identification of arbitrage opportunity between two markets. For instance, the ability of an international securities house or brokerage firm to participate in 24-hour trading and pass a book from Tokyo to London to New York exists only because the technology is available to support it. This ability to bridge markets inevitably serves to eradicate differences between those markets. If the exchange rate between dollars and yen moves in London, so will it soon move in New York, with profitable arbitrage taking place until equilibrium is restored. Every difference creates a profitable trading opportunity that will be exploited until the markets move back into line.

Multinational Clients

Not only do the world's major companies continue to grow in size and strength, but they too are driven by the forces of globalization. Multinational companies have usually operated as decentralized organizations producing and selling for distinct local markets. They have been, in effect, multidomestic companies and have often accepted purely domestic services from those financial institutions with which they have come into contact, be these insurance companies, banks, or advisory businesses. But the tendency now is for a multinational firm to market a worldwide brand or service that makes little if any allowance for local differences.

Starting with the early example set by individual products such as Coca-Cola, whole industries have now become essentially global. These global products include semiconductors, televisions, cars, and telecommunications. But while there is a great deal to be gained by filling a global market niche, the management and organization problems created are often large as well. Nevertheless, companies like IBM which have the capability to manage globally, gain a significant competitive edge over those that have to organize to keep things simple. It should therefore not be surprising that a globally organized company now looks for a financial services company that can complement its global reach. In some areas, a local provider may be able to demonstrate experience with respect to the client or local market sufficient to retain its position. Increasingly, however, this position is likely to be eroded by the superior convenience and facilities that a globally organized financial services company can offer. The treasurer of a U.S. subsidiary based in Sydney, who is able to communicate on-line with his own head office in New York, expects the same degree of sophistication from his bank. As the growth of the Society of Worldwide Interbank Financial Telecommunications (SWIFT) since its founding in 1973 indicates, demand for international services is broadening rapidly. From 239 banks in 15 countries at its launch, SWIFT now has 1257 member banks in 54 countries. The compound annual growth in average daily traffic over the last seven years has been 28 percent.

On top of this, major banks have been developing their own treasury management systems to provide a more elaborate and sophisticated service to their customers. By being able to identify and transfer funds faster, banks can sharpen their investment decisions and reduce their clerical and administrative costs. Because the costs of developing the network are of course high, it is advantageous for many institutions to participate in systems like General Electric Information Services Company (GEISCO) networks for international money transfer and Eurobond clearing, which serve more than one bank.

The influence of multinational companies is not restricted to the debt markets. Increasingly, very large companies are finding that benefits can be gained from raising equity and securing a quotation in more than one market. As large-scale companies in the chemical, pharmaceutical, and electronics industries become increasingly international, investors may become indifferent as to whether they buy Imperial Chemical Industries of the United Kingdom, Dow Chemical of the United States, or Hoechst of Germany, particularly when international investment enables them to hedge their currency, and even their market, exposure. The management of those companies might thus expect to raise equity on the same ratings as their peers. A company like L. M. Ericsson, that wishes to raise money at a competitive price, can avoid the illiquidity of the Swedish home market, where the cost of capital can be extremely high, by offering stock in the much larger U.S. market.

Increasing User Sophistication

The innovation demonstrated by leading financial institutions in designing products to match the desired profile of their corporate customers is being matched also by the sophistication of those customers. No longer will a client accept a less than competitive interest rate on borrowed money when it is able to obtain a more competitive tender from a rival funds provider. As a result, the one-on-one lender/borrower relationship is dissolving in favor of a broadly market-based system, mainly U.S. dollar-related, which large sophisticated companies can tap, swapping the proceeds into their own currency should they wish to. This development has reached the point where some major borrowers are able to raise money more cheaply than banks can. The profitability of using intermediaries when a borrower like ICI can raise money at a margin of one-sixteenth of a point is obviously negligible.

Contributing to this understanding of what markets around the world can offer the customer for financial services is the greater mobility of personnel. Few of the world's top fifty banks do not now have a branch in both London and New York in addition to their home country. With this presence also comes a transfer of skills and techniques applied successfully elsewhere, together with a base of customers to whom these skills can be sold if they are of advantage to the client. Some impression of this eagerness to participate internationally in deregulating markets is provided by the interest shown by outsiders in the London markets. Of the 33 major London brokerage firms that had formed liaisons with outsiders up until June 1985, no fewer than half had done so with non-U.K. partners. And while U.S. partners dominated this list, Canadian, Swiss, French, and Swedish concerns were also represented.

Larger sophisticated clients are themselves responding to the complexity of financial markets by taking upon their own shoulders an increasing amount of work that they previously paid an outside financial adviser to do. British Petroleum has recently set up British Petroleum Finance International as its own in-house bank to handle treasury-bill transactions, foreign exchange, commercial banking, financial planning, and corporate finance. Volvo and GEC have followed suit, and Siemens and ICI have already gone some way toward developing this type of expertise. For large U.S. companies—GMAC, Exxon, Chrysler—the process is already well established. Such developments follow logically from the realization that major companies can often raise money more cheaply than their banks, and can avoid paying high fees for advice by internalizing the expertise.

World Imbalances

There can be little doubt that since the Second World War the increasing cross-border flows of capital to finance trading surpluses and deficits, as well as exports and imports, have served to open up regional markets. The Euromarkets were largely created out of the pool of dollars injected into Europe in the 1940s. In the 1970s, intermediation on a huge scale was required to recycle petrodollars when the price of oil quadrupled. Major recipients of the petrodollar surpluses were the less developed countries (LDCs). At the end of 1984, the Bank for International Settlements recorded a total exposure of $211 billion to Latin America alone. Although the net demand for funds has stabilized considerably in the last two years, it appears unlikely that overall exposure will decline dramatically in the shorter term. The slow growth of a secondary market in LDC debt, and the faster development of a swap market, are examples of the way in which international markets can be developed to fill the collective needs of participating banks by passing on or redistributing risk and exposure.

The expansion of cross-border capital flows is not confined to LDCs. By February 1985, the U.S. current account deficit had reached $100 billion: equivalent to 2 3/4 percent of gross national product. A major contributor to this deficit was the appreciation of the dollar, which undermined the competitiveness of the entire U.S. traded goods sector. The combination of a strong dollar and high real interest rates resulted in massive capital inflows to the United States. At the same time, Japan was running a current account surplus of some $35 billion.

Imbalances of this magnitude are indicative of the need for large-scale financial intermediation between countries. High volatility of exchange rates, interest rates, and inflation together provides an increasing need for risks to be traded and dispersed. There can be little wonder that, against this background in the world's major markets, trading in options and futures has shown a dramatic increase. But although such instruments can be used to spread the risk facing an individual institution, the risk for the financial system as a whole is not reduced.

Deregulation

The belief that free market forces will probably increase the efficient allocation of resources is encouraging governments to open up their financial markets to foreign competition. The governments realize that protectionism is likely to prevent their domestic financial institutions from growing strong enough to participate in the global markets. In Europe, the European Council has assigned "high priority" to the liberalization of capital markets as part of the process of completing the internal markets, a program targeted for completion in the early 1990s. The United Kingdom totally abolished exchange controls in 1979, and moves in France, Germany, and other member countries suggest that full liberalization will not be limited to capital movements that are purely European.

New or broader entry for foreign banks has been achieved in Australia, Canada, Norway, Portugal, Spain, and Sweden. Foreign banks incorporated in West Germany are now allowed to lead-manage Deutschmark Eurobond issues there. Similarly, the Netherlands plans to open its capital market from January 1986. In Japan, awareness that the more open Singapore and Hong Kong financial centers were capturing a major share of the Far Eastern market has resulted in the first steps towards liberalization. Then yen-dollar agreement announced in 1984 began the gradual opening up of Japan's capital markets, most recently in foreign bonds. The Tokyo Stock Exchange has also now permitted foreign firms to buy seats.

In the United Kingdom, deregulation of prices is being combined with geographical deregulation in 1986. Foreign financial institutions (and, indeed, British firms) will be permitted 100 percent ownership of stock exchange members, and the traditional distinction between brokering and market making will disappear in favor of dual capacity. This in turn will result in net dealing and a significant reduction in commission costs.

Removal of legislative and cultural barriers to free competition is a slow, piecemeal process. It will be some time before the world's second largest economy, Japan, is free of major obstacles to full foreign participation. In the United

States, the McFadden Act, the Glass-Steagall Act, and the Bank Holding Company Act continue to distort and limit the range of activities that can be undertaken by U.S. and foreign banks. In Switzerland, Swiss franc issues must still be lead-managed by a Swiss house. Behind it all, however, is a degree of self-interest which suggests that a return to wholesale protectionism is unlikely, barring major economic or political upheaval. Those countries unwilling to open their doors are likely to find business being taken elsewhere.

New forms of business in one country can spur changes in another. For example, in the United States it is now common to deal in major European equities through American depository receipts (ADRs), a vehicle that provides substantial savings in transaction costs. In response to this vehicle, the United Kingdom halved its stamp duty to 1 percent and in 1986 is introducing negotiated commissions, a change that further reduces transfer costs. Pressure is likely to remain until stamp duty is removed altogether: only then will overseas buyers not be disadvantaged when buying and selling U.K. equities on the London market.

Deregulation is thus both a response to changes under way and a stimulus to future change. It is a response to the pressure by international firms and customers to break down traditional boundaries to doing business across borders, and it is a stimulus to globalization. Globalization also brings with it the need for additional safeguards. Paradoxically, reregulation is needed to ensure higher standards for risk control and prudence. Whereas financial collapse might have been restricted in the past to single economies, the complexity of the global system today increasingly places the whole financial community at risk.

Disintermediation: The Financial Institution as Principal

The forces behind globalization—technology, the growth in size and sophistication of customers and providers of financial services, the influence of world imbalances and deregulation—are requiring some industry participants to invest in systems and people and to expand their networks to cover the world's major business centers. But more profoundly, these and other forces are altering the nature of the industry itself, with far-reaching implications. This important stage in globalization can be characterized as the erosion of the traditional role of financial institutions, that of acting as financial intermediary on behalf of large companies, and the evolution of those institutions to positions as principals.

This process is both relatively new—it has really only been apparent in the United States in the last five years—and confined to certain areas of the industry. But there are grounds for believing that the trend will continue. The inescapable problem for the intermediary has been the increasing difficulty of adding value to a transaction to justify a fee or margin. Pressure has therefore been exerted upon the intermediary to add value in other ways. Either the intermediary can attempt to come up with an innovative new product or idea, for which a user may be prepared to pay, or it can step into the role of principal and assume market risk. Thus, a major company will increasingly expect a bank to buy down an entire issue of debt or equity and subsequently make a secondary market in the security.

This development makes distribution and swap skills vital parts of the investment banks' armory in distributing the often major risk that a large issue entails.

Up to now, the advisory businesses of investment management and mergers and acquisitions have been less influenced by this trend. The obvious reasons are that value can usually be added to the quality and content of their advice, although even here there are signs that clients increasingly expect financial support as well. Venture capital proposals now often require an investment by the sponsoring house; management in leveraged buy-outs look to their advisers for provision of debt finance; and companies defending against a greenmail attack sometimes benefit from market intervention by their advising bank.

The transition from intermediary to principal brings with it requirements for much greater capital, a broad, efficient distribution system, and a franchise built on top-quality personnel. For these reasons, it is difficult to envisage more than 25 to 30 major players evolving around the world. These top firms are likely to come from the big US investment banks, the top commercial banks, the large Japanese securities houses and those financial conglomerates having a brokerage or insurance bias.

WHERE ARE FINANCIAL SERVICES NOW?

The process of globalization is not confined to banks, brokers, securities houses, and the markets in which they operate. But it is in these areas that the most visible developments have taken place. Other financial services industry participants are also seeing some of these pressures, even if the symptoms are less apparent or less acute. In the insurance industry, for instance, brokers are merging to expand their global networks (Marsh & McLennan, Alexander & Alexander, and Sedgwick Forbes have all merged with transatlantic partners), while the necessity of spreading ever larger risks further and faster is promoting the development of international underwriting. In the leasing industry, big ticket deals for airlines are increasingly arranged outside the country of origin. Large firms are getting larger, and small firms are seeking more specialized niches in which lack of a global network is of less consequence.

CAPITAL MARKETS

Without doubt, it is the debt markets that have to date been at the leading edge of globalization. The distinction between the different instruments for raising capital—equity, loans, and bonds—has blurred. Similarly, the advent of currency and interest rates swaps has broken down the boundaries between domestic and international markets so that the two are all but indistinguishable today; a borrower can tap a domestic capital market and swap that debt with a foreign counterpart. Indeed, a vital development for global financing has been the growth of the swap market. As swaps presently constitute off-balance sheet risk for the most part, the size of the market is very hard to estimate, but leading players put it at between $150 and $200 billion. (See Exhibit 4.1.)

The liberalization of markets and the greater activity within them has come to provide much more uniform market-determined rates on bank assets and liabilities, at least in the major financial centers. In part this is a product of the securitization of debt, wherein those able to tap the markets can remove their custom from banks unwilling to give a competitive rate. Between 1977 and 1984, the outstanding volume of money-market paper issued by nonfinancial corporations increased five-fold in the United States. Competition has resulted in a narrowing of spreads to such a degree that in the United States, the United Kingdom, and much of Europe, liquid deposits paying market rates extend right down to the individual household.

International bank credit, however, has been almost static in the past three years. Contrast this stagnation with the growth in volume of international bond issues of 40 percent in 1984, to a total of $84 billion net of redemptions and purchases. This rate appears to have held in 1985. A major recipient of the increase has been the Eurodollar bond sector, because of its depth and the proliferation of innovative techniques. From $35.7 billion in 1983, the volume of new issues jumped to $64.3 billion in 1984. As Exhibit 4.2 shows, since 1981, new

Exhibit 4.1 Principal Value Underlying Interest Rate and Currency Swaps—Swaps Growth

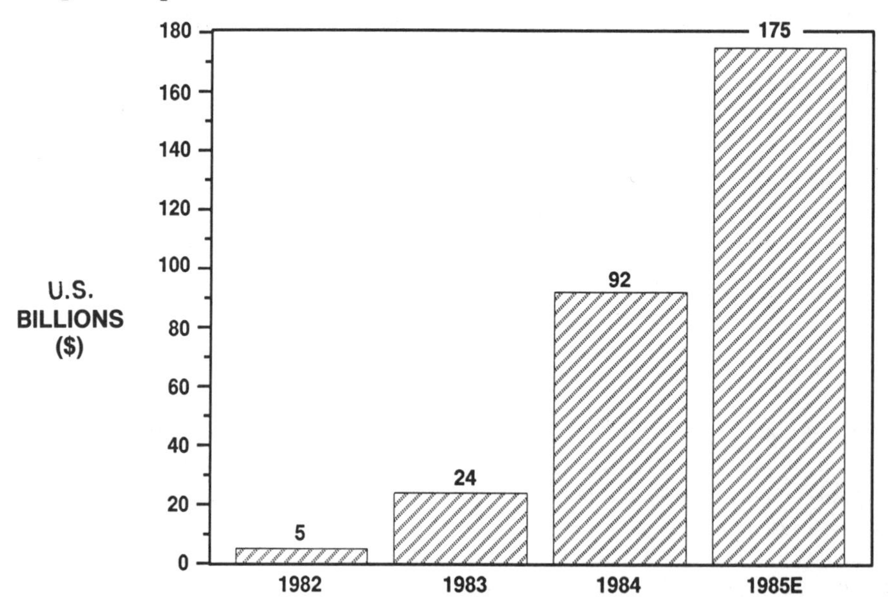

Exhibit 4.2 New Bond Issues

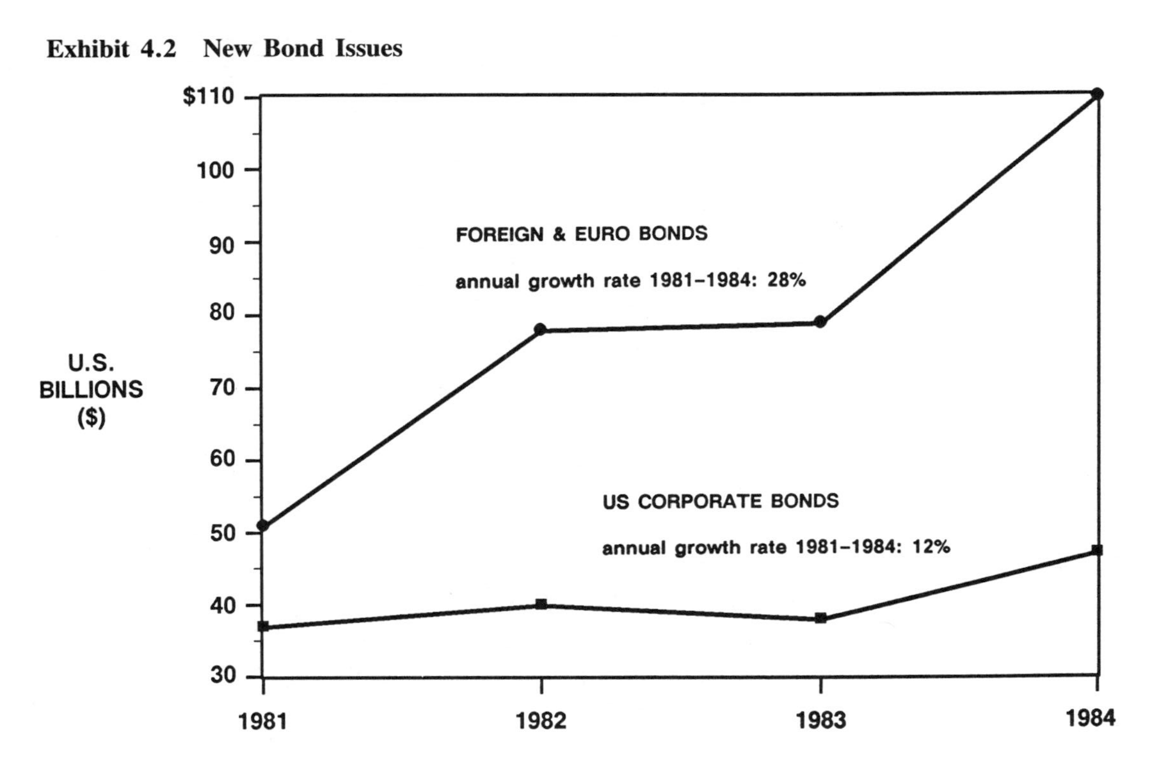

foreign and Eurobond issues have exceeded both the magnitude and the growth rate of new U.S. corporate bond issues.

The growth of the international debt markets has been accompanied by a rapid expansion of the types of instruments offered, including NIFs, RUFs, Euroequities, minimax's, flip-flops, mismatches, caps, WINGs, STAGs. And new packages are being invented every week. In its review of deals of the year, *Euromoney* featured only one plain vanilla syndicated loan; all the rest were more exotic offerings.[2]

One underlying Eurobond issue may be swapped four or more times during its life. The existence of an active swap market has pared down margins. This enables a prime name to act opportunistically in securing the lowest cost of funds, as BMW of Germany did recently, issuing a Euro-Australian dollar bond at a cost of .5 percent below LIBOR for a swap into U.S. dollars. The tendency has been for less prudent houses to try to maintain spreads by attaching swaps to junk bond issues rather than to build up quality exposures or standard dollar interest-rate swaps.

The danger in this building up of off-balance-sheet exposure is the lack of central regulation of what constitutes a prudent level of risk. Put crudely, counterparty risk can be taken on with little regard to the availability of risk capital and at spreads which bear no relationship to credit exposure. Until there is a serious default, there appears little chance that good spreads will return to the market.

Development of the international markets is thus tending to reduce funding costs for all borrowers, with the exception of certain sovereign risks, and is bringing a common standard rate with little allowance for differences in credit rating. The role of the intermediary has thus become increasingly difficult. This difficulty is also evidenced by the development of the global commercial paper market for short-term funding. Corporations simultaneously hold both Euro and U.S. programs, playing the two off to obtain the favorable rates and issuing paper without any underwriting or third-party guarantees. Conditions are stringent, but for a top-quality credit this method is probably the cheapest source of credit available. British Sugar, a major producer, recently launched a U.S. commercial paper program to fund short-term needs for working capital, and is confident that, even after a foreign exchange transaction to swap the proceeds into sterling, the cost of funds will compare favorably with sterling bankers' acceptances or overdrafts.

In summary, the following three factors have created a true global debt market for large borrowers over the last 10 years: willingness to tap whatever market will provide the lowest cost of funds; fierce competition for market share by financial intermediaries; and growth of traded paper and swaps to enable risks to be redistributed. As the process continues, it is constantly spreading downwards to take in smaller companies.

Equity Markets

Compared with the debt market, the international equity market is at a formative stage. But already there are signs that similarly dramatic growth is a prospect.

Pressure is coming from both sides: The major companies wish to raise capital as efficiently as possible, and the end investors wish to balance their portfolios with stocks from more than just their home countries. There are, however, significant regulatory barriers to the coalescence of an international equity market. In countries like the United Kingdom, existing shareholders have preemptive rights on new issues of stock, while in other countries like Japan there has in the past been an embargo on institutional pension fund investment in foreign equities. In addition, an overseas investor in an equity will require up-to-date research on that company to avoid being disadvantaged in relation to an investor in the company's domestic market.

For the company in need of capital, the incentives to seek help internationally are a lower cost of raising equity, a wider base of shareholders, and also, it is hoped, a higher rating on the company's shares. Over the past 10 years, annual returns on U.S. equities, at 15 percent, have lagged behind those in the United Kingdom (23 percent), Hong Kong (21 percent), and Japan (17 percent). (These figures ignore currency movements.) Foreign equities appear even more attractive following the dollar's fall in late 1985. *Euromoney* magazine this year identified 328 internationally traded companies (up from 236 last year), defining this group as companies with at least one active and liquid market outside their home market. Among these it counted 85 U.S. companies, 65 Japanese, 25 British, and 25 Australian.[3] For some time now, foreign companies have been traded in the United States through American depository receipts (ADRs), at least partly because their transaction costs are often lower than those required in dealing on the home exchange. Exposure to another market can serve to raise the rating of a stock, particularly if the domestic exchange is small and relatively illiquid. Norsk Data, a Scandinavian company, entered the U.S. market in 1983, when U.S. investors were placing a high premium on technology stocks. The price of stock rose 15 percent between announcement and pricing of the ADRs.

For the largest companies, the liquidity of the U.S. markets is often a major incentive to a U.S. quotation. The market valuation of IBM alone is now larger than the equity capitalization of all other world stock markets except Tokyo, Frankfurt, London, and Toronto. For large companies like British Telecom, L. M. Ericsson, or Reuters Holdings, the ability to float between $120 and $250 million of equity onto the U.S. markets is both an exercise in international marketing and an opportunity to gain new shareholders.

An important recent development is the growth of the Euroequity market, which is showing marked similarity to the early stages of the Eurobond market 20 years ago (see Exhibit 4.3). This is more than coincidence, as the prime movers in both markets are the same. The advantage is the extremely rapid distribution of securities. Nestle was a pioneer in this market with three Euroequity issues. Others have since followed, including the Swiss Bank Corporation, which formed separate underwriting syndicates in no less than 10 countries.

A parallel movement can be seen in institutional investors' increasing tendency to diversify their portfolios by investing in foreign stocks. Exhibit 4.4 shows the projected nondomestic pension fund investment by the major industrialized countries.

Exhibit 4.3 Eurobond and International Equity Issues[a]

	1963	1964	1965
Eurobonds (corporate sector)	35.0	162.5	381.4
	1983	**1984**	**1985**[b]
International equity issues	83.4	196.4	363.5

Source: Lim, Quek Pek. "Equities Enter the Eurobond Age." *Euromoney*, October, 1985, p. 262.
[a]In $ millions.
[b]To August 1985.

Growth of U.S. ERISA investment overseas to anywhere near $150 million would obviously have a dramatic impact on the global market in equities—and this would still be modest in comparison with the percentage anticipated in other countries. It also presents possible pitfalls for companies and investors, since sales of shares by foreign investors could have a catastrophic effect on prices, particularly if the domestic market is not large enough to absorb the shares. The onus, therefore, is upon companies to keep their overseas shareholders, both existing and potential, fully informed of their strategies and results.

International Mergers and Acquisitions

Corporations, assisted by their financial advisers, are not only actively tapping both the debt and equity markets outside their own country in search of cheaper funds, they are also increasingly looking overseas for potential acquisitions. The

Exhibit 4.4 Projected Growth of Nondomestic Pension Fund Investment

	Nondomestic Investment as % of Total Pension Assets		Volume (U.S. $ Millions)	
	1984	1990	1984	1990
United Kingdom	18%	25%	$20,000	$ 56,000
Netherlands	8	10	6,000	16,000
Japan	8	10	5,000	24,000
Canada	7	10	4,000	12,000
Switzerland	8	15	3,500	16,000
Australia	4	12	1,000	9,000
Germany	3	10	500	5,000
Other (non-U.S.)	8	12	5,000	27,000
			45,000	165,000
United States	2	8	16,000	150,000
Total			$61,000	$315,000

Source: Euromoney, "Corporate Finance."

merger/acquisition trend that has in the United States been characterized by large and aggressive assaults on major companies is now spreading cross-border. As Exhibit 4.5 shows, foreign companies buying into the United States now constitute some 5 to 10 percent of the U.S. merger and acquisition activity, as measured by both volume and value.

U.K. companies like Unilever, Beecham, and Hanson Trust have long been keen purchasers in the United States. Major acquisitions in the last year also involved ICI (the purchase of Beatrice Chemicals) and Nestle (the purchase of Carnation), the latter being at $3 billion the biggest transaction ever consummated by a non-U.S. purchaser. Perhaps the acme of international acquisition battles in recent times was the spectacle of Consolidated Foods, the U.S. giant, and Reckitt and Coleman of the United Kingdom fighting it out for Nicholas Kiwi in Australia. Consolidated eventually acquired control in a deal valued at $327 million.

These international transactions are as much a function of the inventiveness of investment banks as they are of the companies which they advise. With margins being squeezed in their traditional capital-intensive markets, U.S. investment banks and U.K. merchant banks are aggressively looking to generate higher fee income. Mergers are, admittedly, also a product of buoyant stock markets, where highly rated companies have the opportunity to acquire undervalued assets without diluting earnings. But although the level of merger activity will doubtless fluctuate with the general health of the world's markets, it would appear that global merger/acquisition activity is here to stay.

POINTERS ON FUTURE PACE AND DIRECTION

This section examines how the forces driving globalization mesh with the current state of development in financial services, and speculates on the likely future pace and direction of these trends.

Technology

Up until now, technology has been used to improve communication between separate geographical markets around the world. It has been suggested that the

Exhibit 4.5 Foreign Participation in U.S. M&A Activity

M&A Activity in the U.S.	**1980**	**1981**	**1982**	**1983**	**1984**
Volume ($ billions)	45	85	55	75	120
Number of transactions	1,900	2,400	2,350	2,500	2,550
Foreign Companies Buying into the U.S.					
Volume ($ billions)	7	18	5	6	15
Number of transactions	190	230	150	130	150

Source: *Euromoney*, "Corporate Finance."

level of sophistication attained has created what is tantamount to a global market. And in many ways this is true. Certainly the gains have been tremendous. But there is an important difference in format between a thoroughly global market and, say, a Tokyo, a London, and a New York market, among which communication is good, although not perfect. This difference is easily shown. A U.S. investor wishing to sell 400,000 shares in Volvo was quoted prices of 425 Swedish krona in Stockholm, 427 krona in New York, and 435 krona in London. Not surprisingly he chose London. From this seller's point of view, the market lacks homogeneity to the tune of 4 million krona, or about $500,000. As long as buyers and sellers must call on three separate markets, globalization remains at least one step away.

Technology has an important role to play in taking this step. Development of still faster and stronger linkages between exchanges will serve to reduce the differences that exist in pricing: the Stockholm broker would become more aware of the London buyer in the example above, and would thus be able to raise the offer price quoted.

The elimination of market differences will be furthered by the development of computers that can instantaneously identify divergences between markets and "arbitrage out" the differences for a profit without human assistance. The ultimate theoretical development will be a centralized market to which all players have equal access. Such an exchange would have to be computer driven and would have no trading floor—and hence no location, per se. As national markets are increasingly driven by computer systems, and as differences in dealing costs decline, so the tendency will grow for stocks like Volvo only to be quoted on the one market, to which everyone has access. Clearing all transactions through one market has obvious attractiveness, so long as all potential buyers and sellers can be covered. It promotes depth, liquidity, and "best price." While the domestic exchange might be an obvious choice for a company, a dual quotation is likely to remain necessary until the domestic market can match the liquidity and access to buyers and sellers afforded by quotation on a second exchange.

The cost of communication and interpretation of information is a key factor in whether it is cost effective to trade globally. Consequently, the signs are that computerized markets are likely to overwhelm and replace exchange trading floors, steeped though they are in custom and precedent. Perhaps the most vivid indication is the growth of the National Association of Securities Dealers Automated Quotations (NASDAQ) in the United States. From the mid-1970s, when turnover in over-the-counter stocks was around one billion shares a year, volume has soared to over 16 billion shares valued at nearly $200 billion with average daily turnover of four times the U.K. stock exchange. NASDAQ trading in the last four years has grown more than half as fast again as trading on the New York Stock Exchange. The system succeeds by its speed, convenience, and accuracy. Theoretically, the means are already in place for a global 24-hour market—all that is needed is a reduction in the very high cost of communications outside the United States that such a sophisticated system demands.

In London, with the "big-bang" on October 27, 1986, similar pressures have been at work. Although the stock exchange floor seems likely in the shorter term to survive the end of fixed-rate commissions and the removal of certain distinctions between brokers and traders, the pressure is on to move to a screen-based system as soon as possible. Failure to do so on the part of the exchange is likely to lead to more and more deals being done off the floor.

World Imbalances

There is no particular reason to think that the high flow rate of international capital and the volatility of currencies and interest rates are going to decline. On the contrary, dismantling barriers to trade and continuing to move away from "managed" exchange rates is likely to promote rather than reduce volatility: The shrinking cost of transferring funds or exchanging currencies associated with advances in technology and lower commissions will also promote rapid and international transfers of capital.

Under the umbrellas of the gold exchange standard established by the Bretton Woods agreement in 1944, the growth of multinational companies proceeded rapidly. But as national governments increasingly directed their policies towards domestic economic objectives, the system was progressively undermined. It effectively collapsed in 1971, when conversion of the dollar into gold was suspended and replaced by a regime of floating exchange rates. Although many countries would doubtless wish to see a more stable exchange rate environment, there seems little prospect of this occurring while traditional perceptions of national interest persist. The current volume of currency flows makes it extremely difficult, if not impossible, for a government to intervene actively in the market and "hold" a given exchange rate. It therefore seems likely that hedges against exchange rate volatility will continue to be much in demand in the foreseeable future, and that the swaps, options, and futures markets which serve to link the major trading nations will grow further.

The debt situation in the less developed countries makes it difficult to envisage any substantial repayments of principal in the short term, even if third-world debtors continue to bear full interest costs. Banks in the developed world are thus likely to retain substantial overseas exposures in these countries, even if swaps and a secondary market in these debts allow risk to be reallocated between banks.

Deregulation

Deregulation may actually be something of a misnomer. While restrictions on international flows of capital have been lifted and barriers to entry by overseas firms have been reduced, governments have been increasingly preoccupied with protection of depositors and investors from the vagaries of today's fast-moving markets. In effect, many markets have been subject to reregulation. The goal is to balance the benefits of international competition and funds flows against the need to safeguard those who use these markets.

This is far from an easy process. If regulation is felt to be too severe, there is a danger that business will move elsewhere: In London, for instance, the stock exchange has recently encountered such problems of principle in its attempts to regulate international equities dealt out of London. Because many people are only alerted to the need for increased vigilance and control when public catastrophes occur, it must be hoped that future lessons will not be learned too painfully. It was suggested earlier that the risk of contagion in a global system transcends geographic boundaries. It may therefore be that in coming years countries with excessive failures or problems will be partitioned off from the global market until sufficient safeguards are put in place to prevent repetition of such incidents. It would be unwise to speculate too freely on where future difficulties may occur. However, it would appear that at present the risks being taken on the fringes of the very fast-moving debt markets are sometimes not as carefully controlled as those in more established businesses.

IMPLICATIONS FOR STRATEGY

It is important to retain a perspective on the spread of globalization, not just in geographical terms but also in relation to the products and services most concerned. Fundamentally, the process of globalization has been readily apparent only in the debt markets so far. There are strong signs of parallel developments in the equity markets, but these have to date been limited, other than in international investment. There has been an increase in international merger/acquisition activity; but, again, this has still been small in relation to total domestic activity. It has thus been those intermediaries serving larger corporate customers in the debt markets that have been most affected by globalization, at all levels from primary issuing to trading.

An important ingredient in the success of the global debt market has been the ability to package debt into a commodity product that is readily understandable, not only to the "seller" or person raising the debt, but also to the end buyer. Beyond the basic questions of interest rate and maturity profile, the buyer must be fully apprised of credit status; that is, he should be made aware of the risk that an obligation he holds will not be honored. This risk is reduced in two ways: by efficient systems for rating the credit worthiness of customers (which effectively converts risk into margin), and by active trading in the security (which simplifies trading the risk to a third party).

It is much more difficult to capture information succinctly on an equity where the future returns from the investment are dependent on a myriad of factors that demand much closer study. Investors not kept fully informed of circumstances affecting the company can therefore be at an extreme disadvantage.

Long-standing traditions and conventions that exist in the equity markets can also be an impediment to adequate disclosure. Simple structural questions like value dates can cause major processing problems for settlement of international equity dealings: In Switzerland it is two or three working days, in Sweden five, in the Euromarkets seven, and in the United Kingdom it depends upon the period during which the transaction occurs within the (normally) two-week account. It will take time for systems like Cedel and Euro-clear, which cope so efficiently in the Eurobond market, to provide the same service for equities.

Any participant in the financial services industry wishing to servicc the needs of large multinational companies for issuing, distributing, and trading debt must already have felt the effects of globalization. The trend towards increasing concentration of business with the major players has already become apparent in the United States, where around 90 percent of new issues business goes to the top five investment banks. In the Eurobond markets, the top five command about 40 percent. To succeed in these markets it is therefore becoming increasingly necessary to have not only a strong capital base with which to support primary and secondary market activity, but also a global distribution capability backed by expertise in the world's major currencies. At the least, maintaining this capability is likely to demand strong bases in New York, Tokyo, and London. Ancillary centers elsewhere—in Switzerland, Hong Kong, and the world's other markets—would obviously be advantageous as well.

The likelihood is that a group of perhaps 10 to 15 large, heavily capitalized investment banks will emerge, capable of issuing and trading a wide range of securities from the large U.S. investment banks and securities houses, the Japanese banks, and a few of the European commercial banks.

A second tier likely to evolve would be composed of large, well-capitalized investment/merchant banks which would have a major presence in their domestic market and a selective presence in the other major centers. These firms will most likely issue and trade a full range of securities in their home market, and do so on a supportive basis elsewhere. Activities in the other markets will be significant but based on selective development of particular strengths and the need to complement existing activities in their home market. In contrast with the world's major multinationals and governments, this second tier is likely to target international and major domestic clients, for whom lack of a full global network is not a serious debility. The third group, of which many examples already exist, would consist of the medium-sized to large investment banks which have chosen to participate as niche players in those markets where they have strengths and where profitability is good. Their clients are likely to be national companies of all sizes. A fourth group will be the retail sector. This group may remain relatively unscathed by the globalization process, other than possibly by intensified competition as its ranks swell and as larger institutions decide to go "down-market" rather than compete in the above groups. Here, cost and range of product and delivery will determine success more reliably than will global reach.

Financial service companies in each of the first three categories are also likely to be active in the advisory businesses of corporate finance and investment management. As these businesses are fundamentally relationship driven, they will probably be fostered in particular by the niche and second-tier firms that can hope to provide a personalized service not intrinsically inferior to that of global investment banks. With competition within and between categories becoming more aggressive in the face of low profitability in capital-intensive businesses, relationship management will require increasing attention if clients are not to be wooed away by rivals.

Globalization should above all be spurring industry participants to take a critical look at their strategy in the light of the rapid changes taking place in the world's markets. With competition getting fiercer, the uncommitted firm courts a real danger of seeing its market position erode. Firms must increasingly concentrate on what they can be good at, relative to their size and position in the industry. If necessary, they must be prepared to abandon areas in which they no longer feel they can compete.

NOTES

1. Boorstin, Daniel J. *The Republic of Technology*. 1978.
2. *Euromoney* (October 1985). p. 134.
3. Ibid.

SECTION 2 THE CHANGING ECONOMICS OF THE BUSINESS

Understanding and acting in concert with the changing industry structure is only part of the management challenge. Managing the fundamental economics of the business is equally important. The old adage, "revenue minus cost equals profits," is certainly obvious enough, but actively managing the elements of that equation is another matter. Each business has its unique economic model which can be affected by any major strategic thrust. As a consequence, diversified institutions crystallize in very different forms depending on the model from which they start.

The task of understanding the economics of a business is often delegated to a staff group. Ironically, the staff group often knocks itself out doing analyses, but for various reasons (including credibility and communication difficulties), their output is focused on the wrong areas or, in some cases, falls on deaf ears. Managers must get a handle on the key variables which influence profitability in their businesses today and on the ones that will determine it in the future as the profit model changes.

A further challenge to the profitability of all segments of the industry is the current stream of mergers, acquisitions, and affiliations. While analyses have been undertaken to determine the right price to pay, these analyses often stop short of understanding how money is made in the acquired institution. In fact, even after the new business is merged or acquired, little time is spent on the economic issues until a crisis occurs. And then it is often too late for economically based decisions to have a significant impact.

Yet once management understands the economic model of an existing or new venture, it must do something about it. Not all of the profitability levers touch the same areas in the same ways. It takes a skilled executive to learn which ones to manipulate, how to go about it, and when. Reducing overhead, for instance, is a noble goal; but does management really know the best approach? Increasing revenues is equally noble; but are the plans to do this in place? While "reduce overhead" and "increase revenues" are often-sounded battle cries, most organizations find these generalities difficult to translate into concrete behavior. Most often, the only message conveyed to employees is that something must be done, but not specifically what.

Once the key profitability levers are identified, an institution must pay close attention in applying them. Every employee must be told how and what to do to improve the bottom line. How these guidelines are passed down must be appropriate for the organization. Differences in structure and culture will allow varying degrees of flexibility as to what can actually be accomplished.

As will be seen in the following chapters, the authors take very different approaches in analyzing the current and future economics of the various industry segments. There are two reasons for this. For one thing, profitability dynamics differ widely from segment to segment. Dissimilarities in the economics of banking and brokerage, for example, might be said to outweigh the similarities. For another thing, there are many ways to approach the subject of management in any one segment. Whatever the reasons, the practical reality is that some companies do far better than others. The authors provide examples of successful and failing institutions and suggest some of the key revenue and cost elements that were either managed well or ignored.

In Chapter 5, David Cates takes the perspective of a financial analyst in describing the key profitability components with which banks must be concerned. David's firm, which he founded in 1969, monitors the banking industry and advises banks on matters of finance and strategy. Paul Hines, executive president and director of E.F. Hutton & Co., describes the dynamics of making money in the securities industry in Chapter 6. The discussion provided by Richard Shima in Chapter 7 looks at how the insurance industry manages for profitability. Dick's 25-year career has been devoted to the insurance business at The Travelers Companies, where he is now chief investment officer.

Susan Bassin focusses on the profitability challenges of thrifts in Chapter 8. Susan's perspective is one of both a highly experienced consultant and a practicing executive. She is now a principal at King-Casey, the strategic marketing consultants. In Chapter 9, Wylie Dougherty also looks at profitability, but with a focus on credit unions. Wylie was a founder, and the first president, of the U.S. Central Credit Union. Lawrence Fish looks at the major elements of making money in investment management in Chapter 10. Central to his discussion is the development of Dewey Square Investors, which grew out of trust operations at the Bank of Boston, where Larry is an executive vice-president. The issues for finance companies are examined by Charlene Sullivan in Chapter 11. A widely respected observer of consumer credit activity in the United States, Charlene is associate director of the Credit Research Center at Purdue.

While reading this section, readers might think about the various levers the authors describe, and the approaches that might be most applicable within their own institution. Most important, they will want to assess how well their management team has understood and fulfilled its role in shaping the fundamental economics of their business.

5 How Banks Make Money

DAVID C. CATES

The planning efforts of banks center on products, markets, technology, and people. These plans in turn have financial consequences which are periodically expressed in quarterly and full-year financial statements. Funds-providers and investors interpret this evolving financial record to judge the effectiveness of managers and their plans. The chief measure of success is profit on behalf of shareholders, sustainably generated without sacrifice of soundness.

The purpose of this chapter is to show how financial analysis can contribute to strategic planning, by illustrating the "paths to profit"—the profitability dynamic—of any bank. Since plans have financial outcomes, it makes sense to work backward from the financial record to try to discern the plans behind the record. It also makes sense to set forth a method of profitability analysis which can be projectively applied to any set of plans to test its capacity for profit. The task is to design a profit scoreboard useful for planners.

Accordingly, the presentation begins by describing a succinct framework for bank earnings analysis. This framework should have five attributes: (1) it must be generic enough to be applied to all banks; (2) it must be powerful enough to reveal the unique profit dynamics of any bank; (3) it must be simple in outline yet capable of sufficient complexity to reach any level of detail required; (4) it must permit comparison with relevant peers; and (5) it must function in a projection mode as well as permit historical analysis. Once the framework is erected, we will then present and discuss six cases that illustrate the extraordinary diversity of pathways to profit in the banking industry today. One of these cases will show an under-performing bank. We will conclude with some observations about how this analytic model can—and should—be used in the strategic planning process.

(*Editors' note*: By way of introduction, Exhibits 5.1 and 5.2 show an aggregate income statement and an aggregate balance sheet for commercial banks.)

Exhibit 5.1 Consolidated Income Statements: Insured Commercial Banks

	1984[a]
Operating income, total	$ 271,376
Interest, total	241,055
Loans	174,018
Balances with banks	16,493
Gross federal funds sold and reverse repurchase agreements	10,403
Securities (excluding trading accounts)	40,141
U.S. Government	26,000[b]
State and local government	12,050[b]
Other[c]	2,000[b]
Service charges on deposits	6,486
Other operating income	25,835
Operating expense, total	$ 251,980
Interest, total	165,860
Deposits	138,465
Large certificates of deposit	25,288
Deposits in foreign offices	35,687
Other deposits	77,490
Gross federal funds purchased and repurchase agreements	18,957
Other borrowed money	8,438
Salaries, wages, and employee benefits	36,332
Occupancy expense	12,029
Loan-loss provision	13,331
Other operating expense	24,291
Securities gains or losses	(138)
Income before tax	$ 19,397
Applicable income taxes	4,427
Extraordinary items	215
Net income	$ 15,184
Cash dividends declared	7,536

Source: Federal Reserve Bulletin, November 1985.
[a] Dollar amounts in $ millions.
[b] Estimates based on figures for 1980–1983. Numbers do not add.
[c] Includes interest income from other bonds, notes and debentures, and dividends from stock.

AN ANALYTIC FRAMEWORK FOR BANK PROFIT ANALYSIS

The first step is to define "profitability." For banks, the best definition is a triple one: return on assets (ROA); return on equity (ROE); and growth of earnings per share (EPS). In the absence of EPS measures, net income is an acceptable substitute. The key building blocks of net income are also the key determinants of profitability. There are five of them. Together with the ratios built from them (see the following paragraph), they form the basis for an analytic "process of elimina-

Exhibit 5.2 Consolidated Balance Sheet: Insured Commercial Banks

	1984[a]
Assets	$ 2,508.6
Securities, total[b]	385.8
U.S. Treasury, direct obligations	108.2
Obligations of states and subdivisions	120.9
Federal funds sold and securities purchased[c]	110.8
Net loans and leases[d]	1,489.7
Commercial and industrial loans	565.0
Real estate loans	385.6
Loans to depository institutions[e]	72.3
Loans to farmers (excluding real estate)	40.7
Other loans to individuals	266.9
All other loans	176.6
Lease financing receivables	20.2
Cash, balances with banks, etc.	323.5
Other	198.9
Liabilities and equity capital	$ 2,508.6
Deposits[f]	1,962.6
Demand	414.0
Time and savings	1,230.9
Individual partnerships and corporations	1,466.8
Government	96.5
Domestic interbank, foreign government, and other banks in foreign countries	55.6
Miscellaneous liabilities	381.4
Subordinated notes and debentures	10.2
Equity capital	154.3

Sources: U.S. Federal Deposit Insurance Corporation, *Assets and Liabilities: Commercial and Mutual Savings Banks*, semiannual; beginning 1978, *Annual Report*; and unpublished data.
[a] Dollar amounts in $ billions.
[b] Book value, includes other categories not shown separately.
[c] Under agreements to resell.
[d] Excludes allowance for loan and lease losses and unearned income.
[e] Includes loans to foreign banks.
[f] Covers domestic offices only.

tion" or "analysis trail" that managers can use to identify their own sources of profit and those of their competitors and peers. It should also be noted that these categories of analysis have served to describe bank profitability for many years, and as the industry evolves they should continue to provide insight into the determinants of bank performance.

Building Blocks of Net Income

Net interest income is the difference between total interest income (on a tax-equivalent basis) and total interest expense. Until 1983, this formulation—in which interest expense is treated as a "cost of goods sold"—was not mandated by regulators, though it was preferred by analysts and the SEC. It is now universally used as a bank financial reporting model. The level and volatility of net interest income is determined by: (1) the mix of earning assets, as between low-yield and high-yield categories; (2) the pricing and riskiness of loans; (3) the voluntary or involuntary degree of interest-rate risk; (4) the mix of financial liabilities, as between zero-cost demand deposits, low-cost rate-regulated savings and NOW accounts, higher-cost consumer time certificates and "money market" accounts, and large-dollar funding; and (5) the shifts in all these factors over time. Although it is possible to measure and compare all these factors in great detail, an examination of this depth lies beyond the scope of this chapter.

Noninterest ("other") income. This complex body of revenue contains some fees that derive from the balance sheet itself (service charges on deposits, for example). At big banks, the bulk of "other" income is largely independent of the balance sheet. It consists of trust fees, trading profits, letter-of-credit fees, syndication fees, interest-rate swap brokerage, and merchant banking commissions.

Two elements of noninterest income cause analytic problems, since they are discretionary and nonrecurring. The first is capital gains—gains on the sale of bank premises, the repurchase of outstanding debt at a discount, and other income-boosting distortions of true operating profit. The second is net realized gain or loss on sale of investment securities. Since sale of securities is always disclosed (regardless of materiality), the best analytic course is to delete securities gain/loss from "operating income" and restore it to "net income" on an after-tax basis. In this way, the analysis and comparison of operating income is purified of gain/loss distortion, yet the contribution of gain/loss (after tax) to net income can still be analyzed and compared.

The sum of net interest income and noninterest income (excepting securities gain/loss) is operating income; that is, it is the income stream from which all expenses, taxes, and dividends are paid. This sum is occasionally termed "adjusted operating income," to distinguish it from an earlier, now obsolete, definition of total income which did not offset interest expense against interest income.

Loan loss provision. Some analysts prefer to net the loss provision against net interest income or against operating income. But it makes better analytic sense to maintain the loss provision as a separate operating expense. One reason is that the behavior of net interest income by itself usually shows a bank's responsiveness to changes in market interest rates. Whether the loan loss provision is adequate, furthermore, is an important and complex question that requires analysis of the history of charge-offs, recoveries, "nonperforming" loans, the level of the loan loss allowance itself, and other factors relating to the growth and mix of loans. The detail required for a reliable adequacy analysis of this kind is formidable. In other words, loss provision is too discretionary a number to subtract from the much less discretionary data which determine net interest income.

Overhead is a catch-all term for nonfinancial operating expenses, and comprises personnel costs, equipment and occupancy costs, insurance, postage, FDIC assessment, and all other operating expenses required to open the doors every morning. Overhead is occasionally distorted by the costs and writedowns associated with foreclosed real estate; that is, the collateral on former construction and other real estate loans. In regulatory terminology, foreclosed property is OREO (other real estate owned).

Income tax provision. The importance of tax analysis is that occasionally earnings are temporarily overstated by tax credits and refunds are not booked as "extraordinary items." To detect these distortions, it is necessary to restate the tax provision at its fully taxable equivalent—the taxes that would have been provided had all income been taxable—and to divide this figure by pretax net income, also on a tax-equivalent basis. The resulting ratio typically lies between 42 percent and 46 percent, making distortions (e.g., 35 percent) easily discernible. Such distortions, it should be noted, are almost always temporary.

The foregoing five key building blocks of net income form the main architecture of bank profit analysis. Before we can begin this examination, however, we must revisit all five and turn them into ratios that permit analysis and comparison.

Net interest margin is the ratio that relates net interest income to average earning assets. It is rare to find a margin lower than 3.0 percent or higher than 7.0 percent. Contrary to 1980-1981 expectations, deregulation of consumer deposit rates has not led to a sweeping reduction of commercial bank margins, even among retail banks. The two most important ratio components of net interest margin are *earning asset yield* and *break-even yield.* The former measures the blended gross yield on all financial assets (interest income divided by earning assets). The latter measures the blended cost of financing the earning asset structure (interest expense divided by earning assets). The earning asset yield may in turn be analyzed according to the mix and yield of various classes of assets, the most important usually being *loan yield.* The break-even yield may be further subdivided according to the mix and effective cost of each class of liabilities, from zero-cost demand deposits to large-dollar liabilities. One useful ratio is the *effective interest expense rate* on all interest-bearing liabilities (interest expense divided by average interest-bearing liabilities).

Noninterest income-to-operating income is the best measure of the contribution of "other" income to a bank's income stream. It suffers, however, from the "rubber yardstick" problem, since the denominator of the ratio is often unsteady. Thus, variations in the ratio are sometimes determined by the growth and volatility of net interest income rather than by the behavior of noninterest income itself. For example, a bank's ratio of noninterest income-to-operating income may be high for two very different reasons: because noninterest income is above average, or because operating income is below average. Knowing what is driving the behavior of these key performance ratios is essential for appropriate analysis by management. The normal contribution of noninterest income to operating income ranges from a low of 15 percent for smaller banks to a high of 35 percent for larger banks. A "spike" in the ratio usually points to a nonrecurring gain in that year (or quarter).

Loan loss provision-to-operating income is the best single measure of the impact of loan loss upon earnings. The norm of this ratio is between 4 percent and 8 percent of operating income, though in high-loss banks the ratio can of course climb to lofty heights. It is important to keep in mind that banks with a low net interest margin have a diminished income cushion against which to shield a given amount of loss provision. Again, with this type of ratio we must be aware of potential misinterpretation due to the "rubber yardstick" problem.

A supplementary ratio that measures the capacity of earnings to absorb loan loss is *earnings coverage of net charge-offs*. It is computed by dividing pretax net income (prior to loss provision) by net charge-offs. For banks, this pretax income is normally four to six times the amount of charge-offs. Another ratio, useful for testing management's commitment to building or maintaining the loss allowance, is *loss provision-to-net charge-offs*. The recent norm for this ratio is 120 percent-to-130 percent. Lower ratios, however, do not automatically signal under-providing, nor do high ratios automatically signal over-providing.

Overhead-to-operating income is the best single measure of the impact of operating expense upon income. The importance of testing this key intersection of income and expense lies in the fact that overhead normally consumes between 50 and 70 percent of income. Overhead is thus—after net interest margin—the second largest determinant of profit for nearly all banks. It is also important to note that the operating profit margin (pretax profit divided by operating income) is quite high in banking. An overhead/income ratio of 60 percent, in other words, means that 40 percent of income is profit, before loan loss and taxes, of course. Viewed this way, banks enjoy a wide margin of profit.

Since overhead supports the production of net interest income *and* noninterest income, yet is not differentiated accordingly, it is not always possible to know the magnitude of costs attributable to each of these major types of income. For example, a high overhead ratio may be caused by the high cost of producing net interest income or by unprofitable "other" income. On the other hand, if noninterest income is low and foreclosed properties constitute a small percentage of loans (under 0.20 percent), it is safe to attribute high overhead to net interest income production. High overhead is appropriate if it buys a sustainably high net interest margin, but inappropriate if it fails to do so.

One useful supplement to the main overhead ratio is to compare year-to-year *growth of overhead* with *growth of earning assets*. (Note: overhead rarely declines!) Overhead growth typically averages 10 to 15 percent, but is often higher or lower according to the underlying growth of the bank. Another useful, though tricky, supplementary ratio is *net overhead-to-earning assets*. Net overhead (total overhead less noninterest income) is that portion of overhead estimated to be dedicated to the production of net interest income. If the ratio is correctly figured, as should be possible from a bank's internal accounts, the resulting number measures the operating cost of generating the net interest margin. Normal range is between 2.0 and 3.0 percent of earning assets. The catch is that, lacking internal data, outside analysts have no choice but to subtract the total amount of noninterest income from total overhead to get "net" overhead, with the tacit assumption that noninterest income is break-even! Since that is a bad assumption, the value of the ratio would seem to be suspect.

This is not necessarily so, however, as the following illustration will clarify. Suppose a bank enjoys a large contribution of noninterest income. Suppose further that the bank's balance sheet makeup (in particular, the amount of overhead-intensive consumer loans and consumer deposits) points to a likely net overhead ratio between 2.5 and 3.0 percent, judging from peer norms. Yet the net overhead ratio is actually an absurdly low 0.8 percent. This points to the existence of high profit noninterest income! Temporary dips in this ratio can also point to the existence of nonrecurring capital gains booked as income.

Primary capital-to-assets summarizes a bank's capital strength. In this context, "primary capital" is defined to include the loan loss allowance. Conventional though this formulation is, federal regulators are beginning to recognize two crippling flaws in it. First, banks differ in the relative riskiness of their assets, not only by types of assets, but within each asset category. Second, banks differ in their propensity to incur "invisible" risk *off* the balance sheet. For these two reasons, capital adequacy is rather poorly summarized by this government-invented ratio, and it will probably be supplanted by a more sophisticated policy that attempts to relate capital to risk, whether on or off the balance sheet.

The capital formation rate (retained net income divided by equity capital) is valuable in showing the rate of asset growth that a bank can internally finance without a diminution of its proportionate capital position.

CASE EXAMPLES

This section will apply the financial measures just discussed to the recent (1984) performance of six example banks. These case banks have been chosen because they provide the opportunity to show how financial analysis techniques work to illuminate a variety of different strategic situations. Three (Bankers Trust, NCNB Corp., and Core States Financial) are large publicly owned bank holding companies. The other three are smaller banks. In particular, Bankers Trust is interesting among the large banks because of its exclusive commitment to wholesale commercial and "merchant" banking and to the development of significant fee income sources. Two of the smaller banks provide significant sources of insight. Citibank South Dakota lets us look at a bank focused on nationwide credit card banking. Community Bank "X" is chosen because it is not profitable enough to survive as an independent.

In the presentation of each case, reference will be made to pertinent lines in Exhibit 5.3. The purpose of this exhibit is to support the case discussion. Most of the ratios discussed previously are shown in lines 1–16 of Exhibit 5.3. Lines 17–22 present six additional ratios offering a brief but essential glimpse into the composition of the balance sheet. The ratios in lines 23–24 show the disposition of net income between dividends (including dividends on preferred stock) and retained earnings.

Bankers Trust New York Corporation

This large bank holding company is noted for its dramatic repositioning into large corporate wholesale banking, and for its commitment to merchant banking activi-

Exhibit 5.3 1984 Financial Ratios for Six "Case" Banks

Line/Ratio	Bankers Trust N.Y. Corp ($45 Bil)	NCNB Corp. ($16 Bil)	CoreStates Financial Corp. ($10 Bil)	Citibank South Dakota ($7 Bil)	Park National Bank Newark Ohio ($383 Mil)	Community Bank "X" ($675 Mil)
1 Return on assets	0.71%	0.83%	1.17%	3.17%	1.84%	0.85%
2 Return on equity	16	16	18	31	19	14
3 One-year change in net income (%)	19	29	22	22	36	12
4 Securities gain (loss)/net income	0	1.1	(1.0)	0	(1.2)	3.3
5 One-year change in earning assets (%)	14	24	12	50	14	9
6 Net interest margin	2.77	4.43	6.15	9.61	6.28	5.18
7 Earning asset yield	12.02	12.87	13.35	18.99	13.39	12.38
8 Break-even yield	9.25	8.44	7.20	9.38	7.11	7.20
9 Noninterest income/operating income	37	22	24	39	10	12

10 Loss provision/operating income	14	8	7	18	7	3
11 Loss provision/net charge-offs	176	193	191	158	313	173
12 Net charge-offs/loans	0.55	0.35	0.38	1.7	0.28	0.13
13 Overhead/operating income	51	60	61	43	41	68
14 One-year change in overhead (%)	8.6	23	18	62	13	9
15 Net overhead/earning assets	0.6	2.2	3.0	0.6	2.2	3.3
16 Marginal tax rate	46	46	46	47	45	48
17 Large liabilities/earning assets	86	41	29	74	8	21
18 Loans/earning assets	65	69	73	100	57	66
19 :Retail loans/loans	1	30	23	100	59	46
20 :Nonperforming loans/loans	3.0	1.5	1.5	0.8	1.0	4.1
21 :Loss allowance/loans	1.55	1.20	1.32	1.42	2.27	1.02
22 Primary capital/assets	6.3	5.8	7.2	10.0	10.6	6.6
23 Dividend payout of net income	30	30	37	0	39	48
24 Capital formation rate	12	14	11	36	13	8

Sources: Data for Bankers Trust, NCNB, and CoreStates are taken from the holding company annual reports to shareholders. Data for the other three case banks are taken from their financial reports filed with federal regulators. The ratios for all six companies are derived from Cates Bancompare reports, prepared annually by Cates Consulting Analysts, Inc.

ties where regulations permit. Bankers Trust's strategic retooling occurred in the late 1970s, during which time it sold almost all its New York City branches to other banks.

Though Bankers Trust is more profitable per dollar of assets than most of its New York peers, it is far less profitable than the average regional or community bank (see line 1 of Exhibit 5.3). This difference is rooted in several factors. Most important, the net interest margin (line 6) is extremely low, the result of both relatively low asset yields (line 7) and high funding cost (line 8). Bankers Trust's low asset yields result from the highly competitive nature of big-bank lending, a field in which the typical borrower has a choice of many alternative sources, driving down asset yields. Note that the bank has a negligible portfolio of higher-yielding consumer assets (line 19). Bankers Trust's high funding cost is a result of high dependence on large-dollar funding at market rates (line 17). Thus, it lacks the lower-cost deposit base which would strengthen its net interest margin.

Bankers Trust compensates for the disadvantage of its low net interest margin in two important ways that further differentiate it from almost all other banks. First, it derives a large fraction of its operating income from fee income sources, in fact almost two-fifths of its total income stream (line 9). Second, the bank incurs relatively low overhead costs in producing its total income (lines 13, 15). Indeed, Bankers Trust's decision to sell its New York City retail branch network was partially driven by the desire to reduce the bank's overhead cost. This said, it is important to point out that nonrecurring gains in 1984 (disclosed, but not shown in the table) significantly overstate operating income, and similarly understate the overhead ratios mentioned above. Concurrently, the loss provision (line 10) was greatly expanded from prior years, as was the loss allowance (line 21), with the effect that the higher provision considerably exceeded the nonrecurring gain. These complex interactions produce a return on equity (line 2) and a capital formation rate (line 24) that exceed banking industry norms in general, and certainly exceed the norms of money center banking.

The lesson of Bankers Trust is that success as a money center bank requires offsetting the intrinsic disadvantage of a low net interest margin with: (1) substantial profitable fee income; (2) low overhead; and (3) low loan losses. A low net interest margin need not stand in the way of high profit, but management must identify other performance areas where the disadvantage can be overcome.

NCNB Corporation

This holding company is noted for aggressive statewide and interstate expansion in North Carolina, Florida, and South Carolina. NCNB has established a strong reputation for aggressive management and marketing efforts, which have resulted in significant market share and asset growth. Whether this growth by acquisition has temporarily penalized the potential near-term profitability of the company cannot be discerned from the financial record, but it is possible to say that the current profit configuration is strong (lines 1, 2, 3) and that capital retention (line 24) is also solid. The net interest margin (line 6) is somewhat below the average for large regional banks, as is the moderate contribution of noninterest income (line 9). Loss provision (line 10) is a little higher than normal. Given the relatively low level of loan loss and nonperforming loans (lines 12, 20), the loss allowance (line 21) looks adequate, and thus the loss provision is fair (lines 10, 11). As for overhead, the ratios point to below average operating expense, despite the largely retail nature of the affiliate banks (lines 19, 17).

The NCNB "path to profitability" seems to combine successfully two ingredients: conventional banking and aggressive expansion. At the same time, aggressive expansion has a high cost, not only in management time but also in financial capacity. NCNB has so far balanced expansion with performance, and has established a high standard for its regional competitors to meet. The question is whether the interstate banking parade will proceed as smoothly for others.

CoreStates Financial Corporation

In 1983 the Philadelphia National Bank, a predominantly wholesale institution, purchased the Hamilton Bank of Lancaster, Pennsylvania, which is very much a retail operation. The combination, which augmented CoreStates' assets by roughly one-third, produced a 1984 profit profile (lines 1, 2, 3) that is quite distinguished among larger regional banks and exceptionally good within the slower-growth region the company serves. Net interest margin (line 6) is well above large regional bank norms, not only because the earning asset yield is strong (line 7), but also because the overall funding cost is quite low (line 8). This in turn is partly attributable to a relatively low dependence on large-dollar funding (line 17). CoreStates' overhead is low relative to income (line 13), but not low relative to assets (line 15), meaning that the investment in overhead is highly productive. Loan loss provision is a modest fraction of income (line 10), yet contributes generously (line 11) to a loss allowance that seems adequate when set against total loans (line 21), net charge-offs (compare lines 12, 21), and nonperforming loans (compare lines 20, 21). The high dividend payout (line 23) slightly dampens the earnings retention rate (line 24), but this picture looks brighter when the permanent preferred stock dividend is excluded from the equations. The common dividend is then 31 percent of net income, and the earnings retention rate (based on common stock only) 13 percent.

The key to CoreStates' performance is not low overhead as such, but overhead invested to produce a high net interest margin from a wide variety of retail and institutional sources. The example of CoreStates shows this strategic management formula in practice.

Citibank South Dakota

This bank was purchased by Citicorp to handle its nationwide credit card operation. Its extraordinary profit profile (lines 1, 2, 3) is caused by an extremely high earning asset yield (line 7) that reflects the pricing of credit card financing (lines 18, 19). This high yield easily covers a very high cost of funding (line 8) and an untypically high loss provision and net charge-offs (lines 10, 12). Another spur to earnings is the low overhead, which probably does not include Citicorp's full costs of developing and marketing the credit card. Possibly because of the rapid growth of the bank (line 5), no dividend is paid to the parent (line 23), leaving the total of earnings free to capitalize further growth (lines 22, 24).

The value of this case is not as a model for an independent bank to follow, but as a "window" upon the operation of a specialized segment of a very large bank. Other banks, for example, in Delaware, allow similar glimpses into the credit card and other specialized credit operations of big banks.

Park National Bank

This is a classically successful community bank. The profit profile is strong (lines 1, 2, 3), its main determinants being a high net interest margin (line 6) and low overhead (lines 13, 15). Noninterest income is surprisingly low (line 9), and loan loss provision is also low (line 10) despite very aggressive building of the loss allowance (lines 11, 21). The reserve buildup is certainly not warranted by actual or potential losses (lines 12, 20), and may undoubtedly be attributed—together with an extra-strong capital position (line 22)—to managerial conservatism.

The low overhead is remarkable in light of the bank's large proportion of retail lending (lines 13, 19) and the low usage of large-dollar funding (line 17), which implies a consumer funding base. Since consumer products (whether assets or liabilities) are more costly to book and to service, one would expect higher overhead ratios than this bank exhibits. Also interesting is that the bank's net margin was higher in 1984, following consumer deposit deregulation, than in 1980, prior to legislative change!

Park National's performance demonstrates that an established community bank can be a successful and resilient competitor. With its very personal roots in a smaller city, such a bank (of which there are certainly hundreds, if not thousands) is positioned to weather the waves of innovation sweeping the financial industry.

Community Bank "X"

Though adequately profitable on superficial analysis (lines 1, 2, 3), this retail bank (lines 17, 19) shows underlying problems that may have contributed to its recent decision to combine with a larger bank. In the first place, its ROA is significantly below the norm for its local peers (1.0 percent). In the second place, its overhead is quite high in relation to both income and assets (lines 13, 15), and is continuing to grow (line 14). Third, its potential future loan losses are apt to be significantly higher than shown by the recent record (line 12), since nonperforming loans have grown to a high fraction of total loans (line 20) while the loss allowance has remained none too strong (line 21). Fourth, the bank's ability to retain capital is low (line 24) in relation to its asset growth (line 5), pointing to an incapacity to finance a growth strategy.

What makes this bank interesting is that despite its adequate creditworthiness, it is a poor performer from the standpoint of its chances for survival as an independent. Many thousands of perfectly sound banks resemble it. Lacking the financial and managerial resources to acquire a network of other banks, and to finance their modernization and further expansion in a rapidly changing marketplace, they will simply be absorbed by others strong enough to redeploy their resources more profitably.

STOCK MARKET ACCEPTANCE

Expansion, acquisition, and modernization are processes that require financing, whether from internal or external sources. One mode of external finance is term debt or preferred stock placed largely with institutional investors. Another mode of external finance is the issuance of new common shares, either directly to investors or in exchange for the stock of a bank to be acquired. A bank's ability to tap these sources of financing is fundamentally a function of its current performance and future prospects. Both debt finance capacity and equity finance capacity are driven by performance. Each is considered as follows.

Debt finance capacity is measured, for larger companies, by ratings provided by Standard & Poor, Moody's, and other debt rating agencies. The performance factors that underlie the various ratings can be studied in order to discern those companies that are strong or weak within their rating grades, and also to discern strong companies that may lack a rating. The debt finance capacity of banks, however, reflects more on their soundness than their strategic prospects. Stock finance capacity, on the other hand, tends to reflect strategic prospects, whether as an acquisition candidate or as a profitable independent. Stock finance capacity can be analyzed by comparing the relative standing of bank stocks within the bank stock market, and charting the patterns of their rise and fall over time. A simple, reliable method for analyzing bank stock market acceptance is described in the following paragraph.

Stock market acceptance is important because it shows whether an expansionary corporate strategy can be financed, if necessary, with new shares. A banking company whose stock trades at a price disadvantage will probably have a hard time expanding, whether it is underwriting a strategy of internal growth or acquiring other banks on nondilutive terms. Three ratios, taken together, measure the relative market standing of dealer-traded (as opposed to closely held) bank stocks. These are the price-to-earnings ratio (P/E), the dividend yield, and the ratio of market price to book value per share. A "strong" stock will show a high P/E because investors are collectively willing to pay a premium for current earnings. It will also show a low dividend yield because the market is willing to accept an income sacrifice today in return for much higher returns tomorrow. A strong stock will also show a high ratio of price to book, reflecting investor confidence in management's ability to earn an attractive return on capital. Sometimes, of course, investor anticipation of a merger price premium will distort the market.

Because these ratios are changing from day to day, a convenient way to

Exhibit 5.4 Example: Judging Bank Stock Market Acceptance

	1985			1984[a]		
	P/E	Dividend Yield	Price/ Book	P/E	Dividend Yield	Price/ Book
NCNB	8	2	9	6	2	9
CoreStates	4	5	9	3	7	7
Bankers Trust	2	4	6	3	5	6

Source: Cates Bancompare reports, published by Cates Consulting Analysts, Inc.
[a] As of January 31, against financial data of full year 1984 and 1983, respectively.

measure a stock's worth—and to see how this changes over time—is to consider the three ratios relative to an index of other bank stocks and to chart their position in decile terms. A Decile 6 or 7 means that a given bank's P/E ratio, for example, is slightly above average, measured against a cross-section of "visible" bank stocks (those that set the tone for the rest of the bank stock market). Looked at another way, a P/E ratio of 5.6 times may place a stock in Decile 6 during October, but the identical P/E ratio may be a Decile 7 in November, if the market as a whole has receded. The value of decile analysis, then, is that it captures the relative movement of the particular stock against the market, which is also moving.

The population used to compute the benchmark index for bank stocks must be representative of the bank stock market. Fifty market-visible bank stocks compose one representative index, the Cates Index. Exhibit 5.4 shows the decile rankings of the three large holding companies when their stocks are compared to the Cates Index. The rankings display interesting and instructive differences. Clearly, NCNB (like many Southern banking companies) enjoys a premier position among all bank stocks. CoreStates has a lesser standing, but has shown marked improvement in its position over the year's interval. Bankers Trust may have suffered from a stock market concern with money center banks related to the Latin debt crisis that began in 1982. In any case, its shares are held by the market, as of January 31, 1985, to be the least attractive of the three. Theoretically then, Bankers Trust must rely most, and NCNB least, upon internal finance and upon debt finance to underwrite its strategy.

CONCLUSION

Depositors, other funds providers, securities analysts, investors, competitors, acquirors, and acquirees all analyze the performance of banks. They carefully study strengths and weaknesses, and how institutions make money. Managers are increasingly learning to practice the same analysis on themselves that outsiders apply. It is therefore in managers' self-interest to incorporate comparative analysis and financial modeling into the strategic planning process. In this way, the trade-offs between net interest margin, fee income, overhead, and loan loss can be evaluated and projected alongside the studies of products, markets, and technology that make up the core of strategic planning efforts.

The cases presented in this chapter reflect a variety of different strategic plans, objectives, and ways for banks to make money. In Bankers Trust, as one extreme example, we saw that the key source of profit is not the net interest margin, but rather the large contribution of fee income and the low operating expense. Core-States, by contrast, incurs fairly high expenses to generate a very strong net interest margin.

Management has several strategic options in building the necessary financial interrelationships to achieve a final result—return on assets and equity, coupled with a strong growth of earnings per share—which will attract and hold investor attention, a key goal for any investor-owned company. Performance on a wide variety of management criteria is not only measurable but comparable to that of designated peers. Those banking companies that can attain their own demanding performance goals will survive as independents, or sell out at extremely attractive prices, largely because they will have achieved stock market acceptance. Those that cannot achieve demanding goals will be absorbed at less attractive prices by other firms that think they can strengthen performance. The analytic model presented in this chapter, simple as it is, nonetheless has the power to differentiate the survivors, and to serve as a guide to strategic success for all.

6 Making Money in Brokerage

PAUL HINES

To begin with, one fact is inescapable: The securities market is cyclical. That is, periods of active trading give way to quiescent times, and vice versa. To be sure, the overall pattern is never a simple sine curve. Often when one segment of the market—say, equities—is flourishing, another, such as bonds, may be languishing. When money market funds are raking in deposits, mutual funds are generally tailing off. The trick to be explored in this chapter is in maintaining viable levels of profitability during the lean months (or years) while retaining the capacity to surge ahead at peak moments, capitalizing on the high availability of business to be transacted.

As a rule of thumb, firms should be managed to produce operating profits combined with net interest profits that result in the following returns on investment: approaching 20 percent in average times; far above 20 percent in the best of times; and about 10 percent in the worst of times. These relatively high expected returns are a direct result of the nature of the portfolio: The firm's capital is highly leveraged in short-term risk investments, which, by their nature, should yield higher returns than long-term fixed asset investments. This rule holds for firms of all sizes. Real economies of scale may not exist; indeed, absolute profitability does not always seem to vary with size. More to the point for this discussion is that in most instances the underlying economics of firms that are roughly the same size and serve roughly the same segments show little difference. And yet the firms can differ widely in profitability.

The essential distinction between successful and unsuccessful firms seems instead to lie elsewhere—in what might be called, for lack of a better term, "making money management." As shall be seen, making money management has two essential features: (1) a reliance on a sound business model; and (2) the drive of management. A full understanding of why both are essential, and other features are not, needs to be founded on a perspective of how the brokerage world is changing.

ENVIRONMENTAL TRENDS

The brokerage business is becoming increasingly difficult for two reasons. First, consumers, growing more aware of how value is added in financial transactions, increasingly want to see a clearer relationship between price and value. This growing customer sophistication has changed the way customers buy. The proliferation of new financial products and strategies, expansion of credit, and increases in assets invested for retirement have changed customer needs for brokerage and other financial services products. Exhibit 6.1 shows the distribution of real assets among major users.

Second, competition is increasing. Like all financial services firms, brokerage houses compete in the midst of major structural changes to their industry environment. Perhaps the biggest of these changes began in 1975 when federal deregulation of commissions created price competition. On another regulatory front, Rule 415 allows a corporation to structure and register debt or equity issues and inventory them until it receives an acceptable bid from a broker. As a result, a formerly negotiated transaction became competitive. Rule 415 reduced investment bankers' revenues while increasing their capital requirements and risk. Competition is increasing, not only from traditional competitors but also from new competitors, including discount brokers, banks, insurance companies, direct electronic link-ups using personal computer terminals, and direct mail.

Discounters have identified unsolicited securities purchases and sales as com-

Exhibit 6.1 Financial Assets of Households, Personal Trusts, and Non-Profit Organizations: Selected Year-End Outstandings, 1985

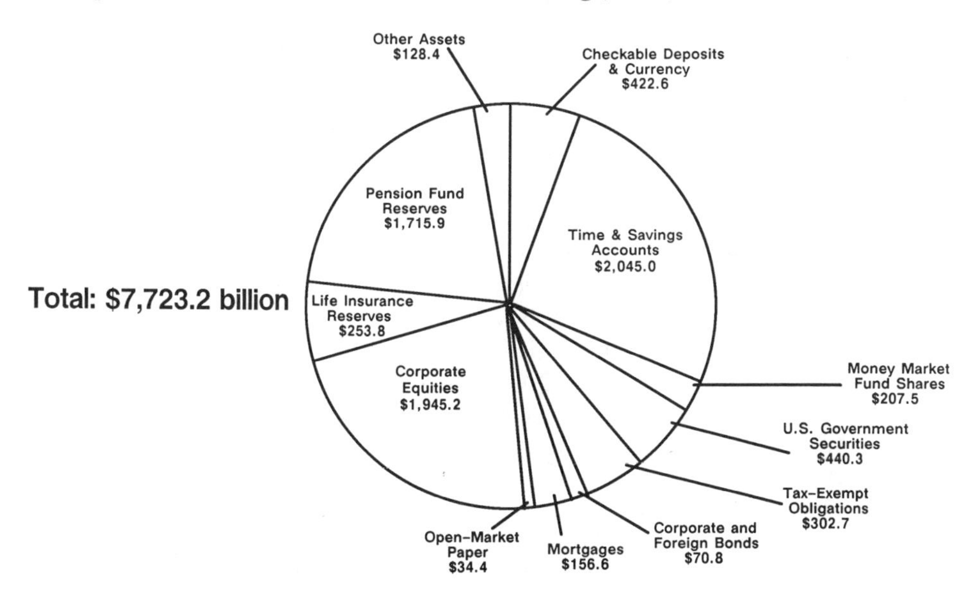

Source: Federal Reserve Board.

modity transactions; that is, the aware consumer has little interest in paying a full service price. Competition for these customers has increased in several industry segments as banks and insurance companies have entered traditional brokerage activities by offering discount brokerage, mutual funds, and other brokerage products through their sales forces. In addition, banks have aggressively entered those areas of public and corporate investment banking permitted under liberal interpretations of the Glass-Steagall Act. These events—and the trends discussed as follows—have changed the basis of competition and the underlying economics of the brokerage industry. Large mutual insurance companies are actively promoting the sale of securities products through their career agents; 60 percent of independent insurance agents have elected to become licensed by the National Association of Securities Dealers, an authorization which allows them to deal directly with the traditional suppliers of packaged investment products such as mutual, real estate, and oil and gas funds.

Technology lies behind the comparatively recent birth of several distribution channels. Most spectacularly perhaps, the personal computer has become a distribution system unto itself. In the hands of competent consumers, it virtually eliminates the need for a full-service broker, or even a discount broker, relationship. A second new retail distribution channel is direct mail. Toll-free sales and service numbers provide faraway or busy consumers with immediate access to customer service reps; PC pilot programs have also been started for active investors. In the institutional market, third-party brokers offer an alternative to the bundled pricing of the traditional investment bank competitors in cash rebates and additional trust and research services. Increasingly, placement of terminals on customer premises is changing the way institutional investors communicate with their brokers. Sometimes, it must be said, these advances are counterproductive for brokers. Although direct electronic connections are only installed after proper justification of future cost savings, brokers' costs may actually increase upon equipment installation. What firms discover is that these systems often require lower error rates, continual on-line access, and other costly features that were not originally anticipated.

The combination of consumerism and competition puts heavy pressure on brokers to lower prices, and consequently squeeze their margins. Given this reduced play in the market, greater care will be needed in setting product prices, which traditionally has been a haphazard process. Indeed, in the retail segment, price now bears little relation to value. If a study were undertaken of agency security transactions at major firms since 1970, it would in all probability reveal that price increases generally result from broker cost pressures—in other words, solely from supply considerations, without regard to demand.

A third environmental change has put at least as much pressure on the brokerage industry as have consumers' growing sophistication and the industry's broadening competitive field. That change is the escalation of economic uncertainty in an already cyclical industry. Markets are becoming extremely volatile as the velocity of trade grows in government securities, equities, and corporate and municipal bonds.

MAKING MONEY MANAGEMENT

Misconceptions of how money is made in the securities industry are widespread, and not confined to the ill-informed. A noted professor at a large eastern business school once described the retail brokerage industry as losing money on operations and only making money on its lending and borrowing activities. Thus it may have appeared to this noncasual observer. However, the reality of brokerage is that to produce earnings on the levels necessary to attract capital for expanding the business, to attract the skilled employees required to compete successfully, and to obtain the cash flow needed for investment in product development and plant expansion, substantial operating and net interest profits are required. Further, an inability to produce operating profits consistently before net interest profits—whatever the phase of the business cycle—is the mark of a marginal firm. A look at the income statement begins to give an appreciation for why this seemingly harsh judgment is true.

Income Statement

Brokerage firms derive revenues from four major sources: (1) commissions on agency activities; (2) spreads on market-making activities; (3) fees for various activities and services; and (4) margin and position interest and dividends. Costs are generated in six major areas: (1) compensation and benefits for sales staff, management, and other staff; (2) communications, for example, phone systems, quote and news services; (3) occupancy, headquarters, and branch systems; (4) marketing and promotions; (5) data processing; and (6) interest expense. These revenue and cost components vary by competitor groups. (*Editors' note*: Exhibits 6.2 and 6.3 show consolidated income statements and balance sheets for members of the New York Stock Exchange. Exhibits 6.4 to 6.5 present growth in assets and liabilities between 1980 and 1984.)

Operating as dealers, by making markets in many securities, and operating as underwriters, creates large funding needs for brokerage firms. Operating as a broker (that is, as an agent for a customer) also requires resources to finance the receivables that are part of any retail business. The strategies brokers use to fund these operations and the rates they pay for funds have a critical impact on brokerage profitability and rates of return. These strategies also affect the firm's ability to comply with government requirements.

SEC regulations require that brokers maintain liquid assets sufficient to repay their debt to customers. Brokers also must meet precisely defined tests of capital adequacy. In fact, their capital balance must remain above acceptable minimums on a daily basis. Reports testifying to actual levels must be filed weekly. Two calculations are particularly indicative of capital adequacy. Indebtedness, measured by totalling most—though not all—debts, is one. Net capital, the "fire-sale" value of the firm, is the other. Net capital is defined as gross capital (equity and long-term subordinated debt) minus "haircuts" (writedowns on inventories, based on historical risk of loss as determined by the SEC), and other assets

Exhibit 6.2 Income Statement for NYSE Member Firms

	1985[a]
Securities commissions	$ 8,238.4
Trading and investments	11,033.5
Interest on customers' debit balances	2,578.0
Underwriting	4,250.3
Mutual fund sales	1,642.8
Commodity revenues	983.0
Other income:	
Related to securities business[b]	8,141.6
Unrelated to securities business	1,758.0
Gross income	$ 38,625.6
Registered representatives' compensation	6,903.6
Commissions and fees to others	1,641.6
Clerical and administrative	6,218.5
Communication	1,921.8
Occupancy and equipment	1,830.7
Promotional	841.5
Interest	10,127.6
Service bureaus and data processing	477.8
Bad debts, errors, nonrecurring costs	365.2
Other[b]	3,952.9
Total expenses	$ 34,281.2
Net profit before federal taxes[c]	$ 4,144.4
Estimated federal income taxes	2,235.6
Net profit	$ 1,908.8

Source: SRI/SIA Database.

[a] Figures in $ millions.

[b] License taxes, dues and assessments paid to exchanges, professional fees, charitable contributions, some officers' and partners' compensation and interest, and other expenses.

[c] Before distributions to partners and federal and state corporate and personal taxes. Year ended December 31.

having little or no market value. For SEC compliance, net capital must be larger than 5 percent of indebtedness. A firm that falls below the 5-percent level is required to stop growing, stop paying dividends, and stop retiring long-term subordinated debt. Maintaining compliance as underwriting and trading activities grow calls for careful and continuous tracking of net capital.

Brokerage firms use repurchase agreements (repos), bank credit, and commer-

Exhibit 6.3 Balance Sheet of NYSE Member Firms

	1985[a]
Assets	
Bank balances, cash, and other deposits	$ 5,441
Receivables from other brokers and dealers	50,504
Receivables from customers and partners	50,049
Long positions in securities and commodities	275,975
Secured demand notes	323
Exchange memberships	258
Land and other fixed assets	2,547
Other assets	8,705
Total assets	$393,802
Liabilities and capital	
Money borrowed	$198,607
Payables to other brokers & dealers	44,572
Payables to customers & partners	33,170
Short positions in securities & commodities	71,458
Other accrued expenses & accounts payable	29,360
Total liabilities	$377,166
Total capital	16,767
Total liabilities and capital as of December 31	$393,933

Source: SRI/SIA Database.
[a]Figures in $ millions.

cial paper to fund the assets required for their operations. Most full-line firms, and an increasing number of investment banks, are publicly held. They issue equity and long-term debt in addition to using retained earnings as a source of capital. The most attractive source, however, is free funds—accounts payable to customers, other brokers, and vendors. Managing such noninterest-incurring liabilities optimally is important to profitability levels.

Cost and Profitability Model

The cost and profitability model reflects the firm as an in-place economic system or set of systems in a specific environment. This model must be balanced in the sense that revenue creation must at least equal cost incurrence, and both must balance with capital and funding availability. Out-of-balance conditions must be corrected and flaws eliminated.

Still, the cost and profitability model is not the ultimate indicator of what firms are doing right or wrong. When in 1973 and 1974 a large federal regulatory organization sent an internal task force of analysts to Wall Street to determine why some full-service brokerage firms consistently made money while many consistently lost money, they began with an operating hypothesis that product mix

Exhibit 6.4 Total Securities Industry Assets

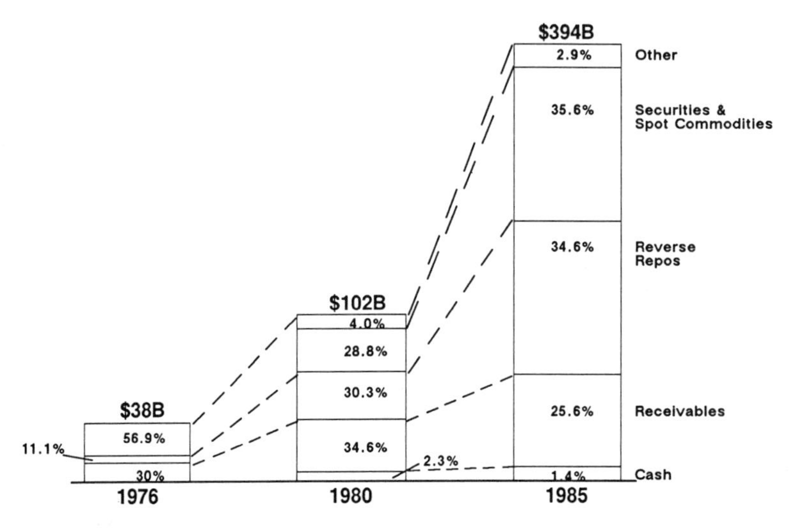

Source: SRI/SIA Database.

Exhibit 6.5 Total Securities Industry Liabilities and Equities

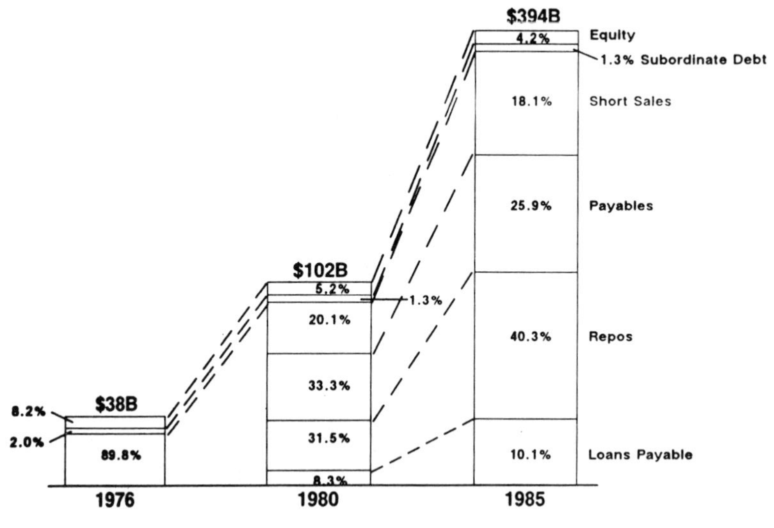

Source: SRI/SIA Database.

was at the root of the difference. At the time, though, there was little real difference in product economics from one firm to another. Rather, full-service brokers principally made money on distribution, and on their borrowing and lending activities. The biggest variable cost was commissions paid to salesmen, while the largest fixed costs were those associated with branch locations and national operations. Hardly any of those costs truly varied with product mix. That hypothesis betrayed an excessive concentration on cost and profitability, and neglected the business model. In reality, it is the business model that should direct decisions and maintain the health of the cost and profitability model, not vice versa.

The Business Model: Key to Making Money Management

The guidelines for profitability set at the beginning of this chapter were: approaching 20 percent return on investment in normal times, rising far above 20 percent in the best of times, and staying at about 10 percent in the worst of times. The key to producing those returns is a business model productive enough to create revenues that satisfactorily outweigh costs. Cost management tactics are not in and of themselves sufficient to ensure survival. Firms that reflexively announce cost-cutting programs in times of economic adversity reveal their lack of understanding of their business. For once they have cut their costs and find they are still losing money, they are bereft of further recourse. Their situation is reminiscent of one portrayed in an old *New Yorker* cartoon: A group of three-piece suited businessmen are watching bubbles rise to the surface of a small pool. Beneath reads the caption, "The day the Ivory Soap sank at Procter and Gamble."

It would be better instead to establish a vision for the firm, agree on and carry out strategies, and track results of key initiatives. Collectively, these comprise a firm's business model. Successful managers are guided by it intuitively. When objectives are clearly stated, managers can recognize which customers to target, which products to stress, which distribution channels to use, and which markets to cover. Firms that possess this perspective regard performance qualitatively as well as quantitatively.

The business model is primarily concerned with the creation of ever more competent customer-focused, profit-driven organizational dynamos of creative energy. The business model begins by defining the client groups or segments to be actively sought, and ends with a desired economic result more familiarly known as the bottom line. Cost and profitability models are anemic by comparison. They are mostly useful in those times—albeit uncomfortably frequent these days—when cyclical forces constrict to the point of asphyxiating the ability of most firms to generate meaningful earnings.

An example of the potential effectiveness of well-conceived business models can be seen during the early period of negotiated rates. Many institutional firms were failing at this time. But others prospered, and it became apparent that they were able to do so because of their business models. The successful firms survived because their business models aimed at getting more than the firms' fair share of business from the highest-potential clients. Strategies involved aggressive solicitation of orders combined with some risk taking and superb research. Customers were looked at in terms of their revenue potential, and products priced so that per-customer revenues were optimized. The successful firms emphasized improving the quality of their services to high-potential clients in their effort to win over this segment of the market. These firms made money, not principally by lowering costs, but by creating sufficient revenue to support their cost bases. Perhaps more than anything, this revenue thrust underlies a born-to-win organization.

It might be added that several marginally profitable major institutional firms at the time had very similar cost and profitability models, especially in relation to their processing and communications costs. What they lacked was a business model capable of generating sufficient revenue.

HOW BROKERAGE WORKS

Brokerage, like Gaul, can be divided into three parts—in this case, distribution, manufacturing, and operations. Relationships between and within those parts vary considerably among firms. The mix ultimately depends upon the perspective the firm adopts through its business model of the market segments it chooses to service. The segments include individuals, institutional buyers, corporations, and public agencies seeking finance capital. Each segment has its own distinct distribution, manufacturing, and operational requirements. Assuming a firm's business attains critical mass with respect to one of these segments, separate and identifiable support systems could be devoted to that segment's needs. However, because firms generally have evolved from originally serving one segment to serving the others as well, many have not achieved sufficient critical mass in all segments to make disaggregating support systems cost effective. And beyond a certain point, firms seem to resist this approach. The larger the firm, the less disaggregated and the more centralized the support systems tend to become.

Interestingly, the culture that produced most firms' initial success continues to dominate after the firms have matured. Thus, two firms which are similar superficially can have very different outlooks on their businesses. Moreover, their cost and profitability models can diverge in important ways.

The best example of this disparity is seen in a phenomenon now underway for a number of years, and that is the full incorporation of electronic technology into the securities business. Especially in the institutional areas, products have become more complex, and successful business models have become more dependent upon the ability to create products. To keep up, some firms have found it increasingly necessary to devote large amounts of their computational capabilities to analytics in support of these complex products (bond swap programs are a good example). These firms have put their technological emphasis on manufacturing. At the other extreme, firms that are predominantly retail oriented have tended to devote their considerable computational capacity to product delivery and service—communications, order processing, and customer and firm record keeping. Comparatively little of their mainframe capacities are devoted to analytics. In fact, one major old-line investment banker, which has developed what it believes is an analytic capability far superior to that of its major competitors, is attempting to enter large new market segments, largely based on what it believes is its computer-based analytics. To the extent that the most successful business models are based on achieving a competitive advantage, especially an unfair one, this firm may succeed in climbing over its analytically less well-equipped competitors.

Distribution

The main manageable dimensions of distribution profitability are productivity, which creates lending opportunities as a by-product, and effective cost management—in that order. Historically, brokerage firms made money only on distribution. In this dimension they are poles apart from life insurance companies, for which distribution is a major cost, and banks, for which distribution became a major cost before the advent of automatic transaction machines and the bankettes that have replaced many full-service neighborhood branch banks. In other words, from an industry-wide perspective, the securities firm is an anomaly as a financial services provider. Thus, it is very much worth considering the economics of brokerage distribution.

The most fundamental way that distribution makes money in retail brokerage is by attracting a disproportionate share of the highest-potential clients in a geographical area, and servicing them with the most profitable products. This means that retail profitability is largely a function of distribution profit. Retail locations should be considered revenue centers, however, and not true profit or investment centers. The reason is that the largest single cost of securities distribution, that of the commission salesman, is variable. A well-run retail branch's location costs can in fact be managed at less than 20 percent of product and service revenue.

Branches further make money by engaging in lending to those customers wishing to leverage their investment activities. Money market accounts and their offshoots have increased the amount of such lending activity; however, it is not yet totally clear that the profit benefit has exceeded the cost incurred to provide such accounts. Assuming that the money lent is borrowed and the branch earns a spread, the resulting location net interest profit will range between 5 and 10 percent of product and service revenues, depending upon product transaction mix. Product transaction mix, for its part, is an important determinant of interest profits, as not all products are marginable by the client. The amounts which can be lent, even on those products that can secure borrowings, are regulated by margin requirements. And these requirements change from time to time.

Discount firms have far more operating leverage than full-service firms, in that they have far lower variable costs, as well as far lower location expenses and investments per sales representative and customer. Fortunately for full-line firms, discounting is not a business strategy. Rather, discounting is but one element in the marketing mix. As a result, it is likely that the more successful discount firms will gradually offer a greater variety of services. By implication, if discounters are not careful, they will end up with cost and profitability models similar to those of the more efficient full-service brokers.

At the same time, competition from discounters is putting pressure on full-service firms to become more efficient. Discounters' strength is again based on their distribution economics, which are dramatically different from those of full-service brokers. Discount sales representatives are paid salaries and bonuses rather than commissions, a practice that normally results in a lower percentage of revenues being paid to sales representatives in discount houses than in full-service firms. The system works particularly well in periods of high volume, when revenues mount steeply while salaries remain flat and bonuses remain proportionate to salaries. Further, discount firms on the whole take orders of listed or unlisted securities without soliciting orders. By foregoing this element of the game they can dispense with comprehensive systems for customer or product information retrieval and marketing support, which are essential to brokers that offer a full line of security and other investment or insurance products. Neither do discounters require the extensive and expensive product marketing and origination support of the full-service broker. Eliminating expenses like these can result in a discount broker's branch operating at substantially lower cost than the branch of a full-service brokerage firm, both on a per-salesman and on a per-customer basis.

The discount brokerage business model is radically different from that of the traditional full-service brokerage firm. The cost and profitability model is radically different as well. Therefore, a certain consequence of intensified competition will be the development of alternatives to traditional distribution systems, where high variable and increasing fixed costs are burdensomely inefficient.

Full-service brokerage unintentionally provides a pricing umbrella under which creative forms of new distribution systems can thrive and flourish. Because dominant firms maintain high prevailing market prices, as their distribution systems force them to do, new competitors introducing lower-cost systems can undercut prevailing rates fairly easily and still recoup their upfront investment in a reasonably short time. For example, with a technology-intensive cost structure more efficient even than that of the discount brokers, it is possible today to offer a wide range of packaged products—still not as wide as full-service firms, but wide enough to accommodate the investment needs of perhaps 80 percent of the investing public. Such a system would combine "almost-full-service" brokerage with more efficient location costs and reduced need for expensive real-time information access and processing. The personal computer has greatly enhanced the availability of this option, to the point where there may be little perceptible difference between the quality of the analytics and other services available through a personal computer and the quality of those provided through the massive communication systems of full-service firms. The customer may even come to feel that such a system gives him the best available service. This perception is especially likely if the almost-full-service sales representative is client rather than product focused.

Manufacturing

Origination, or manufacturing, refers primarily to those activities that create the products to be sold through the distribution system. Classic examples include trading desks that facilitate customer buy and sell activities, departments that create unit trusts by packaging collections of securities, the corporate and public finance departments that create products for sale as a result of their banking activities, syndicate departments that participate in the underwritings of other dealers, and so on. Depending upon a firm's vertical integration, origination activities have expanded to include money management, including origination of mutual funds and creation of real estate investment opportunities, to name only two.

Because distribution profitability is impossible without products to sell, most full-service firms look at origination as an activity which they may have to engage in to ensure a plentiful supply of fully competitive products. Obviously, firms can benefit economically from revenues associated with the manufacture of products. However, the real motivator to engage in origination is the market, not profit. It would be extremely shortsighted for any firm even to contemplate the manufacture of products which are not fully competitive, especially in the realm of quality. For example, trading desks must offer the inside spread, or tightest margin, available. The firm cannot afford to disadvantage its customers when it acts as principal. The sales force, more than any other group, recognizes this fact. And so brokerage firms, especially large ones, are under enormous pressure from their own representatives to offer better products than competitors.

The principal activities of brokerage firms can in some situations become net costs. In periods of adversity, total revenues less direct variable costs and other product-related costs go negative. The pain is usually inflicted by customers wanting to sell back investments purchased from the firm at a time when they cannot be resold to others. As the former head of a consumately successful trading firm observed, "When markets are good, I can never accumulate enough because of the plentiful supply of buyers. And when markets are falling, I can never reduce my inventories enough because of the plentiful supply of sellers." The ability to hedge positions with futures has somewhat alleviated this problem. Still, even the best traders are human and capable of misjudging the market to the detriment of the firm. Traders are the last people who should set trading policy. Expecting a trader to stop trading because of bad markets is like expecting any business manager to recommend closing his activity—a highly unlikely event.

Operations

To the dismay of some, operations has been called the plumbing of the brokerage industry. This is doubtless an exaggeration, yet plumbing is not necessarily a bad analogy. Most operations departments are in a sense large conduits through which innumerable transactions and communications flow daily. At one time this conduit was quite tangible, as departments moved never-ending streams of paper. But the recent past has seen great advances toward certificateless processing. Most back offices of large brokerage firms are now highly automated. With today's sophisticated real-time inventory control systems, any security can be rapidly located at any time. The efficiency that these changes create is extremely important, not only to obtain low unit costs, but also to help the firm earn interest income, and avoid incurring unnecessary interest expense.

SEGMENTS OF THE BROKERAGE INDUSTRY

The preceding framework for understanding the securities industry might be termed conceptual in that it seeks to explain the economic rationale for the structure and orientation of securities firms. There are in fact many different businesses included within the taxonomy of brokerage. The largest are the full-line providers, while the smallest are the boutiques serving either individuals or institutional investors. Other categories could also be cited, but the important fact to note is that the distinctions between categories are blurring.

Publicly available information on the securities industry offers a somewhat organized perspective. A reading of data such as that filed with the Securities and Exchange Commission reveals a diverse group of over 500 firms competing by means of a wide variety of products and services. Some, like the specialist units on the New York Stock Exchange and other trading floors, are brokers' brokers; that is, they do business within the industry only. The majority of firms, however, do business with the general public. This section focuses on these latter firms as they are grouped into the following six major segments by the Securities Industry Association: national full-line, investment banks, New York City regionals, regional firms, discounters, and others. Exhibit 6.6 gives a profile of these six segments.

Twelve national full-line firms compete in both the retail and institutional markets. These 12 underwrite equity and debt offerings for distribution through their own sales forces and by syndicates of other distributors; they position blocks of equities in the secondary market; they position an ever-growing variety of debt instruments; and they package a wide range of products for sale.

About a dozen investment banks compete for corporate and public investment banking accounts and institutional investments. They underwrite equity and private and public debt offerings, commit capital in secondary equity market transactions, and make markets in a full range of debt securities.

The 200 regionals traditionally operating in limited geographic areas often appear to be smaller versions of the national full-line firms. Although most regionals are predominantly retail, many also offer specialized institutional services to local clients, and in some cases to national corporations and institutions attracted by their regional expertise.

Deregulation of fixed brokerage commission rates by the Securities Act of 1975 created the discount opportunity. Discounters compete on price and limited

Exhibit 6.6 Financial Profiles in the Securities Industry[a]

	Revenues		Profit (Before Taxes)		Assets		Equity	
	$	%	$	%	$	%	$	%
National Full-Line	16.7	43	.9	21	122.3	31	6.7	40
Investment Banks	12.1	31	1.8	43	214.4	54	5.2	31
Regionals	4.0	10	.4	10	13.2	3	1.4	8
New York City Regionals	2.1	5	.3	7	12.1	3	.9	5
Discounters	.5	1	—	—	1.8	—	.2	1
Others	3.2	8	.8	19	30.0	8	2.2	13
Total	$38.6	100%	$4.2	100%	$393.8	100%	$16.6	100%

Source: SRI/SIA Database, 1985.

[a] All dollar figures in $ billions.

service for both retail and institutional business. Ten years after deregulation, discounters have about a 10 percent share of individual commission dollars and a 20 percent share of individual volume. Discounters established this substantial foothold by offering trade execution services without the full-service investment advice and personal relationship of traditional brokerage competitors. Core customers are the many sophisticated active investors who make their own investment decisions without professional counsel.

Examining these three segments (national full-line, regional, and discount) in more detail provides an interesting contrast on the levels of profitability and ways of making money in brokerage.

National Full-Line Profitability

In trying to understand how the profitability levers work, it makes some sense to start with the firms showing the poorest overall results, namely, national full-line brokers. The NFLs have a lot of ground to make up on their competitors. Although the arguments for synergy are strong, the NFL results do not show any significant benefit. Profit margins have been running 4 to 5 percent behind industry averages, and 7 to 10 percent behind investment bank performance. (See Exhibit 6.7.)

A number of factors appear to contribute to NFLs' problems. Revenues per employee are low, chiefly because of the relatively large ratio of support personnel to "producers." And variable costs per employee are high: The personal sales force is paid an average of 40 percent of revenues. Fixed costs, in the form of expensive account executive locations and operational overhead, are also high. In addition, one often-cited reason for depressed profitability is that NFLs undertake too broad a set of activities to achieve scale economies. Their retail customer bases are too all encompassing, their account executives have too many products to sell, and their business portfolios are highly, perhaps overly, diversified. National full-line firms cannot be counted out, however. They have large pools of capital amassed from public equity offerings. If they can manage their sales and support costs in relation to reasonably achievable productivity levels, their national presence, customer franchise, and desire to win can pull them through. See Exhibits 6.8 and 6.9 for the aggregated income statement and balance sheet breakdowns on full-line brokers.

Investment Bank Profitability

Investment banks have traditionally made money, and lots of it. Their profit margins have ranged between 11 percent and 18 percent over the last five years, while pretax ROEs were always above 30 percent and rose as high as 57 percent. (See Exhibits 6.7 and 6.10). The reason for this superb performance is suggested by Andre Meyer, head of Lazard Freres, who has called investment bankers "financial engineers," by which he means that they are experts in calculating the large-scale stresses exerted by mergers, acquisitions, and so forth, to determine with precision the risks involved, and the rates needed to compensate for these risks. The agreements constructed are as carefully designed as skyscrapers and

Exhibit 6.7 Pre-Tax Profit Margins

	1976	1977	1978	1980	1982	1983	1984	1985
Total	14.2%	7.7%	14.1%	10.8%	13.1%	12.9%	5.2%	10.7%
National Full Lines	11.5	6.9	10.9	6.9	8.8	8.6	-0.9	5.6
Discounters	N/A	N/A	17.5	12.2	13.6	14.0	3.0	8.9
Investment Banks	20.5	7.6	17.7	15.4	17.4	16.7	11.4	14.6

Source: SRI/SIA Database.

Exhibit 6.8 Consolidated Income Statement: National Full-Line Brokers

Revenues

	1980 ($7.3B)	1985 ($16.7B)
Other Revenues	17.2%	23.8%
Margin Interest	20.0%	8.1%
Under-writing Profits	8.7%	12.4%
Trading Profits	17.0%	27.5%
Com-missions	37.1%	28.2%

Expenses & Net Income

	1980 ($6.5B)	1985 ($13.2B)
Net Income	10.9%	
Other Expenses	15.8%	24.4%
Interest Expense	16.6%	19.1%
DP & Communications	7.7%	8.0%
Floor Brokerage	3.8%	2.2%
Other Comp.	21.5%	21.5%
Registered Rep. Comp.	23.7%	24.8%

Source: SRI/SIA Database.

bridges. Whether engineers or not, investment bankers have clearly found a formula for success, and that formula can be written as equal parts focused business activities, high revenue per employee, sophisticated risk management, and high leverage. The greatest differences between investment banks and the national full-line firms are thus their revenues per employee and their strategic focus.

Another important difference between investment banks and NFLs concerns size and partnership orientation. The largest national full-line firm, Merrill Lynch, has 29,000 employees, a size that makes a bureaucratic operating style and some degree of impersonality nearly inescapable. The largest investment banks, by contrast, have at most a few thousand people. Managements have worked hard to retain a partnership atmosphere, sharing the view that unnecessary additions to staff reduce the profits available for distribution at year-end. In addition to the intangible "cultural" benefits this strategy offers, it tends to translate into a minimum of nonrevenue-producing staff, and consequently, the high revenues per employee noted earlier.

A third major strength of the investment banks is their risk management practices. Investment banks take large positions, in effect making the markets in many securities. Although a trader's natural inclination is to bet the market, the investment banks are more deliberate. They support their traders with sophisticated information systems that provide up-to-the-minute prices and news. They also use sophisticated hedging strategies to reduce risk. The investment banks are highly leveraged, with equity less than 3 percent of liabilities. Their major

Exhibit 6.9 Consolidated Balance Sheet: National Full-Line Brokers

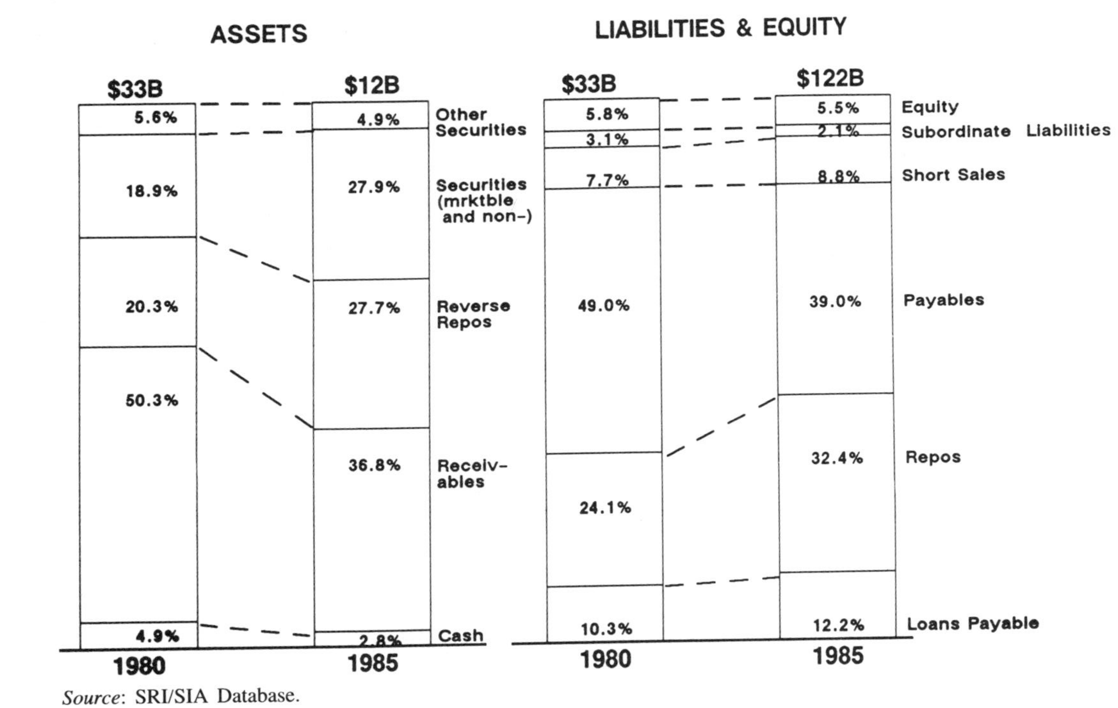

Source: SRI/SIA Database.

Exhibit 6.10 Return on Equity

	1976	1977	1978	1980	1982	1983	1984	1985
Total	N/A	20.7%	49.2%	35.9%	40.5%	36.6%	13.3%	24.6%
National								
Full								
Lines	N/A	N/A	45.0	24.6	29.8	28.1	-2.6	14.0
Discounters	N/A	N/A	N/A	52.2	53.9	46.7	0.8	21.8
Investment								
Banks	N/A	N/A	55.7	56.7	54.8	43.8	31.1	33.8

Source: SRI/SIA Database.

financing vehicle is repurchase agreements, which account for nearly 60 percent of liabilities. Under the terms of "repos," investment banks sell bonds with the legal obligation to buy them back at a specific premium in the future. In most cases, investment firms run "matched books"; that is, for each repo the firm sells, it reverses in a repo of identical maturity. By matching maturities, the firm eliminates interest rate risks, and locks in the investment point spread between the repo and reverse repo rates. As primary government securities dealers in many cases, they put their inventories to good financing use. (For the readers' convenience, aggregated income-statement and balance-sheet information for regional brokers is shown in Exhibits 6.11 and 6.12.)

Discounter Profitability

The discounters are the brokerage industry's new kid on the block. Their margin performance in the four years from 1980–1983 was close to twice that of NFLs. (The discounters, like the NFLs, had a terrible year in 1984 when individuals pulled out of the market.) Discounters' ROEs have also been much higher than the NFLs'. Like the investment banks, they pursue a highly focused marketing strategy, concentrating on the most profitable segment of the retail business. Also like investment banks, they work to keep personnel growth under control. The third element of their formula is a concerted effort to manage noninterest-bearing liabilities.

The discounters define their business as simple and straightforward: they execute trades on behalf of customers who know what investments they want to make. Over 85 percent of discounters' revenues come from commissions and margin interest. In 1984, slightly over 1 percent of discounters' revenues came from trading profits. See Exhibits 6.13 and 6.14 for discounters' aggregated income-statement and balance-sheet data.

Unlike NFLs, which serve their retail customers through highly paid, advice-giving account executives, discounters use "ordertakers" to serve customers. Where account executives regularly call customers and actively solicit new business, discount ordertakers sit and wait for the business to come to them. Paid on salary, not commissions, these sales representatives take only 6 cents out of every dollar of discounter revenue—NFL account executives collect nearly 25 cents on the dollar. And with no solicitation or investment counseling, discounters have also eliminated most of the cost of research analysts or sales assistance.

Another area where discounters improve profitability is in their management of noninterest liabilities, specifically customer and street payables. While the other two segments' balance sheets show receivables and payables netting out, the discounters' payables exceed their receivables, providing them with a free source of funding.

Trends Affecting Future Profitability

Given these results for the past five years, what can securities industry managers expect to experience in the future? The most critical reality is the cyclicality of

Exhibit 6.11 Consolidated Income Statement: Large Investment Banks

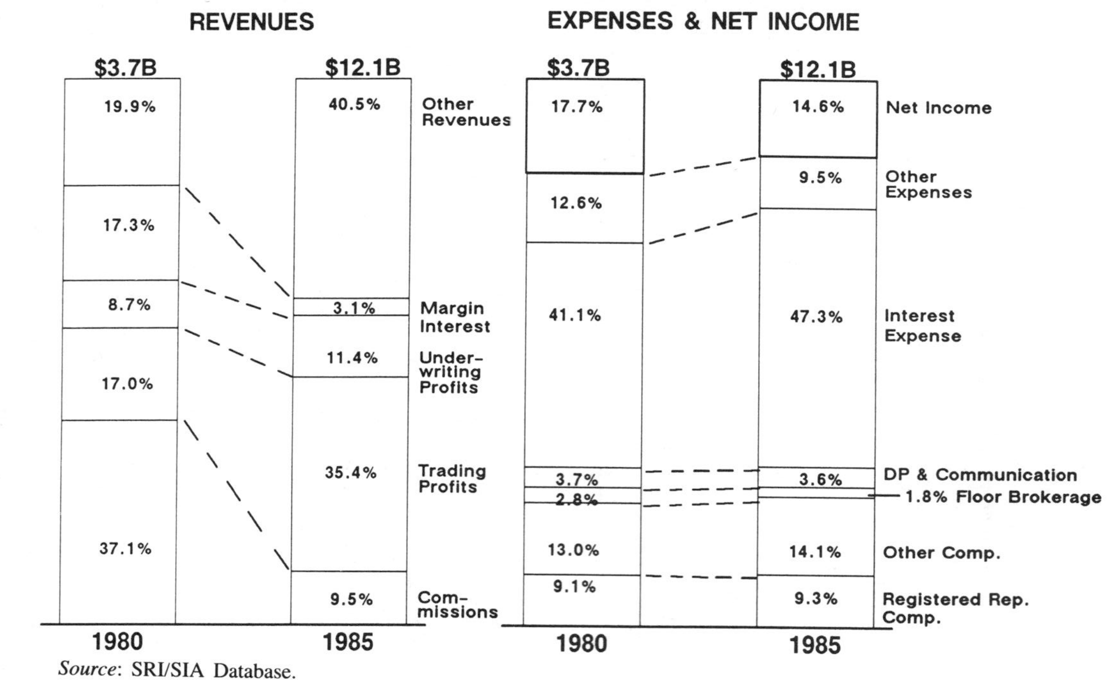

Source: SRI/SIA Database.

Exhibit 6.12 Consolidated Balance Sheet: Large Investment Banks

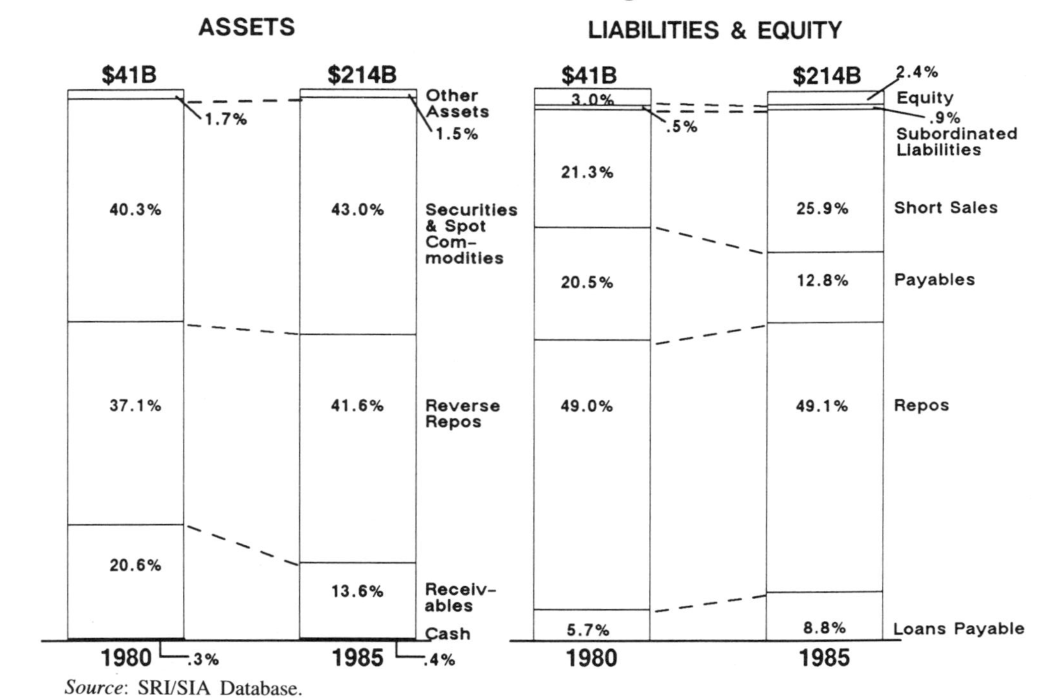

Source: SRI/SIA Database.

Exhibit 6.13 Consolidated Income Statement: Discounters

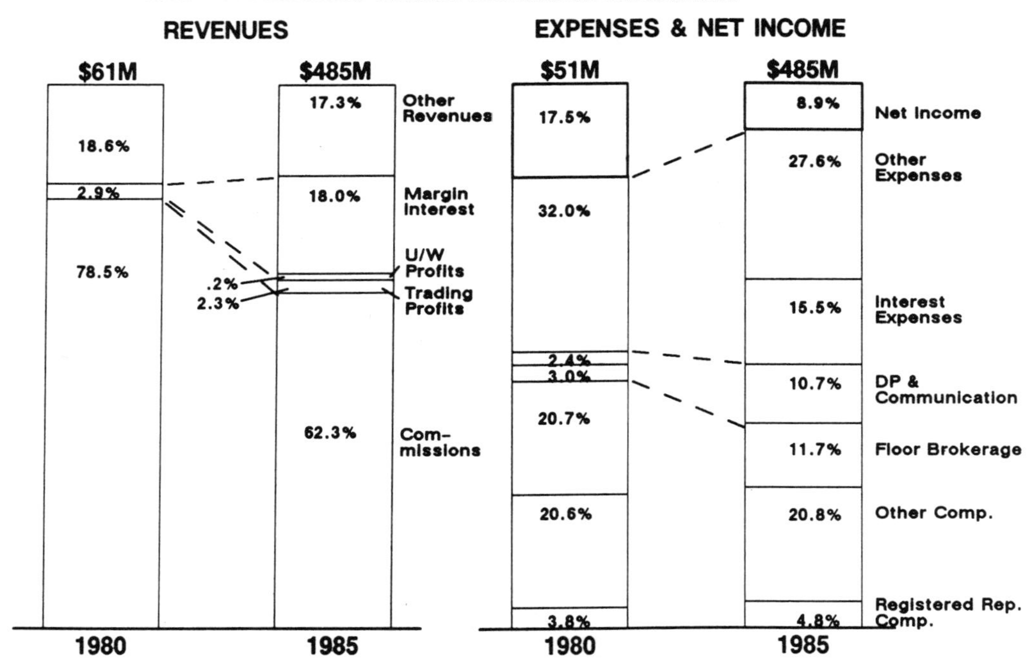

Source: SRI/SIA Database.

Exhibit 6.14 Consolidated Balance Sheet: Discounters

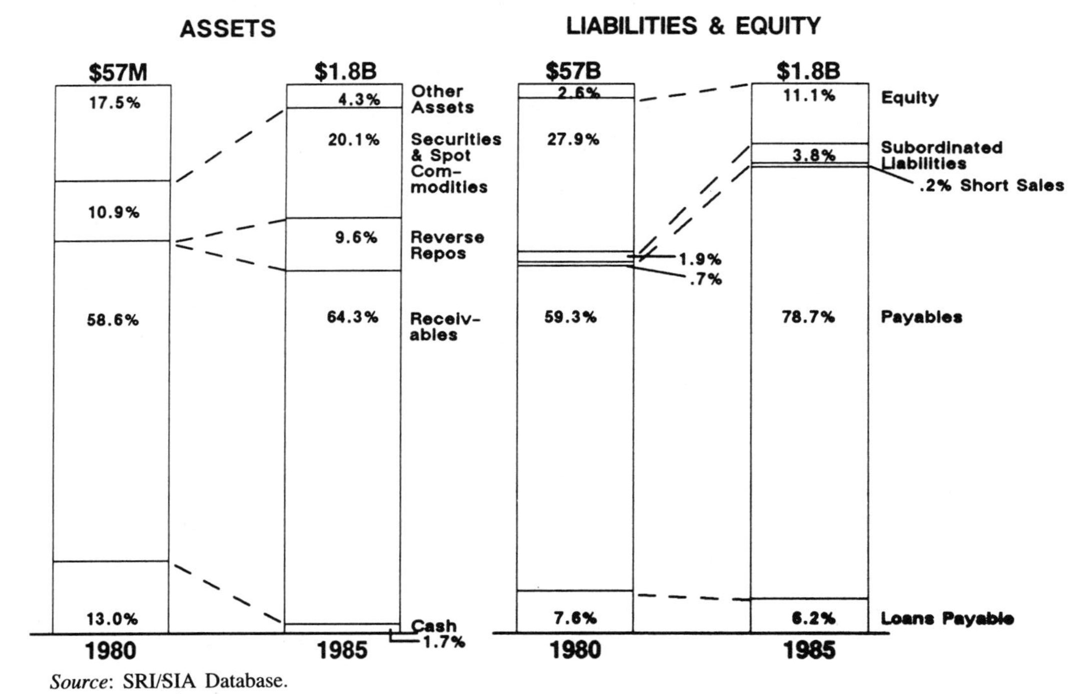

Source: SRI/SIA Database.

the industry, exacerbated by broadening and intensifying competition. Making money in brokerage has become more difficult than ever. Moreover, the patterns of volatility and shrinking margins seen in recent years are likely to continue. Under these conditions, firms need to know more than their revenues and costs. They need to develop thoroughly articulated business models and the conviction of making money management.

What are some of the concrete implications of these trends? For one thing, commission revenues may not grow. For another, banks and insurance companies may progressively gain market share, starting as they are from a small base. While it is true that volume has to date been shifting slowly away from traditional providers, the trend is definitely toward value-priced products and lower-cost distribution options.

Successful NFLs and discounters are adding products; that is, asset management accounts and mutual funds, to their previously narrow product lines. After 10 years of growing by adding customers, discounters have reached the point where they must generate additional revenues from existing customers to maintain growth. Even if discounters continue to rely on salaried reps, new products will mean additional costs. The NFLs, on the other hand, will be working to trim their costs. This initiative may mean experimenting with new distribution channels, cutting compensation to reduce human costs, and questioning additional investments in new products, businesses, and overhead before proceeding.

Investment bankers face a different set of challenges. Even while the Glass-Steagall Act stands, the investment firms' underwriting activities are being challenged by incursions from commercial bankers. Options available for small- and medium-sized firms are disappearing as many brokers scurry to fill niches in which they can prosper. Some successful smaller firms, like Hambrecht and Quist, have focused on the venture capital industry as a source of both venture profits and public offering clients. Industry concentration, which increased over the past five years, will continue. The most obvious area where the concentration trend is seen today is fixed income trading, which is dominated by Salomon Brothers, Goldman Sachs, First Boston, and, in high-yield bonds, Drexel Burnham.

The decline in commissions on equity trading will continue as institutional investors become more sophisticated and demanding. Institutional equity is one principal business in which, perhaps more than in any other brokerage area, the commission is fast becoming a thing of the past. The institutional business is also one that requires capital. Reliance on huge amounts of capital is a strategy available only to already well-capitalized larger players.

CONCLUSION

The messages from this chapter, then, should be clear:

- Different businesses have very different economics and key success factors.

Keeping a fix on the profitability levers is a continuing management challenge. What works today may not work tomorrow.

- The flux in the financial services industry is continuing, and with it come serious challenges to profitability and performance.
- Unless a firm maintains focus and manages the key variables, performance will suffer.
- It is becoming increasingly difficult for smaller players to be competitive. Those that are succeeding have found their niche and are managing the economics of playing in its limited confines.

That massive rearrangement of the financial services industry will come to pass is a certainty on the order of death and taxes. The optimal business models of the future, to say nothing of cost and profitability models, may be unrecognizable. So it should be obvious by now that this chapter's title is in a sense a tease. The models are currently far too dynamic to be described with precision. Moreover, they have never been more dynamic, and are becoming increasingly so.

Managers who aim to succeed will have to anticipate changes, not resist them. No model that is successful today will necessarily work tomorrow. The challenge facing all serious managers of brokerage firms is therefore first, to bet on the business model that they believe will make it in the next five years (or beyond if possible), and second, to ensure that the associated cost and profitability model can provide current results sufficient to attract capital, talented employees, and valued customers. For the moment, there are no convincing models. Rather, there are a number of firms in various stages of evolution, seeking to discover what those models will need to be.

7 Making Money in Insurance

RICHARD J. SHIMA

By all measures, the business of insurance is a pervasive fact of American society. Insurance is fundamentally a mechanism for sharing risk. Through this mechanism, the insurance industry provides protection against financial loss for individuals (life, accident, health, auto, home) and for businesses (property, liability, workers compensation). The insurance industry also offers an array of wealth accumulation products, from pensions to life insurance. Insurance products are sold through a number of distribution systems, including independent agents, company (direct-writing) agents, and, increasingly, mechanisms such as mass marketing and direct response made possible by new data-processing and communications technologies. Insurance organizations may be for-profit stock companies, not-for-profit mutuals, or large non-profit health plans.

In 1985, premiums flowing into the traditional insurance industry (excluding self-insurance, captives, and pension fund deposits) totaled $349 billion. This figure amounts to 8.7 percent of the gross national product. Much of the annual growth of premiums is driven by inflation and increased demand as the economy expands and there are more autos, more homes, more businesses, more workers. Some of the growth is mandated by societal needs and is regulated to varying degrees by the individual states. Auto insurance and workers compensation are prime examples of this type of insurance coverage. Over 3400 property casualty companies and 2000 life insurance companies compete for this vast U.S. market.

The purpose of this chapter is to highlight the elements of successful management for the insurance enterprise, as well as point out several pitfalls facing firms in this highly competitive business.

EFFECTIVE FINANCIAL MANAGEMENT

Managing Assets and Liabilities

In many ways, insurance company operations are similar to those of banks and other financial institutions and, to this extent, have the same considerations for successful operation. Like banks and thrift institutions, insurance companies take in money from customers that later will be paid back to them. Banks accept deposits; insurance companies collect premiums which will be used to pay claims. To be successful, both types of institutions must price their products to attract funds and then invest these funds to obtain the best possible returns. In the process, they must maintain adequate liquidity to meet contractual obligations as they come due.

In other ways, however, insurance companies face issues quite unlike those faced by banks and thrifts, owing to fundamental differences in business functions. While deposit-taking institutions cannot be certain of the duration of their obligations, they can determine their liabilities fairly accurately at any time. Insurance companies also cannot be sure when their liabilities will mature. (For example, the timing of large natural disasters cannot be predicted, and for many liability coverages, claims continue to come in years after a policy is written.) However, insurance companies have a problem that does not concern bankers or thrift managers: insurers cannot know the exact size of their liabilities. Two examples suggest why. An insurance company cannot predict how many hurricanes will occur in a year nor how severe they will be. On product liability policies, a company may find that claims reflect hazards that were unknown when the policies were written. Insurance companies do estimate the likelihood that these, or a multitude of other events, might occur. Making such estimates is a basic actuarial function.

In pricing to compete for deposits, banks and thrifts must take into consideration what can be earned on assets. Insurance pricing decisions also depend on investment earnings. But more critical are the imperfect estimates that must be made of the ultimate size and timing of costs associated with a group of policies. This uncertainty adds to pricing problems particularly during periods of intense competition. Companies that make overly optimistic assumptions about the size and timing of loss payments may be misled into charging too little for coverage. In this highly competitive business, other companies often follow, resulting in depressed profits across the industry.

All successful financial institutions must manage assets and liabilities to obtain maximum returns consistent with their liquidity needs and the degree of risk they are willing to tolerate. Both insurance companies and deposit-taking institutions must hold reserves against losses of assets resulting from bad investments. However, insurance companies have an additional consideration affecting the amount they must set aside as reserves, since their reserves must be adequate to cover possible future adverse trends in loss payments. It is important for an insurance company to estimate its future liabilities accurately. Over-reserving not only depresses current earnings but, by over-estimating claim costs, may cause a company to price its products too high and lose market share. Inadequate reserving can lead to underpricing, which produces inadequate earnings and in the extreme can lead to insolvency.

Beyond this, insurers use a number of methods to reduce the uncertainties inherent in insurance liabilities. These include reinsurance, in which an insurer contracts with another insurer to bear part of the risk, an approach similar to loan syndication; policy exclusions, which specify types of losses which are not covered; and clear statements of policy limits, which define the maximum amounts payable under the policy. Finally, an insurer must be able to recognize when a particular risk is simply uninsurable.

Attracting Adequate Capital

Capital is the engine that drives insurance operations. The risk-sharing enterprise requires supporting capital to assure customers and regulators that contractual obligations will be met. Capital is attracted to or withdrawn from the industry depending on whether the industry's return on capital does or does not satisfy investors' expectations. Indeed, when appropriate returns are not achieved, capital is withdrawn. If there is insufficient capital to support the demand for insurance coverage, severe disruptions can occur in insurance markets.

Achieving Attractive Earnings

Earnings growth is critical to attracting capital. Exhibits 7.1 and 7.2 illustrate the basic income statements for a typical life insurance company and a typical property/casualty insurer. The income statements differ for various reasons, in-

Exhibit 7.1 Life Insurance Company Income Statement

1. Premiums	$ 1,321[a]
2. Net investment income	402
3. **Total income** (lines 1 plus 2)	1,723
4. Benefits paid	871
5. Increase in policy reserves set aside for future payments	660
6. Loss adjustment expenses	20
7. Amortization of deferred acquisition costs	7
8. General and administrative expenses	90
9. **Total expense** (lines 4 through 8)	1,648
10. Net gain from operations (before Federal income taxes) (line 3 less line 9)	75
11. Federal income taxes	28
12. Net gain from operations (after Federal income taxes) (line 10 less line 11)	47
13. Realized investment gains (losses)	(1)
14. **Net income** (line 12 plus 13)	$ 46

[a] Figures in $ millions.

Exhibit 7.2 Property/Casualty Company Income Statement

1. Written premiums	$ 733[a]
2. **Earned premiums**	719
3. Losses	484
4. Loss adjustment expenses	71
5. Amortization of deferred acquisition costs	103
6. Underwriting and administrative expenses	149
7. **Total underwriting deduction** (lines 3 through 6)	807
8. Underwriting gain (loss) (line 2 less line 7)	(88)
9. Net investment income	107
10. **Operating income before federal income taxes** (lines 8 plus 9)	19
11. Federal income taxes (tax-loss carryforward)	(12)
12. Operating income (line 10 less line 11)	31
13. Realized investment gains (losses)	(4)
14. **Net income** (lines 12 plus 13)	$ 27

[a] Figures in $ millions.

cluding regulatory requirements as well as fundamental differences in the businesses. Earnings are derived from the insurance underwriting process, from investment income on the net cash flow, and from investment income on the supporting capital. While earnings come predominantly from these sources, insurers increasingly have been generating earnings from insurance-related services such as claims processing and engineering loss control on a fee-for-service basis.

Appropriate levels of earnings for individual insurance products are achieved by meticulous attention to managing the fundamentals of the risk-sharing mechanism. This process entails:

- Identifying and pooling risks into homogeneous groups
- Assessing the loss potential for each group, and establishing proper prices
- Managing the acquisition expenses involved in creating the pool and the processing expenses in handling the losses
- Managing claims in order to meet obligations promptly and to avoid payment of losses not covered
- Managing the investment of capital and cash flow to match assets and liabilities, maximize yields, and minimize tax liabilities

These activities require expertise in many areas, including marketing, claims, investment, data processing, actuarial, accounting, law, and economics. The process is conducted in an environment which is both highly competitive and closely scrutinized by state and federal regulatory authorities.

Managing Earnings Fluctuations

For any given year, earnings of individual insurance products are subject to a wide variety of external influences, including inflation, interest-rate fluctuations, and the many factors which cause losses. Substantial variation in annual earnings has been a feature in the property/casualty business for many years; now earnings are fluctuating in products which have long been stable earnings producers, such as individual life and group health insurance.

At the company level, net earnings are the sum of the earnings of individual products. A major challenge for insurance company management is to develop an appropriate mix of products that reduces the impact of the earnings fluctuations of individual products. In their efforts to reduce these fluctuations, insurance companies have been adding to their sophistication in technical areas such as pricing and investment management. Besides reallocating their product mix, companies have merged with other insurers and diversified outside of insurance and financial services. In spite of these efforts, fluctuations in overall product earnings have continued to increase.

The fundamental characteristic of the insurance industry that causes this vulnerability to earnings fluctuation is the forward-commitment nature of its contracts. Principally this means that premium rates are set in the present but must accurately reflect the costs of future events. In group pensions and individual annuities, contracts promise to maintain rates of return on invested assets for years into the future. Shifts in economic conditions can make those commitments either uncompetitive or difficult to fulfill. Life insurance contracts permit policyholders to gain access to the cash values built up in their policies through policy loans at a fixed rate of interest, often as low as 5 percent. Particularly during periods of high interest rates, these loans are attractive to policyholders and contribute to instability in company earnings.

On the property/casualty side of the business, liability coverages for corporations and individuals promise to pay future damages and compensation. Losses can prove unexpectedly large, since some hazards are unforeseeable, and changes in legal interpretations of liability further complicate the picture. Of course, certain unanticipated events can be beneficial to a company's earnings. The high interest rates experienced in the early 1980s, for example, provided extra investment income. (However, those high interest rates were associated with high inflation, which raised claim costs and offset some of the extra revenue.)

Competition plays a key role in earnings fluctuations. Insurance is a highly competitive business in a mature market. The growth in total demand for property/casualty products is relatively stable, and is associated with increases in the number and value of autos, homes, business firms and other insurable entities. The total demand for these insurance products is not significantly influenced by price.

Therefore, when profitable times encourage insurers to seek greater market share they often do so via lower prices. Price competition brings about some shifting of risks among insurers, but since the market has little room to expand, "sale" prices do not result in new purchases of additional coverage. Thus the industry as a whole begins to suffer underwriting losses because of inadequate pricing. Those companies that trimmed prices may increase market share temporarily, but generally they do not meet their expectations of higher profit; instead their losses mount. In order to return to profitability, companies then limit losses by restricting the writing of new coverage and by setting higher prices. As with price cutting, these actions do not significantly change total demand; more revenue is derived for the same coverage and profitability improves. After these conditions have existed for some time, companies again seek growth in market share, starting the cycle over again.

This process is called the property/casualty underwriting cycle and is similar to pricing-profitability cycles observed in other commodity-like products. It is a major motivation behind companies' efforts to diversify their product mix and to engage in long-term profit planning.

PITFALLS

As companies seek to achieve growth and profit in today's insurance markets, a number of pitfalls lie in their paths. These include insufficient attention to the basics of pricing, reserving, and investments; failure to take appropriate advantage of technology; and ineffective diversification strategy.

Insufficient Attention to the Basics

Some of the most important "basics" for insurance companies are the same as those in other industries: keep total expenses down, improve productivity, and stay on top of a rapidly changing environment. But the specific areas that can cause insurance companies to perform poorly are pricing, reserving, and investment timing.

Inadequate Pricing and Reserving. Pricing insurance products requires careful anticipation of future events. Proper actuarial analysis is essential to the success of any insurance company. The actuaries determine a price calculated to recover from all insureds a sufficient premium to cover claims and expenses, plus a reasonable allowance for profit. Without a solid understanding of how future obligations are related to current contracts, the underwriters cannot accurately classify and pool risks. And without proper classification (or "underwriting") criteria, the prices set for the various risk groups will be incorrect.

In addition, other forces can reduce profit margins and remove the cushion for unanticipated events. In the early 1980s the pressure for "cash flow underwriting" increased when investment returns were high. It was believed that investment income could more than offset the losses and expenses involved in writing business at depressed rates. While the logic was appealing, the effect was to compound dependence on unpredictable events. Property/casualty companies subsequently were caught by unanticipated high losses and lower investment returns, resulting in extraordinary operating losses in 1984 and 1985. The loss of capital during this period forced companies to limit their insurance writings and/or seek additional sources of capital.

Loss reserving is perhaps the ultimate actuarial exercise, particularly in the property/casualty lines. Reserves are established to provide for future losses; funds are expended and reserves reduced as claims are settled. In principle, total reserves will increase gradually as an insurer's volume of business grows. However, conditions can change in ways that affect basic assumptions that were made when the reserves were established. In recent years there have been court rulings that interpret the policy language to include coverage for situations that had not been intended in the original contracts. In the wake of such events, new estimates of expected losses must be made. Changes in tax policy can also affect companies' reserving practices.

If badly handled, reserving decisions can give a company the image of being poorly managed and, in some cases, can even undermine the firm's solvency. A company's reserving decisions are frequently compared with those of its peers. Sudden, large changes in reserves must be explained to regulators and investment analysts. In such cases, solvency also becomes an issue because increases to loss reserves come directly out of earnings and reduce the capital available to protect against insolvency. Uncertainty as to when the reserves will be paid compromises a company's ability to earn maximum investment income on assets which will ultimately be liquidated to pay claims.

Poor Investment Timing. In life insurance, annuities, and pensions, the policyholder's return on invested funds plays a key role in the competition for business. Earning a competitive return with safety requires making every effort to match investment maturities properly with contractual liabilities. To do otherwise—for example, to offer long-term returns backed in part with short-term investments having higher returns—is a high risk strategy. At times it may show spectacular results, but it may also result in equally dramatic failures. Increasingly, the industry is offering innovative programs of high-yield investments protected against downside risk by options or futures contracts.

Mismanagement of Technology

Insurance companies have long been substantial users of data-processing technology. They use this technology to handle the many statistics required for management, accounting, and regulatory-reporting purposes. Companies doing business throughout the country have become effective users of nationwide communications systems. But advances in competing financial services industries have raised the level of technological sophistication required just to stay in the game. New products demand not only advanced systems and programming capabilities but also require major capital investment in the latest hardware. As costs and complexity have grown, so too have the chances for expensive missteps.

The potential of computer technology for insurance companies expanded as soon as computers could exchange data with other computers or terminals in remote locations. Banks first put this technology to use with electronic funds transfer and automated teller machines. The introduction of Merrill Lynch's Cash Management Account expanded these capabilities into an extensive link-up of banking and brokerage transactions. This account and others like it created consumer expectations for comprehensive information, a direct link to the provider's computers, and procedures to make each transaction as easy as possible for the customer.

Insurance companies have responded to this challenge. They have long sought to improve service and contain costs with "back office" automation. Automation now presents an opportunity to change the nature of the customer interface and potentially save money at the same time. Since the "front office" for most insurance companies is their agency force, the industry quickly moved to provide automation capabilities for its agents.

Some poorly performing companies gained attention by introducing ill-conceived systems for agents, software that could not perform as promised, and timetables that could not be met. In this area, successful companies were not necessarily the ones that were quickest to innovate.

Ineffective Diversification Strategy

A number of insurance companies, like many banks, securities firms, automakers, retailers, and others, have sought to extend their reach into the financial services market. Expansion can occur quickly through merger or acquisition, and many companies have followed this strategy. Unlike the situation in concentrated industries, however, expansion in the fragmented financial services industry must be undertaken piecemeal. The U.S. financial services industry comprises approximately 5000 insurance companies; 40,000 banks, thrifts, and credit unions; 170,000 real estate firms; 5000 brokerage houses; and several thousand loan or credit service companies. Moreover, not all combinations of firms will be successful. Some of the major acquisitions and mergers in which insurance companies have participated have yet to yield the anticipated benefits.

Following the purchase of a life insurer by E.F. Hutton and the merger of American Express with Shearson, Kuhn, Loeb, several insurance companies moved to purchase brokerage firms. The most notable was Prudential's acquisition of Bache, Halsey, Stuart, Shields in 1981. But while such purchases provided insurers with immediate outlets to cross-sell products through affiliated securities brokers, insurers found it difficult at first to make effective use of brokers as insurance distributors for a wide range of products. Although potential synergies may exist, the lack of immediate payoff has slowed firms' drive to acquire.

Some insurers have taken a different approach to expansion into the securities business by purchasing wholesaling intermediaries. Insurance companies also have diversified into totally different businesses with the objective of bolstering profits and reducing earnings fluctuations. The results at this stage are mixed.

Diversification by noninsurers into the insurance market also has potential problems. State insurance regulators are concerned that the purchase of insurance companies by institutions outside the industry could lead to more examples of marketing zeal overwhelming underwriting prudence. Baldwin-United, once a piano company, expanded their sales of single-premium deferred annuities (a high return, tax-sheltered vehicle) by more than 3000 percent in three years, much faster than they could accumulate the capital necessary to meet the legal requirements for financial backing. Insurance regulators placed Baldwin-United's insurance subsidiaries into rehabilitation, and the company filed for bankruptcy.

OTHER ISSUES FACING THE INSURANCE INDUSTRY

Most of the forces prompting major changes for the insurance industry arise from broad societal movements. Changing attitudes toward risk, savings, and compensation for damages have affected both the personal insurance market and the business insurance market. Unforeseen environmental developments, such as the dangers of toxic wastes, have involved the insurance industry in solving major social problems. And changes in the legal interpretation of insurance contracts have altered the very fundamentals of the business in some lines. Some of these shifts are happening slowly enough that companies can adapt. Other shifts require an immediate response.

Individuals' Changing Attitudes

People often seek returns that are both high and guaranteed. Financial markets cannot fully satisfy both objectives simultaneously. Consumers have quickly become aware of alternative strategies for at least partially satisfying their objectives. More than in the past, they move their assets from one product to another as situations change. Providers, of course, have designed their products to minimize the movement of funds among competing products. For example, in the case of individual annuities, withdrawal penalties have been added to discourage cancellation of policies when other products appear more attractive.

Another consumer attitude that has emerged in recent years is the belief that someone else must be liable when there is personal injury, no matter what the circumstances. This view has received support from the courts, reflecting society's general tendency to compensate victims of unfortunate circumstances. From the insurer's perspective, this trend generates substantial added uncertainty in a segment of the business that is already uncertain. Heightened litigiousness increases potential financial burdens—directly to the insurance companies and indirectly to their customers. When a business finds insurance prohibitively expensive or not available, it often responds by curtailing output. For example, the decision by some insurance companies to stop offering medical malpractice insurance placed new financial risks and burdens on providers of medical services. Physicians, in turn, found it necessary to curtail certain services. Thus, insurers are part of a problem larger than their industry.

The widespread consequences of this trend have prompted a nationwide debate on appropriate means for reforming the U.S. tort liability system. The Reagan Administration, Congress, and almost all state legislatures have considered modifications in liability laws. The outcome of this debate will have profound consequences for both the insurance industry and for the businesses and individuals it serves.

Environmental Hazards

Historically, insurance coverage for accidental spills or pollution of various kinds has been straightforward. Whether a local milk truck springs a leak or a supertanker releases oil as a result of storm damage, coverage has been readily available. These accidents are part of a class of events that are predictable in statistical terms.

Where certain hazards are concerned, insurance companies not only can calculate, but also help reduce the risk. Through on-site inspections, insurance representatives make safety recommendations which can lower premiums. Such risk reduction by insurers is in the best interests of all concerned.

Environmental pollution from toxic wastes poses new and special problems for insurers. Annual production of solid waste that is considered hazardous has reached 57 million tons. That volume is handled by between 30,000 and 50,000 hazardous waste dump sites. In addition, more than 2000 abandoned chemical dump sites have been identified by the Environmental Protection Agency (EPA). All these dump sites are potential sources of toxic waste pollution.

Under federal legislation, all contributors to a dump site are required to pay for the eventual cleanup of the dump. The pollution from these dump sites is simply not "sudden and accidental," and the requirement to clean up dump sites is clearly not the kind of bodily injury or property damage which was contemplated by the original policies (despite some recent legal rulings that have declared it so for coverage purposes). The broadening and expansion of insurance coverage by the courts cannot be accurately predicted and therefore the product cannot be accurately priced. Furthermore, there is the additional risk that new chemicals will be defined as hazardous. In that case, insurance companies could be obliged to cover a whole new set of potential claims.

Aggravating this problem is the effect of the older "occurrence" policies. An occurrence policy guarantees that the insurer will pay for any injury that occurs during the policy period—no matter when the injury is discovered, no matter when it is reported. If a newly defined hazardous substance can be traced to an incident years ago, the insurer that provided "occurrence" coverage at the time is expected to pay the compensation even though that risk had not been contemplated when the premium was established.

Once again, provision of compensation for environmental harm is a broad societal issue much larger than the insurance industry. While the issue remains unresolved, some companies have responded by switching policies to a "claims-made" basis. This type of policy limits coverage only to claims which occur and are reported while the policy is in effect. Another alternative is more drastic: companies may simply decline to offer coverage. Such actions are not real solutions. This serious problem has developed into a crisis for those concerned, one that is beginning to receive the attention needed for a permanent solution.

Other Changes in Judicial Interpretation

A further example of changes in judicial interpretation can be seen in developments regarding homeowners' earthquake coverage. Standard homeowners' policies do not cover earthquake damage. In locations of high earthquake risk, individuals can purchase special coverage or simply take their chances without coverage. However, after the 1983 Coalinga earthquake, California courts interpreted policy language in such a way that these policies would, depending upon the existence of certain concurrent conditions, cover earthquake damage even when such coverage is specifically excluded. Subsequently, the California legislature reaffirmed the exclusion of earthquake coverage provided insurers made such coverage separately available; nevertheless, the original court ruling illustrates the current trend toward new legal interpretations of policy coverage. Such changes will pose continuing problems for insurers.

GAINING A COMPETITIVE ADVANTAGE

Successful firms seek to gain a competitive advantage through two major activities: product innovation and new modes of distribution. Both are described below.

New Product Innovation

Attention to the basics of managing existing lines of insurance products is not sufficient for continuing success. Industry leaders must also be product innovators, at least to the degree possible, since flexibility to innovate varies by type of insurance. Coverages closely tied to the public interest such as automobile and workers compensation are constrained by government regulation. Such coverages represent well-defined products; innovation is largely focused on the risk-selection process and on reducing expenses. In contrast, a fertile area for innovation is "asset accumulation" products, which help individuals build or preserve their estates. An excellent example of innovation in this area is universal life insurance, which is a response to consumers' changing mix of security and investment needs.

Prior to the introduction of universal life, life policies offered a limited combination of benefits. Basic term insurance offers protection against premature death but becomes increasingly expensive as the insured grows older. Whole life insurance products offer level premiums by adding a savings element to the calculations; but whole life has limited flexibility. In the late 1970s, economic developments created the need for change: high inflation made the return on the savings element of whole life insurance appear low. Consumers' overall awareness of returns was heightened by the availability of new and flexible savings instruments such as money market funds and NOW accounts. As rates of return and associated levels of risk became more volatile, flexibility became an increasingly important feature of financial products, and flexibility is the hallmark of universal life. Universal life offers flexible premiums, allowing the policyholder to change the death benefit from time to time and vary the amount and timing of premium payments. Each year premiums are posted, mortality and expense charges are deducted, and interest is credited at rates which shift with conditions. The cash value of the policy at any time reflects these credits and charges.

Another new product, variable life, allows the policyholder to select the investment vehicles in which the savings portion of the life insurance is invested. Thus, the policyholder shares a portion of the risk and the rewards of those investments.

Universal life and variable life are direct responses to the demands of the marketplace. Five years after its introduction in 1979, universal life accounted for $330.6 billion insurance in force. Additions to the in-force amount during 1984 alone totaled $179 billion. By this measure, universal life now constitutes over 14 percent of the whole life market.

Product innovation will become increasingly important in the second half of the 1980s. As companies offer new products that challenge existing products, inevitably new will replace old. This trend raises the overall rate of policy replacement. Accelerating replacement puts added pressure on insurers to defray distribution costs. If the expected life of a product is reduced by one half, commission expenses to be absorbed over the life of the product are effectively doubled. Regardless of the replacement problem, successful firms will continue to offer a range of new products.

Flexibility is also key to new approaches to group life and health plans. In the past, employee benefits essentially were sold as a package of preselected coverages to employers, and offered little flexibility to employees. Recent shifts in lifestyles and an increasingly sophisticated workforce have now created a demand for alternatives. Insurers' response has been development of flexible benefit or "cafeteria-style" plans. The essence of these plans is that the employer establishes a limit on the cost of the benefits available to each employee, and the employee then selects the combination of benefits that he or she prefers within that limit. Recent federal government restrictions on certain aspects of these plans have slowed their momentum, but the successful firms are continuing to innovate within these constraints to meet market needs.

Examples of innovation in personal property/casualty products are somewhat less dramatic. When the law requires all drivers to have auto insurance, auto policies become so standardized that they can be viewed as commodities; price and service are therefore the primary differentiating factors. For this reason, the thrust of innovation has been directed toward reducing costs and improving service, mostly through automation of agency and field-office processing, where the bulk of customer servicing is accomplished.

Nevertheless, changes in personal-property offerings have been made. For example, with traditional property coverage insurers settled most claims on an "actual cash value" basis, the value for which the lost item could be sold. Actual cash value, however, is generally less than full replacement cost. In response to consumer demand for coverage that would pay full replacement cost, innovative industry leaders offered policies that provided such coverage. Consumers, they discovered, were willing to pay the extra premium required.

In commercial property/casualty, customers have diverse needs and are careful buyers of coverage. Firms that pay large premiums employ sophisticated risk managers to assess their insurance needs. This segment demands both innovation and low cost in product offerings. In the mid to late 1970s, these customers challenged insurers by electing either to self-insure or to form captive insurance companies. The self-insurance movement was precipitated by large increases in insurance prices and industry capacity problems which followed a downturn in the underwriting cycle. A number of insurance companies responded by offering services for self-insureds. Insurance brokers and insurance companies now provide the claims-handling and loss-control services, while the insured company retains a major portion of its own financial risk. As with universal life, this alternative is less profitable for insurers, and invites a shift in an established book of business. Nevertheless, it provides a response to the needs of the marketplace while rewarding innovators with a measure of success. A final, dramatic example of commercial-market innovation is to be seen in financial guarantee insurance products, such as municipal bond guarantees which insure payments on bonds in case the municipal government defaults. This has been one of the fastest areas of growth in commercial insurance, and one which remained profitable through 1985.

New Modes of Distribution

For many years, much of the insurance industry has depended on a large force of highly specialized agents dedicated to selling insurance. This strong interdependence between companies and agents continues today. Nevertheless, pressures in the marketplace are bringing changes to these relationships. Agents are seeking additional products and services to compete in the world of diversified financial services. Insurance companies see the need to explore alternate distribution strategies already being used by providers of other financial services. If they are to be competitive with other financial services providers, insurance companies must both strengthen the traditional agency distribution system with new product lines, and, through new technology, reduce costs associated with the agency system.

Insurers are also experimenting with alternate distribution systems for products that may not require the high degree of professional expertise and personal counseling available through the traditional agent. Common to many such alternate marketing approaches is the objective of reaching large blocs of consumers as a group rather than individually. The potential gain in efficiency is significant because access to consumers via some intermediate entity can drastically reduce prospecting time. Such approaches work best with products easily understood by the consumer, since there is a minimum amount of personal contact.

One such means of access is mass marketing of individual insurance products through employers. Employer mass marketing differs from group insurance plans in that product prices are determined separately for each individual. Cost savings can be achieved by using established communication channels between the employer and employees such as the payroll process. In conjunction with its use, insurance representatives can be on site routinely to handle applications, questions, and changes. In addition, premium collection costs can be reduced by using a payroll deduction plan in cooperation with the employer. Such cost reductions help employer-based distribution compete favorably with other distribution methods. To date, these programs have not spread rapidly, in part because they require active sponsorship by the employer to be successful. Yet analysts believe that pioneers in employer mass marketing will be well positioned to expand this distribution mode in the future.

Another opportunity for accessing new customers is the practice of cross-selling one product to a set of customers buying a different product. The concept of cross-selling between property/casualty customers and life customers has been part of the strategy of some insurers for many years. It is now being expanded across the entire range of financial services. For example, life insurance products are offered for sale through securities brokerage distribution networks. (The jury is still out on whether stockbrokers can be major sellers of life insurance.) Experimenting with still another way to reach new customers, some companies have entered joint ventures with banks, arranging, for example, to lease space for their agents in the banks' lobbies. Again, it remains to be seen whether this approach will be successful.

Prospects for the Future

It is not clear which approaches to producing and marketing financial services will ultimately be winners. Some observers believe that one-stop shopping for consolidated financial services will require a financial accounts executive, a new species that will evolve from salespersons of various specialities. Others believe that the employer will be the key focal point under a greatly expanded concept of employee benefits. Still others believe that simpler products will be offered to customers in shopping centers or bank lobbies. And others yet are convinced that the insurance company will reach directly into the homes of the buying public through technology: TV, the home computer, or a telephone system of enhanced capability. What is clear is that successful insurance companies will be testing and implementing one or more of these new marketing approaches.

KEY ELEMENTS TO BE MANAGED IN THE FUTURE

Many financial products are now inseparable from their delivery technology. Distribution forces are increasingly linked electronically with their suppliers. Achieving state-of-the-art delivery across a diverse array of products and services will require major support from powerful computer-based customer information systems. Such total systems do not exist today, but they can be expected to evolve over the remainder of this decade. Getting from here to there must be recognized as a key element in current strategic planning.

Making money in insurance in the future will require a creative integration of products, services and distributions systems to meet changing customer requirements. Of critical importance will be an ability to capitalize on technological opportunities for service improvements and cost reductions. Success will require staying on top of the basics of the business with improved management techniques and information. It will also require developing strategies to deal with the changing environment—an environment which will reward those companies that are strong and agile enough to compete with other players in the financial services marketplace.

8 Making Money in Thrifts and Savings and Loans

SUSAN B. BASSIN

On July 26, 1985 *The American Banker* reported that most big publicly held thrifts set record second-quarter earnings. In the same article, the U.S. League of Savings Institutions reported that the thrift industry had earned $1 billion in the second quarter of 1985, and that the industry's earnings for all of 1985 could exceed the 1978 record of $3.9 billion.

Despite this good news, many thrifts are still struggling. For example, most large New York thrifts will be only marginally profitable in the third and fourth quarters, notwithstanding gains on the sales of investments, mortgages, and mortgage-backed securities. Several institutions have recently changed hands. Around the nation, hundreds of thrifts are still on the critical list. "Problem thrifts" continue to fight a combination of potential credit losses, a high percentage of low-yielding fixed-rate investments in their portfolio, a weak competitive position, and tougher regulatory restrictions.

Making money in thrifts and savings and loans has not been easy. Thrifts as a group have been especially hard hit these last five years by both the composition of their asset portfolio and brutal "new" competition from commercial banks, insurance companies, and brokerage houses. But those that are succeeding have accepted the new realities and are changing their attitudes and approaches—to financial management, first, and marketing, second.

To understand how they are succeeding, we need to examine:

- Why thrifts were not making money over the past five years
- Five myths about the business that trapped some unwary managements
- The competitive environment, especially movement by commercial banks into the traditional territory of thrifts
- The critical choice of an asset strategy: shrink or grow
- How financial management and marketing are merging
- Marketing as a key factor for success

[As a quick reference for readers, an aggregate income statement and an aggregate balance sheet for the savings and loan industry segment are shown in Exhibits 8.1 and 8.2.]

Exhibit 8.1 Consolidated Income Statement: FSLIC-Insured Institutions

	1983[a]
Gross operating income	$79,983[b]
Interest—total	71,925
On mortgage loans and contracts	51,913
On MTOE-backed securities, etc.	7,987
On investment securities and deposits	9,020
On nonmortgage loans	3,005
Discounts on mortgages purchased	1,549
Loan origination fees	3,177
Other fees and charges	1,250
All other	2,082
Operating expense	12,298
Compensation and other benefits	5,329
Office occupancy	1,296
Advertising	711
All other (less capitalized interest)	4,952
Cost of funds	67,654
Interest/dividends on deposit accounts	58,274
Interest on borrowed money	9,380
Net operating income after cost of funds	31
Nonoperating income	4,062
Nonoperating expense	1,533
Net income before taxes	2,561
Income taxes—total	593
Federal	421
State, local, and other	172
Net income	$ 1,968
Memo: Dividends on permanent stock, mutual capital, income capital, and net worth certificates	$ 245

Source: Combined Financial Statements/FSLIC-Insured Institutions, Federal Home Loan Bank Board, Washington D.C.

[a] Last year for which income/expense figures were published.

[b] Figures in $ millions.

Exhibit 8.2 Condensed Statement of Condition of FSLIC-Insured Savings Institutions

	1984[a]
Assets:	
Mortgage loans	$599,021[b]
Insured mortgages and mortgage-backed securities	108,219
Mobile home loans	5,284
Home improvement loans	5,583
Loans on savings accounts	3,914
Education loans	3,768
Other consumer loans	18,379
Cash and investments eligible for liquidity	99,924
Other investments	35,716
Federal home loan bank stock	6,200
Investment in service corporations	16,988
Buildings and equipment	12,855
Real estate owned	10,100
All other assets	52,563
Total assets	$ 978,514
Liabilities and net worth:	
Savings deposits:	
Accounts with no fixed term	$ 194,997
Certificates	589,727
Federal home loan bank advances	71,719
Other borrowed money	65,404
All other liabilities	18,746
Net worth	37,921
Total liabilities and net worth	$ 978,514

Source: Federal Home Loan Bank Board; United States League of Savings Institutions.
[a] As of December 31. Figures available at publication are preliminary.
[b] Figures in $ millions.

Why Thrifts Were Not Making Money

Deregulation, competition, inflation, the deficit, bad loans, the dollar, the oil crisis, regulators, legislators, and poor thrift management have all been accused at one time or another of causing the thrift earnings "crisis."

In fact, the thrift earnings crunch of the past five years was caused by the thrifts doing only too well what they had been asked to do during the prior 10 years! Thrifts had invested their 5 percent passbook deposits in fixed real estate investments yielding 7 to 8 percent. Unfortunately, this mix of fixed-rate long-term assets, coupled with the dramatic increase of the cost of money, led to predictable and persistent negative earnings and a dramatic deterioration of net worth. The most progressive of the thrifts, those *most* concerned with profitability in the 1970–1980 period, had elected to invest a chunk of their passbook deposits in preferred stock and fixed-rate corporate and municipal bonds, both because the yields were often *better* than on residential real estate, and because the cost of booking and servicing these assets was considerably less than the cost of making home loans (single-family up to four-family).

The fundamental challenge facing thrifts in the 1980–1985 period was to work out of their legacy of low-yielding fixed-rate assets, and in doing so, to position themselves for the future. Quite simply, the thrift manager had to figure out how to create a business that would be viable when the cost of money over an interest rate cycle averaged 10 percent. When asset yields hovered around 8 percent, however, this was a tough problem.

Five Myths Regarding the Thrift Business: 1980–1985

Failure by many thrifts to respond quickly to abruptly shifting conditions during the 1980–1985 period can be traced to myths about the way things were. These assumptions encouraged thrift managers to pursue their current courses of action, and delayed implementation of strategies that could have lessened the impact of the profitability crunch.

Myth 1: "The volatile rate environment is an aberration." Many thrift managers felt that the underlying interest rate pressures that existed were temporary and would subside. The volatility of rates during the 1975–1985 period was not viewed as normal.

Myth 2: "The new competition is temporary and will stop." This belief caused the thrifts to place low priority on the development of the competitive intelligence necessary to understand what commercial banks, brokerage houses, and insurance companies were up to. Hence, thrifts were often slow to respond.

Myth 3: "Significant asset growth is not a viable survival tactic, and not really possible anyway." With regulators reinforcing this idea, most thrifts comfortably resolved on no growth or slow growth. Once a growth strategy was rejected, thrifts could only "shrink" or "stabilize"—cut costs, shave rates, and wait for a sharp and long-term drop in interest rates to restore profitability.

Myth 4: "Cutting operating costs does not really matter all that much." It was felt that if an institution cut costs drastically enough to make a difference, its competitive viability would be destroyed. The tremendous lever of improved productivity and potential for more competitive pricing was, by and large, not recognized.

Myth 5: "Minimize the cost of deposits by paying less than market rates." The net result of this deposit-pricing approach was to lose customers to the commercials, brokerage houses, and insurance companies that were trying to increase deposits and deposit substitutes as fast as they could.

Given this set of background assumptions, thrift managers were working within an intellectual framework which *deemphasized dramatic change* in traditional policy and *encouraged waiting* for a solution. Not that thrift managers were just sitting around; the internal debates were heated and continuous. But not until 1983–1984 did these myths begin to crumble with the waning expectation that a return to "normal" would save the industry. The thrifts that are viable and competitive today are the ones that challenged the crippling assumptions that had threatened their progress:

- Dispelling Myths 1 and 2, they accepted that the rate volatility and competitive pressure of the 1980–1985 period should be treated as the norm.
- Overcoming Myth 3, they concluded that generating substantial amounts of variable rate assets—either for resale in the secondary markets or for their own portfolio—was critical to their survival.
- Redefining the terms of Myth 3, they also realized that matching variable rate assets and liabilities was a profitable way to grow.
- Overturning Myth 4, they began cutting costs relative to assets, an action they saw as crucial to the major pricing changes required for survival.
- Seeing beyond Myth 5, they realized that theirs had become a customer-sensitive marketing and sales business, and that they were three to five years behind their commercial, brokerage, and insurance competitors in creating a customer-oriented marketing culture.

In addition, progressive thrifts realized that cleaning up the balance sheet, getting rid of old municipals and preferreds, selling off other corporate bonds, hedging, doing interest rate swaps, going public, and borrowing from the Federal Home Loan Bank were important tactics. At the same time, they recognized that diversifying into commercial banking, consumer finance, insurance, and brokerage activities were important sources of *future* profit, but were short-run diversions that postponed a return to profitability.

Commercial Banks Became the Key Competitors

The forces that would cause thrifts to suffer large losses in the 1980–1985 period—high, volatile interest rates; deregulation; the shift from 5 percent passbook deposits to higher rate CDs; expanded checking powers for thrifts; and the removal of usury ceilings on loans—were all evident five years before. But the most dramatic threat to the nation's thrifts came with the strong thrust of the major commercials into retail banking. It was not clear to the thrift industry at first that the commercial banks would get the "marketing zeal" and play such a dramatic role in the national marketplace as fast as they did. What happened in the New York market during the 1978–1983 period is illustrative of what was happening across the country.

While the major New York City commercials had captured most of the consumer checking money in the greater New York City area, the thrift industry controlled some $100 billion of consumer passbook and CD money. The cost of these savings and CD deposits was roughly 6 to 8 percent, not a lot more than the commercials had to pay for NOW account deposits when the costs of reserve requirements and branch operations were added to the interest cost. Consequently, a commercial that wanted to grow its share of the New York City consumer market significantly enough to make its branches profitable would have to start competing for thrift deposits and for thrift customers.

To free up branch staff to handle the planned savings and CD growth, without letting costs get out of control, commercials expanded their ATM programs to move routine checking account transactions away from the branch teller and platform staff to the machines. Citibank was most aggressive in employing this strategy, installing over 500 ATMs in three to four years. The "human capacity" that was created could be turned toward sourcing and servicing savings accounts, CDs, and loans.

In the 1978–1979 period, the commercials began a series of extensive gift giveaway CD promotions and continued these into 1981–1982. Commercial banks also initiated programs aimed at building strong realtor relationships across the metropolitan New York area, a step that was essential to becoming a major force in residential real estate lending. Results were dramatic: Citibank became the largest residential real estate lender in the New York City area, making 50 percent more consumer mortgage and co-op loans annually than the largest thrift lender. The bank's New York area retail deposit balances grew from $4 billion in 1980 to $15 billion in 1985; other major commercials more than doubled their retail deposits over the same period.

While the New York City commercials were acting like successful thrifts, the New York City thrifts were barely managing to hold their deposit bases. Struggling to cope with short-term earnings, and net worth and liquidity pressures, they were unable to match or keep pace with commercial banks' aggressive marketing and merchandising efforts directed at traditional thrifts savers and borrowers.

Choosing an Asset Strategy: Shrink or Grow

During the 1980–1984 period, thrift managers and thrift regulators spent a lot of time debating whether to grow or shrink. Traditionalists in the thrift industry assumed that interest rates and the competition were soon going to revert to "normal." In this belief, the traditionalists had strong support from regulators who were increasingly worried about the effect of rapid growth on credit quality and net worth ratios that were already well under the minimum levels and eroding fast. Financial Corporation of America was cited as eloquent proof that "growth" was an irresponsible solution. Traditionalists favored a "shrink the bank" approach. While waiting to see what happened to interest rates, they would reduce assets, cut costs, and protect the net worth ratio.

Advocates of growth, by contrast, believed a thrift should try to become profitable by adding enough high-yielding new assets to increase the average asset yield from roughly 7 percent to around 10 percent. Growth of this magnitude, however, required doubling the asset base within five years or three years in extreme cases. Not surprisingly perhaps, advocates of growth were in a minority. In addition, the arguments against growth were powerful. These can be convincingly summarized as follows:

- Assets cannot grow fast enough to make any difference.
- Funding asset growth requires bidding up deposit costs so much that maintaining a profitable spread would be nearly impossible.
- Besides, regulators will not let thrifts grow.

Although these arguments are theoretically persuasive, these views did not reflect reality when tested in the marketplace. Great Western in California and other well-run thrifts and commercials were gaining deposits, mortgages, customers, and market share, thus slowly and steadily eating away at the weaker thrifts' franchises. And they seemed to be doing so profitably. It was all very confusing.

In retrospect, building assets at a rate of 12 to 15 percent annually between 1980 and 1985 was the only safe strategy that would have kept a thrift solidly profitable. Greenpoint in New York and Great Western are classic successes in this regard. While it is easy to conclude that more growth is always better than less growth as long as new assets can be booked at a 2 to 3 percent spread, efforts to get growth started tended to stall on the issues of asset quality, rate of asset growth, and regulatory concern. The debate continues today, as evidenced by recent rules limiting troubled thrifts to a 10 percent annual growth rate regardless of the quality of their assets. This growth rate cap is not a helpful tool in the struggle to return thrifts to profitability.

Moving Forward: Financial Management and Marketing Merge

Assuming that thrift management now agrees that a controlled asset growth strategy is more appropriate for survival in today's environment, two funding questions arise:

- Where should thrifts compete on the yield curve?
- What should their pricing policy be?

Historically, consumers looked to thrifts for long-term commitments—a 30-year mortgage or a passbook "for life." But as interest rates skyrocketed and financial markets became less predictable, consumers have adopted a shorter-term orientation and now accept variable rates as a way of life. To alert bankers interested in working on the short end of the yield curve, this consumer trend has been a boon. Since its introduction in 1983, the Bank Money Market Account has been the lowest-cost source of deposit growth for both the thrift and commercial competitors who offered a fair market rate.

The commercials—with as much as 35 to 40 percent of their consumer deposits in bank money market accounts—along with the brokerage houses, have used this product aggressively and consistently over the past few years, even in high-rate environments. As a result, commercials now hold over $300 billion of money market account deposits, as Exhibit 8.3 illustrates.

The logic—which seems to work—is that the money market account will rise and fall fairly quickly with the cost of money. The money market account, if priced to reflect rate trends in the market, eliminates the market timing risk for both the consumer and the bank. It does not lock banks into paying out artificially high rates for long terms, and it does not lock consumers into low yields for long periods. Also, it appears that customers feel reasonably good about receiving a fair market rate on their savings over the interest rate cycle, in troughs as well as peaks.

In many thrifts, the debate between those who advocate extending maturities to guarantee a stable cost of funds, and those who urge funding short to maximize profitability in the near term, has been resolved on the side of extending maturities. However, a strategy to maximize current earnings, get back to profitability, and replenish net worth as quickly as possible, would seem to suggest that thrifts move to more short-term funding, using the money market account matched against short-term (monthly adjustable or six-month adjustable) loans to obtain a 3 to 4 percent spread.

Once a thrift has selected the point on the yield curve where it will compete, the next critical question becomes how high to set rates relative to competitors' in order to get necessary retail funds. While there is no single answer, some pricing suggestions make sense if profitability and long-term customer satisfaction are the goals:

In a rising rate environment, price to increase deposits. As rates rise, money acquired today will cost less than money obtained tomorrow. Lead the market up. The net results will be a lower all-in cost of money, and happy customers.

Exhibit 8.3 Where Savings Are Held

Account	Total	Commercials	Savings Institutions
Money market	$ 475.2	$ 307.3	$ 167.8[a]
Large CD ($100,000 or more)	424.2	267.8	156.4
Small CD (under $100,000)	894.7	390.8	503.9
Passbook	292.0	121.9	170.2
NOW/Super NOW	160.3	—	—
Demand deposit	260.7	—	—

Source: Federal Reserve Board, June 1985.
[a] Figures in $ millions.

In a falling rate environment, lead the market down. Let deposits flow out if necessary. Money lost today can be replaced tomorrow at less cost. Customers will be more forgiving of weak competitive rates in a declining rate environment.

In both rising rate and falling rate environments, keep short-term rates very competitive—close to the top of the market. This tactic helps keep as many customers as possible loyal, while encouraging them to select the institution's lowest-cost source of funds.

The thrift earnings crunch over the past few years came about due to the classic mismatch of short-term deposits supporting long-term loans. The trend today toward short-term lending using variable rate mortgages supported by short-term funding provides a balance that should work for both the bank and the consumer. For thrift managers who want to become profitable and stay profitable, the tactics seem clear:

- Lend short term, or adjustable-rate long term.
- Fund as short term as possible, with funds matched to incremental assets.
- Look for a 3 percent spread.
- Grow fast—20 percent a year—but not so irresponsibly fast as to cause regulators to act to slow growth.
- Use secondary markets to sell loan production in excess of needs.
- Use borrowings wherever cheaper than incremental consumer deposits (although when borrowing rates are appealing, consumer deposit rates generally are too).
- When rates are low enough, reduce holdings in fixed-rate investments.
- Go slow in any major diversifications. Commercial lending, insurance, brokerage, leasing, asset-based finance, credit cards and the like are tempting areas to explore, but could be fatal and unnecessary diversions to any thrift struggling to establish long-term viability.

Last, but certainly not least:

- Stay focused on the consumer as the primary source of deposits and as the primary investment outlet through mortgage lending.

While the strategy is clear, simple, and practicable, succeeding with it will be hard: Most competitors will be trying to do exactly the same things.

Marketing: A Key Factor for Success

With more and more survivors latching on to the winning strategies, pricing and branch location will no longer be meaningful elements of distinction. Thrifts will need to turn their attention to other elements of the marketing mix and take their image with consumers more seriously. When every financial institution offers hot prices to consumers, basic marketing questions that have gone unasked must be raised, and answers found. For instance: Who are our customers? What do they think of us? Is this what we want them to think? What do we offer them? How are we communicating to them? How can we use communications more effectively to shape our identity and attract the customers we want? These questions have to be answered, and fast.

Ultimately, making money in thrifts is little different than making money in any business. In large measure, success comes from being a leader in meeting customer needs, not just from matching assets and liabilities, increasing fee income, or keeping costs down. Meeting customer needs requires careful strategy and disciplined, consistent programs. It calls for employing the necessary financial and marketing tools, even if they differ from the conventional wisdom. The cultural and traditional biases that made some thrifts victims of the 1980–1985 period are not completely gone. But the survivors—the leaders who will present themselves in the next few years—will have managed to make the transition from "thrift" to "business," and will be formidable, profitable competitors.

9 Making Money in Credit Unions

WYLIE R. DOUGHERTY

This topic is a tough one to address because of the nonprofit, service orientation of credit unions. Credit unions are an anomaly in the financial world—their "profits" go to their members. Although credit union management professionals are paid well, and some receive bonuses and participate in so-called profit-sharing plans, they are totally dedicated to serving the needs of their members in a nonprofit manner. A manager may never get rich working for the credit union movement, but many people get greater personal satisfaction from working in this environment.

THE CREDIT UNION DIFFERENCE

The "credit union movement" originated in Europe in the nineteenth century in one form as farmers' cooperatives, and in another form as urban cooperatives. As such, the credit union is very much an institution "by the people and for the people." The major difference between credit unions and other financial intermediaries is that their focus is on service to their members. Profit is a by-product. Credit unions have an old adage which clearly sets out this difference:

Not for profit
Not for charity
But for service

Not surprisingly, credit unions are well positioned in the industry. Alex Sheshunoff, a bank analyst and publisher, once remarked to a group of bankers that they need not worry about credit unions being competitors. After all, he said, credit unions have only three advantages: (1) they pay more on savings, (2) they charge less on loans, and (3) they are just down the hallway from their depositors and loan applicants. These wry observations acknowledge that, in fact, bankers have real cause to keep an eye on credit unions. The cooperative and self-help orientations of the credit union concept have made themselves felt in the world of financial services.

Uniqueness—Members Only

Each credit union serves only the people who are in its field of membership. Several key practices highlight the special relationship between credit union and client:

1. Rarely do officers or credit union employees refer to their clients by any other term except *members*.
2. Even more rarely do those clients refer to themselves as anything other than *members*.
3. Members are the *only* clients.
4. *Only members* can save, borrow, invest, or use the other services offered by the credit union.
5. *Only members* can be elected to the board of directors or any credit union committee.
6. *One member-one vote* is the traditional rule for voting in credit unions. (One or two states have laws allowing cumulative share voting.)

This strong symbolic relationship is the norm within credit unions, and has resulted in uninterrupted growth in credit union membership over the past 50-plus years.

Since each credit union serves only the people who are in its field of membership, dual memberships are not a matter of concern. A set of cooperative principles written in 1844 can still be used today as a mirror of credit union attitudes and behavior, as shown in Exhibit 9.1.

The Rise of Credit Unions in the United States

A recent historical account places credit unions in a populist context shared, at least initially, by the Grange and labor unions:

> The term "credit union movement" correctly implies a historical development characterized by speed, momentum, and idealism. Historical movements are usually based upon ideas whose time has come; so it was with American credit unionism in the early twentieth century. There has been much lip service paid to concepts of economic democracy; protecting the American socioeconomic system by reducing the gap between the rich and poor. By the early 1900s, it was becoming clear that changes in the American economy necessitated new thinking about consumer credit.

Exhibit 9.1 Principles of Cooperation of the Equitable Pioneers (1844)

Primary:

1. A cooperative society shall be democratically controlled; one member, one vote.
2. Money invested, if it receives dividends, shall receive a fixed percentage of not more than the current rate.
3. If a profit is made, it shall be returned to those who patronize on the basis of the amount they participate.

Secondary:

1. A cooperative society shall be composed of members who join voluntarily.
2. No one shall be excluded from membership unless it is known that their purpose is to do injury to the society.
3. A portion of the earnings shall be used for educational purposes.
4. The commodity shall be sold at market prices, the same price to be charged to all.
5. Societies shall be neutral in matters of religion and politics, and offer equal rights to women.
6. At each inventory, reserves shall be set aside to cover depreciation and unforeseen difficulties.
7. Employees of the cooperative society shall be treated fairly.
8. All cooperative societies shall cooperate with each other.

> American farms and factories had reached a point of technical efficiency where they could provide basic and luxury items for all citizens. By the late twenties, more people of modest means were coming to regard the automobile as a necessity, not a luxury reserved for the wealthy, and the increase in cheap electrical power unleashed a horde of home appliances that urban Americans found it hard to live without. The United States was becoming a consumer economy, and low-cost consumer credit was a must. The nation's commercial banks were psychologically and financially disinclined to fill the need. [Loan sharks, of course, were willing.] One practical approach was that of the credit union.[1]

Credit unions were established to provide low-cost installment credit to working people who had no other legitimate resource. Secondarily, credit unions were created to pool the savings of participating workers (credit union members) to fund these borrowing needs. This arrangement continues substantially unaltered today. Members hold their deposits in the form of shares and are called shareholders.

The service portfolios of credit unions now extend beyond loans and savings, however. Services commonly include share accounts (savings), loans, money orders, traveler's checks, mortgage loans, discount stock brokerage, share draft accounts (checking), and credit/debit cards. Initially, services are developed with the member in mind, and only after several years of operations and pricing changes is "profit" generally achieved. Financial success is measured by recovering costs, establishing reserves, and providing adequate capital for expansion. When credit unions have an exceptionally good year, many rebate a portion of interest paid by borrowing members.

Fields of Membership

Participation in credit unions is limited to individuals belonging to strictly defined groups, called "fields of membership." In the New England states and Canada, credit unions were organized along community or parish lines, while in the industrial heartland of the United States, fields of membership consisted mostly of employees of a single employer. It is this second form of organization that predominates today. While there is no strong philosophical reason for employee-based membership, it is easier to organize credit unions on this basis. Whereas finding and attracting leadership for community credit unions can be difficult, businesses have the necessary resources already in place: the comptroller, personnel officer, and other managers of the company. These individuals are charged with protecting the welfare of employees as well as the interest of the company.

Traditionally, a credit union wishing to change its field of membership had to submit the changes to its regulator for approval. It was a long, drawn-out process. However, under the chairmanship of Edgar Callahan, the National Credit Union Administration (NCUA)—the federal government's regulatory body charged with overseeing credit unions—has extended the Reagan Administration's policy of deregulation to apply to credit unions' merger and field of membership activities. As a result of the NCUA changes, as well as corporate mergers, factory closings, and military base closings, heterogeneous fields-of-membership are becoming more commonplace. This shift will surely change the nature of the credit unions involved, as well as their attitudes when the new groups are assimilated into membership and board positions.

Another development along the same lines is the issuance of credit union charters encompassing what are known as "select employee groups." Credit unions holding charters as select employee groups are permitted to serve multiple employers. There need not be any similarity among the industries in which these employers participate. In several instances, more than 2000 separate employers are being served by a credit union of this evolving—and proliferating—type.

These developments, as well as the increase in community-chartered credit unions, will have a great effect on the configuration of credit unions in the future.

Limits to Expansion

Credit unions in the United States have historically served larger companies, those with 500 employees or more. But growth in the U.S. work force by and large results from the spread and expansion of smaller service-related companies. The Fortune 1000 companies as a group have added *no* new jobs to the work force in the early 1980s. Indeed, employment figures at many of these companies have shown substantial decline. Sears, for instance, reduced its work force more than 29,000 in five years—an 8.2 percent overall reduction.

Without penetration into smaller employer groups, then, the credit union movement would probably cease to grow. For this reason, credit unions began expanding their fields of membership in the early 1980s to absorb these groups of workers. Evolution within the last three years has been rapid. At the end of 1984, 34 percent of all credit unions served multiple groups. Twenty-two percent served a geographic area such as a community. As past limitations are removed, prospects for growth are becoming increasingly favorable.

Competition

Although banks and other financial intermediaries are considered competitors of credit unions, rarely do credit unions consider other credit unions as competition. More often, credit unions are likely to join forces with each other to develop an automated teller machine (ATM) or credit card system. Sharing trade secrets and techniques is one way that credit unions can remain competitive in the financial services marketplace without mutually destructive infighting. Since each credit union serves only the people in its field of membership, dual memberships are not a matter of concern.

However, competition among credit unions is a focus of animated discussion among credit union leaders today. As fields-of-membership in urban areas continue to overlap, credit unions will have to adapt in ways that allow amicable coexistence. The state of Rhode Island provides a good example. Here, several credit unions have *state-wide* community charters. The credit unions have prospered and thrived and continue to cooperate on matters such as legislation, Corporate Credit Union Network, and so forth.

BUILDING THE SYSTEM

Today, there are 18,000 credit unions in the United States. Most are quite small: Some 15,000 (or 85 percent) have assets of less than $5 million, as shown in Exhibit 9.2. However, the biggest cannot be ignored. Two-thirds of all asset dollars in credit unions are held by institutions with more than $20 million in assets. And the number of institutions of this size is growing extremely fast. The $20 million-plus category increased from 491 in 1978 to 1129 credit unions in 1984.

These results are the effect of deregulation, greater competition among all financial institutions, and some "merger mania" among larger credit unions.

History of Credit Union Cooperation

Credit union people have a fierce pride in their accomplishments. Still, in an increasingly complex industry, credit unions have a need for specialized support services. Because their self-help orientation leads credit unions to avoid seeking outside help, they have built their own complex and effective infrastructure to provide this support. Originally, state credit union leagues were created to meet

Exhibit 9.2 Distribution of Credit Unions and Assets: 1984

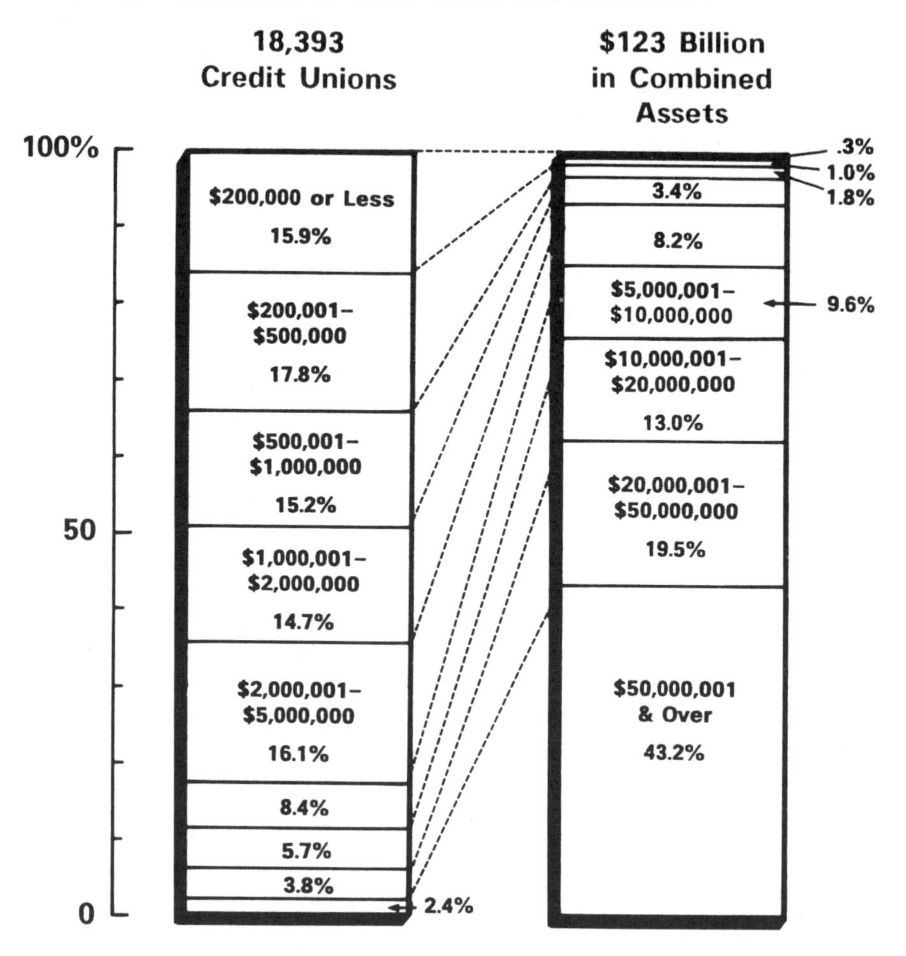

the service needs of credit unions within a state's boundaries. When it became evident that centralization of certain activities would be beneficial, the state organizations banded together and in 1934 formed the Credit Union National Association, Inc. (CUNA), as the national provider of support services. Affiliates include CUNA Service Group and the U.S. Central Credit Union. (See Exhibit 9.3.)

CUNA Service Group (CSG) primarily develops products such as share drafts, IRA account systems, credit/debit cards, and so forth, for distribution to members by credit unions. Delivery from CSG to individual credit unions is through state credit union leagues and league service corporations. CSG services generate many hundreds of millions of dollars of income for credit unions, as measured by the nearly $50 million in revenues that CUNA, CSG and affiliates earned in 1984. CUNA Service Group is the sole arm of the credit union movement that is profit

Exhibit 9.3 CUNA and Its Affiliates

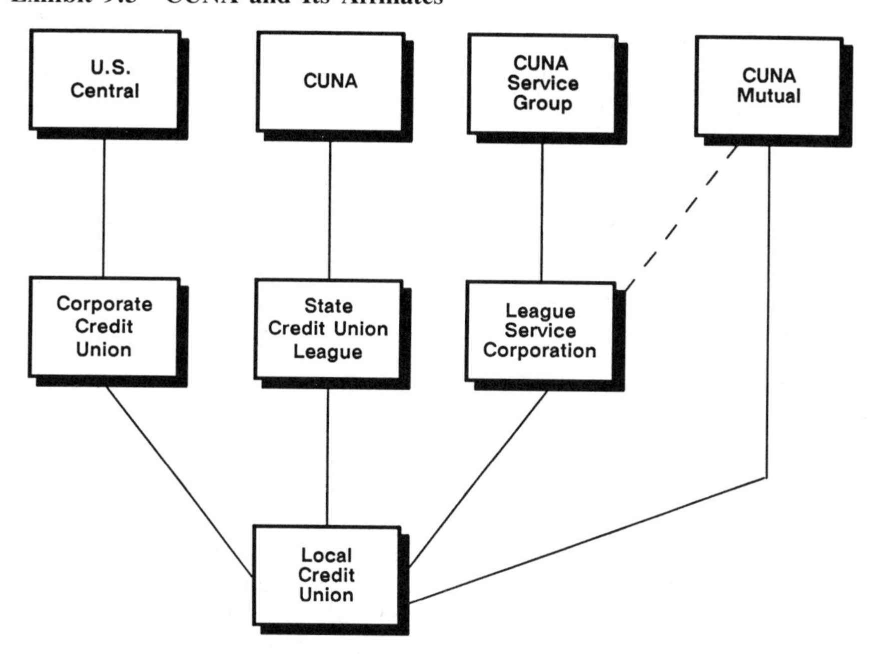

making, and hence taxable. The national organizations under CUNA's leadership provide research and development to keep credit unions in the forefront of the financial services industry.

CUNA Mutual Insurance Group was organized by the national organization in 1935 to guarantee full payment of a loan in the event of the loan-holder's death. In this way, debt could die with the debtor, and life savings could be distributed undiminished through a deceased member's estate. The CUNA Mutual Insurance Group today encompasses seven companies with assets in excess of $1 billion. Although the insurance group is not owned by CUNA, relationships remain close and collegial.

U.S. Central Credit Union is CUNA's private liquidity management and financial services affiliate. It issues commercial paper on behalf of the credit union movement and, at the time of this writing, holds the highest commercial paper credit ratings accorded by both Moody's and Standard & Poor. U.S. Central Credit Union recently received a long-term debt rating from Standard & Poor's of AAA and may now provide additional credit and financing services. Working through 42 states and regional corporate credit unions, U.S. Central Credit Union provides investments, lending, settlement, and payment services for America's credit unions. From its beginning in 1974, this system has developed into a full-service money center operation with nearly $20 billion in combined assets, $15 billion of which are under the direct supervision of the U.S. Central Credit Union. Capitalized by member credit unions at 1 percent of assets, the system is perhaps the best capitalized of financial organizations in the United States.

Government Legislation

Government, for its part, has also enacted legislation to strengthen the credit union system. The Central Liquidity Facility (CLF) of the National Credit Union Association was created by Congress in 1978 to provide credit unions with funds for stabilization purposes and to meet other liquidity needs. Congress provided no capital, simply the vehicle. CUNA spearheaded the effort by which credit unions, through U.S. Central Credit Union and its member corporate credit unions, capitalized the CLF at $250 million. Seen in this light, the CLF is a direct link forged between government and citizens, with the private sector providing both the funding and the delivery system for a publicly created organization.

ECONOMIC VITALITY

Credit unions have always been economically viable. Prior to deregulation, they charged 12 percent on loans, while paying out 6 to 7 percent on savings and suffering only minimal loan losses. This gave them substantial margins and enabled rapid growth over the past 30 years. Since deregulation, credit unions have adapted by offering both variable-rate deposit accounts and variable-rate loans to protect themselves against fluctuations in the prevailing cost of funds. While 3400 credit unions closed by merger or liquidation during this period, the survivors are more firmly capitalized today than they were six years ago prior to deregulation.

Interest Income, Interest Expense, and Costs

Credit unions have typically derived their interest income from loans to members, with some proportion of the assets invested in money market securities. (*Editors' note:* Exhibits 9.4 and 9.5 show the aggregated income statement and balance sheet for credit unions.)

Credit unions are very competitive on lending rates and on credit card programs. The Corporate Credit Union Network provides the flexibility for safe investments with competitive yields.

Credit unions' interest expenses are somewhat higher than those of the marketplace. Passbook savings are typically one-half to three-quarters percent above rates given by banks and savings and loans. Money market certificates and money market deposit accounts rates are competitive. Share draft accounts pay higher rates of interest than available from either banks or savings and loans. Therefore, the net interest margin of a well-operated credit union in the post-deregulation era is around three percent. This margin allows credit unions to cover their operating costs, which typically run between 20 and 45 percent of total revenues.

Credit unions typically have lower loan loss ratios than other financial intermediaries. Historical losses have been less than .3 percent of total loans granted. The field of membership focus on employees no doubt helps keep losses low. This allows credit unions to operate with a fair amount of free reserves.

Exhibit 9.4 Natural Person Federal Credit Unions: Consolidated Balance Sheet

	1984[a]
Assets:	
Cash	$ 1,440,332
Loans outstanding	42,131,728
Allowance for loan losses	(297,936)
Investments:	
U.S. government/federal agency	$ 5,725,101
Commercial banks	2,540,986
S&Ls and mutual savings	5,867,043
Corporate credit unions	3,430,945
Common trusts	420,924
Other investments	582,486
Total investments	$ 18,567,485
Allowance for investment losses	$ (18,645)
Land and building (net of depreciation)	762,824
Other fixed assets	372,978
Other assets	699,265
Total assets	$ 63,658,031
Liabilities:	
Accounts payable	$ 290,775
Notes payable	671,378
Dividends payable	598,557
Other liabilities	125,766
Total liabilities	$ 1,686,476
Equity/savings:	
Regular shares[b]	$ 34,547,563
Share certificates	12,908,289
IRA/Keogh accounts	5,206,294
Share drafts	5,265,288
Total savings	$ 57,927,434
Regular reserves	$ 1,800,469
Other reserves	650,683
Undivided earnings	1,592,969
Total equity/savings	$ 61,971,555
Total liability/equity	$ 63,658,031

Source: Based on 10,547 Natural Person Federal Credit Unions.

[a] Dollar amounts in $ thousands.

[b] Passbook, Regular Money Market, etc.

Exhibit 9.5 Natural Person Federal Credit Unions: Consolidated Income Statement

	1984[a]
Income	
Interest on loans	$ 5,222,868
Less interest refund	(25,960)
Income from investments	2,046,215
Other operating income	206,883
Total gross income	$ 7,450,006
Expenses	
Employee compensation and benefits	$ 1,010,797
Office occupancy and operations expense	510,947
Professional and outside services	169,448
Provision for loan losses	163,539
Member insurance	182,995
Other operating expenses	272,657
Total operating expenses	$ 2,310,383
Nonoperating gains or losses	
Gain (loss) on investments	$ (4,259)
Gain (loss) on disposition of assets	2,620
Other nonoperating expenses	7,713
Total income (loss) before dividends	$ 5,145,695
Transfer to regular and statutory reserves	$ 260,409
Dividends and interest on deposits	$ 4,409,286
Net income (loss) after dividends and reserve transfers	$ 475,928

Source: Based on 10,547 Natural Person Federal Credit Unions.
[a] Dollar amounts in $ thousands.

Investments in technology increased the fixed-cost base of credit unions. (Fixed assets in credit unions are 1.9 percent of assets, compared to 1.8 percent for banks and 2.3 percent for savings and loans.) Nevertheless, rapid changes in technology have been well accepted by credit unions. Approximately 10,000 credit unions use computerized accounting systems, and approximately 2500 credit unions have personal computers. ATMs, payroll deductions, automated settlement through automated clearing houses (ACHs), direct deposit of payroll, debit/credit cards, share drafts, and automated account inquiry are fast becoming routine.

Value of Volunteer Labor

Volunteer labor is a major factor which allows credit unions to operate at lower interest margins than the traditional competitors which pay director fees and employees for these services. Volunteers outnumber paid employers by a ratio of five to two, as shown in Exhibit 9.6. The ratio is much higher in the smallest credit unions, and only in credit unions with assets above $20 million do paid employees outnumber volunteers. Since many volunteers work in supervisory capacities (on the board of directors, credit committee, supervisory committee, and other committees), it is understandable that the value of this volunteer effort has been estimated at between five basis points and 25 basis points in net interest margins.

Employer Contributions

In the early days of an industrial credit union, employer support is of great benefit. The employer usually provides office furniture and offices as well as payroll deductions and staffing. As the credit union grows and becomes self-sufficient, these costs are charged to the credit union. Hence employer contributions, though essential, are largely confined to the start-up phase. Credit unions' cost structures have remained fairly constant as credit unions have learned to adapt to the new deregulated environment in which they live.

Protection of Shareholder Funds

The do-it-yourself philosophy of credit unions has served them well in their dealings with government agencies. Unlike the Federal Depository Insurance Corporation (FDIC) and Federal Savings & Loan Insurance Corporation (FSLIC), which were originally capitalized in the 1930s by the U.S. Treasury, the National Credit Union Share Insurance Fund (NCUSIF) was created in 1970 with no

Exhibit 9.6 Credit Union Personnel[a]

Asset-Size Category	Number of Credit Unions	Full-Time Staff	Part-Time Staff	Volunteers
$200,000 or less	2,568	246	2,045	34,230
$200,001–500,000	2,886	1,183	2,969	41,729
$500,001–1,000,000	2,466	1,722	3,042	37,198
$1,000,001–2,000,000	2,371	3,273	2,649	37,173
$2,000,001–5,000,000	2,607	13,178	2,704	43,927
$5,000,001–10,000,000	1,366	7,716	1,563	34,451
$10,000,001–20,000,000	921	10,174	1,520	16,904
$20,000,001–50,000,000	622	15,323	1,982	12,232
$50,000,001 & more	368	27,274	3,114	8,407
Total	16,175	80,089	21,588	256,251

Source: Economics and Research Department, CUNA.

[a] Based on 16,164 reporting credit unions.

federal capital. Continued funding of the NCUSIF is by assessment, as is also true for the FDIC and FSLIC. As the credit union movement has grown—and with it the size of insured deposits—assessments for the NCUSIF, which are based on a small premium, were reduced to a low level relative to the assets insured. However, the assessment/asset ratio is still higher than the ratios of the FDIC and FSLIC. In an effort to rectify this situation, credit unions lobbied Congress to amend the Federal Credit Union Act such that they could make deposits in the NCUSIF equal to 1 percent of their insured deposits. Congress ratified this change in 1984, and today the NCUSIF, with nearly $900 million deposited in the Federal Treasury, is better capitalized than either the FDIC or the FSLIC.

Pricing

Prior to the passage of the Deregulation and Monetary Control Act of 1980, credit unions had greater flexibility than other financial intermediaries. At that time, credit unions were not covered by the same tight depository statutes as other financial intermediaries. They could, for instance, pay as much as 6 or 7 percent interest on passbook accounts as well as on certificates of varying nature.

Because the overriding concern of most credit committees is to help their members, credit unions go to great lengths to find ways to make loans—even where chances of recovering the funds are marginal. Nevertheless, in 1980, outstanding loans declined for two reasons: (1) credit controls imposed by the executive branch of the federal government, and (2) 12 percent statutory loan-rate ceilings. The second reason merits a closer look. For many years, credit unions used the following simple formula in computing interest on loans: Interest equals 1 percent per month on the unpaid balance. With the cooperative philosophy of a limited return on capital, along with low loan losses and low expenses, credit unions made this formula work exceedingly well—too well, in fact. In 1979, when the prime rate exceeded 20 percent, credit unions, which had a statutory loan ceiling of 12 percent, found themselves unable to attract the funds necessary to lend to their members. That is, the funds they could attract were too expensive to lend at 12 percent.

When the Federal Credit Union Act and most state credit union acts were amended several years later, limitations requiring rates substantially below market levels were removed. Credit unions were allowed the freedom and flexibility of the current deregulated era, and loan volumes once again began to swell in accordance with credit unions' long-term growth pattern.

Impact of Deregulation

Among other things, all financial depositories for the first time were allowed to offer interest-bearing checking accounts to their customers. Credit unions have adapted well to this new era by offering new accounts and services such as share drafts, IRAs, money market accounts, money market deposit accounts, credit/debit cards, ATMs, automated clearing houses, and point-of-sale systems. There was a price to pay for deregulation, however; expanded services and higher depository rates made it tough for smaller institutions to operate profitably. Largely for this reason, nearly 4000 credit unions (17 percent of the 1978 total) went out of existence in the six years ending in 1984.

This trend in part reflects the increasing difficulty of operating profitably, but it primarily indicates a movement toward consolidation. The evidence is that most credit union indicators were quite healthy over this period (see Exhibits 9.7 and 9.8). Between 1978 and 1984, credit union membership grew 26 percent, and shares and deposits grew $50 billion, or 95.6 percent. Loans outstanding grew $26 billion, or 53.1 percent (an absolute dollar decline occurred in 1980 due to statutory loan ceilings in credit union acts). Reserves grew $2 billion, or 76 percent. And total assets grew $52 billion, or 85.5 percent.

Asset/Liability Management

One important effect of changes in services and regulations was to make managing balance sheets, matching assets to liabilities, more critical.

Despite the existence of the associated financial and support systems, many credit unions made unwise investments which resulted in asset/liability mismatches. Some have suffered substantial losses. Beginning in 1970 with GNMA pass-through securities, credit unions were sold billions of dollars of securities which did not fit their strategic plans. In an effort to keep loan rates to members low and yet increase yields on investments, some credit unions stretched out maturities and reduced quality standards. Furthermore, money brokers aggravated the problem by encouraging credit unions with earnings problems to invest in institutions that later failed. Some examples are: Penn Square Bank, Abilene National Bank, and savings and loans in all parts of the country (and in a few cases, offshore).

Exhibit 9.7 Membership Growth and Consolidation

	Number of Credit Unions	Number of Credit Members
1984	18,515	50,388,152
1983	19,097	47,840,386
1982	19,897	46,693,623
1981	20,786	45,313,237
1980	21,467	44,047,759
1979	21,933	41,355,370

Source: CUNA's Economics and Research Department.

Exhibit 9.8 Overview of U.S. Credit Union Business

	Number of Credit Unions	Shares and Deposits	Loans Outstanding	Reserves	Assets[a]
1984	18,515	$ 103,142	$ 75,726	$ 4,842	$ 113,242
1983	19,097	89,693	60,517	4,228	98,327
1982	19,897	74,847	51,488	3,560	82,680
1981	20,786	64,649	50,371	3,339	72,295
1980	21,467	51,748	48,707	3,118	68,996
1979	21,933	55,878	51,230	2,943	64,193

Source: CUNA's Economics & Research Department.
[a] Dollars in $ millions.

In addition, the continuing buildup of liquidity produced by the introduction of IRAs and the growing use of certificates of deposits, share drafts, and so on, placed an added burden on credit union portfolio performance. The loan-to-deposit ratio for credit unions, which had been 94 percent in 1978, dropped to a low of 68 percent in 1983 as total liquidity climbed from $11.6 billion to $37.8 billion. U.S. Central's assets grew from $555 million at the end of 1978 to more than $10 billion in 1984. On a market share basis, that is an increase from 5 percent to 27 percent over a five-year period. Credit unions will need all the tools at their disposal if they are to pay competitive rates while maintaining their financial viability.

Taxation

For the past 50 years, credit unions have been exempt from federal income tax. Congress and various administrations have seen fit not to tax the income or earnings of credit unions for three reasons: (1) credit unions' social purpose, which is to bring thrift and credit to the work force, (2) the costliness of administering the tax, due to the relatively small size and large number of credit unions, and (3) credit unions' status as financial cooperatives, which makes taxation socially as well as financially counterproductive.

Nevertheless, in 1984 the Reagan administration proposed, as part of its overall tax reform package, revocation of this tax-exempt status. While this proposal has been rejected, it will continue to be raised as long as the federal government continues to operate with sizable budgetary deficits. Advocates of elimination of credit unions' nonprofit status argue that credit unions have been given an unfair advantage, one that has allowed many to grow into far bigger institutions than anyone ever anticipated. Credit unions, the administration urges, should now do their part in contributing to government revenues and reducing the deficit. The President's staff also believes, on philosophical grounds, that all financial services providers should be forced to compete on a level playing field.

Credit unions, for their part, hold that their nonprofit charters justify setting them on a different plane from other financial institutions. Moreover, they point out, those who would abolish tax-exempt status have misinterpreted the facts. For one thing, credit unions' chief financial advantage derives not from tax-exempt status but from nonprofit operation, volunteer officials, close sponsor relations, and mutual ownership. For another thing, the vast majority of credit unions have remained small. Ninety-four percent are under $20 million in assets, no more than five exceed $500 million, and only two exceed $1 billion. The largest credit union, Navy Federal Credit Union with $1.6 billion in assets, is barely one-hundredth the size of the biggest bank. And Navy Federal has the most assets for the simple reason that it serves the most members—655,000.

Lastly and perhaps most important, credit unions do play their part in funding government needs. Their technique is not to contribute funds directly, but instead to free the government from spending funds on them in the ways that it must spend on their competitors. Credit unions do this by paying the total costs of the National Credit Union Administration (NCUA), the National Credit Union Share Insurance Fund (NCUSIF) and the Central Liquidity Facility (CLF). No government funds are spent. Further, the capitalization of the NCUSIF and CLF mentioned earlier had the indirect effect of *reducing* the deficit in fiscal year 1985 by over $1 billion.

MANAGING FOR THE FUTURE

In the past, credit unions attracted their key managers from within their fields of membership. This approach worked well for many years because the managers understood first-hand the needs of the group. Besides, financial operations were straightforward—they offered 12 percent loan rates and 6 percent dividend rates, with deposits collected automatically through payroll deduction. Marketing management was also relatively easy because regulations or laws largely determined product lines. These givens left personnel and operations management as the areas needing greatest attention from credit union management.

However, things changed dramatically with the passage of the Deregulation and Monetary Control Act of 1980. In 1982, additional changes in the Internal Revenue Code set the stage for IRA growth, which accelerated already rapid changes in the financial community. With deregulation requiring greater skills in all areas of management, retirements and management changes in key positions have been one major result. The state credit union leagues and CUNA have responded to the need for sharper skills by increasing their training opportunities to strengthen management capabilities in operations, finance, marketing, and personnel.

The shortage of skilled managers has been aggravated by raids on staff by competitors. As savings and loans moved further into consumer lending, credit union and bank loan officers were recruited to fill the new positions created. Conversely, as credit unions and banks intensified their mortgage lending, they recruited savings and loan mortgage-lending officers. Added to this staffing challenge was the development of new products such as IRAs, share drafts, debit/credit cards, and ATMs. In fact, recruitment of new talent became necessary at all levels of the credit union movement. Business and financial backgrounds as well as marketing were sought by credit union recruiters. Improvements are now becoming evident. Increased emphasis on educational background and experience has resulted in stronger management. Then too, mergers between credit unions have brought about staff mergers, and with them the opportunity to become more selective in filling positions. The simpler "good old days" of credit union management and marketing are giving way to sophisticated practices—practices which nevertheless maintain the commitment and responsibilities of old.

CASE STUDIES

The three case studies that follow show the diverse ways credit unions can succeed as their individual fields of membership change. While the subjects are three of the top 10 credit unions, becoming large does not necessarily change the nature or philosophy of a credit union. The experiences illustrated in these three cases is repeated many thousands of times by other credit unions serving their unique, if smaller, membership groups.

Plain Vanilla

United Airlines Employees' Credit Union in Chicago lays claim to being the best example of a "plain vanilla" operation. This credit union has a 50-year history of serving employees of United Airlines exclusively. Services provided are very basic—shares and loans—no share drafts, no debit/credit cards, no ATMs, no traveler's checks, no money orders, no frills of any kind. This strategy is in marked contrast to the practice of most U.S. credit unions over of $50 million in assets: 93.5 percent offer share drafts, 97 percent offer IRAs, and 91.1 percent offer traveler's checks. Only in the past three years has United Airlines Employees' Credit Union offered IRA accounts and expanded their field of membership to include spouses, spouses of deceased members, and retirees. Has this limited product line hurt the credit union's ability to serve its members' needs? Hardly!

Exhibit 9.9 illustrates United Airlines Employees' Credit Union's success, as do the following figures. Participation is well above average—96 percent of the sponsor's employees are credit union members. The average share account—$10,262—is also much larger than the national average, as is the average loan balance, $6,341. Clearly, United Airlines Employees' Credit Union has the full approval and participation of the company's work force.

Exhibit 9.9 Recent Growth of United Airlines Employees' Credit Union[a]

	1982	1983	1984	June 1985
Loans	$ 201	$ 215	$ 272	$ 297
Shares	$ 430	$ 540	$ 637	$ 680
IRAs	$ 17	$ 59	$ 112	$ 159
Total assets	$ 462	$ 611	$ 764	$ 859
Members	60,000	68,000	73,000	76,000

[a] Figures in $ millions.

Expansion by Design

Alaska USA Federal Credit Union began as Elmendorf Air Force Base Federal Credit Union, headquartered in Anchorage. For years, the credit union served members of the U.S. Air Force, as well as government employees working on the base. The Elmendorf credit union was one of the first to see how a broader definition of its membership could help it prosper. In 1968, "once a member, always a member" became the credit union's practice, a shift in perspective that allowed it to continue to serve members wherever they might be, whether in Alaska or not. Later, in the 1970s, the credit union expanded to serve new groups such as enrollees of native corporations, employees of Alyeska Pipeline Service Company, and employees of their contractors and subcontractors. Then, in the early 1980s, as a result of several legislative changes, all Alaska natives were guaranteed permanent membership in Alaska USA Federal Credit Union. Of course, if natives elected to join another credit union, they became ineligible to participate in Alaska USA. When, sometime later, the NCUA began allowing dissimilar groups to be in a field of membership, Alaska USA began soliciting and serving groups of employees across the state. In 1984, the credit union was serving more than 2000 employee groups, managed 28 branches, operated through a subsidiary a shared electronic system of 128 ATMs, and gave full-time employment to 637 people, while serving 206,000 members in every one of the United States. By the end of 1984, Alaska USA had a loan portfolio of $389 million, total assets of $558 million, and $510 million in member shares. Although such growth and redefinition is not typical of credit unions, the example of Alaska USA shows that planning and expansion by design can work to members' benefit.

Biggest "Average" Credit Union in the World

Navy Federal Credit Union in Virginia is the world's largest credit union. But it is also a representative credit union. Its typical loan balances and share balances are proportionately very close to the national averages for all credit unions.

Although Navy Federal uses economies of scale to its advantage, the credit union is totally member-oriented. Because the members live and work around the world, the credit union is open 24 hours a day, 365 days a year. Even on a typical Christmas day the credit union makes some 50 loans. Another factor demonstrating its dedication to members is the uneconomic size of many of the share accounts it services: 135,000 accounts have balances under $10, and 182,000 have less than $100. Actually Navy Federal has no minimum balance requirements, and it charges no fees at all over the full range of its basic financial services. Because the majority of members are enlisted personnel, the credit union concentrates on making credit available on reasonable terms to these servicemen and women who otherwise could not obtain credit easily, if at all. Navy Federal employs 1205 full-time and 83 part-time personnel to serve its members. Twenty members serve in volunteer capacities on their boards, their credit committee, and their supervisory committee.

SUMMARY

Making money, as antithetical as this objective may appear at first glance to the purpose of credit unions, can and does mesh with credit unions' three basic operating principles: Exist not for profit but for service, share large fixed costs cooperatively, and leverage the value supplied by volunteer labor. At one level it is evident that, to remain viable, credit unions must make more money than they spend in interest charges, salaries, rent, and so forth. But more to the point where their philosophy is concerned, credit unions exist in order to make money for their members.

John Naisbitt, in his 1985 book, *Reinventing the Corporation*, says that "the new American work ethic holds that work should be fulfilling and fun, an integrated part of a whole life plan. More and more of us believe that work should accomplish a personal and social mission."[2] Naisbitt's observation effectively summarizes the attitudes of credit union professionals and volunteers. These men and women work out of the belief that they are fulfilling both a social and a personal mission. Profit—while important to credit unions in order to maintain viability—is not what motivates the people who make credit unions work.

NOTES

1. Martin, Kenneth. From the introduction to *Home Port*, the published history of the Navy Federal Credit Union. Bryn Mawr, PA: Dorrance & Co., 1983.
2. Naisbitt, John. *Reinventing the Corporation*. New York: Warner Books, 1985, 172–173.

10 Making Money in Institutional Investment Management/Advisory

LAWRENCE K. FISH

The institutional investment management/advisory business—that is, the management of pension and endowment assets for a fee—has consistently been one of the most rapidly growing and profitable financial services in the postwar period. However, this sustained growth has been far from universal among the increasingly diverse set of competitors; nor have the often high margins—up to 80 percent of fees—characterized all players, even some of the industry's most successful.

This chapter examines the reasons for the successes and failures of investment managers, with particular focus on banks. History has clearly shown that investment management can be a highly marketable and profitable product for banks, when properly carried out. Investment management is a particularly interesting case study in the field of financial services. Unlike some financial services where gains in market share are often made at the expense of profitability, investment management is a business in which the keys to marketability also open the door to higher profitability.

The remainder of this chapter traces the historical development of the investment management business and the changing key factors for successful marketing, then lays out the basic economics of the investment management business. A description of relevant portions of Bank of Boston's program to improve its institutional investment management division are examined in some detail to illustrate the general observations being made. The chapter concludes with a brief discussion of the accrued benefits of the actions taken at the bank.

HISTORICAL DEVELOPMENT AND KEY FACTORS FOR SUCCESSFUL MARKETING

The rapid growth in pension assets and the development of the pension management business began in the immediate postwar period. At that time, most companies viewed pension plans as a means to provide their employees with financial security for retirement. They also sought to keep to a minimum the administrative burden placed on the company. As is normal with new forms of business, corporations turned to suppliers with whom they were familiar and comfortable. So initially the key factors for success were: (1) current relationship with the potential client; (2) a company's strong fiduciary (preservation of principal) image; and (3) smooth administration (custody and recordkeeping) of the pension fund.

It should come as no surprise that the banking industry dominated the pension management business through its early and intermediate development. Pension assets were typically the responsibility of the corporation's chief financial officer, whose ties with banks were well established. Furthermore, the banks had, in the form of their trust departments, an established, functioning entity which was ideally organized to meet the custodial, management, and fiduciary demands of pension management. In contrast, potential competitors had neither the confidence of CFOs nor the administrative know-how to manage pension funds. For these reasons, banks were able to maintain remarkably stable pension relationships into the 1960s.

However, beginning in the 1970s, a number of events signalled the end of the banks' domination of the investment management business. Banks' relationships, as well as their fiduciary and custodial advantages, diminished considerably throughout the decade. Several principal causes can be cited.

Most importantly, the souring of the stock and bond markets created large unfunded pension liabilities for plan sponsors. The perceived fiduciary advantages of bank trust departments had been shaken. While clients had always recognized on an intellectual level that bank investment managers could not assure the preservation of principal, they were now forced to confront the hard realities of that knowledge. And the feeling was distinctly unpleasant.

This gut-level awareness of market vagaries was made still more unsettling by a further development that resulted from the very success of pension programs. The growth in pension assets and pension expense had prompted plan sponsors to focus on pension assets as a source of incremental profit for the company. That is, rates of return, both assumed and realized, were often higher in the funds than were the companies' own return-on-investment (ROI) figures. While fiduciary standards were not compromised, superior investment performance became the primary objective and a proven track record of performance became a prerequisite.

As this view of pension funds' usefulness gained influence, and with volatility in both the stock and bond markets increasing, plan sponsors no longer achieved their investment goals with conservative investment managers like banks. In fact, "safe" instruments, such as long-term bonds and growth stocks, were the source of much of the unfunded liabilities. As a result, plan sponsors developed more sophisticated means of managing risk, diversifying their portfolios by using multiple investment managers. To assure diversification goals, plan sponsors required that investment managers adhere to clearly articulated investment philosophies that fit into their "manager" portfolio. Developments in custody, particularly central depositories and master trusteeships, further facilitated switching between investment managers and using multiple managers. These developments lowered the costs of custody for industry leaders.

Not only were banks' initial advantages in fiduciary and custodial experience reduced during this period, but banks' established relationships with plan sponsors counted for less and less. Plan sponsors were becoming more seasoned buyers and information on comparative performance of investment managers was now widely available. Thus, marketing pension fund investment management services had changed dramatically, and the changes were largely adverse for banks. The key success factors had become:

- Proven track record of performance, supported by a stable cadre of portfolio managers
- Clearly articulated investment philosophy, supported by a disciplined investment process, and professional marketing to articulate the philosophy

Banks made few changes in response to these new market conditions. They also delivered relatively poor performance. Both facts created an opportunity that was quickly seized upon by investment counselors and insurance companies to great effect: Between 1975 and 1985, banks lost one-third of their market share. Growing rapidly, investment counselling firms took personnel as well as business from the banks (in fact, many of today's most successful counselors got their start in bank trust departments). The insurance industry also made inroads using guaranteed interest contract and real estate vehicles.

Although it is a matter of some conjecture, market growth and client stability through the early 1970s may have created an air of complacency in the pension management business. Trust departments ably met their fiduciary responsibilities, but in many instances failed to make adequate investment in the systems and people required to meet the increasing demands of custody and investment management. Because management at the trust department level was focusing narrowly on its fiduciary responsibilities, it failed to grasp the requirements and opportunities of the business. There was also a second, more serious managerial failure: Senior bank management had ignored the need to involve itself in the strategic issues facing trust departments. The very real opportunity that banks had to make profound and beneficial changes to their institutional management business was largely overlooked.

The banks failed to compete for many reasons. In many instances, pension management was a small business relative to the entire bank, or even relative to the trust department, which was often dominated by personal trust. Furthermore, the bank environment, and particularly the trust department environment, was intensely bureaucratic, almost shackled by memos and committees. This environment contributed to a lack of business focus and poor relationship management. Behind all these failures lay a weakness in people management. Particularly damaging was the inability to retain top performers because of gross inadequacies in structure and compensation. The importance of people in this business simply cannot be stated too strongly or too often. Capital, system, and institutional requirements are minor by comparison.

In sum, during an era of rapid change, where the market was calling out for proven, disciplined professionals, the banks were left with a cadre of portfolio managers who showed poor track records (the good managers had departed for counseling firms) and used a hodgepodge of muddled investment approaches. It is little wonder, then, that investment counselors (boasting proven track records and clear disciplines), and insurance companies (offering responsive products, such as guaranteed investment contracts (GICs), tailored to fit into diversified portfolios), grabbed almost half of the banks' market share in the 1970s and 1980s.

The experience of Bank of Boston paralleled that of the banking industry in general. However, the decline in the 1970s was particularly ironic and perhaps more difficult to bear for Bank of Boston. Having been in the forefront of equity investment at a time when most managers failed to appreciate the growth potential of equities and were heavily weighted in fixed income securities, the bank legitimately viewed itself as an industry leader. But by 1983 the Institutional Investment Division was overstaffed and demoralized by a continuing erosion in its client base. Worse, it was performing poorly and inconsistently. Over a period of several years, the bank was only marginally profitable.

Though it is hard to believe in retrospect, the Bank of Boston's pension business had been collapsing around it for a decade, but management had never stepped back and asked "what's wrong?" When we finally did ask, three basic problems were discovered to be adversely affecting the bank's ability to market investment management services. They are listed as follows:

- The investment philosophy and process lacked discipline.
- Key managers were not being attracted and retained in sufficient number.
- Portfolio managers were being forced to perform administrative tasks that distracted their attention from investing.

In establishing a new investment management division for the bank, management sought to overcome these problems. The name given to the division was Dewey Square Investors (DSI).

DEWEY SQUARE INVESTORS

Investment Philosophy and Process

The development of an investment philosophy was the starting point for reorganization into an investment management division. Prior to the creation of DSI, each portfolio manager at the Bank of Boston followed a personal approach to investing, and the individual manager's personal approach was largely unchallenged by bank policy. License of this order may have stimulated individuals to work more energetically, but it also led to a lack of institutional identity. The bank was not associated with any single investment approach. Advice was inconsistent, even conflicting, sometimes to the embarrassment of the bank. Checks and balances that could have assured the "sellability" of investment decisions were absent. The result was a devastating track record of poor performance, with inadequate explanations to the customer.

In contrast, the top-performing investment counselors worked from and projected publicly a clearly articulated investment strategy and strong selling discipline based on a solid core of investment expertise. Furthermore, the top counselors tracked a limited number of securities, and kept fewer still in their portfolios. What the counselors sacrificed in breadth they more than made up in depth of knowledge and timeliness of action. It is a strategy they continue to practice today.

Using the top counselors' approach, DSI developed a clear set of guidelines for both its equity and its bond portfolios. For example, all DSI's equity portfolios now specialize in fundamentally undervalued securities and growth issues. The selection of stocks follows a sequence of applying progressively stricter criteria. To begin with, 6000 equities are screened by computer. The list of 150 issues arrived at is then evaluated by analysts. The analysts choose approximately 75 of these to be included in DSI's portfolios, less than half the number carried back in 1983. Equally important is our selling discipline, which is driven by deteriorating relative valuation, realization of price objectives, and relative performance.

Attracting and Retaining Good Managers

In 1983, DSI's portfolio managers were paid approximately one-half the industry average. Low pay was both a discourager of good performance and an incentive to leave. And in fact some good managers departed. Those in charge at DSI were well aware that success required the retention of key people and that there was a strong linkage between retention and compensation. Therefore, substantial adjustments were made in the base compensation of our top professionals, and an incentive compensation plan was introduced to reward professional staff on the basis of business profitability and investment performance. The rationale underlying the incentive compensation structure was that, in order to be paid like the best, the managers should perform like the best.

A primary focus was the professional requirements of Dewey Square Investors and, to this end, we hired two key people—an equity investment professional who was accustomed to a disciplined investment philosophy, and a marketing professional experienced in working with plan sponsors and their consultants. These key additions helped ignite our restructured team. It is not enough to juggle the lineup on a losing baseball team; the front office must also be willing to trade for a new clean-up hitter or a stopper in the bullpen. Bringing in new talent in this way is likely to raise the confidence factor of the whole team, and it worked for DSI.

Relationship to the Rest of the Bank

The institutional investment division's relationship to the rest of the bank was adversely affecting performance in three ways. First, trading and research capabilities—essential support for portfolio managers—were traditionally shared with other trust functions. But sharing led to insufficient responsiveness and excessive costs for the soon-to-be DSI. Consequently, one of the aims of the reorganization was to provide DSI with dedicated trading and research. Second, portfolio managers were constantly being distracted from their main purpose, investing, by problems associated with the administration of custody services, recordkeeping, and the assessment of fees. To alleviate the burden, both the fees and services of investment management and custody/recordkeeping were unbundled with the formation of DSI.

Third, just as the internal structure of Dewey Square Investors had to reflect its objectives and the unique characteristics of its industry, so did its place of business. Continued operation from the bank's head office was not appropriate. Accordingly, Dewey Square Investors moved to rented quarters specifically designed to its needs. In addition to the obvious practical benefits, this move reinforced the separation between Dewey Square Investors and the bank. It boosted the "can do" attitude of the people and served to remove them from the "memo mindset" that often permeates banks and trust departments. Management held it to be vitally important that this stand-alone concept be clear to DSI clients and personnel, since staff were expected to be competitive and increase their business through their own efforts.

The move also gave the division the opportunity to change the "look" of its business. Internal changes of substance were complemented by external changes in name, logo, and the color scheme of materials. A brochure was prepared introducing the people and philosophy of Dewey Square Investors, and client presentation materials were completely redesigned. Once again, the intent was to reinforce DSI's independent status and its characteristic approach to the demands of the marketplace.

ECONOMICS OF THE INVESTMENT MANAGEMENT BUSINESS

In addition to losing the equivalent of almost $600 million in investment management fees,[1] banks also failed to realize the full profit potential of their pension businesses, in part because they failed to understand where they incurred costs and where they made money. Consequently, banks often failed to recognize at least three types of opportunities to improve profitability:

- Rationalized pricing, in line with the costs of providing services

- Increased efficiency of operations, based on industry standards and the capacity of various functions within the organization
- Heightened consistency of investment, based on the new requirements of the marketplace

Before discussing each of these opportunities in more detail, it should be recognized that achieving these profitability improvements is facilitated by a clear understanding of the costs of doing business, by product and customer group. As shown in Exhibit 10.1, direct expenses are associated with four basic business tasks, each of which can be allocated to individual accounts (and therefore to product and customer group), in a reasonably straightforward manner.

Based on an allocation of expenses to accounts, along the lines of Exhibit 10.1, the institutional investment division of the Bank of Boston was able to identify a number of ways to improve profitability, as described below.

Rationalized Pricing

Basically, there are two different types of investment management accounts—individually managed and pooled. Sponsors of individually managed account

Exhibit 10.1 Components of Investment

Expense Category	Approximate Percent of Total Direct Costs	Basis for Allocation
Portfolio management, including direct costs of managers responsible for designing, implementing, and communicating portfolio decisions for customers.	50	Portfolio managers can only service a limited number of accounts; thus, most costs are allocable on a per-account basis, with some adjustment for account size and trading activity.
Account administration, including preparing customer reports, following through on the recording of trades, and so forth—predominantly a clerical task.	10	Each account requires a certain amount of administrative support; thus all costs are allocable on a per-account basis.
Support services for investment management, such as trading and research.	20	Varies by services; for example, trading costs would be allocated on the basis of the number of trades for the account.
Custody and record-keeping services	20	Costs incurred, in part, by account, and otherwise by the trading and record-keeping activity levels of the account.

plans are provided a portfolio and reports tailored to meet their needs, and they have regular interaction with the portfolio manager. In contrast, contact with portfolio managers is rarely extended to sponsors of pooled account plans, for whom the funds of numerous accounts are intermingled, cutting down on the time required by portfolio managers, traders, and others to service the account.

Not surprisingly, pooled accounts are less expensive to service than comparably sized individually managed accounts. Similarly, larger accounts are cheaper to service (per dollar of assets under management) than are smaller accounts. Consequently, the fees charged per dollar of assets are lower for pooled accounts than for individually managed accounts, and they are also lower for large accounts.

However, until DSI actually went through the exercise of allocating expenses, management did not know whether our price schedule was in line with actual costs. As might be expected, there was considerable variation in the fee/expense relationship among product and customer types, as shown in Exhibit 10.2.

In other words, the bank could not afford to manage small accounts individually—without either pricing itself out of the market or losing money on every account. Therefore, following this analysis, DSI moved to convert smaller individually managed accounts into pooled accounts, and raised its fee schedule at the lower end to be more closely in line with costs. In addition, DSI began focusing its individually managed marketing efforts on profitably sized accounts in the $20 to $50 million range. Finally, the analysis revealed that DSI's custody and record-keeping fees were unreasonably below market prices and did not adequately reflect the costs of high turnover accounts. These problems were soon remedied following the aforementioned unbundling of custody and investment management.

Increased Efficiency of Operations

Another valuable offshoot of the profitability analysis was the identification of surplus capacity throughout the institutional investment division. By looking at fully allocated costs on a per-account basis, management saw that DSI had more portfolio managers than it could afford or than it reasonably needed. In addition,

Exhibit 10.2 Profitability, by Customer and Product Group: Illustrative Examples

	Small Individually Managed	Small Pooled	Small Individually Managed
Assets ($000)	$ 3,000	$ 3,000	$ 20,000
Fee ($000)	6	5	4
Revenue ($)	18,000	15,000	80,000
Expense ($)	45,000	12,000	52,000
Profit ($)	$ (27,000)	$ 3,000	$ 28,000
Margin (%)	(150%)	20%	35%

support costs (account administration and support service) were often in excess of 50 percent of fees, far too high for a business that is capable of generating 50 percent gross margins. Based on these findings, professional and support staff was cut by 30 percent.

Finally, DSI's custody and record-keeping expenses were clearly out of line with both fees and industry standards. Subsequent efforts have focused on increasing the efficiency and effectiveness of this operation through systems improvements and rationalization of staff.

Heightened Consistency of Investment

As noted earlier, unlike many financial services businesses where share can only be recaptured through lower margins, institutional investment is a business in which the changes necessary to prevent further market share erosion can also *improve* profit margins. Such was the case at the Bank of Boston. In particular, a more disciplined investment process requires fewer portfolio managers, traders, and research analysts per account, as discipline limits the amount of independent analysis to a more manageable level. (The assumption is that the operation can support more than a critical mass of portfolio managers.) A related benefit of improved investment performance is the continued growth of accounts and funds under management, which allows the business to make better use of the essential staff.

In addition, the 30 percent cost reduction facilitated the implementation of our investment philosophy by removing individuals who could not accept the philosophy and were therefore unable to make a contribution to the investment process.

BENEFITS OF THE IMPROVEMENT PROGRAM

Almost two years into the operation, it is still too early to proclaim unqualified success for DSI. Yesterday's success is of little comfort in the investment management business, where the future depends on today's effort. However, results so far have been encouraging, benefiting the Bank of Boston as well as the staff and customers of its institutional investment division. Benefits to the bank are evident in a four-fold increase in profit contribution of the division. Margins are now approaching those achieved by successful firms. Benefits to customers are evident in the division's improved track record—from the bottom to the top third of the investment performance rankings in the last two years. Investors' satisfaction is further reflected by the stabilization of the client base and the $100 million that has been added to existing accounts over 1985. For the first time in many, many years, other divisions of the bank have become aware of the dynamics and results of Dewey Square Investors and are developing the confidence needed to promote DSI's investment management skills wholeheartedly. This confidence is not just the result of good salesmanship by senior people. It is directly attributable to improved performance in the bank's pension and profit-sharing plans.

There is every reason to believe that other institutional investment operations can enjoy equal, if not greater success, by systematically reevaluating and restructuring their businesses. The specifics of these changes may well be very different from those implemented for DSI. Still, there is one major point to emphasize; and that is that the ability of any investment advisor to market its investment philosophy and expand its client base is a critical issue. As even the best organizations experience some account turnover, a successful marketing effort is an absolute must. Equally important is the ability of an investment philosophy to provide superior returns over a series of different market cycles. Finally, managements should be alert to opportunities to incorporate new philosophies in spin-offs. This perspective is essential to remaining viable as clients continue to become more sophisticated in the determination of their needs and more specific in their demands for products.

NOTES

1. The figure of $600 million represents a loss of 15 market share points on $1 trillion in assets under management, at an average fee of 40 basis points.

11 Making Money in Finance Companies

A. CHARLENE SULLIVAN

Managing financial services firms has historically been a relatively easy thing to do. Because regulations prohibited free entry into many geographic and product markets, a firm could safely specialize in a particular product market. In the last two decades, however, product and geographic markets have become more integrated. The degree of specialization of financial institutions offering financial services has been reduced, and the various institutions in the market look more and more similar.

When banks came into the consumer finance market, loan rate restrictions or an unwillingness to serve consumer loan customers caused banks to leave a large percentage of the market for consumer loans to consumer finance companies. Somewhat later, however, improvements in credit information, and credit card technology, and the erosion of geographic barriers in the consumer loan market, improved the economics of consumer lending for banks. The combination of banks' below-market cost of money and high use of leverage enabled them to operate with a lower margin than finance companies needed to survive. As banks bid away the best of the consumer and small commercial loan business, finance companies found that they had greater difficulty serving those markets profitably.

In response to the developing forces of deregulation of financial markets in the last decade, independent finance companies have changed to look more like banks. Large independent finance companies wanted to use their national network of offices to the best advantage in the race to deliver consumer financial services in a national market. Their products now include credit cards, ATM services, safe deposit boxes, savings accounts, mortgage loans, and tax preparation and financial planning services. Consequently, there is little reason to believe that making money in independent finance companies will eventually be a much different enterprise than achieving profitability in banking.

This chapter will take a closer look at the ways in which finance companies are responding to volatile markets, pressure on margins, and incursions by other types of financial services providers, notably banks. The evidence coming in daily suggests there are no easy solutions. Survival depends on: (1) lowering operating costs; (2) making the most of available capital; and (3) retaining top-quality management that knows how to identify products and markets that emphasize the strengths of finance companies rather than their weaknesses. Under current conditions, the existing differences in the capital structures of commercial banks and finance companies dictate that both types of firms cannot operate in the same markets in the long run. Finance companies will be forced to develop products where high profit margins are available or ultimately convert to a banking charter.

Conversely, the safety net of deposit insurance has given commercial bank management an incentive to take sometimes excessive financial risks to bolster profit margins that have declined with deregulation of deposit rates. With the regulatory agencies finally realizing the need to price deposit insurance according to the risk of the assets of individual banks, banks may ultimately withdraw from some markets that finance companies once served exclusively.

THE SPECTRUM OF FINANCE COMPANIES

A finance company, in the eyes of the Federal Reserve Board, is any nonsavings institution whose primary assets are sales finance receivables, personal cash loans to consumers, short- and intermediate-term business receivables, junior liens on real estate, or some combination of these. Finance companies vary considerably in the markets they serve and also in their degree of independence. (Nonetheless, it seems helpful to provide an illustration of a typical finance company balance

Exhibit 11.1 Finance Companies Consolidated Assets and Liabilities

	1983[a]
Financial assets	$ 294.1[b]
Checkable deposits	5.1
Mortgages	20.5
Consumer credit	135.5
Other loans	133.0
Liabilities	$ 297.1
Corporate and foreign bonds	78.4
Bank loans, n.e.c.	11.0
Open market paper	101.0
Taxes payable	[c]
Miscellaneous	106.5

Source: Board of Governors of the Federal Reserve System, *Annual Statistical Digest.*

[a] As of December 31.

[b] Figures in $ billions.

[c] Less than $50 million.

sheet. This will be found in Exhibit 11.1. The numbers show aggregate data and thus give a sense of the size of the finance business—*Editors*.)

The consumer finance business as it exists today developed from the first consumer credit law, conceived in 1916 to remedy the "loan shark" problem by creating a strictly regulated, legal consumer money-lending business. This remedial law was called the Uniform Small Loan Law. Consumer credit in the United States at that time was limited to the charge accounts of wealthy customers, Morris Plan Banks that made small loans secured by the borrowers' deposits, a few scattered credit unions, and a few installment sales systems administered by manufacturers of durable goods, like the Singer Sewing Machine Company. The Small Loan Law contained only one permission: the right to charge economically practicable rates. But many stringent regulations were designed to prevent lenders from abusing borrowers and to deter borrowing except after careful consideration.

Commercial banks entered the field of consumer installment lending in the late 1920s. The opening of a personal loan department in 1928 by the then-largest commercial bank in the country, National City Bank of New York, was widely publicized. A year after the National City Bank department was established, about 200 personal loan departments had been established in other banks, although many were discontinued during the period following the Depression. Bankers considered consumer installment lending to be outside their customary field of activity. However, after the Depression the favorable experience of sales finance companies, consumer finance companies and industrial banks showed commercial bankers that consumer installment lending could be both safe and profitable.

The early consumer finance companies specialized in small personal loans, often on an unsecured or signature basis. When security was required, it usually took the form of a chattel mortgage on an automobile or household goods. A few states permitted wage or salary assignment, which enabled the lender to collect from the borrower's employer if the borrower became delinquent. In most states the maximum loan was set by law at $300 or $500. Similarly, the early commercial finance companies made loans to small and medium-sized businesses that banks would not make.

Asset-based lending, which is any loan secured by accounts receivable or inventories or both, was the near-exclusive province of commercial finance companies until the early 1970s. Asset-based loans in this era were short-term and were intended to cover working capital requirements. The size of the loan ranged between 55 percent and 80 percent of the book value of the receivables and/or inventories. The limit depended on the financial condition of the company, how the company collected its receivables, the durability of its inventory, and the volatility of the market for the products held in inventory.

Factoring was another market niche of the early finance companies. Factors provided operating credit to industries characterized by wide cyclical variation in the level of business and considered too risky by banks' credit standards. The process, then and today, involves the transfer of accounts receivable on a continuing basis from the business client to its factor. The factor pays for the receivables at the time they are sold or when it collects from the client's customer. The factor maintains all records necessary to collect debts, and carry out the functions of credit investigation and protection, sales ledger accounting, and actual collection.

Finance companies can be categorized as independents or as subsidiaries of manufacturers or financial corporations. The independent finance company may have one office in one town or several hundred offices in many states. Such offices may offer consumer credit, commercial loan products, or both. Financial affiliates of manufacturers were created to provide sources of credit to dealers and consumers. In many cases, the subsidiaries were established before other reliable sources of consumer credit were available. Given the benefits to the manufacturer of an incremental sale when production is below capacity, providing a stable source of financing for the dealers and customers is potentially a very profitable activity. Today, most of the major financial subsidiaries of manufacturers have broadened their activities to include a whole spectrum of financial services.

PAST PROSPERITY

Finance companies have traditionally been "lenders of last resort." This generalization holds true on both the consumer and the commercial sides of the business. Finance companies have historically made small unsecured cash loans available to their customers at rates substantially above prevailing rates.

Finance companies could justify their high interest rates for three reasons. First, the credit-worthiness of typical borrowers was low, making the riskiness of loans unusually high. Second, the cost of making and collecting small loans was high relative to the dollar amount extended per contract. Third, the finance companies were barred from direct access to low-cost funds such as regulated savings and demand deposits. Giving careful attention to credit and collection procedures, providing friendly customer service, and being a reliable source of funds were factors that contributed to the success of "lenders of last resort." Broadly speaking, then, finance companies were serving a market niche that depended on charging high rates but nonetheless yielded healthy returns.

The healthy returns in part were made possible by the effective barring of potential low-rate competitors, notably banks. Federal prohibitions on interstate banking and state-legislated limits on banks' loan rates made the finance companies' markets unprofitable ones for banks. The finance rates for various types of consumer loans are limited by law in many states. Finance companies in many cases have been exempted from usury ceilings through provisions for special rate structures for small cash loans.

The historic success of consumer finance companies is explained by rather subtle psychological factors as well. It has been generally believed that banks served low-risk borrowers and finance companies served high-risk borrowers. Recent data, however, indicates otherwise. In a state where both banks and finance companies operated under a nonbinding and identical rate ceiling, the risk characteristics of each group's borrowers were not significantly different.[1] The intriguing question was why one group would pay the finance companies' higher rates.

Another study suggests that consumer finance company customers place greater importance on the size of the monthly payment than the annual percentage rate. Bank customers are more likely to rank the APR above the size of monthly payments in terms of importance. Finance company customers apparently have a lower perception of their own credit worthiness and have greater trouble saving in advance for purchases. So it seems that the difference between bank loan applicants and finance company applicants stems from differences in consumers' perceptions of their own credit worthiness, and their financial sophistication.[2] This means that some of the finance company customers were low-risk borrowers who could qualify for less expensive credit. More to the point, it means that consumer finance companies were serving a group of customers which included both high-risk and low-risk borrowers. Thus, the risk of the portfolio of finance company loans was somewhat lower than would have been the case had finance companies acted strictly as lenders of last resort.

WORSENING CONDITIONS

The conditions of the early days have changed. Banks have discovered that making consumer loans can be a highly profitable business. And credit cards have provided a means for lowering the costs of extending small cash loans. Additionally, as commercial banks have begun to pay market prices for their funds, they have moved into higher risk product markets, creating more competition in what had once been the exclusive domain of finance companies.

The increased competition is reflected in finance companies' diminishing market share. In 1930, finance companies and retail outlets held 93 percent of total consumer credit outstanding, with finance companies holding 44 percent of the total (see Exhibit 11.2). From 1950 to 1970, finance companies held about one-third of total consumer credit outstanding. From 1970 to 1980, finance companies' share of that market shrunk to about 22 percent of credit outstanding. Since

Exhibit 11.2 Market Share: Consumer Credit Outstanding

Year-End	Commercial Banks	Finance Companies	Credit Unions	Retail Outlets	Others
1930	7%	44%	0%	48%	1%
1950	39	34	4	20	3
1965	41	33	10	14	1
1970	44	27	13	14	2
1980	49	21	15	9	6
1985	46	21	15	8	10

Source: Federal Reserve Board

1982, finance companies have not been extending net new credit at a rate sufficient to regain, or even maintain, their market share (see Exhibit 11.3). Outstandings at commercial banks, by contrast, have been growing rapidly.

The data breaking down sources of new consumer installment credit between 1980 and 1985 reveal the dramatic volatility in market share that has recently characterized that submarket. In 1980–1981, finance companies captured a large share of new credit outstanding when financial affiliates of auto manufacturers offered below-market interest rates to improve auto sales. Commercial banks, which normally originate a large percentage of new auto credit, were restricted during that period by binding loan rate ceilings and an inability to compete with the rates offered by the finance companies. Some perceive these shifts in market share as evidence that modern consumers have little loyalty to a particular supplier of credit. Rather, they switch readily to the low-cost supplier.

Asset-based financing and leasing products are available from most major banking organizations. Commercial banks discovered that making loans to small and medium-sized businesses was highly profitable, and during the 1970s they got into the high-risk commercial lending business, bidding down profit margins in the factoring market. The effect on one of the major players, Walter E. Heller, Inc., was severe. In 1982, following a downgrading in its credit rating, Heller was put up for sale. Its nonbanking operations were acquired by Fuji Bank Ltd. of Tokyo in January, 1984.

Increased willingness to grant high-risk loans is not the only source of banks' impact on finance companies. Their introduction of credit cards has also cut into

Exhibit 11.3 Market Share: Sources of Net New Consumer Installment Credit to Households (Seasonally Adjusted)

	1981		1982		1983		1984		1985[b]	
	$[a]	%	$	%	$	%	$	%	$	%
Commercial Banks	301	1.8	3,794	24.7	19,463	40.8	39,754	52.1	17,570	53.4
Savings & Loans	2,613	15.7	3,406	22.2	7,135	15.0	6,878	8.9	3,697	11.2
Finance Companies	9,184	55.3	5,703	37.1	9,034	18.9	9,761	12.8	6,037	18.4
Credit Unions	2,073	12.5	1,309	8.5	6,115	12.8	14,331	18.8	4,715	14.4
Others	2,446	14.7	1,156	7.5	5,984	12.5	5,642	7.4	847	2.6
Total	16,617	100.0	15,368	100.0	47,731	100.0	76,366	100.0	32,876	100.0

Source: Federal Reserve Board.

[a] Figures in $ millions.

[b] January–April.

finance business from another direction. Credit cards provided a vehicle by which consumers desiring small amounts of money for short periods of time could be efficiently and profitably served. In effect, the most creditworthy customers could now get a bank line of credit that substituted attractively for a cash loan from a finance company. As a consequence, only high-risk consumers who could not qualify for a bank credit card tended to remain with finance companies.

Banks are not the only institutions eroding the customer base of finance companies. Beginning in 1950, the credit union movement virtually exploded. Between 1950 and 1975, the number of credit union members increased from about 4 million to approximately 27 million as credit unions' market share of credit outstanding increased from 4 percent to 15 percent. Being nonprofit, deposit-taking organizations, credit unions had a low cost of funds and charged the lowest loan rates in a local market. Credit unions were typically sponsored by companies whose employees were heavily blue-collar, the segment of the market previously served primarily by consumer finance companies.

Plainly, competing institutions were grabbing finance company customers to a serious extent. Furthermore, banks did not content themselves with going after the customers—they have gone after the finance companies themselves. In approving the creation of bank holding companies, The Federal Reserve Board specified that consumer finance was one of the businesses in which bank holding companies were permitted to invest. Over the period from 1971 through mid-1973, the Federal Reserve Board reviewed 86 applications by bank holding companies to acquire finance companies, a high number by any standard. The basic reason for the wave of acquisitions was the desire of major bank holding companies to position themselves for a nationwide banking system. Finance companies had not been restricted, as banks had been, from having offices in many states. By acquiring a finance company, a bank holding company immediately gained a market presence in several states.

Relaxation of the law on a wholly different front, creditors' remedies, also hurt finance companies. Following the passage of the 1978 Bankruptcy Reform Act, the rate of personal and business bankruptcies increased dramatically, placing severe limits on lenders' ability to make profitable, unsecured loans. Bankruptcy losses, as a cost of doing business, are normally reflected in the rates charged to high-risk consumers. However, when the cost of bankruptcy to the borrower are unusually low, all borrowers become high-risk. In such an environment, lenders' best recourse is to readjust the characteristics of the credit contract by raising the cost of default. Intensifying competition has militated against this corrective.

RESPONSE

Finance companies have attempted to meet these challenges in a number of ways: changing their lending policies, changing their funding policies, and reorienting their strategies.

Lending Policies

In the 1970s, finance companies, especially the large national companies, moved to diversify their portfolios between consumer and commercial business. There was a particularly compelling reason to do this. The operating income streams of small loan companies and commercial finance companies are negatively correlated.[3] There was a dramatic increase in business receivables relative to consumer receivables held by finance companies (see Exhibit 11.4). Diversification into both areas, which leverages management expertise into apparently countercyclical businesses, is one of the most prudent methods of guaranteeing stable cash flows.

Another dramatic change in the lending activities of finance companies was the move away from the unsecured personal loan business toward real estate-secured lending. In mid-1975, real estate-secured loans represented slightly more than two percent of total finance company loans; by April 1985, that share had risen to 10 percent. When the market is restricted to loans to individuals, fully one-fifth of finance companies' cumulative lending is real estate-secured.

The "move to security" was motivated by two forces. The first, mentioned earlier, was the explosion of losses on unsecured borrowers following the passage of the Bankruptcy Reform Act of 1978. The second force was the rapid growth of real estate equity during the high inflation period of 1970–1979. Consumers quickly discovered that an equity-secured loan had become a relatively inexpensive way to finance consumption needs.

Funding Policies

An important source of funds for finance companies is commercial paper. In fact, these institutions issued about 70 percent of all commercial paper offered in 1984. This funding emphasis can have significant implications for financial strategy. For example, some finance companies have strategically restricted their leverage ratio to protect their high credit rating and their ability to raise capital at the most

Exhibit 11.4 Gross Receivables at Finance Companies

	Dollars[a]			Percentage Change			Share of Total (percent)		
Type	Mid–1975	Mid–1980	Apr–1985	1970–1975	1975–1980	1980–1985	Mid–1975	Mid–1980	Apr–1985
Consumer	40.0	77.3	101.3	28.5	89.3	31.0	47.5	42.1	37.2
Business	39.3	86.1	143.3	70.8	119.1	66.4	45.7	46.9	52.7
Real Estate	1.9	11.8	27.5	n.a.	n.a.	133.1	2.3	6.5	10.1
Other	3.9	8.2	n.a.	68.6	107.3	n.a.	4.6	4.5	n.a.
Total	86.0	183.3	272.1	50.6	113.2	48.4	100.0	100.0	100.0

Source: Federal Reserve Board.
[a] Figures in $ billions.

advantageous rates in the commercial paper market. Although bank loans also represent an important source of funds (especially for small finance companies), the finance companies are becoming proportionately less reliant on this source of funds—as they must if they are to survive (see Exhibit 11.5).

Business Strategy

Major finance companies anticipated banks' entry into a national market for consumer financial services, and tried to realize the value of their nationwide branch network. Their strategy was to position themselves in bank markets through the acquisition of thrift institutions and the establishment of nonbank banks. The largest firms, such as Household International, Beneficial Corp., Avco Corp., Lowes Corp., and Transamerica, now compete with banks in most product areas. Indeed, they are able to offer some products, such as insurance, that banks cannot sell. Some bankers view the ability of these diversified financial firms to sell insurance as a major competitive disadvantage for the banking industry, and some objective observers (for example, Rosenblum) agree.[4] Nonetheless, finance companies' higher cost of funds puts them at a distinct disadvantage to banks. Thus, a major thrust of finance company strategy has been to reduce operating costs. In this regard, there is much catching up left to do.

One important way to become competitive with banks has simply been to get bigger. Consolidation of the finance industry has proceeded at a steady pace since 1960. At that time, 6424 finance companies were in existence and 87 percent held receivables of less than $1 million (see Exhibit 11.6). By the end of 1980, only 2775 finance companies were in operation. Of these, firms with more than $25 million in receivables made up 11 percent of all finance companies. Yet this top tier held fully 97 percent of all consumer receivables—and 98 percent of all business receivables held by finance companies.[5]

Relatively speaking, the growth strategy has been successful. The operating

Exhibit 11.5 Liabilities and Capital Outstanding at Finance Companies

	June 1980	April 1985
Loans and notes payable to banks	$ 15,458	$ 18,648[a]
Commercial paper	52,328	81,189
Other short-term debt	10,627	
Other long-term debt	52,898	172,291
All other liabilities	18,363	
Capital and surplus	25,350	
	$175,025	$272,128

Source: Federal Reserve Board.
[a] Figures in $ millions.

Exhibit 11.6 Number of Finance Companies by Size

Size of company, by consumer and business loans outstanding	1960	1975	1980[a]
Under $1 million	5546	2482	1749
$1-5 million	631	500	484
$6-100 million	220	306	395
Over $100 million	27	88	148
Total	6424	3376	2776

Source: Federal Reserve Board.
[a] As of June 30 each year.

expense ratios of the largest finance companies are barely half those of the smallest, while return on equity is almost 3.5 percent higher (see Exhibit 11.7). But when the results of individual giants are stacked up against the performance of the real competition—banks—the situation is often bleaker. In the first half of 1985, Citicorp earned 15 percent on equity, Barnett Bank earned 17.5 percent, and J.P. Morgan and Co. earned 15.3 percent, while Household earned 14.2 percent and Beneficial earned 12.2 percent. General Electric Credit Corporation, a notable exception among finance companies, provided a 20 percent return to its parent.

Managements at the larger finance companies have long recognized the difficulty of battling commercial banks on unequal ground and have therefore often

Exhibit 11.7 Expense and Net Income: 1983

	All Reporting Companies	Companies with Receivables of $1 Billion or more	Companies with Receivables of less than $1 Billion
Total operating expenses as percent of gross income	31.5%	30.8%	43.5%
Net income as percent of gross income	13.1	13.3	11.2
Noninterest operating expenses as percent of year-end assets	4.5	4.4	8.7
Net income as percent of year-end equity	17.8	18.1	13.7

Source: American Financial Services Association.

diversified their operations as they grew. The diversification routes followed have been quite dissimilar, however, reflecting the differences in strategies of the finance giants. A quick look at three of these—Household International, Beneficial Corporation, and General Electric Credit Corporation—will give a rough idea of the possibilities. Household and Beneficial diversified out of financial services in the 1960s and 1970s, but are both now retrenching in this area. General Electric Credit stayed closer to its core business, but has also closed ranks somewhat in recent years.

Household has acquired savings and loan associations and industrial banks to broaden the range of financial services it offered to middle-income Americans. Currently, the firm offers checking and savings accounts, loans for education, first mortgages, credit cards, and electronic funds transfer services in addition to unsecured personal loans and second mortgage loans. In 1979, Household bought receivables from Chrysler Financial. Two-thirds of these receivables were retail accounts, and one-third were dealer accounts. Beneficial, also anticipating deregulation of the financial markets and interstate banking, bought two savings and loan associations in Texas in 1979 and 1981. Then, in 1983, Beneficial established the Bencharge Credit Service to provide large-ticket retailers with a private label revolving credit program.

Household is today a much more diversified company than Beneficial. In 1983, Household comprised 43 companies in four industry groupings. Management at that time predicted future distribution of earnings from the four groups to be 40 percent from financial services, 25 percent from merchandising, 25 percent from manufacturing, and 10 percent from transportation.[6] However, in 1985 they divested their merchandising business.

The management of Beneficial, on the other hand, thought that growth of finance companies in a deregulated environment would be hampered by nonfinancial businesses, since debt-rating agencies discourage heavy borrowing by companies that mix finance with manufacturing or retailing. And to compete with banks that had very high leverage ratios, management at Beneficial believed that finance companies would need to convert to high leverage ratios. Beneficial therefore sold its Western Auto and Spiegal operations, which had contributed over a quarter of Beneficial's sales, and reverted to an exclusive focus on financial services.

General Electric Credit Corporation had quite different origins, as the financial services subsidiary of General Electric Company. Diversifying within financial services, General Electric Credit has become a dominant force in the industrial and equipment leasing segment of financial markets, with almost three times the lease receivables of the next largest competitor. In 1984, the corporation embarked on a search for profitable financial businesses to house in a new holding company, General Electric Financial Services Corp. Its traditional specialty of loans to small and medium-sized businesses had become crowded with banks and other industrial companies' finance subsidiaries, and the resulting competition had cut margins substantially. As GECC deemphasized its traditional commercial business, it also withdrew from direct consumer lending, mortgage banking, and mobile home finance in 1984. Today, GECC's commercial real-estate financing is developing rapidly, while another profitable niche is providing financing in leveraged buy-out situations.

General Electric Credit maintains a low leverage position: an asset/equity ratio of eight as compared with banks' range of 14 to 20. The philosophy of the corporation is that this low leverage position has two strategic implications: General Electric Credit must find financial product markets where the level of competition is low, and the corporation should serve those markets until competition becomes excessively intense.

FUTURE

The presence of intense competition in the changing financial services industry bodes well for improvements in the efficiency of consumer and small business loan markets. However, it forces finance companies to abandon strategies that were once well adapted, replacing them with new ones suited to developing conditions. The foregoing examination shows much diversity in strategy among the largest competitors, yet one basic conclusion can be ventured: Finance companies have to break with their pasts. Basically there are three options. Either finance companies can become quick on their feet, staying one step ahead of competition; they can diversify away from traditional finance operations; or they can become more like banks. Remaining essentially a "lender of last resort" is no longer viable.

Like it or not, finance companies are already out of their traditional business. Consumer finance companies were largely in the business of making debt consolidation loans in 1973, with 46 percent of their loans made for that purpose. In sharp contrast the recent figure, for 1983, is only 20 percent. This drastic shift away from high-interest loans makes tight control of operating expenses critical. All three major companies examined previously have recognized this fact, and acted.

In 1982, both Household and Beneficial reduced the number of their offices in operation and reduced branch office employees by a significant percentage. Beneficial reported having reduced noninterest operating expenses/receivables to 4 percent from 4.5 percent in 1982. At General Electric Credit Corporation, noninterest expense as a percentage of assets was pushed down from 4 percent in 1979 to 3 percent in 1984, revealing control of overhead expenses as one of General Electric Credit's basic strengths. Commercial banks of all sizes were already well below 4 percent by 1983, when Federal Reserve figures showed their total noninterest operating expenses in the installment loan function ranging from 3.8 percent down to 3.5 percent of outstandings.[7] The roughly comparable figure for a sample of finance companies was 4.7 percent of total receivables.[8] Tellingly, companies with less than $1 billion in receivables reported an average operating expense ratio of 8.7 percent.

The leverage issue is one that each institution must resolve for itself, and the issue is pivotal. Finance companies do not have as much leverage as commercial banks, a factor that restricts their ability to compete in product markets where slim margins are the rule. The industry average leverage ratio for finance companies in 1980 was six (total debt/capital plus surplus). For commercial banks, it was between 14 and 20.

To offset their cost of funds disadvantage, successful finance companies that do not convert to a bank charter will avoid markets where financial products are viewed as commodities. There are more terms in a loan contract than the annual percentage rate (APR). Surveys of consumers and small-business borrowers show that "availability" of credit is frequently more important than cost of credit. Finance companies have been quite successful at attracting customers to pay higher APRs in return for quicker loan processing, and more lenient terms on loan rescheduling. Profitable finance companies will stay with that strategy.

Experience at evaluating low-probability events, coupled with a knowledge of the severity and duration of cycles in old and new industries, is critical to the profitability of all lenders and to finance companies especially. The lender's role is to make a realistic assessment of the probability of default and the net worth position of borrowers and to price credit accordingly. Finance companies can achieve success in new markets by applying their strengths to new lending activities. For example, the financial affiliate of a manufacturing company may be able to use information collected by the parent, placing it at an advantage in evaluating risk in industries related to the parent's. More generally, finance companies have to make the most of their well-honed skills in managing the credit risks of less financially steady borrowers.

By now it should be apparent that in the coming years finance companies will need one resource badly, and that is depth and breadth of management skill. Although financial services managers are well versed in their field, the industry has not always attracted the best and brightest. Brilliance was not needed to make money in what was once a protected business. But the financial services industry is more like most other businesses now. It offers few protections from competition. Financial products have taken on the aspect of commodities, rather than unique services. And all competitors are paying market (deregulated) prices for inputs to their product.

In the area of business development, managers must formulate strategies and diversification efforts to move their companies forward. In the area of business control, management must maintain a tight rein on the growth of new areas of business. Cost control and growth in profitable activities has become much more important than growth of assets. In the provision of financial services, researchers have found limited economies of scale. On the other hand, they suspect that considerable economies of scope, the result of broadening an office's array of services, can be attained. The catch is that successful management of a broad array of products requires an entrepreneurial spirit in addition to sharp administrative skills. Finance companies are relatively strong on administration. However, their willingness to try new approaches will need further development.

Well-directed reorganization may help stimulate a spirit of enterprise. Successful firms do not operate as monoliths. Most exhibit few management layers, few executive privileges, and a strong commitment to employee training. They emphasize careful selection of employees and establish working channels of communication between management, employees, and customers alike. These are not, generally speaking, characteristics of firms providing financial services. They must be, however, if these firms are to survive.

NOTES

1. Sullivan, A.C. "Competition in the Market for Consumer Loans." *Journal of Economics and Business* (February 1984) 36, pp. 141–149.
2. Johnson, R.W., and A.C. Sullivan. "Segmentation of the Consumer Loan Market." *Journal of Retail Banking* (September 1981) Vol. 3, No. 3, pp. 1–7.
3. Stover, Roger D. "A Re-Examination of Bank Holding Company Acquisitions." *Journal of Bank Research* (Summer 1982) Vol. 3, No. 2, pp. 101–108.
4. Pavel, C., and H. Rosenblum. "Banks and Non-banks: The Horse Race Continues." *Economic Perspectives*. Federal Reserve Bank of Chicago (May–June 1985) Vol 9, pp. 3–17.
5. "Survey of Finance Companies 1980." *Federal Reserve Bulletin* (May 1981) pp. 398–409.
6. Editor's note: on October 22, 1985, Household International announced the sale of its merchandising business to an investor group. Donald C. Clark, Household's chairman, stated publicly that, "They approached us; we have no intention of selling. . . . It seemed to us that it was an opportunity to maximize the value of a subsidiary for our shareholders and concentrate on our other three businesses." Chicago *Tribune*, October 23, 1985.
7. *Functional Cost Analysis 1983 Average Banks*. Federal Reserve Board.
8. *Finance Companies in 1983*. American Financial Services Association Research Report and Second Mortgage Lending Report.

PART 2 MANAGING FOR SUCCESS

SECTION 3 THE MARKETING OF FINANCIAL SERVICES

Understanding the changes occurring in financial services and in the fundamental economics of the businesses is a necessary, but insufficient, condition for success. Financial services executives must also develop themselves and their organizations into effective marketers and managers of technology. Implicit in both these skills is becoming more effective in the art of general management. This section of the Handbook discusses various ways to become more effective marketers. Sections 4 and 5 cover technology and general management.

Over the past decade, it has been fashionable within the financial services sector to talk about becoming "marketing oriented." And certainly, becoming a good marketer will require a major shift in attitudes for most institutions. But has anything really changed? The truth is that all too often little has changed. In some institutions, however, dramatic changes have occurred. The question is, why have these few institutions recognized the need for change and embraced the marketing orientation?

First of all, successful firms have recognized that customers are fast becoming more sophisticated, and that the industry's traditional product orientation cannot respond to this change. No longer can the industry simply produce whatever it is capable of producing, and then offer the product unmodified to customers. That practice may have worked well within a regulated environment, but with the relaxing of controls it was no longer viable. Successful firms saw that products and services had to be expressly designed to meet customer needs.

Another differentiating factor in successful institutions is that their line divisions have accepted marketing as a way of life. Even when the resources of a strong centralized marketing function exist, the line division feels a sense of ownership and takes responsibility for its customers' welfare. By contrast, institutions that have been less successful typically have marketing plans that were developed independently by the marketing department. As a consequence of this black-box approach, the marketing department often has a difficult time persuading others to take ownership.

A third reason why the marketing orientation has had a major impact in some institutions is the credibility of market research. Managers who understand the value and limitations of research data are committed to high-quality research to assess changes in buying patterns, desired product attributes, and competitive position as well as a variety of other market characteristics and needs.

The authors in this section describe the key role that marketing plays and will continue to play in the future of financial services. In Chapter 12, John Steffens describes a spectacular success story in the marketing of consumer financial services. The case is based on personal experience with the development of the Cash Management Account—Launny is president of Merrill Lynch Consumer—and may provide a useful model for other firms to follow. In Chapter 13, Christopher Lovelock, a leading professor and consultant in service marketing and a long-time faculty member at the Harvard Business School, provides an overview of the key elements of marketing financial services in the corporate arena. James Smith and Philip Wilson provide practitioners' viewpoints on marketing corporate financial services in Chapter 14. Both now serve in top-level marketing capacities, Jim at Marine Midland Bank and Phil at Bankers Trust. In Chapter 15, Eileen Friars, William Gregor, Lucile Reid (all officers of the MAC Group), and Mark Johnson (Senior Associate in the MAC Group) describe how distribution systems are evolving with the changes in industry structure. In Chapter 16, Ralph Kimball, also of the MAC Group, and Rowland Moriarty, of the Harvard Business School, discuss the importance of relationship management, the necessary equation. Finally, in Chapter 17, William Schrempf describes the challenge of international marketing. Bill has practiced marketing throughout his executive career, which has included senior positions at Johnson and Johnson, CIGNA, and now Teledyne, where he is President of the Property and Casualty Insurance Group.

Readers will find that each of the authors keeps returning to "the customer" and insisting on the importance of heeding customer wishes. This unanimity is by no means a coincidence. Customers are the ultimate decision makers. It is they who will choose with their dollars the losers and winners in the evolving financial services industry.

12 The Marketing of Consumer Financial Services

JOHN L. STEFFENS

The financial services industry has rapidly evolved into a business far different from what it was just a decade, let alone a century, ago. Over the last 20-odd years, an individual could have worked for the same firm on Wall Street and have told his friends that first he worked for a stockbroker, then a securities firm, after that an investment firm, and most recently, a financial services firm. And all the time he would have been working for the same company. For example, the sign outside the door at Merrill Lynch has always said "Merrill Lynch," but the structure and strategy inside have changed significantly.

Many observers refer to this transformation as the cash management revolution. In the same breath they cite the Merrill Lynch Cash Management Account (CMA) financial service as an explosive volley in the battle for consumers' minds and investment dollars that is now being contested on a broad competitive front. This chapter describes Merrill Lynch's success in developing and marketing the CMA to the consumer. Specifically, the chapter examines how this brokerage firm reassessed the nature of the financial service market for consumers, and then proceeded to develop a product to meet the needs of its customers. While there have obviously been other success stories in financial services, the one described here provides a model which may be useful to other institutions as they consider marketing strategies for a variety of consumer financial services.

Deregulation, and before that, the skirting of regulation, have played major roles in creating turbulence within financial services.

Deregulation swamped the investment market with new competitors. Competition squeezed profits and margins began to erode. At the same time, many traditional securities firms discovered that success demanded ever-increasing capital infusions—an investment not all had the power to make or could afford to risk. The financial services business was becoming one where success was never final, but failure—given the capital requirements—could often be fatal. Consequently, while the competition intensified there was a steady decline in the number of competitors. Moreover, this trend is likely to continue: Some observers feel that the current 50,000 purveyors of investment advice and services could drop 50 percent by the early 1990s. But while there will likely be a sizable contraction in the number of entities providing financial services, the quantity as well as quality of available services is expected to increase substantially.

That is because emerging mega-institutions, with nationwide networks of trained professionals offering a wide variety of financial counsel in one or a few service areas, are well capitalized and highly automated. Some in the industry would argue that these octopuses have already made the transition to genuinely full-range "financial services" providers and are spreading their tentacles at a rapid pace. Today, Merrill Lynch and others (Sears, Prudential, Equitable, American Express, and Citicorp, to name just a few) are clearly establishing their credentials in the "mega" category. Others, entering slowly but cutting big paths as they do, include such giants as General Motors and General Electric. And not to be overlooked is Japan's Nomura Securities with its growing beachhead in the United States. Each of these companies is unveiling a strategy for expanding its own financial services business. All are beginning to target markets and to communicate with their audience.

Sears, through its financial network of Dean Witter, Allstate, and Coldwell Banker, appears to be targeting its traditional customer, perhaps hoping that middle-class Americans will transfer their trust in the long-established retail relationship to the Sears financial relationship. American Express, on the other hand, is letting each of its financial services group members approach their own markets; cross-pollination is minimal. Emphases at American Express range from a targeting of the middle-class by Investors Diversified Services to a gathering of assets from the upscale market by Shearson. Citibank for its part is spreading nationwide, crossing borders with the aid of technology when the alternatives are limited by law. BankAmerica, the first banking company to go after a discount brokerage firm, is finding Charles Schwab & Co. to be one of its most profitable operations.

It was with a vision of this competitive market ahead that Merrill Lynch began to develop its strategy back in the 1970s. It began with questions, with research, with a look at Merrill Lynch's existing customer base, and with an eye to the potential for adding new customers. New competition was also examined. In a broad sense the strategy that evolved, and which continues to evolve, presumes that success depends on Merrill Lynch's ability to establish and maintain long-term relationships with a targeted group of clients. It also places a great deal of emphasis on what management feels is a demand by these customers for personal service from a professionally trained person. This strategy is widely referred to as being "all things to some people."

In Merrill Lynch's research, it was found that a small fraction of clients provided most of the firm's revenues. Other research confirmed that such disproportionate contribution is not unique to the securities business; it holds true for every other sector of the financial services industry as well. The rule of thumb, "80 percent of business comes from 20 percent of clients," is highly applicable. Moreover, in financial services there is tremendous overlap among clients. Merrill Lynch's "best" clients tend also to be the best clients of banks and insurance companies. Therefore, the goal was to find ways to induce Merrill Lynch's best customers to loosen their relationships with bankers, insurance agents, and other financial representatives. These customers included a significant share of the nation's most affluent households, which account for a large portion of the total expenditures on financial services in the United States. When this group is the target, the rewards for being "all things for some people" can be quite dramatic.

Getting to know these potential key clients early in the game is extremely important. Some institutions forget that. But one can't be a narrow-minded elitist in the brokerage business; new clients have to come from somewhere. Often they come from the ranks of those who are just beginning their savings career.

A related fact gave this point particular urgency for Merrill Lynch and other brokerage firms: Most households consume the products of nonbrokerage financial competitors' lines *before* they begin to invest. Notably, for instance, most young families buy houses and life insurance before they think of stocks. While Merrill Lynch's best clients were and are typically in their late forties, the average American family spends significant sums on mortgages and insurance much earlier in its life cycle. With baby boomers just beginning to settle down with families during the late 1970s, the "business as usual" brokerage firm was going to miss out if it waited for this group to reach its earnings potential. The firm therefore set out to meet the financial needs of these young people before they entered the affluent segment that Merrill Lynch was targeting. Nothing secret about this approach—in fact, banks and insurance companies are increasing their efforts to expand their products and services, with objectives similar to those of Merrill Lynch.

Two characteristics of both top clients and high-potential prospects suggested inviting opportunities to Merrill Lynch management. First, these people are busy, and so they value convenience. Second, they are accustomed to paying well for quality services. Clearly, to succeed with them meant doing certain things better, such as identifying the clients most worth reaching, carefully determining their needs, and developing products to meet those needs. But the key was to provide them with comprehensive, innovative solutions to their financial problems. Merrill Lynch had to create packages of services that offered so much value-added that clients would be induced to move their business. These packages would provide day-to-day convenience and truly sophisticated financial advice. Management viewed the latter—sophisticated advice—as crucial. The focus of Merrill Lynch's efforts therefore became the relationship between the client and the financial consultant.

In the competitive arena of major financial services organizations Merrill Lynch had, in addition to its franchise in the upscale market, a second formidable strength: a nationwide sales force experienced and successful at providing personal financial advice. To capitalize on these strengths, it was felt that Merrill

Lynch's financial consultants would have to be able to tailor their approaches, using a variety of products and services to meet the specific needs of each client. The firm's consultants had to become highly skilled financial planners and advisers—not product pushers.

The task of making the transition from brokers to planners was complicated by the fact that many of these products would extend beyond the traditional range of the brokerage business. In training its representatives to be the genuine financial planners they had to be, Merrill Lynch began by establishing a clear set of values, and distilled these into the following list of business principles:

- The interests of our clients must come first.
- We are committed to innovation as a way of life.
- Our products and services will be of the highest quality and will be marketed with a consistent overall strategy.
- Our employees are our most important asset.
- Maintaining our profitability and a fair return to our shareholders is essential.
- We are always fair competitors and never denigrate other firms.
- Integrity and honesty are at the heart of our business.

The Cash Management Account (CMA)

Introduction of the Cash Management Account, often called the opening volley in the financial revolution, actually started out quietly. In an age of high-tech the CMA was first conceived in mundane, age-old fashion by forward-thinking individuals using market research. Ultimately it was born of hard work, innovative technology, and luck. As with any significant innovation the concept, once grasped, seemed childishly simple. But making it work wasn't simple at all.

Thursday, May 1, 1975 marked the end of fixed commissions for all equity and bond transactions. Known on Wall Street as May Day, it increased the momentum of a relentless consumer movement and signalled that the good old days of putting a product on the table with a take-it-or-leave-it attitude were over.

Wall Street received this signal slowly and reluctantly. But some firms soon began adjusting. Merrill Lynch was one that realized it had to offer the product and price the consumer wanted, otherwise there would be no sale. Its Chairman, Donald T. Regan, was an early advocate of deregulation (Regan would later become Secretary of the Treasury and then White House Chief of Staff). At Regan's direction, the firm commissioned an in-depth survey by the Stanford Research Institute (now SRI) to discover what the market wanted most in financial services. SRI's questions identified four basic needs that investors and prospective investors have:

- Easy and quick access to their money

- Increased credit availability when necessary
- Assurance that their money is working for them at all times
- Consolidated information about their financial situation

To meet these needs, Merrill Lynch began with the traditional brokerage margin account. Three other services were then added. These were: (1) a money market fund; (2) a checking account; and (3) a Visa debit card. At this point Merrill Lynch had four services on the table. What was needed were the links to put the parts together. These links would come in the form of computer hardware, software, and related organizational systems. With a nothing-is-impossible attitude, Merrill's systems professionals created the necessary systems and software. Although the computer apparatus, designed and later patented by Merrill Lynch, created some headaches at first, after a few years of research and development, it met Merrill Lynch's high standard. The new account based on this system, the Cash Management Account, was truly more than the sum of its parts. It was a whole new way of managing assets. It promised to change the way people managed their financial lives.

CMA was packaged for convenience. The customer received a brokerage account with a margin capability, a choice of four money market funds (from the original money fund to a tax-exempt fund), government securities, and an insured savings account. He had access to his money via a checking account or a Visa debit card, a service made possible through Merrill Lynch's affiliation with Bank One of Ohio. He could also conveniently make deposits by mail. He had the prestige of Merrill Lynch. And, most important, he had a relationship with a Merrill Lynch financial consultant.

When Merrill Lynch looked at pricing with its affluent customer base in mind, the firm decided to make CMA a premier-priced product. Marketers established a high initial entry requirement ($20,000 in cash, securities, or combination of both) and an annual fee of $28. In 1982 the fee was increased to $30, in 1983 to $50, and in 1986 to $65. Each increase was justified by specific product improvements that provided increased customer benefits. The small cancellation rate after each increase suggests that customers agreed.

Once packaged and priced, the CMA still had to be promoted and distributed. But before it could be marketed to the public, it had to demonstrate its value to Merrill's financial consultants. The consultants were reluctant to embrace CMA, an understandable feeling as they earned not one penny for opening an account. Fortunately, however, once they worked with the account and realized it was a simple, easy way to gather more assets from a customer or a new prospect for future investment they became CMA's strongest advocates.

Promotion and distribution of CMA was handled conservatively. There were three reasons for this restrained approach. First, the public had to be educated in the use of this new product, and that would take time. Merrill Lynch management reasoned that to learn how to instruct customers it would be best to proceed gradually, one or two steps at a time. In this way, improvements could be made easily at each step. Second, Merrill Lynch wanted to verify that its systems performed as predicted when the work volume increased. The product had to be free of major defects—otherwise it would be dropped. Third, Merrill Lynch knew there would be major legal hurdles, especially from banking interests. Banks were apt to view the CMA as a direct attack on territory they felt the Glass-Steagall Act had clearly staked out as theirs.

Educating the public and testing systems were time-consuming processes. Establishing the legal basis to offer the product was also time-consuming, and more. Merrill Lynch moved carefully, using public relations to soften the resistance. In the end, even the toughest legislators were swayed by the realization that CMA provided a real benefit and was demanded by consumers. Just as no one could turn back the tide created by May Day, no one could or would deny consumers their opportunity to manage their money better and more conveniently. Of course, the high inflation of this period, which made money funds a hot product, was also a major contributor to government approval as well.

Despite all efforts, market success came slowly. Four months after CMA's introduction, Merrill Lynch had a mere 350 accounts. A full year later, customers still numbered only 4000. A year after that however, the figure was 52,000. Then in 1980 Merrill Lynch more than tripled the previous year's total and momentum took hold. By the end of 1983 accounts had topped 1 million.

As this article is written, in early 1986, the total stands at 1,300,000 accounts, with nearly $80 billion in assets. The average client's assets are approximately $70,000. The financial profile of these customers is indeed affluent. More than half have a net worth of over $250,000, and almost a quarter have a net worth of $500,000 or more. About half earn $50,000 a year or more. About a quarter earn $75,000 or more. As to their personal profiles, over three-fourths are over 45 years old, and more than half are over 55. Sixty-nine percent are college graduates. What is most important in this context, though, is that the CMA customer generates three times as much revenue as does a customer with one of Merrill Lynch's traditional brokerage accounts.

Since 1977 a lot has changed. Some changes are visible, some less. Those who directed CMA were never satisfied. They constantly strove for better software, a more precise statement, new and more useful features. Modifications were made to benefit the customer and often in response to customer requests. Initially there was only one money market fund. Three were added to address different needs of different customer segments. Later, insurance protection to $10 million was added, as was a direct deposit feature for social security and payroll checks. A toll-free 800 number was also introduced, and still later, access to automatic teller machines.

There were also product line extensions. If the CMA was good for individuals, it might well be good for business. So Merrill Lynch brought out Business CMA, a cash management account designed to serve the special needs of commercial enterprises. Business CMA was followed by a CMA for pension and profit-sharing plans, and by an International CMA. In 1985, Merrill Lynch began testing the Working Capital Management Account, or WCMA, a Business CMA with a line of credit designed for small corporations and businesses. Recently

Merrill Lynch has introduced its latest CMA-related account, called "Capital Builder" (CBA), which was tested nationwide for nearly 18 months, as was the CMA.

Capital Builder was targeted at the market composed of emerging investors, a group that many in the industry felt was substantial but hard to approach. CBA was designed with a lower initial entry requirement of $5,000. Also, unlike CMA it offered fewer money fund options and charged for some transactions, in addition to assessing an annual fee of $40. Merrill Lynch's financial consultants are enthusiastic about CBA, and the consumer market appears responsive even before heavy promotion begins. In fact, over 50 percent of CBA accounts opened thus far involved people who previously had done no business with Merrill Lynch. What is more, the business they are doing is highly attractive.

After CBA? Merrill Lynch does not believe it has saturated the market for CMA, so the firm is continuing to promote it heavily, in spite of at least 14 competitors who now offer similar, central assets accounts. Merrill Lynch is slowly moving pieces of the processing and all of the debit card issuing into its own *de novo* bank, both to ensure quality and to capture more of the revenues.

CONCLUSION

Where does Merrill Lynch go from here? Who knows. The *Economist* magazine may have set the direction for the industry a while ago when it said "in financial services, you either innovate or die." In the 1970s, it was the consumer who led the revolt against inflation, against low-yielding savings vehicles, against cumbersome and fragmented delivery systems. In the 1990s the cash management revolution will continue, and the consumer will be both the driving force and the beneficiary.

You can't sit still in a tornado. At Merrill Lynch, management has learned you can't sit still in an industry as volatile as this one either. Change is the only constant, and it drives everything we do.

13 Marketing Corporate Financial Services

CHRISTOPHER H. LOVELOCK

The 1980s will be seen in retrospect as the decade during which marketing became an integral management function within the financial services industry. As in many other industries, expertise in consumer marketing has preceded the development of corporate and institutional marketing efforts. Sophisticated consumer marketing efforts can be seen in strong industry players such as Citicorp, Merrill Lynch, and American Express. Now the pressure is on to develop an equally strong marketing orientation within corporate financial services.

Corporate financial services fall into two broad categories. There are services designed for consumption by corporations and other institutions, and there are services designed for retail consumption which are sold in wholesale volumes to retail intermediaries, which then resell them to individuals and households. Some of the key factors differentiating corporate from retail marketing include: much larger and more frequent transactions; more individuals involved in influencing and making purchase decisions; and relatively more rational and less emotional decision-making criteria. As a result, the development of a marketing orientation by suppliers of corporate financial services will produce strategies and tactics that are very different from those practiced in the market for retail financial services.

SCOPE OF THE CHAPTER

This chapter begins by reviewing briefly the factors that are driving change in the corporate financial services. These include international developments, electronic technology, evolving customer expectations, and deregulation. All of these factors have contributed significantly toward creation of much greater competition in corporate financial service markets. New players have entered, many existing players have merged or redeployed their resources, and customers have become more sophisticated and demanding; hence the emphasis on marketing as a key functional element in competitive strategy.

The chapter continues by outlining a marketing perspective that can be applied to corporate financial services. It then turns the spotlight on the key tools of marketing management and the elements of the marketing mix. The balance of the chapter is devoted to competitive positioning strategy. A good understanding of these topics can provide insights into how to answer several key questions facing providers of corporate financial services, such as: How can a financial services firm compete effectively in today's fast changing environment? In particular, what types of customers should it seek to attract and retain? What specific services should it offer each of these target segments? How should the firm distinguish its services from those of the competition?

THE CHANGING CORPORATE FINANCIAL SERVICES ENVIRONMENT

The development of marketing strategy starts with a review of a firm's environment. The strategist must ask what external forces are shaping the size and composition of the corporate financial services marketplace, the nature of competition, and the ways of doing business. Some of the key forces for change are described below in broad-brush terms; their specific implications will naturally vary from firm to firm.

Changing Client Expectations

Corporate clients have become increasingly sophisticated in recent years, especially in larger firms. Capital-raising clients are more aware of the alternatives open to them, institutional investors have become more aggressive, and the corporate treasurers of today tend to be better informed and more demanding than their predecessors. An excellent example of changing client expectations was manifest in the changing competitive environment for corporate securities underwriting following the establishment of 415 shelf registration. As a result of regulatory changes, major corporations have been able to "self-service" their securities underwriting needs. Thus, the major underwriters have experienced significant declines in their underwriting commissions. As will be shown later, these trends have created an environment in which many clients—although not all—value performance above relationships.

Advances in Electronic Technology

Modern technology has had a remarkable impact on the ways in which financial service firms do business. During the 1970s it led to the creation of new products, such as electronic cash management and treasury management systems. At the same time, it began to open up new channels for the distribution of corporate financial services. Since the arrival of commercial satellite communications, financial and informational data can be transmitted around the globe within seconds.

Innovative financial service firms have recognized the value to customers of providing real-time access to both financial information and their major transaction accounts. Today a significant proportion of corporate banking activities is carried out from computer terminals in the offices of corporate treasurers. Even the small business owner is realizing significant advantages from this technological revolution in the market for corporate financial services. Chemical Bank has introduced a personal/computer-based banking product specifically for small businesses.

The development of new technologically oriented products and distribution systems has also created an important opportunity for banks to develop the fee-based income necessary to replace declining net interest income. Investments in computer technology were initially based on the need for rapid data processing, improved documentation, and quality control. Many institutions are now attempting to pursue the opportunities for competitive advantage available through the application of computer technology. The development of new products, the creation of research data bases used to identify opportunities for cross-selling additional services to existing clients, and the automation of back-office operations to reduce operating costs, are all examples of how financial services firms are seeking to harness technology to better serve their corporate customers.

International Developments

The growth of international trade, the move to flexible exchange rates, the removal of foreign exchange controls in many countries, and the advent of global electronic funds networks, are combining to create a global financial market. Although the Euromarkets were seen as a minor and temporary phenomenon by many observers during the mid-1960s, they have evolved into a large and permanent "supra-national" market which falls outside the jurisdiction of the Glass-Steagall Act. The linkage of the various national capital markets with the Euromarkets, accompanied by aggressive arbitrage on rates and terms, have established money as a truly fungible commodity whose movements around the world are increasingly difficult to regulate.

Many financial institutions have long operated on an international scale, and this is especially true of British and U.S. firms. But the pace of international operations has accelerated in recent years. More and more financial service firms have opened branches in countries where they previously had limited representation or none at all. For instance, by 1980 there were 76 foreign bank branches in New York City. Five years later the number of foreign banks in New York City stood at over 125. The total number of foreign bank offices in the United States now exceeds 900. In the United States, competition is intensifying as international banks become "domesticated," seeking corporate (or retail) business locally in addition to serving the needs of existing clients from their home countries. Foreign bank expansion into the United States has also resulted in a number of notable acquisitions of U.S. banks, including Hong Kong & Shanghai Banking Corporation's acquisition of Marine Midland, Allied Irish Banks' acquisition of

First Maryland Bancorp, and Midland Bank's acquisition of Crocker. Not all these acquisitions have proven equally successful, as evidenced by Midland Bank's subsequent resale of Crocker to Wells Fargo.

Multinational corporations (MNCs) have both stimulated and capitalized on the globalization of money markets and financial networks. During the early 1970s, MNCs greatly expanded the number of their banking relationships. But as the decade progressed, they began to handle their banking relationships on an increasingly competitive basis. In 1980, Greenwich Research Associates' survey on European multinational banking showed that the typical MNC had relationships with 19 banks but did the bulk of its business with just seven key banks. Paralleling the increasing performance orientation of U.S. domestic corporate banking relationships, more recent survey data suggests that the typical MNC today has over 22 banking relationships, and considers eight banks to be of principal importance to it, but makes all buying decisions based on competitive assessments.

Deregulation

In recent years, changes in government regulations have substantially reshaped several major service industries. The air, truck, and rail freight, passenger airlines, telecommunications, and financial services industries have all undergone dramatic change as the result of deregulation. In each instance, reduced regulation has sharpened competition by allowing new players to enter markets for once-protected product categories, and by enabling some existing players to expand their geographic scope of operations. Deregulation has also permitted greater pricing flexibility, thereby forcing many firms to choose between competing on price as the low-cost producer and competing on added benefits as a higher-cost producer.

"Deregulation" is perhaps too sweeping a term to describe what is going on in the financial services industry, since many state and federal restrictions remain in force. Moreover, these regulations apply unequally, with banks typically being more constrained than insurance, brokerage, and credit card companies. Electronic distribution networks and the "nonbank" status enjoyed by many financial service providers allow many players in this industry to make an end-run around certain current regulations. Equally important from the perspective of commercial banks, industry participants are increasingly finding ways of penetrating the so-called "chinese wall" created by the 1933 Glass-Steagall Act. The entry of commercial banks into securities underwriting and dealing will place competitive pressure on the investment banking industry equal to that experienced by the banks with the expansion of the commercial paper market during the 1970s.

The net result has been a steady erosion of the barriers that once divided financial service providers into several discrete segments. The resulting opportunities for expansion fall into three broad categories: new products, new geographic markets within the United States, and new customer groups (see Exhibit 13.1). The marketing challenge lies in selecting only those routes for expansion that best

Exhibit 13.1 Expansion Opportunities in the Market for Corporate Financial Services

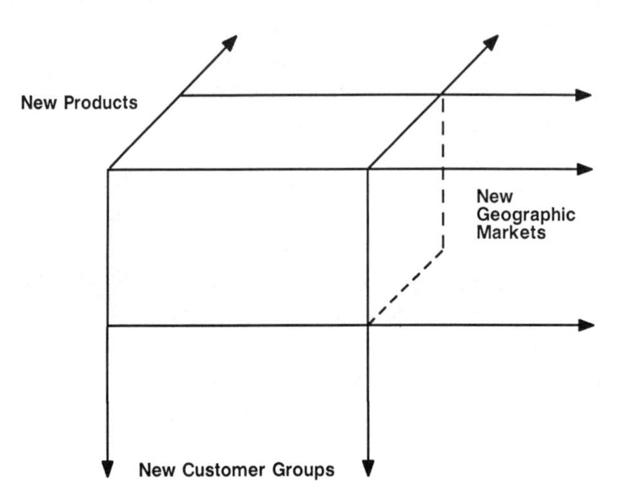

fit the capabilities of the individual firm relative to the competition that it can expect to face.

THE MARKETING PERSPECTIVE

The marketing function goes beyond the activities performed by the marketing department in most financial service firms. For marketing is more than just a set of activities concerned with research, planning, program development, and implementation. It is a critical bridge that links the organization with its external environment. Marketing provides an orientation towards customers and helps management to position the firm effectively against competitors in the same marketplace. Developing a successful marketing strategy requires an understanding of the following important concepts: transactions, customer decision making, and segmentation. Each will be looked at briefly in turn.

Transactions

At the core of modern marketing thought is the concept of a transaction, defined by Philip Kotler as "the exchange of value between two parties." According to Kotler, "marketing is specifically concerned with how transactions are created, stimulated, facilitated and valued."

The importance of this concept is that it focuses attention on the quid pro quo of marketing activities. Instead of simply noting which customers purchase what products at what price from which suppliers, it is often more revealing to ask what benefits customers seek to obtain from a transaction and what costs—time and effort as well as money—they are prepared to pay in return.

Segmentation

Understanding benefits and costs from a customer perspective provides an important input to market analysis. Most financial service firms have learned to segment their markets along various dimensions. Corporate customers are easily differentiated from retail customers and can quickly be further segmented along such lines as geographic location, size, industry, profitability, and growth rate. Many firms wisely choose to target certain types of customers and/or geographic regions, thereby developing expertise in the financial needs of clients in those chosen categories.

However, even within the types of categories described above, important differences may be found among the management styles and preferences of otherwise "similar" firms. In the development of marketing strategy, it can be misleading to segment the market on the basis of readily identifiable criteria. It is important that a segmentation scheme lead to a higher level of understanding regarding how a customer behaves and how a supplier can expect to build a profitable relationship with that customer. For example, a recent study by the MAC Group unearthed that some corporate treasurers value relationships and prefer to buy a package of services from the same financial institution. Other corporate treasurers emphasize performance against key cost/benefit criteria for each service that they buy; as a result they may use a different financial institution for each financial service and be quite willing to change suppliers each time a new service requirement arises.

Segmentation analysis can be very useful for identifying opportunities within the marketplace and for selecting target prospects. But it would be a serious mistake to assume total homogeneity of needs and preferences among customers or prospects within any given segment.

Customer Decision Making

One of the keys to successful segmentation is understanding how customers make decisions. This involves detailed knowledge of the client company's needs and of the individuals who will influence or be involved in the buying process. Members of this group are often referred to in marketing terminology as the *buying center*.

As shown in Exhibit 13.2, the buying center encompasses individuals who separately or collectively play up to five different roles:

1. *Users* of the service(s) to be acquired
2. *Influencers* of the decision who provide information and selection criteria
3. *Buyers* who have formal authority for contracting with suppliers
4. *Deciders* who have the authority to choose among alternative courses of action and suppliers
5. *Gatekeepers* who control the flow of information to the buying center by identifying acceptable suppliers and limiting their access to participants in the buying center

Exhibit 13.2 Roles of Buying-Center Members by Decision Stage

	User	Influencer	Buyer	Decider	Gatekeeper
Identification of need	X	X			
Establishment of specifications	X	X	X	X	
Identification of alternatives	X	X	X		X
Evaluation of alternatives	X	X	X		
Choice	X	X	X		

Source: Frederick E. Webster, Jr., and Yoram Wind, *Organizational Buying Behavior*. Copyright 1972, p.80.

One person may play several roles in the buying process. For instance, the user and the influencer may be one and the same. On the other hand, several individuals may play the same role, yet bring different perspectives, needs, and criteria to that role. In such instances, it is very important for the marketer to understand the relative power of each individual to convince (or overrule) colleagues.

The size and composition of the buying center and the scope of its activities tend to vary with the nature of each purchase decision. In general, when a client is dealing with important decisions in an unfamiliar area that is fraught with risk, there is a greater likelihood of top management involvement and extensive discussion among a large group of buying center members.

Providers of corporate financial services have traditionally underestimated the importance of the differing roles of buying-center members in purchasing financial services. Providers of such services may need to establish relationships at multiple levels within the buyer organization to ensure a secure competitive position. They must recognize that the selling process extends beyond the single contact point to which many are accustomed. A critical competitive issue in the future will be how to best coordinate and manage multilevel relationships.

TOOLS FOR ACTION: ELEMENTS OF THE MARKETING MIX

Almost 40 years ago, Neil Borden, a Harvard Business School professor, heard one of his colleagues describe the marketing manager as a "mixer of ingredients." Thus was born the concept of the marketing mix, which identifies and classifies all the different elements comprising a marketing action plan (as distinct from the research needed to create and evaluate the plan). The five elements of the mix are product policy, pricing strategy, choice of distribution and delivery systems, sales management, and communication efforts.

Product Policy

The products of a manufacturing organization are not difficult to identify. They are physical objects that can be seen, touched, and sometimes heard, smelled, and tasted. Once produced, they can usually be held in inventory for a while until ready for pick-up or shipment to customers and wholesale or retail intermediaries.

The products of a service organization, by contrast, are more ephemeral. Physical manifestations of corporate financial service products are usually confined to hard-copy documentation of a service, or to production and delivery systems in the form of buildings, equipment, officers, and staff members. But as with physical goods, the purchaser of a service is basically buying the benefits that service will provide.

In designing financial service products for corporate customers, the marketer can engage in far more customization than is feasible in most retail services. Since customization necessarily entails personal discussions and consultations with the client, the *process* may become almost as important as the *output*. In situations where it is difficult to differentiate the core service from those of competing firms, astute marketers often seek out meaningful ways to offer superior performance on supplementary product elements.

Customers often define and perceive service differently from the provider. All service firms would do well to follow the lead of Federal Express, which some years ago redefined service as "all actions and reactions that customers perceive they have purchased." Although that company's core product was transportation and delivery of small packages, managers recognized that customers also evaluated Federal on such supplementary product elements as information provision, billing procedures, documentation, and problem solving. Consider in contrast how many commercial banks would seek to have their problem-resolution capabilities perceived as the basis of competition. One of the marketing challenges facing providers of corporate financial services is how to integrate customer service into their approach to providing financial products.

The array of financial service products is large, and growing larger. Particularly significant in recent years has been the growth in fee-based services. Exhibit 13.3 shows a representative list of corporate financial services.

Collectively, all the different services sold by an individual firm constitute its product line. Marketers often distinguish between the *depth* of a product line, meaning the number of available versions of the same product category (plain vanilla plus 30 other flavors in four different sized servings), versus its *breadth*, which refers to the number of different product categories offered (ice cream plus an array of other general store merchandise). A key product policy issue facing financial service firms today is whether to go for depth, and the expertise that this implies, or for breadth, with its implications of full service. The full-service approach to the market for corporate financial services is being pursued by providers such as Citicorp and Chase Manhattan. In contrast, Bankers Trust, Security Pacific, and Mellon Bank have achieved arguably stronger results with narrower, but deeper product lines. The obvious management challenge is to build a product line in concert with the other elements of the marketing mix.

Pricing Strategy

As in many service industries, the pricing of financial services has not always been addressed from a marketing perspective. The tendency has been to focus on

Exhibit 13.3 Corporate Financial Services Products

Advisory Services	*Credit Products*
Financial Risk Assessment	Lines of Credit
Capital Structuring	Revolving Credits
Overseas Network	Bankers Acceptances
Merger & Acquisition	Secured Lending
Foreign Exchange	Equipment Finance
Industry Expertise	Commercial Paper
Economic Information	Euronotes
Tax Based Transactions	Private Placements—Domestic
Regulatory Based Transactions	Private Placements—Euro
Investment Advice	Leverage Leasing
	Project Finance
Transaction Services	Asset Purchases
DDA Services	Public Debt—Domestic
Letter of Credit	Public Debt—Euro
Insurance	Convertible Debt—Domestic
Barter Transactions	Convertible Debt—Euro
Investment Management	Preferred Stock—Domestic
Cash Management	Preferred Stock—Euro
Commercial Paper Insurance	Common Stock—Domestic
Precious Metal Vault	Common Stock—Euro
Investor Services	Loan Syndications—Domestic
	Loan Syndications—Euro
Money Market Services	Vendor Leasing
U.S. Governments	Venture Capital
Municipals	
Money Markets	
Asset Intermediation	
Interest Rate Products	
Foreign Exchange Products	
Trading/Positioning	
Blocked Currency Transactions	

financial and cost criteria, rather than taking a customer viewpoint. Historically, both regulatory restrictions and tradition led many firms to avoid price as a competitive weapon. For many years, competitors in the commercial banking industry shared the same pricing benchmark—"the prime rate"—for pricing credit to primary customers. Competition in the investment banking industry during this same era of nonprice competition evolved around the maintenance of long-term relationships. This situation has since changed significantly.

Realistically, pricing decisions should reflect the three key inputs of cost, value to customers, and competitive price levels. The *cost* of producing the service sets a floor to the price: charge below cost and the firm will lose money. The development of reliable cost data may require detailed cost analysis and represents a major challenge for the financial services industry, given its limited investment in management information systems.

The *value* of the product to the customer sets a ceiling to the price: No customer will pay more for the product than its perceived value. Understanding this value—which may vary sharply from one customer to another—requires insights into the benefits that the customer expects to obtain. In some instances, research may show that customers are paying much less for a product than they would actually be willing to pay—a situation known to economists as consumer surplus. This situation most frequently occurs when nontraditional providers move into new product areas. These firms, lacking any intuitive sense of value, tend to price at cost. Many observers see this beginning to happen as commercial banks begin to offer corporate financial advisory services in competition with investment banks.

Moderating the firm's ability to engage in value pricing is the impact of *competition*. Competition may be direct or indirect, involving another firm, another product, or another marketplace. If a competitor charges a lower price for a similar product, some clients who are aware of this option are likely to purchase the competitive offering instead. Price competition, historically unknown in the market for corporate financial services, has become a major driver of both customer and provider behavior.

A firm's ability to price up to the full extent of perceived value is a function of the number of meaningful ways in which the product can be differentiated. Adding extra benefits may enhance perceived value and thus allow the firm to charge more. The traditional approach to institutional brokerage sales relied heavily on extra benefits to secure long-term service relationships. This is a particularly desirable strategy when the cost of adding these benefits is significantly less than the increase in price that they command. With the increasing practice of unbundled pricing, however, very few customers still seek "packaged value."

As more emphasis comes to be placed upon developing fee income from financial services, firms will have to develop greater sophistication in pricing. Some of these fee-based services result from this same practice of unbundling complex services into several components. When firms are forced to compete on rates and the spread diminishes, one way of recouping the lost income is to start charging for formerly free or extra services. An interesting example of unbundling complex services into discretely priced components is the "revolution" that has occurred in the corporate market for basic transaction and cash management services. In the less competitive, less profit-conscious past, explicit pricing was never applied to transaction services. Compensating balances were always assumed to be sufficient. With the advent of corporate cash management "sweep" accounts, however, charging fee-based pricing has become essential for the providers of corporate cash management services. Fees for specific transactions—wire transfers, checks, account inquiries—have become essential for recouping the cost of providing services that were long taken for granted.

Distribution Study

Distribution strategy centers on where and when the service is available, and how to get it to the customer. The advent of electronic systems has provided enormous convenience in terms of access, helping financial services firms to leapfrog geographic and regulatory barriers, and to minimize execution time on many transactions. However, for many services involving face-to-face interactions and detailed market knowledge, geographic proximity to customers remains essential. In many instances, geographic proximity may not be as important as maintaining a credible physical presence. Citicorp has been building regional physical presences not so much to provide for face-to-face interaction, as to symbolize their commitment to doing business in a given region—hence the rapid growth of branch offices both domestically (where permitted under current regulations) and internationally.

For many institutions, decisions regarding distribution strategy have historically been ones of establishing the best way to serve the customer in a physical sense. With today's thin margins, providers of corporate financial services are necessarily beginning to scrutinize the costs of current and alternative distribution strategies to identify opportunities to improve both their financial and their marketplace performances.

In addition, most financial services institutions historically have both "manufactured" and distributed their own products. Now there is a growing trend toward separation of the production and distribution functions. Within specific product categories, firms are making choices between being (1) both producers and distributors, (2) producers who sell to distributors, and (3) distributors who purchase financial products created elsewhere and then resell them to other intermediaries or to the end-user. This has been the traditional structure of the corporate underwriting market. Today, asset securitization and commercial loan packaging are driving a similar separation of production and distribution functions in the commercial banking industry.

Sales Management

A key element in the distribution of corporate financial services is managing the sales force and managing customer relationships. Since relationship management is discussed in detail in Chapter 16, this chapter will focus on sales management. Unlike customers in retail financial markets, corporate and wholesale buyers must be sold one by one, and one on one. When a calling officer visits a prospect, he or she must do more than just "show the flag." To the extent that calling officers can follow up leads previously generated by advertising, telemarketing, or personal referrals, their chances of turning prospects into customers will be commensurately higher. Further, such visits are much more likely to be fruitful if calling officers have done their homework in advance by learning all they can about the prospective customer.

To an increasing degree, financial services institutions are developing a professional approach to managing calling officers and other individuals involved in personal selling efforts. Much can be learned from studying the sales management practices of successful industrial firms that sell goods and services to a variety of corporate customers.

Industrial salespeople are selected with an eye to their selling capabilities, and are put through often rigorous training and apprenticeship programs. Moreover, a key element in effective sales management is the development of appropriate compensation policies. Most sales representatives receive a combination of base salary plus commission on those sales for which they are responsible.

Adapting sales compensation policies to the corporate financial services industry requires separating individual performance from that of the organization as a whole, and relating it to the incremental profitability of the services sold by that individual. Further, strict controls must be placed on credit quality and loan approval, since bad decisions on customer screening can have serious adverse results.

One example of an apparently successful incentive program comes from Industrial Valley Bank and Trust Company, located in the Philadelphia area. Officers receive 20 percent of the profits obtained from acceptable loans, fees, and demand deposits that they generate through calling, up to a maximum (in 1984) of $8,000 annually. To control the quality of credit relationships being developed, officers must submit loans for review by both their superiors and a loan committee. Only loans of above-average quality earn incentive pay. In addition, account officers are penalized for any loans that, although they met incentive criteria, subsequently turned bad. To encourage high performers to remain with the bank, commission payments are distributed once a year, and the account officer being rewarded must still be employed at the bank at that time.

Compensation is an important motivator. Sales bonuses and commissions can be very useful in providing direction and focus to selling efforts. Paralleling the changes occurring in both brokerage and insurance companies, compensation policies may need to be changed to give appropriate selling emphasis to the different products and services that financial services firms offer in the marketplace.

Managing sales efforts requires skills in selection, training, evaluation, and counseling. Sales management also requires the collection and analysis of data to pinpoint sales opportunities, the planning of selling activities, and the monitoring and evaluation of sales performance. This is where marketing research and information systems support become so important. Leg work in the field should always be preceded and followed by desk work in the office.

Among the problems associated with rapid rotation of calling officers through account assignments is the tendency to focus the officers' attention on short-term sales of the products for which they are personally responsible, rather than on building relationships and cross-selling other products. In either case, valuable information acquired by the officer may be lost once he or she moves to a new assignment. The solution lies in capturing these data through call reports and lead referral systems. Once again, there is a need for a strong sales management function to ensure that busy calling officers do not neglect these responsibilities.

Communication Efforts

The various forms of marketing communication collectively perform three roles: to inform, to persuade, and to remind. Although communication tends to be associated with persuasion and the creation of brand preference, it may also play an important educational role, especially where new products are concerned. Several different types of communication tools are available to the corporate marketer, including advertising, personal selling, brochures and promotional literature, and public relations. Each form of communication has its own strengths and weaknesses, and an effective campaign will seek to integrate all communication efforts for maximum synergy and impact. In many firms, unfortunately, this integration is left to chance rather than being planned.

As a general rule of thumb, impersonal communications, such as advertising and placement of news stories through public relations, are the most efficient way of building awareness and generating leads. However, creating a preference (for an organization or a specific product) and moving the customer to a purchase decision require person-to-person communications.

Financial services firms have tended to mismanage their advertising efforts, due to lack of clear objectives and inadequate knowledge of the different capabilities of alternative media. Common errors include running conservative "me too" image-building campaigns that fail to set the organization apart from its competitors; failure to deliver a specific message to a specific target audience concerning relevant organizational strengths and/or product performance features; and running the right messages in the wrong media. Much financial services advertising is probably wasted, since it appears in large-circulation publications, most of whose readers are unlikely to be in the target market. The advertiser is paying to reach them anyway, however. Use of more tightly focused publications, such as industry-specific or regional magazines, may represent much better value for the advertising dollar. In corporate markets where prospects can be identified individually, use of customized direct mail efforts, followed up by telephone calls, has proven quite effective. A major advantage of direct mail is that the advertiser can more easily measure response, and can evaluate the impact of alternative messages and formats.

A key factor in using all five elements of the marketing mix (product policy, pricing, distribution, sales management, and communication) is knowing how the institution wants to position itself in the marketplace, and then ensuring that all marketing efforts are consistent.

FORMULATING A COMPETITIVE POSITIONING STRATEGY

Understanding the concept of positioning is the key to developing an effective competitive posture. This concept is certainly not limited to services—indeed it had its origins in packaged goods marketing—but it does offer valuable insights by forcing service marketers to provide specific answers to the questions: Who are our target customers? How well do our products and services meet the needs of customers in different market segments? How do our offerings compare with competitive offerings?

What Positioning Is

Positioning is the process of establishing and maintaining a distinctive place in the market for an organization or its individual product offerings. Repositioning involves changing an institution's existing position, such as when Bankers Trust sold its retail branches and moved into investment banking.

Many marketers associate positioning primarily with the communication element of the marketing mix. This perception reflects the widespread use of advertising in packaged goods marketing to create images and associations for branded products in order to give them a special distinction in the consumer's mind. Examples include the visual imagery created for a major cigarette brand by the Marlboro man, and the positioning of Seven-Up as an alternative to cola products through the use of the term "unCola."

In guiding development of marketing mix strategy for services, positioning is more than just imagery. The positioning process entails making decisions on substantive attributes that are known to be important to customers and that relate to product performance, price, and service availability.

Role of Positioning in Marketing Strategy

Positioning plays a pivotal role in marketing strategy, since it links market analysis and competitive analysis to internal analysis. From these three—market analysis, competitive analysis, and internal analysis—a position statement can be developed that enables the organization to answer the questions: Who are our target customers? Whom do we want to target in the future? What marketing actions must we take to get there?

Because of the intangible, experiential nature of many services, an explicit positioning strategy is valuable in helping prospective customers to get a mental fix on a product that would otherwise be rather amorphous.

Failure to select a desired position in the marketplace, and to develop a marketing action plan for achieving and holding this position, may result in one of several undesirable outcomes. The organization (or one of its products) may be pushed into a position where it faces head-on competition from stronger competitors. Or it may be pushed into a position nobody else wants to take because of little customer demand. Or if the organization's or product's position is fuzzy and ill-defined, buyers will not know what its distinctive competence really is. Even worse, the organization or product may have no position at all in the marketplace because nobody has ever heard of it.

Steps in Developing a Market Position

Exhibit 13.4 outlines the basic steps involved in identifying a suitable market position and developing a strategy to reach it.

Exhibit 13.4 Developing a Market Positioning Strategy

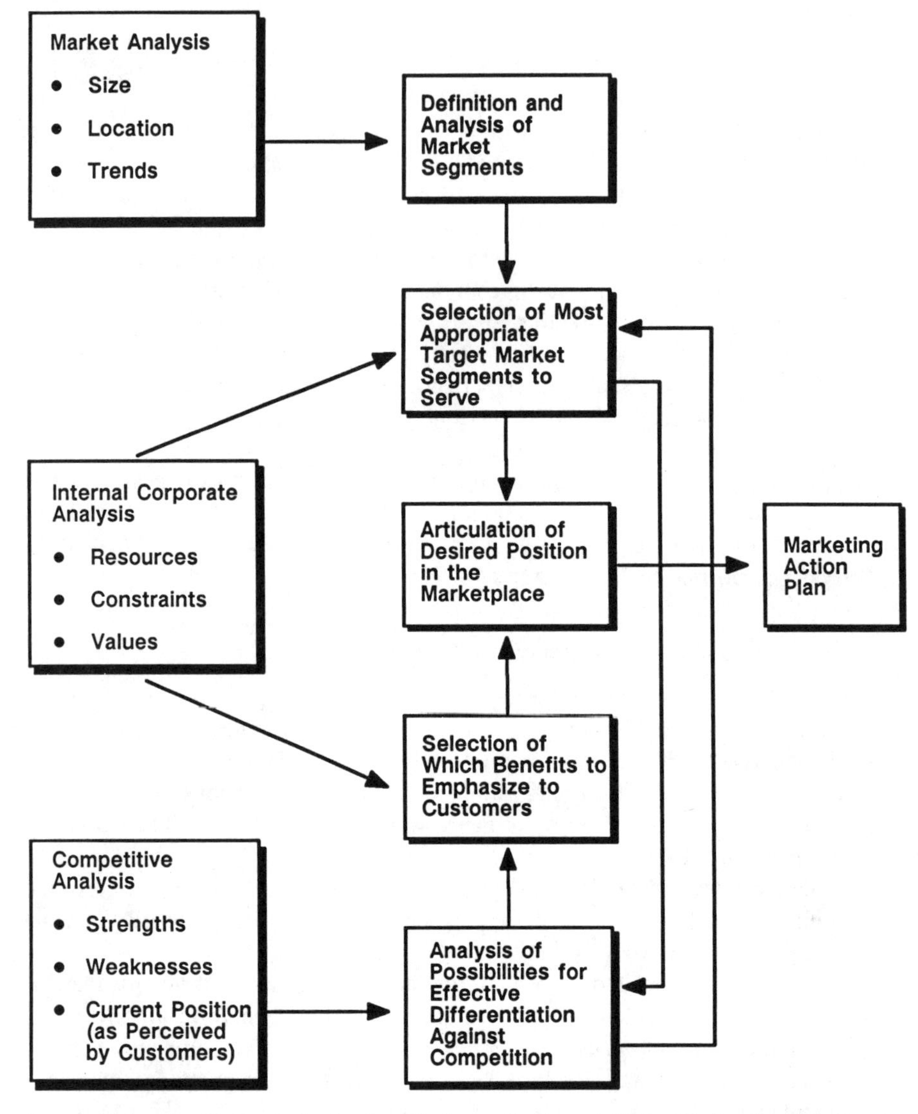

Source: Christopher H. Lovelock. *Services Marketing*. Englewood Cliffs, NJ: Prentice-Hall. Developed from an earlier schematic by Michael R. Pearce.

Market analysis is needed to determine factors such as the overall level, trend, and geographic location of demand. Then alternative ways of segmenting the market should be considered and an appraisal made of the size and potential of the different segments. Additional research may be required to generate insights into the needs and preferences of prospective customers within each of the different segments, and how they perceive the competition.

Internal corporate analysis requires identifying the organization's resources (financial, human labor and know-how, and physical assets), recognizing the limitations in these areas, and understanding the values of its management. Based on the insights gained from this analysis, the organization can select a limited number of target market segments that it is willing and able to serve with new or existing services. Finally, through identification and analysis of competitors, a marketing strategist can gain a sense of strengths and weaknesses, which in turn can suggest opportunities for product or organizational differentiation. Relating these insights back to the internal corporate analysis should suggest which benefits to offer to which target market segments.

The outcome of integrating these three forms of analysis is a position statement that articulates the desired position of the organization in the marketplace and, if desired, that of each of the component services offered. Armed with this understanding, the marketer should then be able to develop a specific marketing action plan. The cost of implementing this plan must, of course, be related to the expected payoff.

A key factor in developing a defendable competition is having the information necessary to make decisions. Good market research and effective use of internal information are required.

Marketing Research and Information Systems

Many people associate marketing primarily with communication efforts such as personal selling, advertising, and public relations. But in practice the contents of the marketer's tool chest are much more extensive. As shown in Exhibit 13.5, the marketing process is a loop that begins and ends with collection and analysis of data. Information is needed not only to plan strategy but also to evaluate subsequent performance against the plan. The design and management of marketing information systems are an integral part of the marketing task, as is interpretation of the resulting data.

Making sound decisions requires access to the most accurate and meaningful information. Strategy must be based on an understanding of market structure and competitive activities, and on the needs and expectations of individual customers. Information is also needed to evaluate the effectiveness of a particular strategy and to monitor performance in the marketplace over time.

Data Collection and Storage

Most financial services firms collect a vast amount of data about their customers for operational and credit approval purposes. Although this information may have significant marketing value in terms of profiling customer characteristics, needs, and behavior, it is not always stored and formatted in ways that make it accessible and useful.

Further, information about corporate clients is not always gathered together in a single location. Some of it may be unrecorded, stored only in the personal

Exhibit 13.5 The Marketing Loop

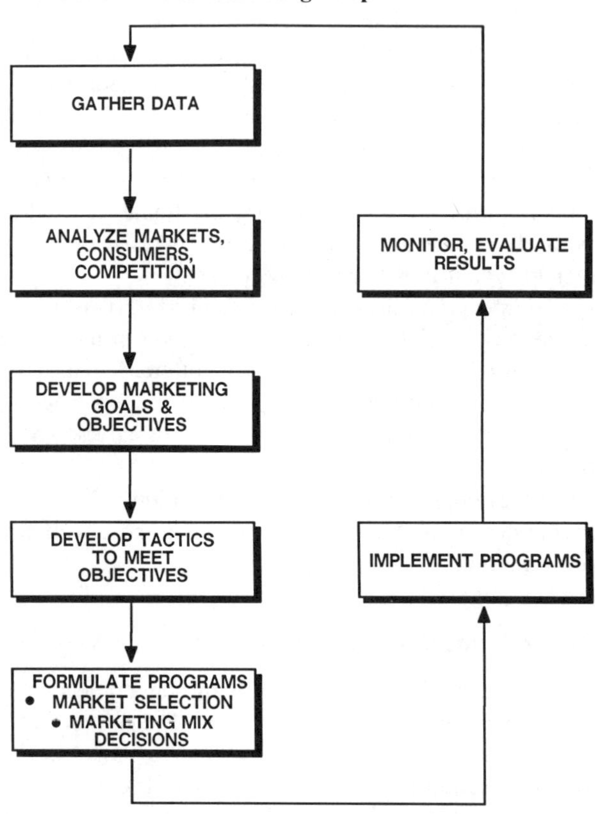

memories of calling officers; consequently, the rapid rotation of individuals through account officer positions may result in failure to develop and record detailed information about customers' needs and preferences. Other information may be diffused among different departments or branches, reflecting regional or product-based organizations that do not always communicate with each other as well as they should. Similarly, information may be stored in an inaccessible repository; the commercial banking industry, for instance, generally maintains most of its customer information in customer credit files, usually buried away or stored in the basement fireproof vault. Whatever the case, firms need to develop a disciplined process for capturing, evaluating, and acting on client-specific data that could prove useful in making strategic marketing decisions.

Information to support decisions regarding markets, competitors, and individual clients may require special research studies. *Primary data* collection involves doing research to collect data that was not previously available. *Secondary data*, by contrast, refers to published sources such as articles, books, industry and government statistics, and so on. Reliance on secondary data may well yield much or all of the information that is needed, quickly and at low cost. Intermediate routes to information are also possible; subscription to proprietary research findings (such as the surveys conducted by Greenwich Research Associates, Lou Harris, TransData Corp, or Synergistics), provides a way of sharing the cost of research among participating institutions. Unfortunately, using syndicated research may not yield the insights that could be gained by commissioning tailored research studies, since each institution tends to face distinctive challenges.

Customer and market information must be combined and analyzed to support management decision making. An effective marketing information system brings the information together in a central location, updates it on an ongoing basis, and makes it accessible to authorized personnel. Firms that are known for taking a proactive stance toward marketing not only keep files on their current clients and on the industries and regions in which these clients are active, but also on prospective clients which have been targeted for future acquisition efforts. Additionally, regularly updated files may be kept on key competitors or prospective competitors, as well as on new product developments. Customer prospecting systems can be developed internally, or can be purchased from a variety of different vendors. Creating such a system is an important first step in leveraging the use of marketing information to improve performance in the marketplace.

CONCLUSION

Old ways of doing business in the marketplace for corporate financial services will no longer suffice. Faced with a much wider array of both services to offer and customers to service, firms are going to have to make choices among both categories. The marketing concepts discussed in this chapter offer a framework for structuring an analysis, but each institution will have to collect data relevant to its own situation. Analysis and interpretation of the resulting information should yield insights for a marketing strategy that is at once economically viable and competitively defensible.

BIBLIOGRAPHY

Hedges, Robert B. Jr. "Managing Your Customer Relationship Portfolio." *Commerical Lending Review* (Spring 1986).

The MAC Group. "The Market for Corporate Financial Services—Solving the Profit Puzzle." (Independent research (Fall 1986).

Kotler, Philip. *Marketing Management*. Englewood Cliffs, NJ: Prentice-Hall, 1980.

14 The Marketing of Corporate Financial Services: A Banking Perspective

JAMES J. SMITH, JR.
PHILLIP WILSON

Over the past few decades, banks have approached the financial needs of their corporate customers and prospects with varying degrees of attentiveness and marketing intensity. Marketing efforts have ranged from fairly passive accommodation on credit and other product requirements to, more recently, a highly aggressive selling approach. Efforts to gain a competitive edge have generally centered on such variables of the marketing mix as personalized attention, service innovation, quality and delivery, pricing product features, and other means of differentiation.

However, marketing served a less critical role in the pre-1970s corporate banking world when availability of adequate credit strongly dominated the corporation's buying decision. It was also a time when alternative sources of funds were fewer, and corporate dependency on banks as a prime source for short- and intermediate-term borrowing was much greater. At the same time, with generally lower interest rates and less competitive intensity, corporate treasurers were satisfied to continue the time-honored practice of maintaining relatively high interest-free balances with their banks, only a portion of which were required to compensate for funds being borrowed or for other services their companies received. How, then, did the role of marketing develop in this environment?

Changing Market Conditions

Market conditions that had long been stable began to change dramatically in the early 1970s, in roughly the following sequence: As a depressed stock market created a relative scarcity of bank capital, bank managements were pressured to produce the higher earnings required to attract additional capital. Scarcity of capital in turn forced banks to place limits on borrowings, which served to inhibit their own asset growth. Slow growth caused banks to scrutinize more carefully the ways in which they allocated scarce resources. As a result, better resource utilization and greater focus on the most attractive profit opportunities became the watchwords.

Capital scarcity also changed bank management perceptions about business decisions, time horizons, and customer relationships. As with a vast cross-section of American industry, management now had to demonstrate above-average returns not just over the long term, but from quarter to quarter. A "quick hit" mentality came to be emphasized over an "invest for the future" perspective. Still, in those banks generating above-average returns, farsighted management was able to commit to product development programs in cash management, securities processing, trade services, and other evolving financial services businesses. By contrast, those with average or below-average returns were placed at a competitive disadvantage, lacking as they did the ability to undertake such important investment spending.

Scarcity of lendable funds also reshaped the practice of "relationship" banking, wherein a designated officer strives to identify and serve a client company's needs either directly or by drawing on bank specialists. Banks tended to curtail lending to those companies with which they had only marginal relationships, and, conversely, sought to ensure that the credit needs of their best or "lead" customers were well served. Overall, the importance of relationships was strengthened. The reverse pattern became more evident in the mid-1980s, when lendable funds became more generally available. As senior bank managers have sought to maintain or increase return-on-asset levels, reduced corporate borrowing demands on commercial banks, along with increasing competitive pressures, have worked against them and brought about thinner spreads. Relatively speaking, lending became a buyer's market, and buyers exercised their option to choose. Consequently, in place of relationship banking, lending tended to be conducted on a transactional basis whereby designated specialists in credit, trade services, cash management, and other areas marketed these services directly to their counterparts within the company.

PRESSURES OF THE CORPORATE MARKET

Faced with capital pressures not unlike those of commercial banks, and with tightening availability of funds by the banking system during the mid-1970s, corporate treasurers were impelled to begin an active search for alternative sources of funds so as to reduce their dependency on commercial banks. This search sparked financial markets to respond with imaginative vigor both in terms of new types of credit instruments and through the emergence of new competitors.

The late 1970s witnessed a surge in the commercial paper market, vast expansion in the Eurodollar arena, and growth of other domestic and overseas sources of funds. Significant new competition also emerged from foreign banks and insurance companies. Historically, insurance companies directed the majority of their lending efforts toward long-term markets. With the sharp general rise in interest rates during the 1980s, the distinctly more volatile nature of these rates, and increasing reliance on interest-sensitive sources of capital, however, insurance companies began to channel their lending programs toward the intermediate three-to-seven-year range which had traditionally been the almost exclusive province of commercial banks. As for foreign banks, they had always been a presence in the U.S. market. But it was only in the 1970s and 1980s that they came to recognize the potential for servicing the enormous capital requirements of the vast U.S. economy and to prize its political and economic stability. As such, these banks began to attack the corporate and institutional banking markets with great zeal.

Faced with growing competitive pressures, and with corporate treasurers able to raise short-, intermediate-, and longer-term funds in a much broader variety of ways, the commercial bankers saw their traditional supremacy as a source of funds erode sharply. The impact of market forces mentioned above has manifested itself in several ways.

- The average number of principal banks used by companies in the Fortune 1000 range has declined sharply.
- Use of foreign banks for U.S. domestic business has measurably increased in the large corporate market.
- Lending based on the prime rate has become more the exception than the rule; that is, below-prime rates are being offered to big customers (although small business and middle market companies still pay the published rates).
- Lending spreads have been severely squeezed, thereby prompting increased efforts to control costs better and improve productivity.
- Non credit and other noncapital-reliant, fee-based products have emerged as vitally important alternative sources of revenue.

EMERGENCE OF MARKETING

Until the middle 1970s, marketing within the corporate banking environment was modest and conservative by the standards of industrial America. It consisted primarily of small-scale image advertising, limited cross-sell efforts with existing customers, some organized calling programs on prospective customers, and various forms of corporate entertainment designed to enhance relationships and build good will. But with conditions changed as previously described, the need for vastly more sophisticated marketing of corporate credit and noncredit services has become urgent. Most importantly, banks have ceased to view marketing in the narrowest sense, as equivalent to selling. No longer able to serve the broad cross-section of potential markets with reasonable spreads, banks have begun to examine their market systematically and view it as a collection of smaller markets which need to be understood and prioritized. Pricing, products, and people also have emerged as significant marketing variables.

MARKET SEGMENTATION

The corporate market for credit and noncredit services comprises a highly diverse array in terms of size, industry, and geographic segments. In small businesses and professional concerns (annual sales of $5 million or less) owner/managers assume a fairly active role in selection of banking and other outside support services. The owner/manager typically looks to his or her banker to serve both personal as well as business financial needs. The confidences required to achieve a good banking relationship generally lead to a high degree of loyalty to the existing financial services provider. With time a scarce resource, owner/managers show a strong tendency to select a bank with branches or commercial banking facilities located in close proximity to the business itself. Dominating the service needs of this market segment are credit and simple depository, investment, and transactional services.

Middle market companies are variously defined to have sales as low as $10 to $50 million or as high as $120 to $250 million. Unlike the small business segment, middle market and larger companies generally base their buying decisions for financial services on the requirements of the business, rather than upon combined business/personal credit and noncredit needs of owner/managers. Credit availability is an essential criterion for bank selection among mid-sized businesses, along with perceived caliber of the bank's account or relationship manager. The basis for obtaining credit is to some extent dependent on the maturity of the business. As the company grows, it makes a gradual transition from secured borrowing based on inventory and accounts receivables, to unsecured borrowing based on rising cash flows. With greater size and business activity, many companies also begin to require cash management and international services.

The large corporate market, often defined as the Fortune 1000 industrials plus the nonindustrial companies of comparable size, comprises some 1500 to 2000 firms. This upper end of the corporate banking market presents the financial services provider with more professional and knowledgeable buyers of credit and noncredit services.

THE LIFE CYCLE OF BUSINESS

Bank marketers must be sensitive to the gradual increase in complexity of clients' financial requirements as companies grow and diversify through their life cycles. This increasing complexity is, of course, a direct result of the broadening scope of their business activities.

Small businesses, logically enough, generally derive most of their sales revenue from a relatively narrow cross-section of neighboring buyers, while large corporations market products and services across immense geographic areas, at the same time dealing with an extensive array of national and overseas suppliers and end-users. As corporations pursue domestic and international diversification and growth, their needs for credit, processing, and information services change and magnify. Not only do these expansionary efforts increase the volume of services required, but they also directly impact the complexity and timeliness of financial services requirements. Other events shaping the demands of the corporate market include increasing volatility of interest rates, changing value of the U.S. dollar relative to overseas currencies, efforts to cope with growing foreign competition via overseas diversification, and more recent moves toward growth and/or improved capital resource use via acquisitions, leveraged buyouts, and so forth. Not surprisingly, large and diverse corporations find it essential to rely on skilled, specialized financial teams. Typically, such a team comprises not only a treasurer, one or more assistant treasurers, and a chief financial officer, but also specialists in cash management, foreign exchange positioning, acquisitions, and a myriad of other specialties. This splintering of responsibility complicates the financial decision-making process, creating special challenges for those who sell financial products. These challenges include decisions about which products and services to develop and offer, as well as how the financial services provider should best organize to address this opportunity. Some banks have chosen the relationship manager approach, others a transactional approach.

PRODUCT OFFERINGS

The needs of the corporate markets for financial services should be seen as falling into four distinct categories. These are the needs for: (1) credit-related services; (2) processing; (3) information; and (4) "value-added." Except for a few cases, banks are beginning to specialize or niche in their market emphasis and in the mix and delivery of these product offerings.

Credit-Related Services

Credit-related services include traditional forms of bank credit and newer, more innovative credit products. Examples range from established offerings such as short-term lines of credit, revolving credit, and secured and unsecured financing, to newer forms such as commercial paper backups. Corporate demand for credit services tends to be a function of the client company and its stage in the business cycle.

Credit products have historically been a primary source of commercial bank revenue, supplied in the form of net interest income. In recent years net interest income has become a less reliable source. Margins have been shrinking as corporate treasurers avail themselves of alternate sources of funds. Pressures, especially on large banks, have also grown to maintain attractive earnings levels as a means of preserving and building the capital base. For these reasons, most regional and larger banks have become more selective in their policies toward asset growth. Thus, with quality rather than volume of earnings becoming the determining performance criterion, emphasis is shifting toward generating assets selectively, in many cases for securitization or future sale. As a result, net interest income from traditional credit offerings has become a shrinking portion of overall revenue for many banks.

Processing Services

Processing services—funds transfer via fed wire or automated clearing house (ACH), check deposits, check clearings, collections, concentration, disbursements, securities processing and custody, and so on—are basic transactional services. Traditionally they have been seen as a means to attract a deposit base to the bank. Almost indispensable, they are used by all corporate market segments. What differentiation in usage does exist tends to be a function of client volume (size), sophistication of transaction input (automation), and pricing. Costs and resultant profitability differ widely from bank to bank. Investments in these products are often substantial, with short economic life cycles.

Application of bank capital to these products is seldom understood. Delivery is obviously becoming a systems-engineering task, even to smaller customers. These services are often poorly marketed. Sometimes they involve little or none of the principal selling officer's time. Buyer decisions are often located in distant areas of the client corporation. Until about five years ago processing was primarily the engine that supplied the customer with information confirming the accurate and timely execution of financial transactions, which are the purchased service. Today the information itself can be a key service provided by financial institutions.

Information Services

Information services have become banks' greatest growth business over the last decade. For some, these services actually represent an entry into a "new business" as they test the limitations of regulation. The services that banks offer run the gamut from simple account statements to on-line access, to an increasing array of customer, economic, and capital market information stored at the bank.

Historically, most information services were an outgrowth either of processing products or of the systems designed to manage them. But the impetus for new services has now moved from the supplier side to the demand side. Customers' data requirements now clearly spur product development. Products such as cash management, for instance, have become highly automated and are often combined with additional outside data for the convenience of customers.

As with processing products, systems development to support information services is seldom understood. Information is commonly viewed as a non-capital-intensive aspect of business, most often sold by specialists in the bank. Moreover, such services are often bought by multiple buyers within one customer organization, presenting a whole new dimension to bank marketing.

Value-Added Services

Value-added services are relatively new offerings for commercial banks, ones that may eventually expand bank activities into once off-limits new businesses such as investment banking. This category includes such diverse services as international currency management, merger and acquisition services, debt swaps, interest-rate hedge transactions, private placements, syndications and asset sales, and many more esoteric products. This group is characterized by high fees or upfront income. As such, most realize their full value quickly, with little if any reliance on capital.

Value-added service offerings operate on the fringe in two respects. First, they fill the void between traditional bank activities and the limits to activity defined by government regulations. In some instances, this practice leads to the relaxation of the limits. Second, value-added products lead banks into new areas of competition, even occasionally into conflict with their own traditional customer bases. Customer use of these services is limited (but growing) and reaches from the multinational corporate market down into the middle market. Buyers tend to be at higher levels in the customer organizations. Value-added products are generally sold by specialists or, to some extent, by more sophisticated account officers.

ATTRACTIVENESS OF THE CORPORATE MARKET

There are many ways of grouping current banking services, but doing so by the four categories above tends to highlight trends in supplier thinking and buyer attitudes. Clearly, substantial expansion of product lines, whether grouped this way or in other ways, is providing bank customers with many alternatives. Regulation (e.g., the Glass-Steagall Act, DIDC, ERISA) appears to be the only real limitation to continued expansion of product lines to corporate customers.

Hand in hand with product extension and diversification has come radical market expansion, or at least access to new geographical markets. Market expansion has partly resulted from the easing of regulations. But possibly the greater aid to expansion has been the application of data automation and system developments which fall outside the dated categories laid out by current regulatory definitions of banking. Geographical business expansion has also been enabled by removal of certain state regulations. Some states now permit out-of-state banks to purchase troubled thrifts; they sanction the formation of so-called industrial and nonbank banks; and they grant thrifts permission to place up to 20 percent of their assets in commercial loans. Acting in groups, states have also signed pacts that dismantle barriers to mergers and acquisitions across state lines.

Do these reforms constitute a banking bonanza? Do they say "yes" to any product, any market? They may do so in theory, but not really. Few, if any, banking organizations have the capital or human resources to profitably pursue wide-scale market/product diversification. Some have tried, however. Although there have been glaring cases of failed attempts to stretch resources too thinly while operating in an expansionary mode, most often the real costs are not seen publicly. Indeed, much goes unrecognized even by management. Expensive investments in processing technology applied to the wrong markets, data systems marketed too early or too late, and credit extended in the wrong forms to the wrong segments are examples of this. Market and product diversification dictates "choice" from the supplier side. The opportunity to make many of these choices began to exist a decade ago. However, some banks have not made them. Today the opportunity has become an outright need—banks must make these choices soon. The challenge here is to assure that management decisions are truly market driven; that is, that they do not unconsciously reinforce existing prejudices in the organization.

DEVELOPING CORPORATE MARKETING STRATEGIES

How is it then that banks search for, choose, and pursue the ideal combination of products and customers? In the past, a wide cross-section of regional and larger banks operated with a firm conviction that they had the capabilities and the capacity necessary to serve all the financial requirements of companies within their defined areas of marketing influence. Resources and energy were thus directed toward these "opportunities" on a fairly simultaneous basis. Experience has shown, however, that a marketing approach based on "force" strains financial and human capital. Few banks have been able to sustain the required investment for long.

What is interesting is that many smaller banks have utilized marketing more effectively than larger banks, which more often have relied on force than finesse. Finesse essentially yields effectiveness. It requires the skill to conceive and describe a strategy for the most economically efficient allocation of resources. Finesse recognizes that making the right decision is only part of the task—being certain that the decision is effectively implemented is equally important. The question of what to do and how to do it are now more often becoming explicit marketing responsibilities. Where the what and how tasks fit into the organization is not particularly important. Management recognition that they must be accomplished is, however.

The "what" is often described as strategic marketing or planning. Within financial institutions these functions require definition, discipline, and dedicated resources. The key functions are information gathering and analysis, creative planning, and program development. A variety of inputs can be used by a good marketer. Using these inputs effectively requires knowledge of corporate capabilities and managerial skills and resources on one hand, and market dynamics and segmented buyer behavior on the other. Some key techniques are:

Market Research. Purchasing and analyzing readily available syndicated research as well as designing, arranging, and analyzing research that may be proprietary to the institution or may be product/market specific.

Market Analysis. Reviewing internal and readily available external data to identify the composition of markets and the requirements of constituent customers.

Market Segmentation. Defining by revenue and/or profit potential the markets which will shape the strategic marketing approach. Segmentation might be based on client location, size, or industry. For example, one perspective which in recent years has caught the eye of several banks is service sophistication or responsiveness.

Market Feasibility. Recommending what customer groups to pursue, what product investments to make, what product extensions or modifications to invest in, what delivery mechanisms, and so on.

Research, analysis, segmentation, and feasibility studies should be performed to assure that explicit choices are made and well-informed strategies are set. But a sensible strategic marketing process is not by itself sufficient to guarantee desired results. It has been said that a bad strategy well executed may be worth more than a brilliant strategy poorly executed. While this formulation is undoubtedly exaggerated, it does hold a grain of truth.

The second major area of marketing tasks therefore deals with how to increase effectiveness. Functions associated with building the business are as diverse as data management and human resources. Managing them as an integrated unit entails supplying pertinent sales management information, building internal and external awareness, generating leads, getting at the buyer effectively, closing the sale, and ensuring effective after-sales service.

The relationship manager who knows the company best should undertake to prioritize both the customers and prospects for which the manager is responsible. To do this, he can use as a benchmark the normal credit standards of the commercial bank for information on noncredit service usage and profitability. He can then use this data to decide which companies to do business with. Prioritization should be based upon a preliminary forecast of the revenue and profit potential of the company. Having prioritized the companies with which to do business, relationship managers next need to put together a detailed plan for companies that appear to represent the most attractive potential. This plan should set forth the specific measurable objectives the relationship manager intends to pursue, and the optimal strategy for accomplishing those objectives. The objectives should themselves derive from an earlier, careful review of where the company has decided it intends to direct its future energies. Of course, the financial strategies, as well as the specific credit and noncredit opportunities associated with that direction, would also have to be considered. Customer/prospect priorities should be adjusted where appropriate to make a thorough determination of profit potential align closely with broad corporate strategy.

Training for relationship managers is an important ongoing element of the sales process. Not only should it be designed to ensure that selling skills are finely tuned, it should also make certain that these people have a good understanding of the evolving products and services the bank has determined it wishes to emphasize and sell. To ensure ongoing effectiveness of the selling effort, as well as the various sales support programs, performance must be continually measured. Such measurements will allow the bank to continually fine tune and improve its various programs. They will also make it possible for the bank to give proper recognition to its above-average sales performers.

In addition to direct sales efforts, a variety of techniques can be employed to generate specific sales leads. These include direct response programs via advertising or through the mail, telemarketing, and development of business referral networks. Awareness and reputation are built through many internal and external efforts of the bank. Some of the more common tools include advertising, newsletters, seminars/brochures, and public relations.

In addition to evaluating the performance of their sales forces and their various marketing programs, banks that aspire to long-term success should also institute programs to monitor the quality of the service they are delivering to their customers. It is axiomatic that exceptional companies continually strive to deliver to their customers what they have promised. Through customer service units, through attentive, inquiring relationship managers; and through various proprietary and syndicated surveys, it is relatively easy to determine how well the bank is doing in the eyes of its customers.

CORPORATE MARKETING—A LESSON IN DYNAMICS

Even nonmarketers can easily see the interaction between the strategic/analytical and the dynamic executional dimensions of corporate marketing. Product/customer profitability should provide grist for the market analysis function, while market research should contribute to framing target segments, selecting marketing strategies, and identifying sales training requirements. Most important, the whole process should be geared to continuous monitoring and fine tuning in response to changes in market behavior, competitive moves, and other forces. Analysis and research should provide a fix on the potential market universe, product requirements, and product profitability. The process should lead to decisions and choices which, in turn, ought to shape changes in selling techniques and adjustments in products and services.

Changes detected in the profit contributions of customers and products should send signals to keep the adjustment process going. The hackneyed expression a "living strategic plan" probably has even more meaning at the market level than at the corporate level, simply because customers are human and their preferences and needs change. Disciplined use of market data lies at the heart of corporate marketing. After all, customers are where revenue comes from and must therefore be the centerpiece in the design of any marketing strategy.

15 Distribution: A Competitive Weapon

EILEEN M. FRIARS
WILLIAM T. GREGOR
M. LUCILE REID
MARK D. JOHNSON

TOWARD MARKET-FOCUSED, PROFIT-BASED DISTRIBUTION STRATEGY

The current turbulent environment is forcing financial institutions to search for new competitive weapons. Firms have expanded their product lines and are now encountering an unfamiliar set of competitors and even less familiar distribution systems. Historically, most financial institutions sold a limited range of products through one major distribution channel. For example, checking accounts and loans were sold through branches of banks and thrift institutions; investment products were acquired through account executives of securities brokerage firms; and insurance policies were available through sales agents of insurance companies. Today, as deregulation removes restrictions on products, and technology offers new ways to serve customers, managers face an ever-enlarging number of tradeoffs, among the many new channel options that continue to emerge. The way managers reconfigure their firms' distribution systems in the 1980s to cope with new environmental change will have a telling impact on their ability to serve their markets—and stay profitable—into the 1990s.

Challenging Distribution Myths

A firm operates under a set of assumptions about how its business works and how it makes money. When the competitive dynamics and basic economics of a business change, as they have for financial services firms in the 1980s, these assumptions may no longer hold true. Yet old assumptions die hard, and they stymie many companies. The three following assumptions seem to be prevalent among financial institutions. These myths can threaten to undermine even carefully thought out distribution decisions.

Myth: More is better. Believing that "more is better," some financial institutions continue adding products to their distribution channels in hopes of improving profitability. But not all products suit the existing distribution channel or customer base. The more-is-better myth has led some banks to become discount brokers—a strategy that has met with only mixed success. One bank entering discount brokerage added $100,000 in distribution costs, but garnered less than $10,000 in fee revenue for its trouble. Research by the MAC Group indicates that customers seek a particular set of benefits when purchasing a product (such as specialized expertise or personalized service). Because customers select providers on the basis of the product benefits as well as the method of distribution, simply pushing more products through existing distribution systems may not be the answer.

Myth: Old is bad. Realizing that distribution systems must change, many industry observers simply conclude that old is bad and traditional systems are dinosaurs destined for extinction. Bankers and thrift executives may view the branch system as expensive and ineffective, while some life insurers see career agents as inefficient. Such views can lead to large-scale modifications of the existing channels, which are often a major source of revenues. When market share declines, as sometimes happens, results are disappointing.

An analysis of market and profit data will often dispel the old-is-bad myth. Customers value many attributes of established systems, such as their many convenient locations and knowledgeable, personalized service. However, customers may not be willing to pay the costs of overhead and services that systems have acquired over the last several decades. To survive, aging systems will need to be refocused and reconfigured. If managed effectively, the old system can in fact prove to be a tremendous asset.

Myth: New customers are more profitable. The "new customers are more profitable" myth is visibly at work in the industry today. Banks are chasing thrift and brokerage customers, thrifts covet bank and insurance customers, and insurance companies are pursuing bank customers. Yet by allocating too much effort toward acquiring new customers, firms reduce the resources they have to cross-sell and maintain existing customers, and the expected jump in profits often fails to materialize. This happens for two reasons: First, the high cost of convincing consumers to switch institutions can offset the revenues new customers bring. Second, established customers may become disillusioned with the changing character of the institution and sever their relationships. Often the existing customer base offers significant potential to deliver additional volume and profitability. Initially, most financial institutions would be wise to be sure they are maximizing the potential of what they have, and seek to attract new customers on a very selective basis.

What Customers Want

One way of rising above traditional assumptions about distribution is to take the customer's perspective. Leslie R. Butler, Executive vice-president of First Pennsylvania Bank, has written: "Financial institutions have to stop following each other and start following the consumer."[1] Those that do will be successful in increasing the efficiency of their distribution systems without compromising effectiveness. As noted earlier, it is easy to view distribution narrowly as branches, agents, and account executives. But when customers select a provider, they look for the distribution value they want, such as knowledgeable advice or convenient hours. Customers do not pay for tellers, ATMs, brokers, or career agents. They pay for the value of service, convenience, and advice that each of these options delivers.

Distribution systems have varying capacities for delivering value to consumers through information, personal service, access, and advice—but it is the customer who sets the ultimate value. A wealthy individual with complex financial service needs may find that a private banker is indispensible when he or she is making decisions about tax shelters or credit. A different person may have no need for personal attention, preferring instead to use ATMs that can process standard transactions any time of day. These two attitudes are undoubtedly extremes, but the point is unassailable: Consumers determine the value they want from a distribution system, and they choose the provider that delivers it.

Distribution systems also vary in their ability to enhance different products. When life insurance companies attempted to sell IRAs to their service-oriented customers by direct mail, for example, most did not respond; these customers wanted a higher level of service and advice for their purchase of IRAs than direct mail can provide. Bank branches, on the other hand, can deliver the information that service-oriented IRA customers want through their traditional channels. Although opening mail is more convenient for the customer than making a trip to the branch bank, providers who got into the customer's shoes reasoned that convenience is not as important to service-oriented IRA purchasers as advice. Fidelity, which has identified a group of convenience-oriented customers, was successful in marketing to this group because it had already built a strong customer franchise.

Redefining Distribution

In developing marketing strategies, the financial services industry needs to adopt a broader definition of retail distribution. Traditionally, financial services firms have defined distribution in terms of the primary channel outlets they used—branches, agents, or account executives. But distribution is not just outlets and sales forces. It is the complete range of distribution activities involved in acquiring and maintaining customers. It is also the combination of people, technology, and outlets involved in the industry's myriad efforts to acquire customers and maintain a customer franchise.

Acquiring customers, for example, entails such distribution activities as promotion and sales. It includes incorporating sales-promotion materials with account statements, and generating sales leads by computer, direct-response advertising, and cross-selling efforts. Most often involved in these activities are marketing and sales staff, and less frequently customer service people. Customer-maintenance activities—transaction delivery, customer service, and revenue collection—are generally handled by bank tellers, customer service representatives, operations clerks, and accounting staff.

Retail distribution, therefore, can be thought of as activities critical to serving markets at a reasonable cost. Distribution activities are important from a *market perspective* because they form the essential two-way link between the provider and the customer. From the provider's standpoint, distribution is the conduit for products, services, and revenues, and from the consumer's point of view, the distribution system gives access to the desired products and services.

Distribution is also critical from a *profit perspective*. Financial firms are above all service organizations. For that reason, distribution almost by definition constitutes a very large proportion of their operating costs. Analyses conducted as part of MAC Group research show that distribution costs range from 45 to 80 percent of operating costs, depending on the particular business. In the discount brokerage segment, for instance, the cost of customer-acquisition and maintenance activities makes up fully 60 percent of operating costs (see Exhibit 15.1).

Finally, distribution decisions often require major investments in people, technology, real estate, or all three. Because of these investments, the decisions take time to implement, have long payback periods, and cannot be changed without incurring substantial added costs. Given the scope and importance of retail distribution in financial services and the risks involved in making poor choices, it is easy to understand why managers are seeking answers to the difficult questions this environment poses.

Exhibit 15.1 Distribution Costs

Participant	Operating Costs Percent
Retail banks	45–50
Personal trust	50
Discount broker	60
Direct marketing insurance	70
Career insurance company	75
Full-service broker	80

Source: The MAC Group.

A Package of Benefits: The Offering

Consumers buy more than just products or convenient delivery—what they really buy is a package of benefits. That is, they make purchase decisions based on the total value they receive for a given price. For convenience, this package of value might be called "the offering." The offering is the product delivered through a particular distribution channel to a selected consumer. Thus, 24-hour cash access (the product), combined with an ATM (the distribution system), represents an offering directed to the convenience-oriented customer.

When purchasing a stock trade from E. F. Hutton, the customer purchases an offering that differs vastly from one purchased in a stock trade through Rose and Company's discount brokerage service. At E. F. Hutton the broker provides advice, research, information, and trade execution. Rose and Company only provides the trade execution, without information or advice. The same "product"—a stock trade—thus becomes two different offerings by virtue of the way it is delivered to the customer.

The industry is rapidly embracing this concept. U.S. Trust, for instance, has advertised an offering that explicitly featured both its product and distribution attributes. Representing elements of the financial services world as interlocking puzzle pieces, the ad shows how a home computer terminal, personal account officer, and a broker fit together with five separate products to create the U.S. Trust Master Account (see Exhibit 15.2). The bank has demonstrated our point explicitly: customers view products and their mode of distribution as a unified whole.

Viewed as part of an offering, distribution can become a source of competitive advantage. Professor Louis W. Stern of the Kellogg School of Management at Northwestern University buttresses this view:

Exhibit 15.2 Master Account Offering

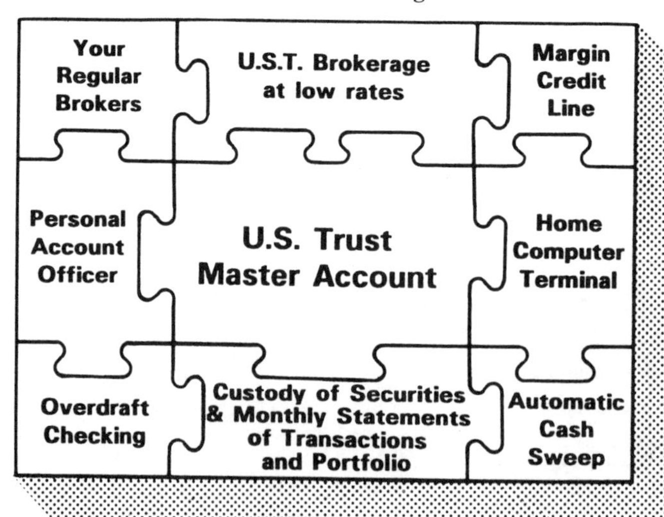

Source: U.S. Trust Company.

> In financial services, competitive advantages have been few. Distribution decisions, coupled with a thorough understanding of the customer are among the only sources of competitive advantage available. Financial services firms have far to go in applying this lesson.[2]

For most financial providers, making distribution a competitive weapon will require, above all, a capacity to make the right decisions. The rest of this chapter will bolster that decision-making capacity by examining new tools and perspectives.

BE MARKET-FOCUSED: THE CUSTOMER'S VIEW

Taking the customer's view is the critical first step for a provider seeking to become market-focused. It is difficult for providers to view what they produce and deliver as a package of product and distribution benefits. Yet what a customer wants and pays for is just that—an offering that combines product and distribution features. Shell and ARCO, for instance, distribute the same commodity product, refined gasoline. But each has tied that commodity product to a different distribution system—ARCO emphasized the low prices of self-service, while Shell emphasized the convenience of a no-fee credit card. This gave customers a choice between two very different alternatives. Firms like these have grasped the supremacy of the offering concept and enriched their understanding of how customer needs are satisfied. Based on this understanding, they can next construct the product and distribution portions of their offerings to better meet the needs of targeted markets.

The Offering Grid

To help managers visualize the offering from the customer's perspective, we have developed the offering grid (see Exhibit 15.3). This tool juxtaposes two dimensions of an offering, product complexity and distribution value-added, both from the customer's perspective. The offering grid allows you to see how product and distribution benefits are inseparable, from the customer's point of view, and shows that explicit decisions about matching a product and a distribution system are essential in meeting a target consumer's needs.

Product complexity is arrayed across the top of the grid, ranging from customized to commodity products. Customized products are tailored to each individual's financial needs—for example, a personal trust, key-man insurance, or real estate investment. At the other end of the continuum are simpler, commodity products. Checking accounts or airline flight insurance are two products that are well understood and widely available. These are commodity products that are usually standardized.

Distribution value-added—shown on the vertical axis—is the level of benefits the consumer receives from the distribution system. In financial services these benefits include personal service, advice, information, execution, and conve-

Exhibit 15.3 The Offering Grid

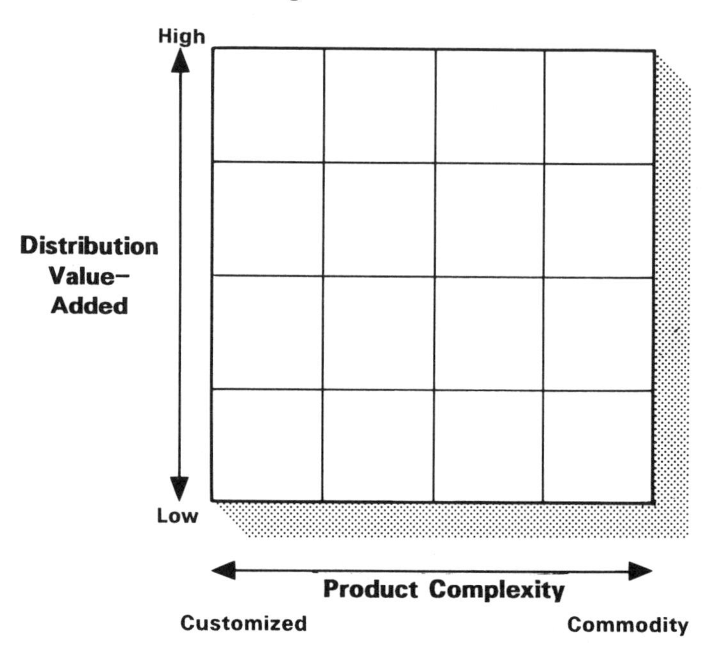

nience. At the high end are channels such as a personal banker, full-service broker, or a door-to-door insurance sales agent. Each of these distribution options provides high levels of advice, personal service, and information. Low value-added alternatives include mail, telephone, and other direct-response distribution channels. These alternatives supply little advice and personal service. Instead, they provide in-home, self-service convenience.

Offerings that have matched distribution and product components are represented by the diagonal line running from the upper-left corner to the lower-right corner of the grid (Exhibit 15.3). These offerings combine custom products with high value-added distribution systems, and commodity products with low value-added distribution.

Two Examples

The variety of offerings in the restaurant industry makes it attractive for illustrating the customer's view and showing how the offering grid works. On the diagonal line in Exhibit 15.4, the upper left-hand corner of the grid shows an offering of custom-prepared gourmet French cuisine served in an elegant establishment. Lavish attention from a coordinated team of waiters, along with advice in interpreting the elaborate menu, makes this a high value-added distribution system combined with a customized product. We have named this offering position after the exclusive Paris restaurant, "La Tour d'Argent."

In the lower right-hand corner of the grid in Exhibit 15.4 is a meal from a fast-food outlet. The food is completely standardized, and the restaurant chain has simplified or automated the preparation and service. This is appropriate; the product is easily understood and little information or advice is required. This offering position is named for the all-American favorite, McDonald's. The very different offerings of La Tour d'Argent and McDonald's both succeed. Their managers have skillfully matched product and distribution attributes to customer needs.

Different Customer Needs, Different Offerings

As indicated by La Tour d'Argent's offering, consumers are often willing to pay for a high level of advice and personal service when they are purchasing customized products. As a product becomes simpler, however (and its position thus moves toward the commodity side of the horizontal axis on the offering grid), most consumers do not require—and will not pay for—a high level of distribution benefits. For a hamburger most customers prefer McDonald's to La Tour d'Argent. Nonetheless, some people do crave hamburgers served in gourmet restaurants—offerings that would be positioned toward the upper right-hand corner. Still others have a yen for gourmet take-out food—an offering situated in the lower left-hand corner of the grid.

This example suggests that while offerings in most areas of the grid do have markets, the important question is the size of those markets. An offering whose

Exhibit 15.4 La Tour d'Argent's & McDonald's Offerings

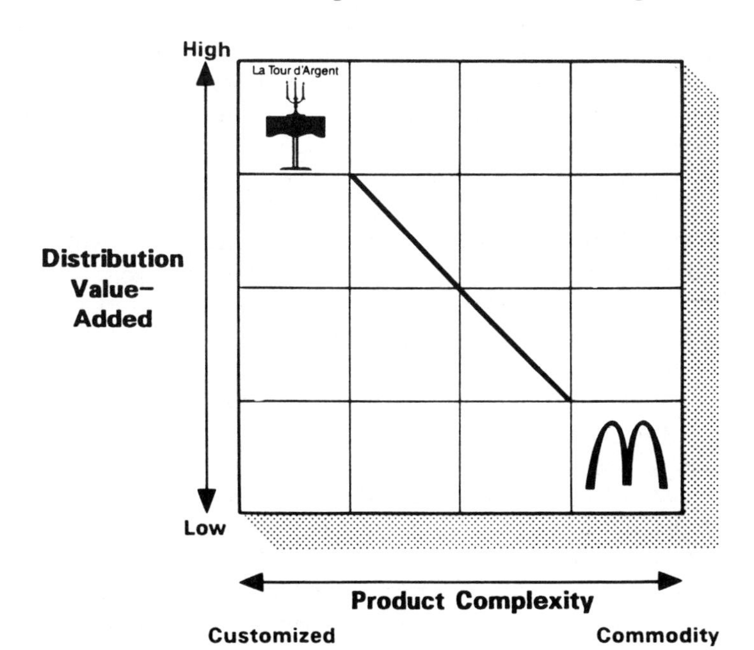

attributes place it off the grid's diagonal line generally addresses the needs of smaller consumer segments. Many firms have followed one another in creating banking or brokerage services for upscale customers, for instance, only to discover the market is too small to support them. Firms that construct offerings that would be well off the diagonal on the grid can see at a glance that business volume will be generally lower, and that their cost structure will have to be adjusted accordingly.

Segmenting the Market

To further illustrate the differences in consumer preferences, the MAC Group has developed a simplified approach to characterizing the distribution needs of financial services customers based on a range of retail segmentation schemes being used by financial institutions we studied. Because our research indicates clearly that an individual customer's preferences for distribution attributes varies by product, the scheme described here, though based on customer behavior, cannot be entirely representative. Firms need to understand the distribution benefit tradeoffs made by their unique customer base, and conduct their own original segmentation analyses.

This simple scheme identifies three customer segments that characterize behavior for most customers. Each segment has very different distribution needs. We have indicated these different needs by shading the areas where offerings purchased by these segments would fall on the offering grid (see Exhibit 15.5).

The first group is made up of the *"service shoppers."* They account for one customer in 10 at most. These customers are willing to pay premium prices for higher distribution benefits, preferring to cash checks using human tellers to ATMs, for instance, and buying insurance from professional agents. Significantly, although some service shoppers are wealthy, many are not. Several insurance companies' most profitable business is door-to-door insurance sales in rural areas. Service shoppers demonstrate that buying behavior does not always correlate with demographic measures such as income, age, or occupation.

The second group is composed of *"selective shoppers,"* who account for a little less than half of all financial services customers. The selective shopper purchases offerings while making price/benefit tradeoffs that depend primarily on the nature of the product. These consumers will use a full-service broker—E. F. Hutton, for example—for option trading, where advice is important, but call a discount broker like Quick and Reilly for simpler transactions.

"Price shoppers" make up the bulk of the remaining financial services customers. For a given product, they will search out the least expensive offering and avoid the costs of high-benefit distribution systems. Price shoppers are willing to learn about products on their own instead of asking a broker or banker to explain them. Price shoppers will, for instance, purchase universal life insurance policies by mail on the basis of a price advantage.

On the offering grid, service shoppers make purchases that fall in the upper right area, selective shopper purchases fall along the diagonal line, and price

Exhibit 15.5 Customers

shoppers prefer offerings below the diagonal, where products are combined with low value-added distribution options.

Traditional Approaches

The well-established practices of many financial services providers do not address the variety of tradeoffs being made by more and more consumers. Looking at Merrill Lynch illustrates this point. Merrill Lynch has a high value-added, full-service brokerage distribution channel, the account executive in local offices. The firm distributes its securities products primarily through the account executive, or broker. As a result, Merrill Lynch's offerings fall horizontally on the offering grid shown in Exhibit 15.6. This set of offerings will appeal to affluent customers in each of the three customer groups—service, selective, and price shoppers. Merrill Lynch's stated strategy of "being all things to some people"—consistent with "serve selected markets"—built a distribution system that was also some things to other people. In recent years increasing consumer sophistication has reduced the number of service-oriented customers. At the same time, the recent multiplicity of offerings has revealed the willingness of many to forgo once-unavoidable services. Merrill Lynch has announced new efforts to target several customer groups and to construct separate offerings using new distribution configurations for each. This suggests that the firm has recognized a problem with its current offerings and is working to remedy the situation.

The distribution systems of many financial service firms—regional banks, thrifts, and insurance companies—also offer a broad range of products with varying degrees of complexity through one channel. These firms' offerings would

Exhibit 15.6 Merrill Lynch

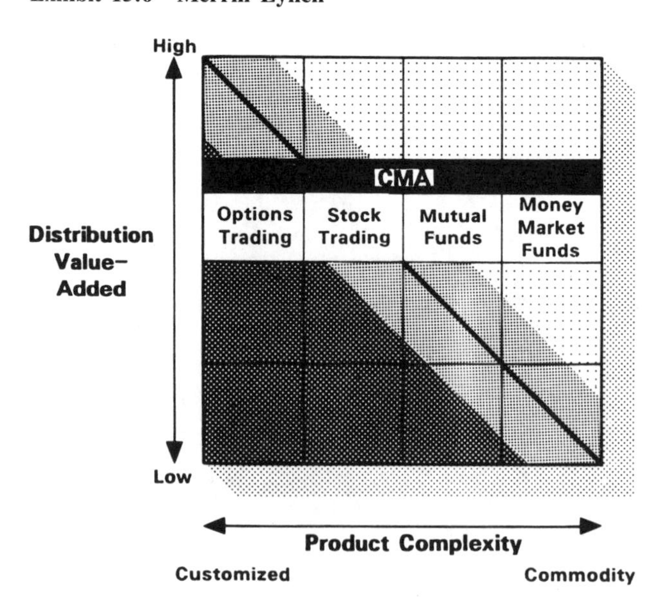

look much like Merrill Lynch's offerings on the grid. By focusing on only one channel, however, these firms may not be meeting all of the needs of any of their customers.

Multiple Approaches

Some firms are abandoning the single-channel approach and are developing multiple channels to address the needs of customers. Citibank seems to be going in this direction, as the positions of its three offerings illustrate (see Exhibit 15.7).

Each of the offerings meets the needs of a customer group that prefers a distinct level of distribution benefits for a range of products. One of these—Private Banking—is a group of customized asset management, lending, and deposit products aimed at the wealthy consumer and distributed through personal bankers in posh surroundings. The high level of advice and personal service is appropriate given the customized nature of some products and the service preferences of the targeted customer group. Focus, another Citibank offering, combines investment and banking products with an account officer available either by telephone or personal computer. It provides a lower level of personal service, but still accommodates consumers who want some customization. Finally, Citibank's Electronic Banking delivers commodity transaction products through ATMs that provide no personal service or contact.

Sustaining Differentiation

To sustain differentiation, firms must recognize that distribution is dynamic. *Deregulation* stimulated a high degree of change in the industry, but even in

Exhibit 15.7 Citibank Offerings

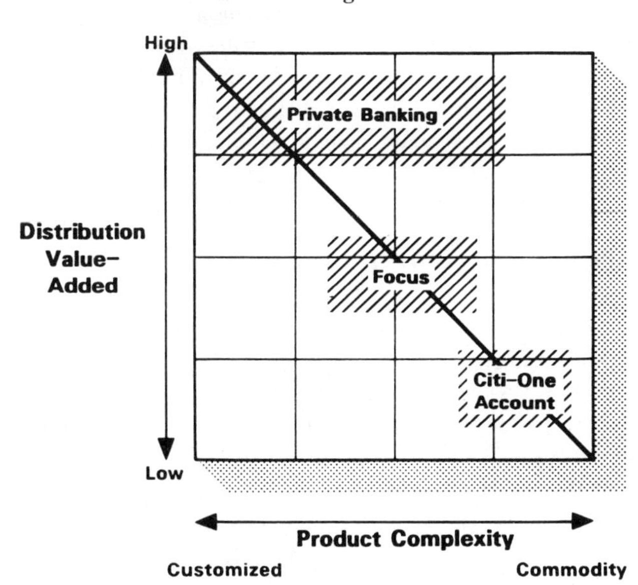

calmer times, offerings have a natural evolution. As more and more competitors enter the fray, products eventually evolve into commodities, and less advice and personal attention is required from their distribution systems. This evolutionary process is driven by:

- *Customer knowledge*, which decreases the need for high value-added distribution systems as customers require less information and advice
- *Competition*, which allows new entrants to establish and target niches of customers whose needs are not well met
- *Technology*, which facilitates the development of standardized products and lowers distribution costs

The history of the brokerage industry illustrates the evolution of distribution systems and the difficulty of remaining distinct from the competition. As recently as 1975, virtually all stock transactions took place through national, regional, or local full-service brokers such as Merrill Lynch and A. G. Edwards, which offered personal advice and research. But deregulation opened the door to a new group of competitors, the discount brokers. These companies, beginning with Charles Schwab, created low-cost, low-price offerings with considerably less distribution value-added (see Exhibit 15.8). Customers traded over the telephone or in a local office where customer service representatives took orders but provided no investment advice or research.

Discount brokers show up in the lower part of the offering grid; their offerings are intended to attract price shoppers and selective shoppers. Rose and Company went a step further, providing an even lower value-added offering—pure trading, no advice, and no offices—by removing local offices from the distribution system. The most recent step in the evolutionary process was first taken by C. D. Anderson in San Francisco: trading directly from home by personal computer, an offering made possible by an outside supplier called Trade Plus.

To sustain differentiation, a firm must continually monitor its offerings, customers, and competition. Firms that succeed will become market-focused. But being market-focused is not enough. There is another constituency that most firms must satisfy—the shareholders.

BE PROFIT-BASED: THE PROVIDER'S VIEW

For a provider to please the shareholder, its offerings must make a profit. In the regulated environment of the past, competition was held in check and pricing was prescribed, creating wide, virtually guaranteed profit margins for major financial service products. Based on these wide profit margins, firms were in a position to emphasize revenue growth. More important, perhaps, they were able to build expensive distribution systems to move a small number of products and offer high levels of service and convenience to all their customers. The safety offered by wide margins, combined with the fact that—with limited competition—customers

Exhibit 15.8 Distribution Evolution

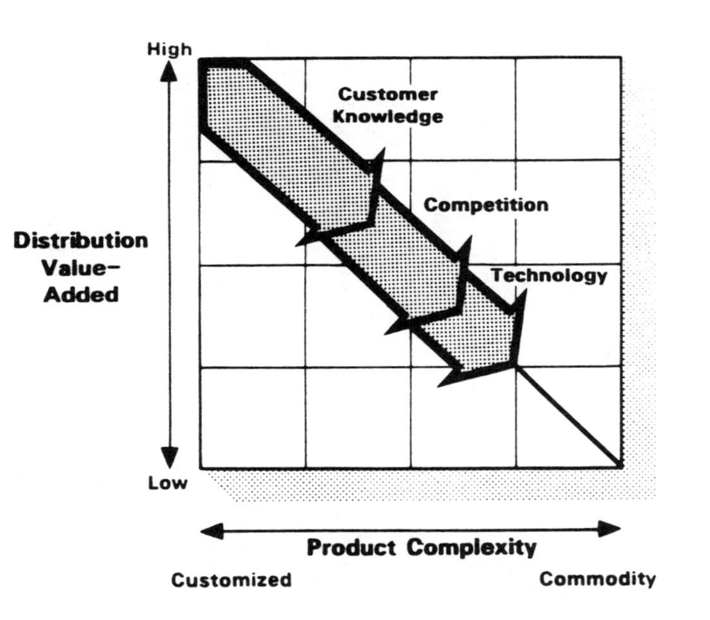

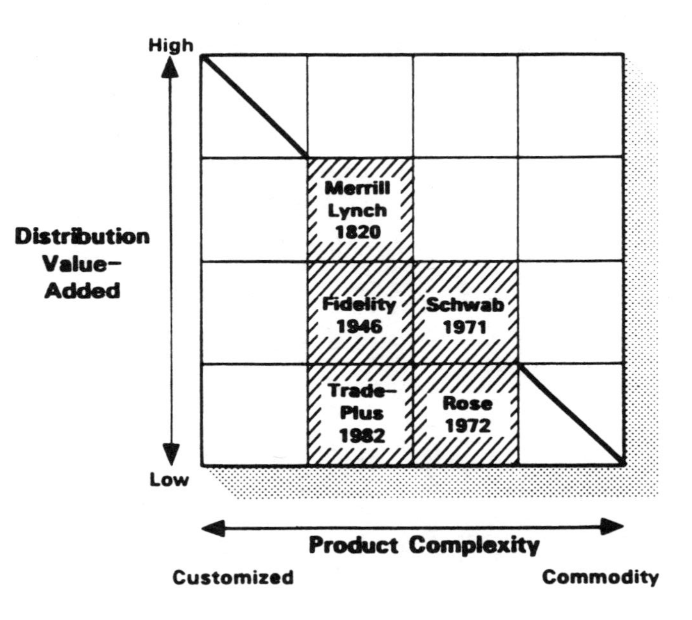

tended to stay with the same bank, broker, thrift, or insurance company, left managers free to focus their attention on building volume by attracting new business.

Under deregulation, however, fat margins have become thin, as low-cost competitors have driven prices to bedrock levels. Managers have had to shift their attention from just generating new business to generating profits. The new thin margins of existing products and services no longer support expensive distribution systems offering the same high service to all customers. As in the retail gasoline industry, financial services firms face the dilemmas involved in reconfiguring their distribution systems. Understanding and managing the delicate balance between revenues and costs has become more vital than ever. In many cases, firms must now deliver higher volumes of lower margin products to stay profitable.

The previous section concentrated on techniques for structuring offerings that give specific groups of customers what they want and need. This section takes a closer look at the reverse side of the coin—the provider's perspective—and examines the issues involved in making sure a firm's offerings are profitable.

Given the way financial and cost data are reported in most financial institutions today, it is not easy to assess profitability below the business unit level or identify the underlying drivers of costs and revenues. The necessary database is admittedly cumbersome to assemble, and managers often avoid the task. This reluctance results from management's traditional orientation toward revenue or asset growth, to the neglect of profitability considerations. It also stems from the difficulties managers encounter when defining and documenting revenue/cost relationships. Since many managers recognize that a high proportion of costs are fixed, they presume that any attempt to allocate these costs will ignite internal conflicts over allocation techniques and transfer pricing. To avoid this quagmire, more and more firms are putting measurement in a strategic, not an accounting, perspective, and measuring profitability on the basis of both contribution margin and fully allocated costs.

Early in this chapter we introduced the offering, a concept we believe is essential to making market-focused distribution decisions. The offering concept is relatively new and is developed from the consumer perspective. Profits are usually calculated from the provider's perspective, and generally stop at the business unit level. This means data do not include profit information for product lines by each channel used. The firms we have studied, save for a few using a single distribution system, were not able to produce an offering profitability analysis. Knowledge of offering profitability is desirable, but not usually feasible. As the next best thing, the most astute firms break their profitability analysis into three parts: product profitability, customer profitability, and distribution profitability.

Starting with Product Profitability

Most firms have the basic information available to conduct product profitability analyses. Revenues are collected and tracked by individual account, individual product, or product line. Direct and overhead costs are then allocated by account or product and subtracted from revenues.

The results of product profitability studies are often alarming. We have found that anywhere from 20 to 40 percent of an individual institution's products are unprofitable and up to 60 percent of their accounts generate losses. This high percentage of unprofitable products and accounts emphasizes better than anything how important it is for financial services firms to have the data they need to understand product profitability. Only then they can take effective corrective action by altering the product's cost or revenue structure.

Dependable product profitability information is also needed if products are to be managed effectively as a portfolio. Many managers defend continuing to provide products they intuitively believe are unprofitable on the grounds that these products are "loss leaders." But such loss leaders can only be justified if sacrifices are outweighed by contributions from other products in customers' portfolios.

Looking at Customer Profitability

Successful strategic plans depend on identifying profitable customer segments. Analyzing individual customer or customer group profitability is the link that connects profit-based decision making to market-focused decision making. Customer profitability analysis involves assembling data on revenues generated by a customer or customer group, and subtracting the associated product costs from those revenues. Our research has shown that in most firms, more than half of all customer relationships are not profitable, and 30 to 40 percent are only marginally so. It is frequently a mere 10 to 15 percent of a firm's relationships that generate the bulk of its profits.

Stopping at product profitability analysis can be misleading. One large retail institution, for instance, discovered through a product profitability analysis that 70 percent of its retail checking accounts were unprofitable. But customer profitability analysis revealed that roughly half of these unprofitable checking accounts belonged to customers who also held regular savings accounts. The final decision to revise the pricing structure of the checking product, therefore, required combining the checking and regular savings product profitability analyses.

Distribution systems cannot, however, be reconfigured just on the basis of product and customer profit information. In order to know what steps should be taken, distribution cost structures must be clearly understood as well.

Assessing Distribution Profitability

Distribution profitability can be analyzed by channel and by individual outlet. This involves measuring the revenues generated by an individual or group of retail outlets—be they branches, sales representatives, agents, brokers, direct marketing, or third-party marketing—and subtracting the costs associated with maintaining an outlet or group. Though it seems straightforward, the process of gathering and analyzing the data is time consuming, and the conclusions can be surprising.

Channel Profitability. Channel profitability measures the return on a type of retail outlet, for example, a branch system, a force of door-to-door sales agents, a network of offices, a WATS-line order system, a linkage to electronic terminals, or association marketing. Just as revenue/expense relationships differ from one product line to the next, they differ substantially among various distribution channels. Analyzing each channel will expose the profitability drivers that can improve efficiency. Furthermore, understanding the fixed/variable cost structure for alternative channels assists managers in selecting the best delivery system for new products.

Financial services firms that have limited capital or investment funds must often make hard choices about which channel to use to distribute a new product. One life insurance company, after making a substantial systems investment in a new universal life product, started to build three new and different distribution networks: a brokerage system, an agency system, and an employer-sponsored system. When investments ended up being higher than expected and growth turned out to be slower, resource constraints forced a choice.

The firm elected to continue funding brokerage—the group that had the lowest margins over the long term. The principal reasons behind this counterintuitive decision were that brokerage held the highest probability of fast volume growth. Because a fixed investment charge was figured into each policy, the number of policies mattered more than margins over the short term. Moreover, emphasis on the less competitive market for small policies facilitated the pass-through of costs.

Individual Outlet Profitability. Examining profitability of individual distribution outlets identifies differences in profitability across individual outlets and provides the basic information required to reconfigure the distribution system. In addition, such studies reveal the drivers of distribution outlet profitability.

Our profitability research into the branch system of a regional bank turned up some counterintuitive results, later confirmed by studies at other institutions. Thirty percent of the bank's branches were unprofitable—a revealing discovery, but not particularly helpful by itself. Of greater interest was the revelation that it was not low-cost deposits, high loan/deposit ratios, or the mix of profitable to unprofitable products that accounted for the profitable performance at the branch level. Instead, the key factor was volume—specifically, total deposits per branch (see Exhibit 15.9).

In fact, results point to substantial economies of scale at the branch level; tripling the deposit base, for instance, only doubles branch expense. Based on this information, the bank concentrated on building volume in its major branches to keep its profit high, at the same time scaling back on services offered by its smaller branches.

When a major securities firm analyzed its broker network profitability, it followed up with a study calculating individual office profitability. On the local

Exhibit 15.9 Branch Profitability

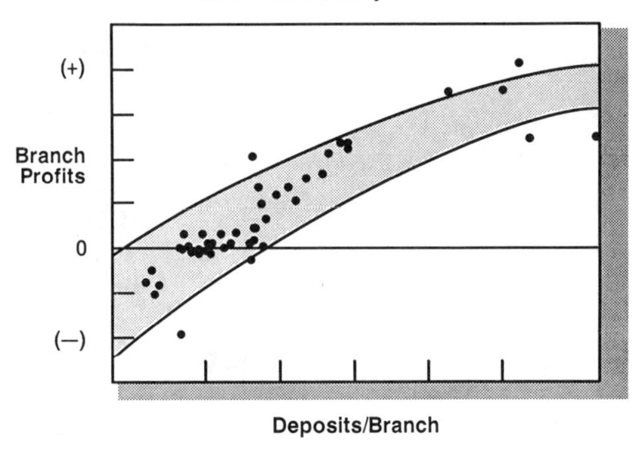

level the key determinant of profits was found to be length of brokers' tenure. The longer a broker had been in the business, the higher the office's contribution to the profits of the firm. The study's implication was that brokers should be retained and not laid off through low-volume (bear) markets, as was the widespread industry practice. Long-term gains in revenue, together with reduced need to train new brokers for high-volume (bull) markets, outweighed the cost of paying salaries through the lean times. (See Exhibit 15.10.) Overturning traditional logic, this revised view of office profitability regarded a large proportion of the commission-based broker network as fixed.

Beyond this, the study revealed that the primary ingredient in building and maintaining a high average length of service was the quality of office management, particularly the individual in charge. In the past this area had not received much attention from executives. Office management had been considered more as a necessary part of overhead costs than as a key driver of transaction volume and profits. As a result, distribution revitalization focused on deepening management capability at the office level.

Functional Cost Applied to Distribution. An especially critical driver of distribution profitability is functional costs. As indicated earlier, distribution costs are a significant portion of operating costs (see Exhibit 15.1). A functional analysis of these costs highlights the major types of activities in the distribution system and the expenses related to each, exposing potential opportunities for reducing costs as well as increasing effectiveness. The major functions—customer acquisition, customer maintenance, and administration—are common to every distribution system, but their relative importance varies substantially with the mix of offerings provided by an institution.

Functional analysis is particularly useful when firms are restructuring offerings and must decide which technologies to invest in. Many firms spend large sums on what they hope are cost-saving technologies—but base these investments on an intuitive understanding of the potential savings. One institution we studied, for

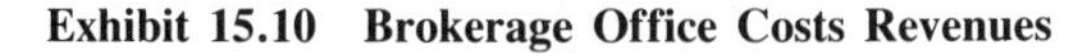

Exhibit 15.10 Brokerage Office Costs Revenues

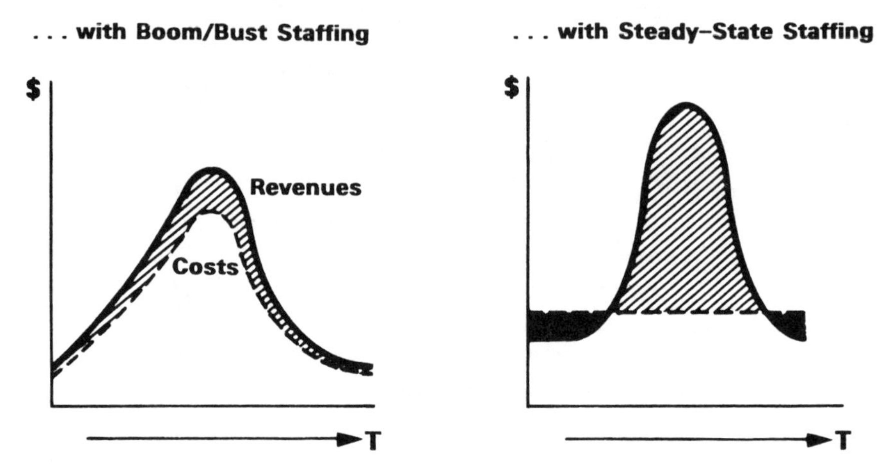

example, was preparing to make substantial expenditures to automate the teller line, installing additional ATMs in an effort to replace people. Fortunately, a functional cost analysis revealed that teller salaries accounted for only half of branch salary expense, and that tellers spent less than one-fourth of their time cashing checks—the activity ATM transactions handled (see Exhibit 15.11). The institution consequently shifted its efforts toward automating the platform in a more rational approach to holding costs down.

Having built a strong base of data around the key profitability drivers, and the profitability of certain products, customers, and distribution options, managers are well equipped to begin explicitly managing the relationship between costs and revenues.

PULLING IT ALL TOGETHER

The challenge to financial services executives now is to take a hard look at their retail distribution systems and develop product/distribution offerings that are profitable and provide a real competitive advantage. In designing distribution strategies, they must follow the needs and desires of the consumer—not blindly follow the rest of the industry. This chapter has arrived at four guidelines that should help management put distribution to most effective use in their marketing strategies.

Guideline 1: Serve Selected Markets. Companies succeed in these highly competitive environments by selecting target groups of customers (market segments), and serving them better than anyone else. Accomplishing this requires a precise definition and knowledge of market segments and a willingness to allocate resources to those that are chosen. Although many financial

Exhibit 15.11 Functional Analysis

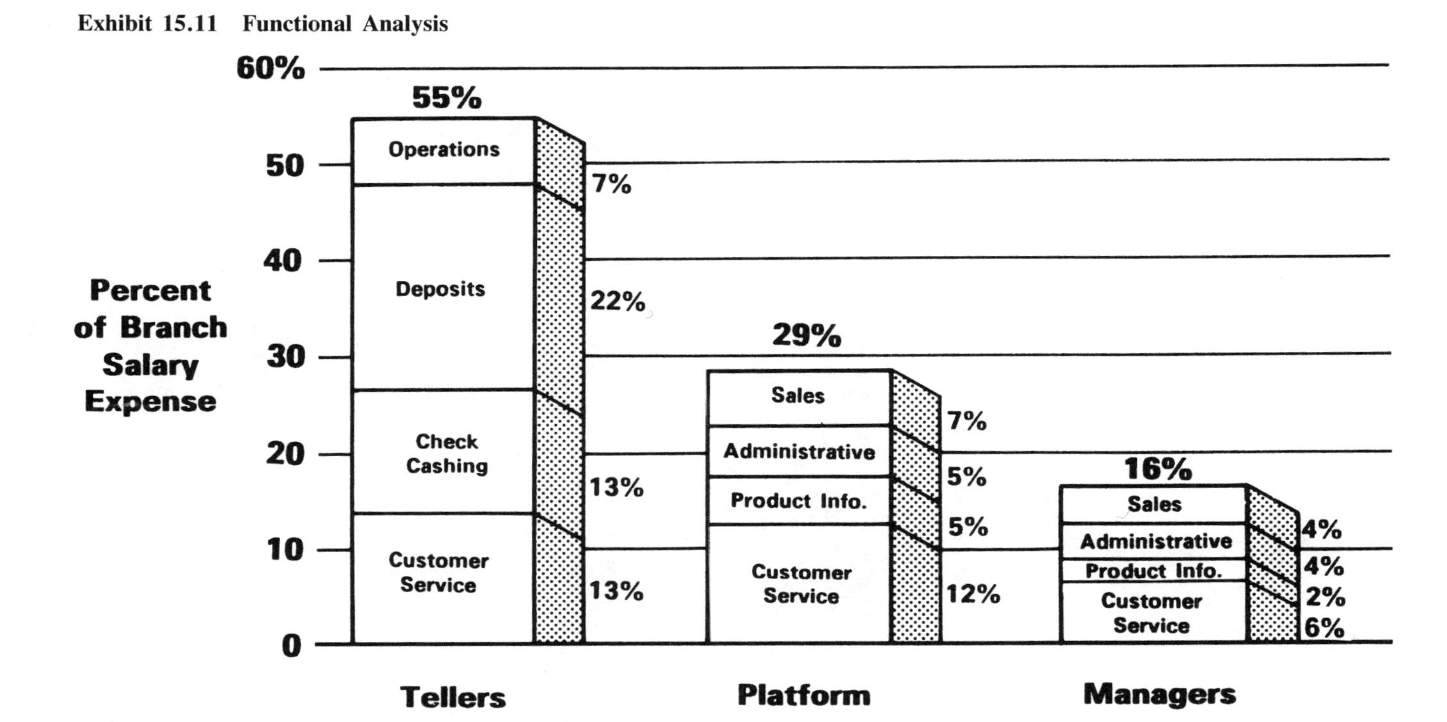

Source: The MAC Group.

services firms have segmented their markets, few have taken the next steps and been selective about who they want to serve, or translated their choices into concrete distribution decisions.

Guideline 2: Differentiate through Distribution. Another action taken by market-focused companies is to use distribution to differentiate an offering from the competition's. Merrill Lynch's CMA account used computer technology to link together products in a way that provided convenience to its customers. The investment in processing technology cannot be quickly imitated, and as a result Merrill Lynch managed to accumulate nearly a million accounts in the late 1970s and early 1980s before its competitors could introduce similar accounts. Failure to adapt to industry change, on the other hand, can leave a competitor with an undifferentiated image and no clear customer franchise. Designing the distribution system to position the institution uniquely in the eyes of the customer can create a competitive advantage that is very difficult to copy.

Guideline 3: Manage Costs and Revenues. Margin reduction is to be expected following deregulation. This lesson has been made abundantly clear in airlines, retail gasoline, trucking, and now financial services. In almost every case, firms must lower and control their cost structure to survive. Some will need to restructure their pricing as well.

Guideline 4: Make Informed Decisons: Markets and Profits. Because distribution is the link to the customer, distribution decisions must be driven in part by the needs of specific customer groups. At the same time, these decisions must contribute to the firm's bottom line. Successful companies create blueprints that carry a single lesson: Distribution choices must be both market-focused and profit-based—even though these two principles raise inherent conflicts. Successful firms have learned to analyze both dimensions and make decisions that keep them in balance.

Companies that neglect the insights contained in the successful blueprints often end up saddled with expensive distribution networks unsupported by their revenue potential. They ignore, or are unable to adjust to, new market realities and a new set of profit rules. Although different firms have translated being market focused and profit-based into different strategies, applying the lessons learned from others can help managers make the hard decisions they face in financial services today.

CONCLUSION

Clearly distribution decision making is complex. The difficulty in balancing market and profit motives in today's environment makes it essential for managers to reach decisions armed with a full knowledge of their firm's current positioning and future direction. Executives can become market-focused by systematically selecting target customers on the basis of their wants and needs, and structuring offerings to meet those needs. Firms become profit-based by understanding the key profitability variables and identifying specific areas where they are making and losing money. Then, and only then, will they have the knowledge and the commitment needed to implement difficult, but needed, distribution changes.

NOTES

1. Bulter, Leslie R. "Bank Branch Offerings: Dinosaur or Dynamic Opportunity," *Credit Union Executive* (Fall 1983).
2. Stern, Louis. Privately transcribed interview with one of the authors (Johnson), September 12, 1984.

16 Relationship Management

RALPH C. KIMBALL
ROWLAND T. MORIARTY

As a result of changes in competitive and market conditions, many financial services firms today are placing increasing emphasis on establishing and maintaining relationships with important corporate customers. Such efforts have often become the primary focus of their strategy aimed at the corporate market, but are also being applied to customers as well. New programs to establish relationships, however, have varied widely in terms of the amount of energy and resources devoted to them. Some banks, for example, have simply renamed their calling officers "relationship managers," and have placed more emphasis on cross-selling bank services. Other financial services firms have extensively restructured organizational units and have made substantial investments in management information systems and other support systems. In the past these relationships were handled on an ad hoc and intuitive basis. But competitive and environmental developments are now pressuring firms to conduct such relationships in a more systematic manner. The different approaches taken by various financial services firms are attempts to develop effective processes for establishing and maintaining these relationships.

Even though conducting business on a relationship basis provides substantial benefits to both the provider and the corporate customer, both parties must understand the benefits if the relationship is to endure. In addition, while relationship management can be used to increase the profitability of large and small corporate customers as well as consumers, the firm's approach must be consistent with other elements of its strategy, such as market segmentation and product development.[1] Finally, although relationship management often improves customer profitability, it is not appropriate as a primary strategy for all financial services firms because

---

Portions of this chapter are reprinted from "The Management of Corporate Banking Relationships," by John H. Gay, Ralph C. Kimball, and Rowland T. Moriarty, *Sloan Management Review*, Vol. 24, Number 3, by permission of the publisher.

of the resources required and the varying attitudes of corporate customers toward relationships.

Although the many issues connected with relationship management cannot be covered in-depth here, this chapter will raise and briefly discuss some of the more important ones. The chapter's first half describes the concept of relationship management and the environmental and competitive factors that have led to its current importance in the strategies of many large financial services firms. The benefits to both customer and provider are examined and the provider/customer relationship life cycle is discussed. Based on these analyses, some implications for strategy are described. The second half of the chapter examines the organization of the relationship management function, including the role of the relationship manager and common problems connected with the implementation of a relationship strategy.

What Relationship Management Is

In its simplest form, relationship management is a recognition that the financial services firm can increase its earnings by maximizing the profitability of the total customer relationship over time, rather than by seeking to extract the most profit from any individual product or transaction. Because most customers purchase many financial services products, and do so on a recurring basis, a provider must build and maintain a number of product relationships to reach the full potential of a customer. In some instances, a bank or insurance company may be able to produce and deliver two products at a lower unit cost than can two firms each producing a single product. Such economies of scope in the production and distribution of financial services make it possible to increase profits when product lines are broadened and more products are sold to each customer.[2] Relationship management, therefore, emphasizes deeper penetration of the existing customer base. Exhibit 16.1 lists some ways in which a marketing program based on relationships differs from more traditional, transaction-oriented selling programs.

Over time, as product linkages between firm and customer multiply, each party becomes more valuable to the other. Initial product linkages often give rise to personal relationships that transcend the sale of individual financial services products and act as a conduit for the creation of new product relationships. These personal relationships generate certain intangible but substantive benefits for both the provider and the customer. For example, in a corporate banking relationship, the customer is assured of preferred access to credit and is relieved of other perceived risks attached to the purchases of complex banking products. The provider in turn gains access to information about the firm's business plans and banking product needs, which provides a substantial competitive advantage in selling more of the bank's products to that firm.

Such strong and complex relationships are usually formed over relatively long periods of time. In such cases relationship management involves more than an emphasis on total customer profitability and cross-selling; it includes an acknowledged perception of mutual interdependence between the financial services firm

Exhibit 16.1 Relationships Versus Transactions as a Basis for Conducting Business

	Relationship	Transaction
Objective	Profitability of total customer relationship	Profitability of individual transaction
Strategy	Penetration of existing customers	Volume of new business
	Cross-selling of a variety of different services	Single product emphasis
Marketing	Emphasis on adding value in the selling phase	Emphasis on superior products
Functions	Management of internal and external relations	Sales
	Coordination of efforts	Go-it-alone

and the customer. In effect, the various personal and product relationships are institutionalized. The perceived interdependence of both parties is often based on mutual trust and openness, shared objectives, and a commitment to doing business with each other on a long-term basis. In its most developed form, relationship management involves the establishment of complex psychological and interpersonal relationships across multiple levels of functions, products, and locations. Over time these multiple links constitute an institutional relationship that, ideally, will persist for generations.

The Impetus for Relationship Management

New or improved financial services have proliferated as a result of deregulation, technological innovation, and increased competition among financial services firms. Since these factors have shortened the expected lifetime of most financial products, a customer relationship based on the sale of a specific product may be short-lived. For many firms it is therefore desirable to establish long-term institutional relationships with their customers. While specific provider/customer linkages fostered by individual products may come and go, the institutional relationship will persist and lead to successive new product linkages.

The establishment of stronger institutional relationships was certainly a key factor behind the development of Merrill Lynch's Cash Management Account, as John Steffens discussed in an earlier chapter. Brokerage firms, banks, and insurance companies have developed similar packages which aim at getting consumers to consolidate their financial accounts and develop stronger ties with their institutions.

Commercial banks' recent emphasis on relationship banking in the corporate market is at least partially attributable to declining interest margins on loans. Both the entry of foreign banks into domestic loan markets and the establishment of loan production offices by nonlocal domestic banks have increased pressures on interest margins. Many larger corporations, furthermore, have begun to borrow directly in the commercial paper market, reducing their dependence on commercial banks. As a result of this decreased demand and increased supply of bank credit, spreads on loans have narrowed sharply. Banks' reaction to this decline has been to cross-sell noncredit services to generate additional fee income. Similarly, declining margins associated with risk management have caused insurance companies to emphasize the design and administration of employee benefit plans.

Finally, relationship management has been stimulated by some corporations' increasing tendency to concentrate their financial services purchases among fewer providers. For example, the development of complex cash management systems linked by telecommunications networks makes it advantageous for a firm to concentrate its banking activities at fewer banks.

Benefits for the Customer

From the consumer's point of view, a solid relationship can mean less paperwork and more time saved, because fewer financial institutions are dealt with. In cases where explicit incentives have been provided, it can also mean a better financial return for reasons ranging from lower loan rates and fees to higher deposit interest rates. It may also allow the consumer to get better service and advice, since the institution has a clearer picture of the individual's financial situation and needs.

From the corporation's viewpoint, an institutional relationship offers several important benefits not usually received when financial services are purchased on a single transaction basis. Perhaps the most important of these is the provider's implicit commitment to provide ongoing credit and assistance. In effect, this commitment is an insurance policy, assuring the customer of access to credit during periods of restricted availability or financial distress.

The exact nature of this commitment has varied over time as financial market and customer needs have developed. In the early years of the twentieth century, when financial panics were common, preferred access to credit was vital to the customer to ensure survival during such crises. In the 1960s the imposition of Regulation Q ceilings—legal ceilings on rates paid to depositors—hindered the expansion of bank liabilities at certain points in the business cycle, and many banks were forced to ration credit among customers. Preferred access to bank credit was thus important to avoid cyclical disruptions in corporate business plans.

Today, larger banks are managing their liabilities so that deposit growth does not constrain credit funding. Other factors, however, may still make preferred access to certain types of credit an important consideration. For example, prudent country risk management may limit a bank's credit exposure in a particular foreign country. Preferred access to this limited credit may be critical to the success of a customer's operations in that country. Similarly, a bank's appetite for the purchase of tax-exempt industrial revenue bonds is limited by the size of its tax liability, and it will tend to allocate purchases of such bonds according to the nature of its relationship with the customer. A corporate customer hoping to utilize this low-cost form of financing usually must have a well-established banking relationship.

Preferred access also benefits firms seeking property and casualty risk protection. The appetite of a property and casualty carrier for certain types of risks may be limited, and this limited underwriting capacity is allocated to customers perceived as important to the insurer. Similarly, brokerage firms will tend to allocate popular, over-subscribed new issues to those customers with whom they have strong relationships.

The value of a banking relationship is frequently made explicit to a customer when some traumatic event jeopardizes his survival. A bank that is willing to assist the customer through such a crisis often establishes an extremely strong and long-lasting relationship. For example, during the Franco-Prussian war of 1870, when Paris was beseiged by Prussian armies, J. S. Morgan & Co. underwrote $50 million of French bonds to help the provisional French government purchase war supplies. This incident established a special relationship between the Morgan interests and the French government that has persisted for over a century.[3] Similarly, the assistance of the Guaranty Trust Company was a major factor in the survival and growth of the Computing-Tabulating-Recording Corporation (CTR) during the first decades of the twentieth century. This assistance was of particular importance during the recession of 1921, when an overextended CTR faced a serious cash-flow squeeze. Today, Guaranty Trust's successor, Morgan Guaranty Trust, is still the lead bank for CTR's successor, IBM.[4]

In addition to ensuring access to credit or underwriting capacity, establishing an institutional relationship benefits the customer by reducing the perceived risk associated with the purchase of financial services. The proliferation and increasingly technical nature of financial services, and the customer's substantial commitment in purchasing such products, have increased the risk of buying an unsatisfactory product. The credibility of the institution selling the product has therefore become increasingly important, and the ongoing, long-term nature of the relationship fosters confidence on the part of the customer that he or she will not be supplied an inappropriate or nonperforming product. Or if such a product is inadvertently sold, the customer is assured that the institution will take effective corrective action.

Finally, the customer's importance to the institution often stimulates special treatment in the form of customized services. These services take a variety of forms from product improvements such as special telecommunications links to facilitate data transfer and transactions, to personal services for senior corporate executives, such as an automatic teller machine placed in the corporate headquarters.[5]

Benefits for the Financial Institution

For most banks, the long-term goal of relationship banking is to establish a stable source of revenue and a profitable base of customers. With consumers, this often translates into higher balances and greater product usage. These benefits are even more prominent in the corporate market, where the goal of a banking relationship is to be lead bank for the corporate customer. Most large corporations do business with a number of different banks. A Greenwich Research Associates study estimates that the top 2000 corporations did business with an average of 17.6 banks in 1982, and were called upon by an additional 13.4 banks. These large corporations usually group their banks by "tiers," with the bank's tier position determining the volume and type of business awarded. Under such intense competitive conditions, it is critical for a bank to obtain a position of distinction as a leader or first-tier bank to gain a greater share of a customer's business.

In some cases, attaining lead status means the bank is the preferred supplier of banking services, and it will continue to be chosen as supplier as long as the customer perceives its products, services, and price to be approximately the same as those available from competitors. In cases where the customer has more than one lead bank, each lead will be permitted to bid on new business, and, in some situations, "to have a last look" and rebid to meet the competition.[6]

As a result of these substantial advantages, lead banks received 43 percent of large corporate noncredit-related business and 37 percent of credit-related business in 1982, according to Greenwich Research Associates. Lead relationships are so important that other proprietary research has shown a bank's market share of noncredit services to be closely related to its share of lead relationships.

In addition to winning a greater share of the customer's business, a lead bank is also able to realize higher margins on business with relationship customers. The greater customer penetration enjoyed by lead banks allows them to realize economies of scope in both the manufacturing and delivery of bank services.[7] Also, because customers receive significant intangible benefits from the relationship, the demand for banking services by a relationship customer is less sensitive to price than is the demand by a nonrelationship customer.

Achieving lead status usually means that the bank is able to obtain more detailed information about the customer's business plans and financial service needs. This information is of significant value when the bank is preparing its own business plans, and it can also be useful in product development efforts. Indeed, where particularly close bank/customer relationships exist, the bank and customer sometimes develop business plans jointly. Such activity is usually a clear sign that both parties recognize a mutual dependence.

Finally, lead status confers on banks some immunity to cyclical cutbacks in customer loan demand. Customer demand for credit is often related to the business cycle. It increases during expansions, as working capital and inventory are built up, and falls off during recessions, as inventory liquidation provides funds to the firm. During cyclical downturns, a lead bank is likely to suffer lower cutbacks in loan volume than is a nonlead bank.

Insurers that can establish an institutional relationship are able to enjoy many of the same benefits as commercial banks, such as a larger share of customer business and wider margins. A large property and casualty insurer has found its most profitable customers to be those customers who prefer to purchase coverage on a global basis from a single provider.

The Relationship Life Cycle for Corporate Customers

While many of the same principles apply to both consumer and corporate relationships, the remainder of this chapter will focus on the *corporate market*, where relationship approaches have been used by more institutions for a longer period of time.

Although most relationships are based on a perceived interdependence, the relative dependence of the financial institutions on the customer, and vice versa, may vary over time. Among the factors affecting the perceived value of the relationship to the customer are:

- *Competition.* Firms solicited by a number of competing financial institutions that are capable of meeting their needs are likely to place less value on relationships.
- *Need for Credit.* Firms requiring large amounts of bank credit value banking relationships to a greater degree. In contrast, firms that have primarily deposit relationships or have access to the commercial paper market do not value banking relationships as highly.
- *Need for Complex Products.* Firms involved in complex or unconventional businesses value relationships, since these relationships assist them in obtaining the customized services they require. The ability to structure and finance large projects in foreign countries, for example, is a skill appreciated by many large firms.
- *Financial Health.* Firms that are not strongly capitalized, that have low earnings, and that are engaged in lines of business perceived as risky, will place a high value on relationships.
- *Attitude Toward Management of the Financial Function.* Some firms prefer to concentrate their managerial resources on their own line of business, while others prefer to integrate backward whenever possible, absorbing internally some of the functions previously performed by financial services providers. Firms that prefer to purchase financial services rather than produce them in-house will place a higher value on relationships.

To some extent, the value placed by customers on banking relationships is correlated with the size of the firm. Larger firms are usually in a stronger financial position, have access to alternative sources of credit, are more capable of internalizing financial functions, and are solicited by a greater number of banks. However, the effect of these factors is often offset by an increasing need for noncredit products and customized services. In contrast, the value the bank places on the relationship usually increases as the customer grows, since larger customers use a greater number of credit and noncredit services. While there is a general relationship between the size of the firm and the value it places on banking relationships, the greater variation in individual circumstances can create substantial differences among firms of the same size.

Exhibit 16.2 illustrates typical bank/customer relationships. The vertical axis of the matrix measures the customer's need for the bank, while the horizontal axis measures the bank's need for the customer. Thus, in quadrant I the customer values the banking relationship to a greater extent than does the bank. In quadrant II, both value the relationship highly, and in quadrant IV the bank values the relationship more. The shaded areas of quadrants I, II, and IV indicate where both customer and bank needs are sufficient for a banking relationship of some sort to exist.

The life cycle of various customer/bank relationships is shown in Exhibit 16.2 by the solid and broken curves. At its inception the firm is at point 0, but moves toward point A as it grows. During this period, the firm values the banking relationship highly, especially for the access to credit needed to finance its growth. As the firm grows, the value of the relationship to the bank steadily increases. Having reached point A in quadrant II, several paths are possible. The firm may continue to value the relationship highly, so that further growth would be represented by the track AB, lying within quadrant II. Alternatively, as the firm gains access to other sources of credit and begins to internalize banking

Exhibit 16.2 Bank/Customer Relationship Life Cycles

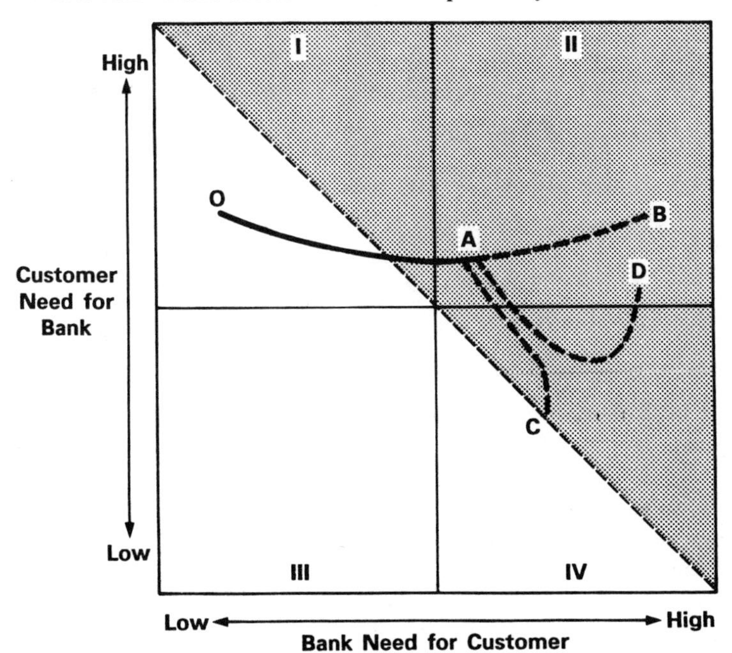

Source: Moriarity, R., R. Kimball, and J. Gay. "The Management of Corporate Banking Relationships." *Sloan Management Review*. (Spring, 1983) Vol. 24, No. 3.

functions, it could begin to place less value on the banking relationship. In this case the curve would fall downward into quadrant IV, as shown by the segment AC.

The value placed by the firm on the relationship may fluctuate over time, as shown by the curve AD. One large energy firm, for example, experienced substantial positive cash flows in the late 1970s and accumulated large deposits at its banks. As a result, the firm began to conduct its banking business more aggressively on a transaction basis. A series of business reverses and falling energy prices in the early 1980s depleted the firm's cash position. Now more dependent on banks as a source of liquidity and long-term funds, the firm has begun once more to make financial services purchasing decisions on a relationship basis.

When Relationship Management Is Appropriate

Because of the greater costs of relationship management and differences in customer attitudes, not all corporate accounts should be assigned to a relationship management program. Criteria must be developed to screen potential or existing corporate customers to ensure the best use of scarce managerial resources.

Customer Attitudes. The most desirable customers are those who value the institutional relationship over time, and who do not seek to exploit temporary conditions that give the firm an advantage over the financial services providers. These firms have an institutional memory that causes them to continue to appreciate the value of a relationship during periods when the immediate benefits are small.

Among the factors affecting the development of a firm's institutional memory are the tenure of the chief financial officer, and the career paths within the company.[8] Firms with frequent turnover among financial officers are less likely to develop institutional memories than are firms where financial officers hold their position for longer periods. Similarly, firms that hire financial officers from outside or transfer personnel across functional areas are less likely to develop institutional memories than are firms that select candidates from within who have spent their whole careers in the financial area.

A firm with little need for current bank credit and with confidence in its future ability to secure credit is likely to place a low value on its banking relationships. Such customers tend to be transaction oriented, purchasing banking services on the basis of price and quality rather than on a relationship basis. These transaction-oriented customers are usually more aggressive in managing their financial services needs, buying unbundled products from numerous banks, or what is becoming increasingly common, internalizing banking functions within their own organizations.

Similarly, multinational firms operating in a number of different countries may differ in their attitude toward relationships with property and casualty insurers depending on the degree of centralization of the risk management function. Those multinationals with a highly centralized risk management function are more likely to purchase coverage on a global basis, and thus to place greater value on relationships with insurers than are multinationals with a decentralized risk management function.

The different attitudes of customers toward relationships, and the effect these attitudes have on buying decisions, have implications for a provider's strategic stance with respect to its corporate customers. In particular, decisions about product development and breadth of product line are dependent on the financial services firm's approach to relationship banking.

Understanding Risks and Resource Constraints. If a provider's strategy emphasizes relationship management, the provider identifies customers with relationship potential and concentrates on developing business ties with them. But in order to realize the full potential of these relationships, the provider also needs to develop an appropriate product line to facilitate cross-selling. In addition to adding customers with relationship potential, a systematic and sustained effort must be made to upgrade existing second- and third-tier relationships.

One difficulty with this strategy is the uncertainty and risk involved in upgrading nonlead relationships to lead ones, especially when those customers have a long-established relationship with a competitor. Gradual penetration may lead to improved tier position, but the opportunity to become the lead provider may depend on the existing lead making a major error, or on some adverse and traumatic event occurring that forces the customer to need assistance that the existing lead provider is unwilling or unable to offer. In the latter case, the move to lead position may involve substantial risk exposure. The recent experience of Continental Illinois with AM International illustrates this risk:

> When Richard B. Black took over as AM's chief executive in early 1981, Continental's Baker called the officer handling the account to ask about the company's credit status. According to insiders, he was told that the bank's exposure at AM was being gradually reduced and that it would be almost eliminated by year end. Baker's order: Lend AM more money. He had faith that Black would be able to turn the company around. But AM entered bankruptcy proceedings last April, owing Continental $15 million.[9]

In any event, a strategy based on improving tier position requires patience on the part of the provider and may yield benefits only after a long period of persistent effort. Thus it may not appeal to management seeking visible results within a one- to two-year time frame.

Another drawback of this strategy is the resources required to develop and maintain an appropriate product line for very large corporate customers. For example, when purchasing banking services such customers usually purchase a broad range of credit and noncredit services. The investment in products and systems necessary to develop a full range of products may exceed the resources of all but the very largest banks. Unless a bank already has a sizable number of lead relationships, the volume of sales of individual products may not be sufficient to compensate the bank for its investment in these products. One response is to trim the product line to those products where volume is break-even or better. But if the bank does so, its larger lead relationships are vulnerable to penetration by competitors offering broader product lines. Thus a relationship-oriented strategy aimed at very large corporate customers may require a substantial investment in resources if lead relationships are to be established and successfully defended.

Focusing Relationship Strategy. Financial services firms lacking the resources or patience to implement a relationship-oriented strategy aimed at large corporate customers have developed several alternative approaches. One is to focus on developing a limited number of advanced or low-cost products for sale to transaction-oriented customers. The intention here is to expand sales and displace other providers by offering a superior product or a better price. This strategy is common among regional banks that lack the resources to offer a complete product line but nevertheless have the capability to develop specialized products for sale to major corporations. Among the regional banks that have followed this strategy successfully are Wachovia, State Street, and Mellon.

This product-driven strategy has its drawbacks, however. In preparation for new product introduction, the provider must commit substantial resources to identifying unmet needs of a target segment, developing an appropriate and superior product to meet these needs, and organizing a specialized distribution network to market it effectively. Since the number of products a provider can develop is limited, a product failure can involve substantial adverse consequences for the provider. Second, the provider must be alert to moves by competitors, and must be prepared to devote considerable resources to maintaining its competitive advantage. Thus this strategy not only requires substantial resources but also involves significant risk, both during product development and subsequently from moves by competitors.

The strategies of relationship management and a specialized product focus can be combined in some circumstances. For example, many banks and insurance companies concentrate on a chosen market segment, such as a particular industry or group of related industries, and develop a product line suitable for the special needs of this market segment. Thus a regional bank may not have sufficient products to pursue a relationship strategy aimed at all large corporate customers, but it may very well be able to develop appropriate products to support a relationship strategy aimed at utilities, transportation, or energy firms.[10] Also, because middle-market customers usually have simpler product needs than do larger customers, a regional bank may be able to apply relationship banking to this segment, while using a specialized product strategy to generate business from larger corporate customers.

Finally, at least one bank has created a dual marketing program for relationship- and transaction-oriented customers. A large New York bank has segmented its corporate customers in two large groups: (1) those who have either a current relationship or the potential for a future one; and (2) those who are not appropriate candidates for relationship banking. Relationship managers are assigned to the first group of relationship candidates, directing all marketing and delivery of services toward these customers. Product managers are given responsibility for the marketing and delivery of products to all customers except those in the relationship-banking program. The principal difference between relationship managers and product managers is that the former emphasize maintaining and improving the profitability of a single customer, while the latter focus on the volume and profitability of individual transactions. Thus their marketing approaches and pricing strategies may differ significantly.

The Relationship Management Function

Because the marketing and pricing approach appropriate for relationship customers will differ from that of other customers, and because relationships with large corporate customers are usually quite complex, successful implementation of a strategy emphasizing relationships will require that a relationship management program be organized in a systematic fashion. While a central function of the relationship manager is to increase customer penetration through cross-selling, relationship management involves additional managerial functions as well, both with respect to specific customers and internally within the financial services providers. The complex nature of many customer relationships and the managerial functions required of the relationship manager are the two factors that make relationship management more than a synonym for cross-selling. Unless these managerial functions are systematically organized, the financial services provider will jeopardize its ability to build and maintain the complex customer relationships that typify more profitable accounts.

Complex Customer Relationships

The principal impetus for relationship management is the increased complexity of relationships with larger customers. This complexity arises from a number of different causes. For example, the customer's decision-making process is often complex due to the customer's organization structure, the size of the transaction, or the nature of the product. Decisions about the level and type of pension investment services purchased by a corporate customer, for instance, are often influenced by both the customer's human resources and treasury functions. Similarly, the treasurer of a foreign subsidiary often reports to and is compensated by the subsidiary's manager, but his career advancement is determined by the treasury division of the parent company.

Another source of complexity arises in organizations where purchasers of financial services are not the users, or where the product will be used by different functional units of the customer. For example, while a lockbox is primarily a cash management tool used by the customer's treasury function, information is also generated for use by the customer's accounts receivable department. In situations where there are dual users, the relationship manager must create multiple relationships within the customer's organization structure.

Relationships are also more complex in organizations where the functional or operating units of the customer are geographically dispersed. For customers operating on a national or global scale, financial services have to be delivered at different geographical points. In this case also, the relationship manager not only has to coordinate product delivery but also must ensure that policy is consistent throughout the world. Providing foreign exchange services, for example, often requires a provider to work with the customer's subsidiaries in numerous different countries.

The complexity of the relationship increases further when customers purchase multiple products produced by different functional units of the provider. For example, most large relationship customers may purchase a variety of credit, deposit, and noncredit services from a bank. The relationship manager must coordinate the delivery of these products in order to guarantee a consistent level of quality service. Inadequate performance by one product or in one market adversely affects the overall relationship and can endanger the bank's ability to maintain or expand other product sales to the same customer.

Managing Relationship Managers

As relationship management is itself a complex process, implementing a relationship management program may require extensive staff training, difficult organizational changes, and the development of special techniques to motivate, evaluate, and compensate relationship managers. Relationship managers generally need training in areas such as relationship planning, competitor analysis, and negotiation skills. Similarly, organizational units may have to be restructured to give relationship managers sufficient authority relative to their responsibilities.

For example, what is the authority of the relationship manager relative to product managers, country managers, and support staff? If there is a dispute between the relationship manager and a product or country manager concerning pricing or the availability of resources, how will the dispute be resolved? Careful consideration of such issues is critical, since financial services providers implementing relationship management programs often assign responsibility for profitability to the relationship managers without giving them the authority to command the resources and make the decisions necessary to carry out their responsibilities.

Existing cultural norms may also hinder the implementation of effective relationship management. When there is a widespread belief among staff that it is important to defend one's management prerogatives, or that managers are evaluated only on the basis of their own reported profit contribution, the relationship manager's ability to organize and coordinate actions by diverse areas of the provider will be impaired. Even if detailed management processes are put in place that specify decision procedures or the division of revenues among units, staff from different areas must be able to work together on an informal and mutually trusting basis for results to be satisfactory.

Another issue arises from conflict between the financial services provider's goals for the relationship and the relationship manager's personal ambition for rapid career advancement. A critical variable in maintaining and strengthening a customer relationship manager's personal goal of gaining a broad and varied work experience or moving up to more responsible management positions will conflict with this. Career paths and compensation practices must be structured so that the best staff do not view substantial time spent as relationship manager to an important customer as a dead-end position. One solution to this problem is to have relationship managers keep their more important accounts as they move up in the organization.

A similar problem arises from the inherent conflict between performance measurement systems and the temporal nature of institutional relationships. Relationship managers are usually evaluated annually on the profitability of the relationships they manage. But the establishment of a successful relationship may take many years of persistent effort before profit objectives can be attained. How can the efforts of the relationship manager be measured and evaluated during the interim period when customer penetration is not yet significant?

The Role of the Relationship Manager

A key internal management function performed by relationship managers is the coordination of sales efforts and the delivery of services. While coordinated, intensified selling efforts are critical to the generation of income, they can adversely affect customer relationships unless they are well organized. Often customers complain that they are called upon by two or more officers of the same bank who give conflicting advice. An intense but uncoordinated calling program often gives an impression of disorganization and lack of professionalism, and it can seriously affect the provider's credibility. Moreover, as mentioned above, the proliferation and greater technological complexity of financial services have complicated the delivery of banking services. Delivery problems are further complicated if the customer should have geographically dispersed domestic and foreign offices, as is becoming increasingly common. Thus, to maintain service levels, the relationship manager must also coordinate delivery of products.

The relationship manager performs additional functions with respect to individual customers. One of the most important of these is the development of strategies for account penetration. Large corporate customers usually purchase financial services from several different providers. In order to displace competitors and increase his share of the customer's business, the relationship manager must identify individuals within the customer organization who make or influence decisions about financial services and persuade them that his firm wants their business and can offer quality products and services. Analyses of the customer's financial services needs must be conducted and appropriate products selected for them. Pricing strategies must also be developed. In short, a detailed relationship plan must be developed that meets the specific needs of each customer.

A second function of the relationship manager is to reduce the customer's transaction costs. Acting as a central contact point for all transactions with the provider, the relationship manager provides information, arranges for technical specialists when needed, ensures that errors are corrected—in short, performs all functions that would prove burdensome to a customer not intimately familiar with the provider's organizational structure. The relationship manager's understanding of the customer's business, furthermore, reduces the time and effort expended by the customer in communicating problems or product needs.

The relationship manager also builds and maintains personal relationships across functions, levels, operating units, and time. Establishing and maintaining these relationships is crucial because individual decision makers within the customer organization change as a result of retirements, promotions, and separations. Thus the relationship manager must ensure that the institutional relationship is not terminated by a change in personnel. To preserve the personal network that sustains the institutional relationship, the relationship manager must identify likely successors and build personal relationships with them.

Finally, the relationship manager must work to attain a position of influence over the customer's buying decisions. By demonstrating an in-depth knowledge of the customer's financial service needs and those of the key decision participants, and by delivering superior service, the relationship manager establishes credibility. Having earned the trust and confidence of the customer, the relationship manager can assume an advisory role and can then influence the customer's financial services purchases.

Problems with Relationship Management

In order to establish and maintain an institutional relationship, the provider may have to trade off earnings in the short term for the long term. As mentioned previously, the customer wants an institutional relationship to ensure access to services despite economic or political conditions or business setbacks. A relationship-oriented bank must, therefore, be prepared sometimes to furnish credit even if its risk exposure is increased or some opportunity for short-run gain is foregone. Prudent country-risk management, for instance, may prevent a commercial bank from meeting the credit demands of both indigenous borrowers and multinational corporations that wish to do business in certain foreign countries. In such circumstances a country manager might want to allocate the scarce available credit to indigenous borrowers, thereby obtaining greater net interest margins and enhancing the bank's local reputation. But effective relationship banking stipulates that the bank allocate its credit to multinationals with which it has lead relationships. From the bank's perspective, the immediate loss of revenue will be offset by other business generated by the relationship. A related example of this tradeoff is Morgan Guaranty's deliberate operation with a capital-to-asset ratio above that of its peer group so that it will have the capacity to raise additional funds should customers need them.[11]

The cost of an effective relationship management program is significantly greater than conventional calling programs, resulting from greater skills required of relationship managers, more intensive personal selling involved, and special support systems needed. In addition to the product knowledge, customer knowledge, and selling skills normally required of calling officers, relationship managers must also possess management skills to mobilize and coordinate technical specialists; analytical talents to assess customer service needs and to formulate plans for account penetration; and relationship skills to identify the customer's decision-making process, to build personal contacts and influence, and to maintain the relationship over time. The provider must develop these additional skills among its own staff.[12]

In addition, in order to gather needed information on the customer's business, financial needs, and purchasing decisions, and in order to maintain personal contacts, the relationship manager must make frequent and often lengthy calls on the customers. Consequently, the number of accounts that can be handled by a relationship manager is significantly less than the number of nonrelationship accounts serviced by calling officers.

Finally, to measure and control the profitability of their relationship customers, relationship managers need information systems that provide detail on the various services purchased by the customer. The cost of developing such support systems can be significant. As a result of the greater variable costs of using more skilled staff and more intensive calling, and the greater fixed costs of developing specialized information systems, relationship management is only appropriate for those larger customers whose long-term profitability is sufficient to offset the increased costs.

Conclusion

Individual financial services providers have varied widely in their approach to relationship management. Some have adopted a "toe-in-the-water" approach, appointing relationship managers for a few customers on a trial basis, or increasing their emphasis on cross-selling and overall customer profitability. But overall, organizational changes or investment in support systems have been avoided. Such superficial programs may be initially successful, but they often founder as organizational conflicts emerge, skill deficiencies become apparent, and senior management begins to lose patience because no immediate results occur. Thus, the validity of relationship management as a strategy depends critically upon how effectively it is implemented. Effective implementation requires that the provider's management processes, support systems, human resources, and marketing program be consistent with a relationship-oriented strategy. Above all, relationship management is not a "quick hit" strategy that can be implemented quickly or at a low cost. Rather, relationship management is a strategy requiring greater patience and a substantial investment of resources before it becomes successful. Perhaps these factors explain why, despite a fairly widespread intuitive understanding of the dynamics of institutions' relationships, very few financial services firms have been able to implement an effective relationship management strategy.

NOTES

1. Although the concept of relationship management can be applied to retail customers, this chapter focuses on the corporate customer. For a treatment of relationship banking applied to the retail customer, see Berry, L. L., and T. W. Thompson. "Relationship Banking: The Art of Turning Customers into Clients." *Journal of Retail Banking* (June 1982) pp. 64–73.
2. For a review of this concept, see Bailey, E. E., and A. F. Friedlaender. "Market Structure and Multiproduct Industries." *Journal of Economic Literature* (September 1982).
3. See Allen, F. L. *The Great Pierpont Morgan*. New York: Harper, 1949, p. 36.
4. The recession of 1921, although short-lived, was particularly sharp. See Sobel, R. *IBM: Colossus in Transition*. New York: Truman Talley Books, 1981, pp. 49, 65–66.
5. This special treatment of important customers was epitomized when a New York City bank placed a statue in the garden of a new branch in Manhattan. The statue shows a trust officer walking a customer's dog.
6. Although Greenwich Research Associates reports that Fortune 1000 firms receive an average of 136 sales calls per quarter by commercial banks, or two every working day, such firms are likely to seek bids from only three or four banks when considering the purchase of new banking services. Being invited to bid is obviously of crucial importance to the bank.
7. While economies of scope may give the provider a competitive cost advantage, this may be offset by the additional costs of managing complex relationships.
8. This is illustrated by the statement of the treasurer of a troubled drilling concern: "I know if we get through these things, we'll stay with Continental as long as I'm here." See "Big Continental Illinois Hopes It Will Recover as U.S. Economy Does." *Wall Street Journal* (January 5, 1983) p. 17.
9. See "Continental Illinois' Most Embarrassing Year." *Business Week* (October 11, 1982) pp. 89–90.
10. The development of an industry specialization also benefits the provider by increasing the credibility of its marketing programs, and sometimes in the case of banks, the effectiveness of its credit analysis. The specialized product focus in corporate relationship banking has an analogue in the "core service" of retail relationship banking. See Berry and Thompson (June 1982), pp. 64–73.
11. An additional factor that may explain Morgan's balance sheet policies is its mix of business. The lack of a large retail deposit base and its dependence on a small number of large corporate customers may make it prudent for Morgan to operate conservatively in order to be able to raise funds if an important customer should withdraw its business.
12. Research has shown that efforts to short circuit this training process and hire qualified individuals from outside the bank tend to fail because these individuals lack the influence, credibility, and other skills necessary to manage delivery of services within the bank. Thus, "relationship managers" must be developed rather than bought.

17 Challenges in International Marketing

D. WILLIAM SCHREMPF

The market for international financial services represents a tremendous opportunity. Revenue growth for these services has been greater than that of most of the developed economies. Taken overall, profitability has also been better than that experienced in most of the major economies of the world. All of this is true. But there is another side. Few companies have successfully realized the potential for growth and profit that the international markets offer. Regulation, nationalism, the problems of managing a diverse and far-flung network—all of these factors and more have conspired to block the aspirations of many internationally minded corporations.

This chapter will explore the nature of the international market—its characteristics and some of the important trends that should be considered in establishing an international strategy. The opportunities inherent in the market will be considered along with the risks that must be evaluated by any potential market entrant. Finally, the task of selecting and implementing a successful international strategy will be explored, along with the management issues with which an international organization must deal.

On the assumption that organizations with extensive international operations will already have benefited, perhaps painfully, from their experience, the primary focus will be on issues that will be faced by companies with little or no international business and on the decisions they must take as they consider entering international markets or expanding their international operations. However, many of these same problems confront large, global companies which are considering entering a new market, product line, or customer segment. Special considerations applying to companies with large, existing international networks will be highlighted whenever possible.

PERSPECTIVE ON THE MARKET: OPPORTUNITIES

Although it is common shorthand to talk about "the international market," the belief that there is one international market has been the downfall of many a company. Unfortunately, there is no such animal. Instead, there are literally dozens of separate markets, each with its own unique characteristics. Virtually every country has its own laws and regulatory structures. Most have their own currencies and languages. These factors alone create enough diversity to assure that no two markets will be alike.

When cultural differences are added to variations in business practices, it becomes clear that each local market must be approached separately by any company considering doing business there. Some part of the company's historic formula for success in its home market may be applicable, but the formula will almost certainly have to be adapted to local conditions. A good nonfinancial example of this is McDonald's. The company has strict standards around the world for quality, portion size, and so forth. However, protective legislation prohibits McDonald's from either importing or growing its preferred potato (for french fries) in much of Europe.

The problems of regional variation facing a financial services company are perhaps even greater. Business practices, regulation, and market economics seem to differ much more markedly from country to country than do eating habits—and traditions are much harder to change. Anyone thinking on a global scale must be prepared to cope with the intense nationalism of Japan, many of the developing countries, and even Australia and Canada. On another dimension, collection and payment standards vary enormously from country to country. In some developing countries 180 to 270 days might be considered prompt payment, whereas in countries like Australia governments legislate strict payment standards for insurers, brokers, and others. Any company considering an international strategy must also recognize the tremendous differences in economic growth, development, and market sophistication from one country to another. Such variations can be seen even within the same region (or among countries considered comparably developed, developing, or underdeveloped) that legislate strict and very tight payment standards for insurers, brokers, and others. The list of such variations is virtually endless, and almost every country takes its own approach. Plainly, the world market represents a segmentation problem of the most complex dimensions.

Notwithstanding the difficulties associated with classifying international opportunities, the potential for growth and profit is unquestionably great. One need only to look at Citicorp or American International Group (AIG) to recognize the impact that a successful international operation can have on a company's bottom line. For a number of years Citicorp's Brazilian company alone produced more profit than all of its U.S. operations combined. AIG's Japanese, Philippine, and Malaysian companies similarly have produced profits out of all proportion to their revenue, and the insurer's total international operation has been its most profitable, consistent, and fastest growing business for many years.

What is it about international markets that make them so profitable? While it is difficult to generalize about a particular country, patterns emerge when one looks at a large cross-section of countries. First, many countries regulate financial services businesses very closely. Pricing is often regulated, with price levels generally set to protect the least efficient companies in the industry. Approved products may be specified along with payment terms in order to minimize competition. In such an environment, a well-positioned, well-capitalized, or particularly efficient company may take advantage of these market inefficiencies to the benefit of its bottom line.

A second factor in many countries is a lack of local capacity (capital, ability to syndicate large exposures, and so on) or technical expertise. This deficiency is particularly true of smaller underdeveloped or developing countries where local competitors lack the ability to serve the larger and more complex corporate or governmental risks in the country. Large multinational companies operating in these economies may be able to create a significant competitive advantage for themselves in this kind of environment, particularly if they can combine access to capital and international financial networks with local underwriting or other technical talent.

In economies where local financial institutions, or even the local economy itself, are so fragile that local consumers or businesses lack the confidence to place their funds with indigenous companies, foreign companies may be viewed as a very attractive alternative. Foreign life insurers in a number of African countries have enjoyed the advantage of being considered as safe local havens—among the only secure places for individual savings.

Finally, a few large multinational financial institutions have been able to compete on the basis of their unique global capabilities. These companies can provide services that no local company, virtually regardless of size or capability, can provide to local industries doing business abroad. Although such a network would be difficult to create today, it was not always so. British companies that formerly expanded to serve their customers throughout the Commonwealth, and American companies that expanded all over the world to serve developing U.S. multinationals, have enjoyed the benefits of the unique services they could provide.

Non-U.S. markets for financial services have also grown faster than the U.S. market for many years. This trend is illustrated by the following graphs (see Exhibits 17.1 and 17.2), which show the growth of American versus non-American insurance premiums in recent years.

This attractive pattern of growth is attributable to a number of factors. In many countries in Southeast Asia, Latin America, and Africa, growth rates have substantially exceeded the global average. Countries like Korea, Singapore, Colombia, and the Ivory Coast have enjoyed the benefits of industrialization and development of their natural and human resources. This growth has required a concomitant expansion of financial services and financial capacity. So financial industries in these countries have grown as well.

At the same time, the worldwide market for financial services has become increasingly sophisticated. Led by the United States in most cases, the products and services offered by financial institutions have become broader and more

Exhibit 17.1 U.S. Share of World Insurance Premiums

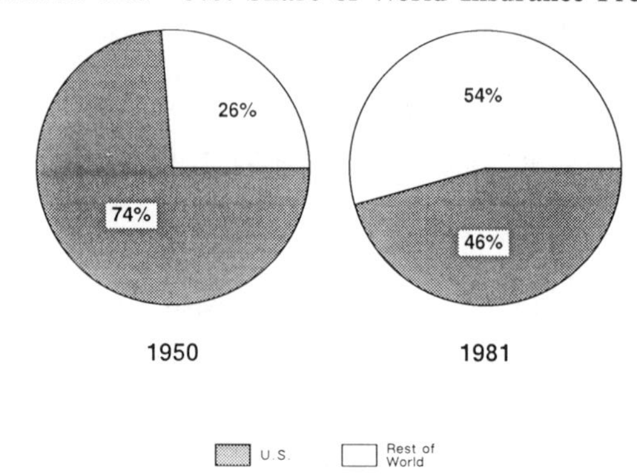

complex. Parallelling this growth, financial markets have increasingly shifted from locally isolated institutions to components of one integrated global market. This increasing sophistication, combined with globalization, has caused financial service industries in general to grow even faster than their local economies.

A final contributor to the rapid worldwide growth in financial services has been the development and proliferation of multinational companies since World War II. U.S. direct foreign investment has grown considerably faster than GNP for a number of years. Today, European direct foreign investment is also outpacing U.S. growth, with most of the funds moving into the United States and Latin America. Thus, even in the relatively stable developed economies of Europe and the United States, there have been significant growth opportunities in foreign financial services.

These are the underlying trends that have made the market for international

Exhibit 17.2 Global Markets—Premium Growth

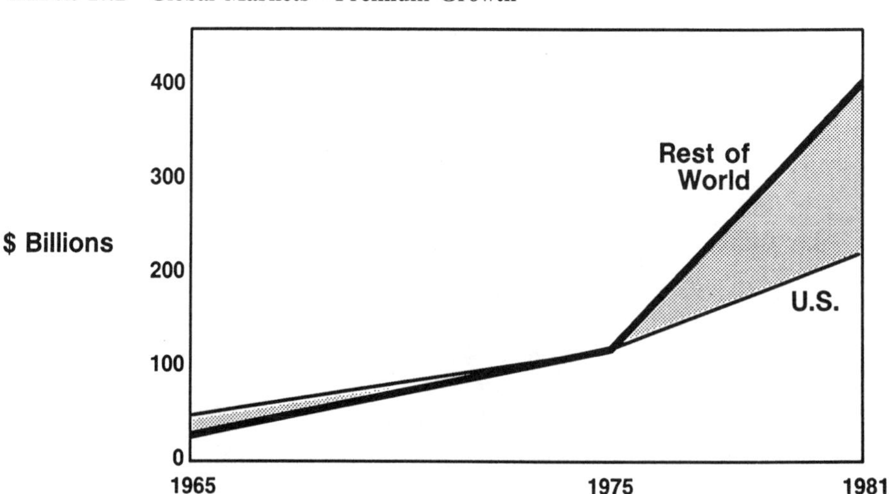

financial services so attractive over the last 30 to 40 years. What is the prospect that they will continue for the next 20–40 years? The factors that have created the pattern of growth are still present and are likely to be there for years to come. They include regulation, economic expansion, and increasing market sophistication. The real question is, "who will be able to take advantage of these attractive circumstances?" The answer requires a look at the risks and barriers faced by any company entering, operating in, or seeking to expand in foreign markets today.

PERSPECTIVE ON THE MARKET: RISKS

Probably the first concern of any company contemplating international activities should be its own attitudes toward international markets and the needs of international customers. As with any other marketing situation, a low probability of success and profitability will attend the company that expects to provide foreign customers with the same products and services it provides at home, especially if it plans to provide them in the same way. This expectation is a significant problem, particularly in American companies. The American market is so large and, relatively speaking, cohesive, that we often lose sight of (or lack incentive to be concerned with) the need to vary our products and strategies from market to market. A good example of this mistake in the financial services industry is Allstate Insurance Company's attempt to enter several European markets using the same strategy and approach that had served it so well in the United States. Allstate's subsequent losses and withdrawal from these markets are clear demonstration of the financial and personal pain this erroneous, but seemingly reasonable, assumption can produce. This problem has been much smaller for companies headquartered outside the United States, where markets are often so small that a company must serve customers in several countries in order to survive.

The corollary to this first risk is that no company should readily assume that its domestic managers or its domestic management and control systems can be used without modification overseas. Many companies have fallen into this trap to their later chagrin. We will discuss the management issues related to foreign operations in more detail later in the chapter.

Regulation

The regulatory environment to be encountered in the host country or countries must also be carefully evaluated by any company contemplating international activities. The restrictions that can be encountered can prevent entry, make the cost of entry prohibitively expensive, make a later withdrawal virtually impossible or very costly, and more. Management of the foreign operation may be quite limited in its ability to affect critical performance areas such as local salaries, work methods, office locations, or the number or type of employees. Finally, the government may also control product mix, ability to compete with distinctive products or services, the form of organization that may be used, and the local partners or managers that may have to be brought into the business. The reality of international business is that in many countries the government is a silent partner whose concerns and interests must be considered by any prospective market entrant.

The significance of the impact of regulation cannot be overestimated. In Japan, for example, the Kemper Insurance Company sought to obtain and, after considerable delay was granted, an insurance license. Since all rates and forms of insurance are standardized by the government, insurance agents are very loyal to their existing companies, and buyers tend to favor Japanese companies. Kemper therefore sought to identify a unique capability that might enable it to establish itself. The American company applied for permission to market a special policy for highly protected risks—covering large factories equipped with loss-protection systems which could justify much lower insurance rates than those paid by normal customers. This type of policy was not available in Japan and might provide a way to penetrate the corporate insurance market there, something which no foreign company had yet been able to do. The Japanese government, after due consideration, approved the policy form. However, it also ruled that Kemper could not charge less than the standardized price for regular insurance—effectively negating Kemper's potential advantage.

Sometimes government rulings can be favorable to outsiders. A few years earlier the government of Japan had created a fantastic windfall for an American company through an administrative ruling. It had permitted the American Family Insurance Company to market cancer insurance in Japan. For a number of years the company was the only provider in the country allowed to market this type of insurance. In post-Hiroshima, cancer-sensitive Japan, the product was an overwhelming success. No one can really be sure why one product was allowed and another refused. The point is that a company's success, in each case, was determined by governmental action over which the company had little control.

Japan exercises very tight control over financial services, but it is not alone or an isolated example of regulatory control. In Malaysia, the government is now requiring all existing foreign financial services businesses to hand over at least 70 percent ownership in their entities to Malaysians by 1990. At least 40 percent of the ownership must be in the hands of Bumiputras (literally "sons of the soil," those viewed as native Malaysians). New foreign entrants must start at a maximum of 30 percent equity. All contracts and documents and all proposed partners must be submitted to the government for approval. Even as western a country as Australia strictly regulates foreign insurers and prohibits foreigners from controlling a majority of a life insurance company.

Government policy and regulation need not be aimed directly at financial services companies to have a significant impact on their operations. Currency controls such as those experienced recently in the Philippines, various Latin American countries, and Nigeria can have a substantial impact on the success and profitability of a foreign company. They can also make it very difficult to withdraw all or part of a company's capital should the company desire to shrink its entity, withdraw from the market, or repatriate dividends to use elsewhere in the organization. Similarly, labor and wage regulations may take decisions on compensation, layoff, or work methods out of the company's hands. Somewhere in the world a government controls almost any type of decision a company might want to make. Business can be sure that if the decision is crucial to success in that country, Murphy's law will apply: "If things can go wrong, they will!"

Marketing

Against this backdrop, the marketing issues associated with international operations seem relatively tame. Having mastered internal chauvinism and the host government, one need only be concerned with the nationalism of the buyer, and local differences in product, pricing, distribution, and so on—not to mention the need to compete against entrenched local and foreign competitors. Nationalism is a particular problem in large developed economies like Japan, France, and Germany, where history and culture produce a strong preference for local suppliers and where local financial services firms are large and sophisticated enough to meet most needs, even those of the largest local corporations.

Local Competition

Local firms may also be able to command the best technical talent in the market and the best branch locations or representatives. Their long experience in the market alone is an advantage against most foreign firms, especially given the fact that regulation in many of these countries minimizes the rate of change and innovation in the financial services industry. Any entering company must study the market carefully in order to understand the competitive exposures it will face and the unique marketing characteristics to which it will have to adapt. If it cannot identify some way in which to differentiate itself against other competitors in the market (e.g., by lowest costs, special products or services not easily duplicated, ability to handle overseas needs of local customers), the prospective entrant would probably be well advised to consider another country.

Exit

A final concern to any potential entrant derives from the barriers to withdrawal that may exist. Some are regulatory; local governments may require that large reserves be maintained for many years after operations cease or may deny permission to repatriate capital. In addition, some businesses have inherent barriers to withdrawal while others do not. For example, fire insurance policies typically last for one year. A company writing fire insurance in such a market might be able to wind up its operations within a year or two. However, if local custom is to write three- to five-year policies (as in the Netherlands), withdrawing can take much longer. A life insurer might have to remain in the market and maintain staff for the lifetime of its longest living policy holder. Since many foreign operations are ultimately unsuccessful, the wise company looks to the possibility of a reasonably simple exit even if it does not expect to exercise that option.

In summary, operating overseas is far from simple. The difficulties are easily and often underestimated. However, the opportunities for growth and profit are tempting. The trick is to recognize the opportunities without overlooking the potential perils so that a sound strategy can be developed. Once these considerations are balanced, business should look at the issues associated with selecting and implementing a sound international strategy.

SELECTING AND IMPLEMENTING AN INTERNATIONAL STRATEGY

Selecting a strategy is a little like one of the old cartoons where the hero tries to shut the drawers in a dresser. Every time one is closed, another one pops open. With international strategies, the question is not how to shut all of the drawers at once, but to decide which ones to leave open. No strategy can minimize all risks and cover all contingencies. Thus, selection becomes a process of evaluating combinations of risk and opportunity, and choosing the set that seems to offer the best overall tradeoff between exposure and reward. Although they may sound trite, a few maxims should be applied by any company in developing or evaluating an international marketing strategy:

Maxim One: Be clear about the time frame. If the strategy under consideration is an opportunistic one—capitalizing on a short-term market situation to make money for a few months or years before withdrawal—management will want to choose ownership options, distribution channels, and countries other than those suited to developing a long-term market position. Also, use of expatriate management might be much more attractive than using local management (despite the cost and the expatriate's lack of local knowledge), simply because the local managers would be harder to eliminate a few years down the road. But some short-term situations may not be viable. It would probably not make sense to try to operate in countries with a history of regulation in which license applications take from two to three years to process. Neither would it be advisable to choose a product or market that involved substantial exit barriers. These examples illustrate how important a clear understanding of time horizon is to a sound strategic choice.

Maxim Two: Recognize that only a few countries really matter in most strategies. In a global sense, 10 to 20 economies account for almost all of the world's GNP. Insurers' revenues reflect this. AIG's international earnings are heavily dependent on its operations in Japan, the Philippines, and Malaysia despite its globe-girdling organization. For CIGNA, the countries are different, but the numbers are the same. The good old 80/20 (or maybe 90/10?) rule applies in international business, too: Eighty percent of the income comes from 20 percent of the business. In addition, the worst problems and earnings drains usually come from a few operations as well. All too often, while a company is congratulating itself on outstanding results in a few countries, two or three small entities turn up with enough losses or other problems to more than offset the contributions of the winners. Successful companies recognize the countries that are crucial to their success and focus on them. They also realize that the global environment is a rapidly changing one and watch to see if those changes are likely to produce new problems or exposures that can only be ignored at a very high potential cost.

Maxim Three: Know yourself. It is crucial to know what the company's own strengths and weaknesses are, to have a good sense of its present and future capabilities, and to understand the ways in which they might be applied to an international opportunity. A company that is struggling to develop enough managers for its domestic operations may not be in a position to manage an overseas entity. If capital is limited or cash flow is marginal already, it is probably not the time to add a new operation. A new international entity added in these circumstances, while it may be seen wishfully as a way of escaping the present peril, could in fact jeopardize the parent's future.

On the other hand, a company with a large, stable, and profitable domestic business may be well positioned to experiment with foreign operations, especially if they are of a size which does not risk large amounts of corporate capital or management. An institution with a large branch network and a sophisticated computer system to which foreign offices can easily be added may be in an ideal position to expand. In fact, the computer system may be the basis for a competitive advantage if it can provide a productivity edge against smaller competitors in foreign markets. Thus, a clear view of corporate assets and liabilities—along with an understanding of the ability of the corporate culture to absorb the differences and respond to the challenges raised by international activities—is a prerequisite to any strategic decision.

A corollary to "know yourself" is "stick to what you know." A completely new and unknown market is a poor place in which to develop new products, information systems, distribution techniques, or management styles. Some variation in each may be essential to account for the inherent differences in foreign markets, but the wise institution will probably seek as little variation as possible. It should adjust just enough to meet the customer and regulatory requirements in the country.

Maxim Four: Know the customer and know the competition. This is part of any marketing strategy, but cultural and other variations found in international markets complicate the process considerably. Sometimes market statistics are available for only a few of the countries under consideration; other times, the statistics are old or of questionable accuracy. Moreover, investigations will probably have to be conducted in foreign languages by people who have little knowledge of the market. Otherwise, they will need to be delegated to people in the local market who may have little or no knowledge of the product or service. And management, lacking exposure to local people or any knowledge of their performance history, may have only limited confidence in the accuracy of their conclusions. Developing the necessary knowledge base is a daunting task, especially if a number of countries are involved. It is a task that is never fully achieved, and one that continues as long as the company is active in the market.

Maxim Five: Understand the nature of the risks and exposures being undertaken. Many firms, in considering an overseas operation, look at annual revenue or their direct investment as their total exposure when they evaluate their overseas position. That may be a reasonable evaluation of exposure to a hazard like expropriation, but it may also lead to gross errors.

A European banker entering the U.S. market a few years ago might have assumed that his initial investment represented his total exposure and that his risk was nominal. However, if his American unit became involved in something like the Penn Square debacle, his potential for loss was considerable. Given that the bank's name and prestige were committed to its foreign operation, the management might decide not to limit its liability to that permitted by law even if it could. If the American operation were a branch, no such protection might exist. Midland Bank's much publicized purchase of, and subsequent capital and management contributions to, Crocker National Bank is an example of an exposure to loss and a capital drain that may have been substantially underestimated by the bank's U.K. management.

In the insurance industry, many foreign insurers have found themselves with massive financial commitments in the United States related to asbestos exposures, toxic substances claims, and environmental pollution liability among others, perhaps partially because the European companies did not fully understand U.S. liability laws and litigation processes. These liabilities undoubtedly far exceed the exposure to loss that the parent anticipated when it entered a new foreign market. If the lessons of history are heeded, financial services institutions will make every effort to understand the markets in which they intend to operate. They will try to accurately define the risks involved in operating there. And they will develop control mechanisms and contingency plans to ensure that financial and nonfinancial exposures can be contained within limits that are acceptable to the corporation.

OTHER MANAGEMENT ISSUES

When it has developed a strategy, management must be concerned with a host of practical issues as it prepares to enter a foreign market. What will the ownership of the entity be? Will the business be essentially local or global or both? How will the business be managed in relation to domestic operations? There are many more, but these questions serve to highlight the issues that must be faced. Each will be briefly explored.

Ownership

There is a range of ownership and affiliation options open to a financial services company operating overseas. The simplest is probably an informal marketing agreement in which a Japanese company and a British company, for example, decide to market each other's services to their clients. The Japanese company might thereby gain British clients interested in Japanese investments, and vice versa. While some form of licensing or franchising might seem to be the next step upward, such arrangements are relatively uncommon. The reason is simply that little in the financial services area is tangible enough to be protectable. Consequently, licensees may be licensees only as long as it takes them to learn the business and copy the products and systems involved.

Minority ownership is fairly common today because many countries now require that majority ownership of financial institutions be held by their citizens. Malaysia and Australia have already been mentioned in this regard. The United Kingdom and France are among many others with formal or informal barriers to majority ownership of some or all of their financial services companies. Although they may be mutually beneficial and profitable, minority ownership arrangements also involve substantial risks. The foreign company must often provide all or most of the capital for the new company, as well as the technical knowledge and computer systems that may be required. Despite this, there are few ways for a minority owner to protect its investment or to control the destiny of the entity.

As in any partnership, there is a considerable risk that the parties will disagree about goals or methods. In such an event the minority foreign partner is likely to lose out. In the Middle East it is even possible to hold the foreign partner's employees in the country without an exit permit until a dispute is resolved to the local partner's satisfaction. If a minority partnership is to be considered, it should be based on the most equal possible contribution by the partners—of both capital and expertise. In addition, potential partners should be carefully investigated and time should be taken to get to know the principals personally. In short, the partnership should be approached like a marriage—one wants it to be long and happy.

A majority position, or at least a 50/50 arrangement, offers somewhat more protection depending upon the local legal environment. However, the same potential for disagreement exists, and unless the contributions of the parties to the success of the venture are reasonably balanced, there is a strong likelihood that the majority partner will feel that it is creating the earnings while the minority partner sits by idly and benefits. True or not, this perception can lead to serious problems in the relationship and great frustration for the majority partner.

Despite the potential problems, however, it should be recognized that there are situations in which partnerships can be highly attractive. A local partner may have the political or business contacts necessary to ensure the success of a new operation. Partners may have a great deal of market expertise or offer a unique distribution channel. Examples of such an arrangement include the partnership between Allstate Insurance and the Seibu department store group, which distributes insurance in Japan for Allstate. Another example is the partnership between

Prudential and Sony in Japan. There, Prudential products have been marketed to Sony's employees, and Sony's business connections used to gain other contacts for the new company.

Wholly owned branches or subsidiaries are a solution to the problems presented by partnerships, but they also involve complications of their own in many countries. Regulations may discriminate against 100 percent-owned entities. In Argentina, for example, the government operates a monopoly reinsurance company to which every direct insurer in the market must cede a mandatory portion of its business. The terms under which foreign companies must cede their business are such that Argentinian companies can write local business much more profitably than can their foreign competitors. In some countries, foreign-owned institutions may also have special capital or reporting requirements or pay taxes that are not applied to locally owned companies.

On the other hand, a subsidiary may be one way to minimize the problems of customer nationalism. CIGNA's acquisition of the Crusader Insurance Company, PLC gave them a well-known local name and management team in the United Kingdom. Their marketing position in the life insurance and employee benefits markets was considerably different than it might have been had they operated a branch of the Life Insurance Company of North America or the Connecticut General Life Insurance Company in Great Britain. Furthermore, a company like the Crusader is regarded as a Common Market company and can branch into the European Economic Community with fewer restrictions than can an "American" company. Even a subsidiary created by the parent can have some of the same marketing advantages enjoyed by local acquisitions. A local name and/or identity can be established. There may also be tax advantages for subsidiaries in some countries. In addition, local managers are often more readily attracted to a subsidiary and its titles (e.g., president, managing director, etc.) than to a branch manager position. In many countries, titles are as important as compensation in attracting management.

Branches, on the other hand, also have their own set of advantages. Capitalization requirements are often lower than those for local companies, reporting requirements may be simpler, and the branch carries with it the financial security of the parent company. Where the name of the parent is well known and would be an advantage in the market, a branch offers a direct link to the parent's reputation.

There are clearly many ownership options for the firm considering foreign marketing ventures. The right choice must ultimately be related to the objectives, financial capabilities, and reputation of the parent company in the particular market or markets where it may decide to do business. It is one of the choices which can have a substantial impact on the risks assumed by the parent and the ultimate probability of success in the markets to be entered.

Organization

The needs of the selected customer group and the nature and type of market to be entered also merit careful consideration. Clearly a very different organization is required to serve a multinational client than to accommodate the requirements of medium-sized French industrial customers. Choosing one country to enter and developing and implementing a successful strategy for the market and customer groups to be served is not an easy task, especially in countries where relatively little market data is available. However, the task is simple compared to the need to operate in many countries at once, particularly if each country requires unique products, distribution channels, and so on. Any firm contemplating multicountry activities would do well to evaluate the risks and the organizational demands that a large international activity can generate.

The need to serve multinational clients adds an even more substantial layer of complexity to the task. In general, a far-flung organization is required to serve such customers. If the services to be provided are such that a few mobile specialists can provide them wherever they are needed (for example, investment banking analysis), a global marketing effort may be reasonably manageable. However, in many businesses significant local capabilities may be required to provide the needed services.

Property-casualty insurance is one such industry. Effectively serving a multinational insured requires local claims capabilities, and probably engineering services, in virtually every country where potential clients do business. These requirements mean the company seeking multinational business must usually have offices in many countries. The costs of providing these services to a few large clients is excessive in relation to the premium charged for property-casualty insurance. Consequently, servicing multicountry clients is often profitable only when the company also has a large organization of local companies producing local business in sufficient volume to cover the required overhead. The potential competitor needs to create an organization that can, at once, flexibly serve many diverse local markets and provide the uniformity of service and information required by its global clients. This can be difficult: The requirements of global and local customers almost always diverge, creating unavoidable stresses within the organization and significant management challenges for the parent company. Serving multinational customers can also place unanticipated stresses on partnerships when partners believe local earnings are being compromised because of profits being earned elsewhere.

Management

It is difficult to think of anything that more closely correlates with success in a country than the quality of the local management and the way those managers relate to their superiors and to the parent company. Unfortunately, it is very difficult, if not impossible, to predict which manager will be successful. Expatriate managers may not be familiar with local markets and customs. Their families often have difficulty in adapting to the inherent differences and stresses of a foreign environment. On the other hand, expatriates will probably be much more familiar with the parent's management, control systems, and objectives. At the least, this knowledge can be important in maintaining the confidence of the parent's management. It can also enable the organization's informal networks to be brought into play to support the distant entity.

Indigenous managers lack these advantages, but they know the local customer, language, and culture. In addition, use of indigenous staff in senior management positions can be highly motivating to local staff who might otherwise feel that there is little opportunity for them to advance within the company, whether locally or internationally. Unfortunately, it is often difficult for headquarters executives to evaluate the quality of local managers. A national who speaks one's own language poorly or with a severe accent can appear less bright or less technically qualified than an equally attractive expatriate candidate. Furthermore, indigenous candidates may be unfamiliar with the management styles and language of the parent company's country and can easily be judged to be lacking in "appropriate" management skills.

In the final analysis, some combination of indigenous and local management is probably inevitable. The current tendency is to put expatriate managers in new ventures because of the need for parent confidence. Over time, however, the knowledgeable international organization will make the investment necessary to recruit and develop skilled indigenous managers who are committed to the company and who have the confidence of the corporation's managers.

In assessing and choosing various management options, it is important to recognize the normally dynamic nature of international businesses. Companies typically start out with small organizations operating in one or a few countries. In the financial services business, the foreign activity often starts out as a liaison office for domestic customers or as an isolated subsidiary serving one local market which has, for some reason, been deemed particularly attractive. This type of operation is generally tucked into and subordinate to one of the company's large domestic units. Kemper Corporation, for example, operated a direct insurance subsidiary in Brazil for many years through the company's reinsurance division, presumably because that division did some business overseas. There are two major risks at this early stage: (1) the foreign operation may be subservient to domestic activities, making it unable to adapt and grow, or (2) the foreign operation may be ignored, possibly getting out of control and becoming a major corporate liability. Also conceivable is that both possibilities could arise in the same foreign operation.

As a company's international operations grow, perhaps through the addition of offices or subsidiaries, these operations become more complex and demand considerably more time and attention. The overseas businesses are not yet seen as vital to the company's success and may still be part of a domestic unit rather than reporting directly to the CEO. Now, however, they are large enough to justify a dedicated management team. At this more advanced stage a company frequently chooses to create some kind of dedicated international organization to manage its growing global activity. Furthermore, although the nature of the risks changes, their magnitude probably alters little.

When a company first enters this stage, it may assign a trusted executive to manage its international units. This executive often knows nothing about foreign business and fails to learn quickly enough. These shortcomings can create management vacuums and control deficiencies, as well as serious morale problems among international managers who feel that the corporation does not understand or appreciate them or their "unique" problems. As a result, the international unit may break down into uncontrollable individual fiefdoms, or it may wither due to weakened management.

On the other hand, the company may choose an experienced international manager with few ties to the corporation, its culture, or its managers. This choice may produce a rapidly growing and successful international division that is viewed with distrust by the rest of the management team. Ultimately, growth may be squelched by the company's attempt to socialize its young upstart. In such a situation, international management may become almost paranoid about the corporation's interest in its activities, and resistant to efforts to coordinate its activities and strategies with those of the other corporate units. This posture can be very destructive to management morale and may lead to the erection of organizational barriers or to management restructuring. Recovery can take years.

If a company's international operations continue to grow and mature such that they have the potential to make a major contribution, they should probably be formed into a strategic business unit with management reporting to the CEO. At this stage, resistance from domestic managers may be encountered as they reassert their dominant role in corporate affairs. However, unless there are compelling corporate reasons to the contrary, maintaining the international unit separate at a very high level is almost a necessity if international activities are to be assured the attention and resources they deserve. At one level, this necessity is no different from the need to separate out any large and growing business within a company. However, at a more concrete level international operations are unique, worn out as this justification may sound. International operations in fact differ much more from their domestic counterparts than do domestic units from one another. Corporations will be tempted to deny these differences and to try to make the international strategic business unit look and act as much like their domestic counterparts as possible.

A second major risk at this stage is that the newly powerful organization will itself seek standardization. In doing so, it may become so bureaucratic that it gradually destroys its ability to adapt to the local markets and key customer segments which provided its initial success. This failure to recognize the different operating modes, strategies, and cultures required in a successful international operation can significantly curtail the international business's ability to realize its full potential. This problem is intensified when combined with failure to place the business in a position of high visibility or when deprived of the resources and priority it needs to grow.

International organizations also have a tendency to concentrate on geography—organizing around regions or focusing on specific countries as opportunities. But some of the best opportunities in international financial services are tied to global factors. Like the automobile industry with its hopes for a world car, multinationals have the potential to capitalize on the common denominators among their far-flung businesses. Transnational products and services can be developed, as can low-cost or service-oriented global processes for back-room operations. Likewise, regional or worldwide systems can be created to deploy more power and information than those of local competitors, at a lower initial cost and lower continuing costs. These are the types of things that can be overlooked or underutilized by a company that is unduly focused on specific geography rather than business dynamics.

There are no simple answers to the management issues presented by a large and growing international business. Each solution has within it its own risks and problems. Even if effective, a solution will almost certainly succumb to the dynamic changes that are required as the business grows, enters more markets, or adds new customer segments. The most successful companies in international business seem to use various matrices to try to make sure that all of their "bases are covered," and that changes are recognized and responded to. Combinations of expatriate and local management produce one such matrix. Organizational structures that blend domestic or global product or technical expertise with skilled international line managers yield another. Regional staffs can add another dimension to the matrix. Worldwide or regional management forums may also be used to ensure that local and global perspectives are considered by all concerned managers.

In short, managing an international entity is a process of customizing local operations while constantly integrating the information produced with corporate goals, strategies, and objectives. No wonder the effective international staff is constantly on the road. Without continuous integrative activities, strategic implementation would probably be much less effective. It might even be said that, under certain circumstances, integrative efforts become a determining factor in the international unit's profitability or lack thereof.

CONCLUSION

Perhaps the best way to summarize the challenges of international marketing is to note the inherent tension in what has been said in this chapter. On the one hand, international marketers should "stick to what they know." On the other, they must recognize that everything about international activity must be considered to be different. There is peril in copying domestic formulas; in standardizing too much. Similarly, it is important to know as much as possible about the markets in which the firm will operate and the customers it will service. But lack of data, language barriers, and so forth make it very difficult to obtain even minimal information. These are the contradictions (or compromises) of international marketing.

In the final analysis, the successful international entity is one that provides meaningful economic benefits to each customer it serves, no matter where they are. These benefits are at the core of the sustainable competitive advantage from which the corporation gains its own benefit—long-term growth and attractive returns on its investments. Finding the strategic and management formula that will achieve this system-wide synergy is the true challenge of international marketing. Like the famous lost gold mines of the western United States, the right strategy is elusive and implementation takes an enormous amount of time, energy, and management discipline. Unlike the lost mines, however, there are real and proven opportunities for growth and profit for the company that can combine the management skill, common sense, flexibility and ingenuity necessary to negotiate the international rapids and reach their goal. The challenge, and the opportunity, are there for those who dare to pursue them.

SECTION 4 THE ROLE OF TECHNOLOGY AND OPERATIONS

As suggested in the previous section, another key element in managing for success is defining and managing the role of technology within the institution. Most executives of financial services firms are still struggling with this issue, and with the related issue of operations. Many have grown up on the customer side of their organizations, and so have dealt with the back office principally when customer problems arose or management reports were circulated. As a consequence, they are not intimately familiar with the intricacies of technology and operations. At best, these executives view technology as an indistinct opportunity and as a critical strategic variable about which they wish they were more knowledgeable. At worst, they view technology as an unnecessary expense competing with their own favored projects for a limited pool of resources.

In all fairness to these managers, the technologists have sometimes gotten out of hand. This is true even in those progressive institutions that have allowed technology and operations to play important roles. Because the users are either unsophisticated, or because they are too busy chasing customers, some institutions have allowed their technology initiatives to ride roughshod over the organization's strategy—instead of working in concert with it. As a consequence, it is not uncommon to see product development driven entirely out of the technology area, with little analysis of need at the customer level.

One of the key issues for management, therefore, is trying to balance the influence of technologists and the rest of the organization. Doing so can sometimes be as simple as restructuring reporting lines and relationships. In other cases it requires a fundamental change in the culture.

One of the obstacles to changing the culture is lack of a common vocabulary for technology and operations. With younger managers, this snag is becoming less significant, as their education has begun to give them a grounding in applied science. But older managers are in great need of a massive dose of training—not to convert them into technologists, but to give them the vocabulary to deal with the programmers, systems analysts, engineers, and others responsible for putting technologies to work. A similar effort needs to be undertaken to give the technologists a business vocabulary.

A second critical issue for management as it relates to technology is defining its role in the institution. For some institutions, technology and information management will be the strategic weapon which can offer a competitive advantage. The business of these institutions is the packaging and management of information for their customers. For other financial institutions, technology is going to offer efficiencies and cost reduction opportunities. (However, many organizations have found that capturing those savings has been far more difficult than planned.) For yet other institutions, technology will become a complement to existing businesses. For example, automation may be used to enhance customer service (but not to substitute for human contact).

This section describes the strategic use of technology as well as the need to manage both technology and operations within an organization. Max Hopper in Chapter 18 discusses the emergence of technology and its effect on strategic alternatives for an institution. Max has been a guiding light of information systems automation, notably at BankAmerica and American Airlines. In Max's tenure, American showed itself to be one of industry's foremost innovators in computerized network technology. In Chapter 19, David Blackwell addresses the issue of how best to manage the technology function and information flows within an organization. Dave speaks from his perspective as chief administrative officer at Massachusetts Mutual Life.

In Chapter 20 Richard Rizzolo, group head of general services at Chemical Bank, discusses operations management in the services sector, with particular attention to how it differs from its equivalent in the manufacturing sector. Since most executives are taught to visualize business activities in manufacturing terms, it is important to reinforce these distinctions, as Dick has done here. Next, in Chapter 21, Ira Gregerman reviews productivity issues, a topic he is well qualified to answer, having devoted 25 years of his career to it, most recently at State Street Bank where he is senior productivity officer.

In all likelihood, most institutions will assign different roles to technology for different parts of their businesses. The key is to decide what role technology should play in the firm's business strategies, and how the technological resources should be managed to achieve the technology position the company desires.

18 The Strategic Use of Technology in Financial Services

MAX D. HOPPER

THE IMPACT OF THE NEW INFORMATION SYSTEM TECHNOLOGIES

Over the past decade, commercial banks, brokerage houses, and savings and loan institutions, among many other financial service entities, have experienced changes that are undoubtedly the most dramatic in the history of the financial services industry.

In the process of having to adjust to rapid technological and marketplace changes, many financial service institutions have had to give serious attention to their internal managerial cultures and decision-making structures. Many now realize that practices that may have been adequate during the era of extensive government regulation have become obsolete as a result of the new information system technologies. These technologies have leveled most of the "restraining walls" of anticompetitive state and federal legislation erected over the past century.[1]

Though changing consumer preferences were partly responsible for this revolution in financial services, it was mainly the new information systems (IS) technologies that battered down the doors to market entry. Developments in microprocessors, high-density data storage techniques, satellites, microwave transmission, and fibre optics—among other electronic data processing (EDP) and telecommunications innovations—finally pushed many commercial banks, thrifts, brokerage houses, and some other providers back into the mainstream of American business practice.

The isolated occupational cultures (symbolized by an internal, rather than market, focus) that once characterized banks and other financial services institutions had to give way to the recognition that survival in the more competitive marketplace of the 1970s and 1980s required much the same strategic decision-making tools and professional expertise found in other business enterprises. Bankers, for example, suddenly found that they had to *sell* their products. While deregulation forced this discovery, technology simultaneously emerged to support sales efforts: Brokers learned that stock investors wanted competitive practices and would trade off advisory and other services for lower commissions. Advances in microprocessor-based data processing and lower cost telecommunications have led to dramatic changes in product offerings and price structures in the securities industry.

The world had changed. The world had gone "on-line." Indeed, as Walter Wriston pointed out, the globalization of financial markets via speed-of-light electronic funds transfer (EFT) systems has led to the emergence of an "information standard" in place of gold and other exchange control arrangements intended by governments to regulate investment flows and exchange rates.[2]

Some industry observers argue that information services, including information about financial matters, have begun to match the traditional roles of banks in payments and lending services.[3]

Responding to the Information Explosion

Financial service institutions have begun to alter their business practices in response to these changes. For example, as recently as 1970, fewer than 10 percent of commercial banks having $100 million and more in assets had formal business planning systems. What little "planning" banks engaged in consisted mainly of the annual operations budget review. By the late 1970s, however, a *majority* of the banks surveyed reported having installed formal (strategic) business planning systems. By 1983, fully 97 percent claimed to have such systems.[4]

The growing trend towards longer-range *strategic* planning dovetails with the growing acceptance by bank and other financial services managements of the new EDP decision-making tools used by other businesses today. In a study conducted by Peat, Marwick and Mitchell in 1984, fully 73 percent of the banks surveyed reported that their managers were using microcomputers for over 20 different planning and evaluation operations. Most of the remaining 27 percent said they would be installing micros in the near future. Although micros are being used mainly in traditional operations areas—for example, asset-liability management, budgeting, and financial reporting—there is a growing trend toward other uses, including commercial credit analysis, loan pricing, cost of funds calculations, human resource planning, product development, marketing, and so on.[5] Also, financial services managements are finding it advantageous to network their microcomputers to external data bases supplied by outside vendors.

Accessing external data bases not only provides low cost information not available in-house, but also allows innovative problem solving that would not have been economically feasible before. For example, calculations of interest rate swap arrangements can now be undertaken without the hazardous guesswork that was formerly required. Banks are also reducing the hazards of marketing credit products in distant and unfamiliar geographical areas by tapping into macroeconomic forecasting data specific to a given geographic area.[6] Ironically, the new data processing and telecommunications technologies have clearly added to the complexity of the decision-making *environment* of financial services firms—by placing an ever-expanding array of analytical tools and data base sources at managers' fingertips. With so much knowledge available, managers must become skilled at knowing what they need and how it will help them. On the other hand, when used properly these technologies provide important strategic planning controls that can reduce investment and other business risks.

A clear and fairly uniform trend in recent years is the shift from loose and haphazard technology policies toward more centralized management of technology development, a trend that most industry observers favor because of the cost savings and operational efficiencies made possible by more centralized controls.[7] Lack of centralized coordination of technology policy has often led to *redundant* systems, which add to a firm's costs and increase the dispersion of its system-engineering talent.[8] The trend, though, is toward a more centralized and coordinated management of technology architecture and policy.

"Architecture"is defined here as the total corpus of hardware and software applications and the systems that unite them. Architecture can be thought of by its users in almost purely technological terms as the infrastructure that links all of the pieces together. Policy, by contrast, is very much business oriented: It is management's playbook for making architecture serve the ends of the corporation.

As will be discussed in more detail later, managements of financial services institutions must set the policies appropriate for the organization and achieve the right balance between centralized and decentralized information systems architectures if they hope to use the new technologies as *strategic* rather than just tactical resources.

INFORMATION SYSTEMS TECHNOLOGY: FROM TACTICAL TO STRATEGIC DEPLOYMENT

Until the 1970s, the impact of evolving data processing technology was tactical rather than strategic. The distinction is important because it marks an important watershed in the use to which financial service managements are putting the new EDP and telecommunications technologies.

During the 1950s and 1960s, electronic technology was typically applied to *vertical* areas of the business (restricted to one or a few departments) and to limited problems. The main thrust was in the area of back-room processing. Because products were standardized and markets walled off by regulation, efforts aimed at raising productivity through expense control became the main arena for innovation.

In the case of banking, the limited tactical use of technology to improve productivity is easy to understand. The dramatic post-World War II economic boom led to an explosive increase in paper-based transactions. Household checking accounts grew in popularity and as a result banks faced serious bottlenecks due to the rising check volume. Because these systems were labor-intensive, service quality was as much a consideration as expense control in motivating banks to seek new solutions.

In 1956, Bank of America worked with the Stanford Research Institute to develop the Magnetic Ink Character Recognition (MICR) technology, a check-encoding system that became the industry standard for automated check processing. Two years later, in 1958, Bank of America developed the Electronic Recording Method of Accounting (ERMA) in collaboration with General Electric. Both innovations spurred dramatic back-room productivity gains.

The first *horizontal* extensions across departmental lines of the new EDP technology occurred when BankAmerica encouraged the development of the first automated clearing house (ACH) in 1972. BankAmerica's interest in a more cost-effective electronic payments system is not difficult to understand when one considers the bank's very large California corporate and retail customer base, and the heavy transactions volume resulting from that base.

By contrast with back-room applications in the paper-intensive transactions area, there was little incentive to push for technological applications in *product* development, because banks and thrifts were tightly regulated in product markets. Interest rates were stable, market share growth reasonably predictable, and foreign competition next to nil. However, computers made it possible to align traditional transactions and investment products in marginal ways by providing, for example, daily compounding of interest on savings accounts (in the case of commercial banks, thrifts, and credit unions) or, in the case of insurance firms, by offering a greater variety of annuity and insurance products. Mainframes also enabled the security industry, which was beset by a rising torrent of transactions in the 1970s, to automate stock registration, transfer, and safe-keeping—much the way banks are now using check truncation to alleviate processing pressures.[9]

Technology finally came to be used as a *strategic* resource only when markets came under intense pressure during the 1970s and 1980s, and banks and other institutions had to develop a more outward-looking and market-responsive posture. Throughout the entire history of the industrial revolution one would be hard put to find capital substitutions that achieved the productivity gains of the new digital impulse processing technologies—gains reliably estimated at 20 percent per annum in recent years!

Also, the precipitous decline in data processing costs meant an open season on financial service markets. With the escalation of both inflation and real interest rates beginning in the late 60s and accelerating during the 70s, financial service entrepreneurs discovered that data processing economics enabled new IS technologies to be used as siege guns to level market barriers right and left. Unregulated entities such as money market mutual funds used IS technology to punch through the statutory protections surrounding the depositories' payments and investment products. The money market mutual funds (MMMFs) offered integrated investment/transaction accounts paying market-sensitive interest rates with reasonable safety. With a large mainframe, reliable software, a few good system programmers, and a toll free 800 number, the MMMFs and other low-overhead entrants were able to rapidly build market share during the 1970s.

TECHNOLOGY AS PART OF THE CORPORATE STRATEGIC PLAN

Just as the new IS technologies were first used to level entry barriers, financial services managements now see them as opportunities to rebuild the competitive strengths of their firms. However, by itself, the new technology will not deliver competitive market advantages. Among other things, technological diffusion is sufficiently fast that technology-based market leads have very short half lives (perhaps one to two years at most). To be used effectively for competitive advantage, IS technology must be integrated with a corporate business strategy that uses the technology as a *tool* for leveraging the firm's other comparative advantages. Correctly applied, the technology can *enhance* whatever comparative advantages the firm already enjoys. These advantages may stem from highly sophisticated expertise (learning and experience curve barriers) or from a favored position as the high volume producer of certain products (scale barriers).

However, the financial services firm that seeks to apply the new technologies as a a strategic resource for increasing revenue growth and profitability can do so effectively only if the technologies are *fully integrated* with a corporate-wide systems strategy and business unit strategy that directs the firm into its most advantageous market niches.[10] Strategy leads, and technology follows—usually. Sometimes strategic reviews are initiated because technology suggests itself as a tool with which to execute new strategies (i.e., the presence of the tool itself suggests a job to be done). But neither technology nor strategy will get the firm anywhere unless they are properly hitched together.

What some financial service firms have done, however, is to allow decentralized acquisitions of "off the shelf" IS technologies by individual departments and business units within the firm. This is a carry-over from the 1950s and 1960s, when applications were designed to solve ad hoc productivity problems. This often results in incompatible systems and costly attempts to provide appropriate linkages.

The Development of a Technology Policy

Today, IS technology cannot be used effectively as a strategic resource unless the system architectures are properly designed from the start so that the data base resource, communications, and security requirements are fully taken into account. This poses an awesome challenge for financial services managements because, in addition to the inherent technical complexity and rapid pace of new electronic innovations, the systems must be interfaced with a dizzying array of new products and delivery systems. Even when the right hardware/software design has been developed to create or deliver a new or modified product, managements must consider the impact on other products and delivery structures. Will an ATM in a supermarket chain, for example, preclude acceptance of a POS debit system? Will growing ATM usage rates diminish sales opportunities by reducing face-to-face contacts between customers and customer service representatives? Today's marriage between a given systems design and one or more products may well foreclose a more suitable product and marketing strategy later.

For example, a technology policy must be able to anticipate future growth in usage volumes and related software peripheral requirements. Systems planning in the *present* cannot be effective without a careful assessment of the potential *downstream* applications and development resources that will be required. Second, the new architectures must allow for extensive *horizontal* networking by end-users, both within the business entity itself but also beyond, in linkages with other institutions. The importance of this requirement becomes clear when one considers the evolution of EFT systems over the past five years, including automated teller machines, automated clearing houses, and point-of-sale debit networks. Although EFT systems account for probably no more than 10 percent of all payments transactions, their *growth rate* has begun a sharp acceleration in recent years. Nationwide, there were 42 percent more electronic payments in 1983 compared with the preceding year. The use of ACHs for business-to-business payments, government transfer payments, and so forth, has been increasing at 80 percent a year! Though only 9 percent of U.S. households used ATMs in 1976, fully 33 percent now use them, and a recent survey conducted by the Bank Administration Institute and Arthur Andersen Co. projects ATM usage rising to over 50 percent of all U.S. households by 1990.[11]

Third, careful planning of IS architectures is also necessary to capture scale and other advantages in product marketing and delivery of services to the firm's customer base.

In view of the substantial investment required for major system architectures, centralized and coordinated *policy planning* is absolutely essential for making effective strategic use of IS technology.

Any firm that goes on a "buy from the shelf" high-tech spending spree without centralized policy guidance risks ending up with a jerry-built aggregation of systems. It will harvest a "spaghetti bowl" of DP systems that will be hard to integrate for networking. Invariably, unintegrated systems built piecemeal must be merged. This involves data base, communications, and security facilities.

Operational efficiency may be the first casualty. Not very long ago, First Tennessee Bank realized that it had too many different DP systems for maximum operational efficiency. There were four different systems being used for its installment loan processing product line alone; the main bank used systems different from the affiliate banks, and so forth. Each time changes were required, programmers had to make the changes in each of the multiple systems.[12]

Some other financial service providers that began with a decentralized technology policy approach have also come to have second thoughts. In the mid-1970s, Chase Manhattan initially saw advantages in decentralizing its DP systems management. It believed decentralized purchasing decisions would give line units greater flexibility while also spurring its management to become more computer literate. But now Chase has come to realize that the price one pays for a decentralized technology policy is systems that are either incompatible in design or malintegrated when installed. Chase's solution has been to recentralize system investment decisions involving over $400,000. A "third party" review committee consisting of senior management end-users and systems people seeks to make sure that compatible systems are being bought and that a *company-wide* perspective will be brought to bear on each decision.[13]

BankAmerica is another example of a financial services institution that decided to centralize its systems policy making after it realized that it had amassed a "spaghetti bowl" of EDP networks that were not as well suited to the firm's strategic plan as a more centralized system would be. (There were over 60 DP systems in BankAmerica's North American Division alone.) Centralized technology policy was required not just to guarantee that the major architectures would fit the strategic game plan, but to ensure that mainframe and peripheral purchases throughout the corporation would be both cost-effective and suitable to the needs of end-users.

Given the complexity of today's technology, along with the tremendous range of options offered by vendors, common sense dictates that systems professionals have major input in reviewing and coordinating technology decisions.

CREATING THE RIGHT STRUCTURE

In late 1984, BankAmerica formally established BASE (BankAmerica Systems Engineering) as the organizational infrastructure for managing its technology infrastructure. BankAmerica's systems architecture contains both centralized and decentralized components. Transactions processing and telecommunications are both highly centralized. By contrast, product applications such as treasury management information tools and customized IRAs, among other new products, require a decentralized format that involves systems technologists working in close collaboration with line business managers. Indeed, at the product level, the systems people are attached to the line business divisions, maintaining a dotted line reporting relationship to their functional managers at BASE.[14]

However, almost all resource allocations decisions are centralized at the top of the policy pyramid in the Strategic Information Resource Committee, a technology policy committee chaired by president Sam Armacost. The SIRC also resolves disputes between systems and business units that could not be resolved lower down the chain of command.

Under BASE, BankAmerica's systems engineers are not technology "czars" who impose their writ on line business managers; rather they are more akin to internal corporate consultants who develop appropriate systems in close consultation with business managers. Because they are knowledgeable about the multiple IS technology horizons and the compatibility requirements for networking, they are able to assist other departments in avoiding costly investment mistakes.

The firm that wants to get its systems and strategy ducks lined up for the purpose of maximizing revenues and profits would do well to consider using this or a related kind of policy-making format. It requires *integrative* teamwork and a willingness to let technical expertise decide troublesome disputes on their merits rather than giving the prerogatives of turf and rank the edge in dispute resolution. Because today's IS technologies are synergistically interdependent, managerial cultures and structures must be adjusted to this technological imperative. Turf defense and the "not invented here" attitude, which have characterized old-line, segmented, corporate structures, are incompatible with the strategic deployment of today's EDP and telecommunications technologies.

Planning for Technology

To carry out IS technology deployment effectively, financial services managements would be well advised to consider a step-by-step planning process to make sure that the new systems are brought on stream at the correct time. As Jerome Svigals, former vice president of strategic planning at BankAmerica, has observed, it is still something of a "magic act" for financial managers to reach out more than six months in anticipating market needs. Svigals recommends that managements develop "plan process" teams made up of specialists from all sides of the business, including DP hardware and software engineers, experts on industry trends, line officers knowledgeable about branch operations, and so on. Together they should develop a growth plan that has benchmark progress measures ("quantifiable events") to insure that the EDP systems mix is appropriate to the strategic business plan, and that the various system components are phased in at the most economically optimal times. For example, if a bank management decides to undertake partial automation of its branches, it needs to know the approximate ratio of customer service reps to ATMs for any level of volume, among other possible substitutions.[15]

In larger firms that can afford the expertise, an effective program of horizontally integrated technology deployment also requires specialists who can scan and match up multiple horizons of opportunity. For example, a systems R&D group within the firm may scan the evolution of the applicable technologies and develop a *proactive* approach to relations with commercial vendors along with researchers at nonprofit universities and think tanks. If a purely *reactive* approach is used ("show us what you've got and explain to us how we can use it"), the firm risks becoming captive to vendors wanting to sell "off the shelf" products. But while vendors are often useful in alerting managements to new industry trends, they cannot anticipate the specialized business needs of a given financial services firm. As a result, there are good justifications for retaining in-house R&D expertise sufficient to evaluate the applicability of vendors' products along with their servicing and R&D competencies. If the bank, brokerage house, insurance firm, or other firm, is a very large business entity, then it may be able to "motivate" customized R&D by hardware and software suppliers.

A few large financial services institutions have themselves invested in software R&D facilities. This is very aggressive technology policy that goes well beyond proactive scanning. It may be justified as a means of developing technological *confidence* as much as competence, or as a way of motivating scarce systems personnel to remain with the firm. The drawback, however, is that many financial services firms are unlikely to be willing to provide in-house R&D with the funding that would be required to develop and maintain state-of-the-art technological leadership. In a few cases, for example, at Security Pacific National Bank, the systems engineering group has been spun off as a separate profit center to compete head-on with other nonbank vendors of telecommunications services. That kind of uncoupling strategy makes eminent good sense if the division is to meet the test of a highly competitive marketplace.

But whether established as a functional department within the firm or as an autonomous business entity, it is clear that systems engineers must synchronize their R&D scanning with the product development and marketing decision making of the line business units. If one maxim holds for strategic technology deployment it is surely this: "*Systems architectures and other DP facilities must be based on a flexible balance between technological and business requirements.*" For example, in the case of BankAmerica's BASE infrastructure, this maxim is followed by making sure that customers are involved in all systems design decisions from the very start of the planning process. In the case of the corporation's treasury management products, for example, corporate treasurers and other end-users become initiators of new software innovation. The bank's corporate marketing and systems staffs bring users together in focused group discussion to learn about their experience in using the bank's treasury management products.

Although many banks and other financial services institutions can purchase fairly reliable "turn key" systems solutions and expect outside vendors to fine tune the applications to their specified needs, those firms having more esoteric or complex systems requirements will want sufficient in-house systems expertise to develop and maintain their systems. Increasingly, professionals from other industries are being hired because their generic expertise in marketing, personnel, and systems engineering is needed in house by financial services firms. Differences in occupational culture may produce strains. In time, however, this infusion of new systems and marketing professionals from outside the industry, along with increasingly computer-literate bankers, brokers, insurers, and so on, will erode the traditional occupational insularity that has been characteristic of many financial service managements.

Illustrative of the way financial services firms are looking outside their industry for the expertise needed to rejuvenate their operations, is BankAmerica's approach to coping with its growing paper-based and electronic transactions volume. BankAmerica is beginning to approach a level of 1000 banking transactions per second. The current 2.5 billion transactions per year are projected to double to nearly 5 billion by 1990.

When the bank's senior management realized that a new systems architecture was required to cope with the rising transactions load, it decided to study the systems architecture that American Airlines had adopted to cope with its rising reservations volume. Because high-speed electronic processing architectures have generic applications that can be transferred from one industry to another, BankAmerica was able to design its new high-speed transaction processing facility based on the American Airlines reservation system prototype. Just as paper-based systems continue to pose bottleneck problems, increasing electronic transactions will also create processing load pressures in search of information system solutions. To help solve these problems, systems specialists and systems architectures will continue to migrate to financial services institutions from other industries until managements have had time to accumulate their own base of experience.

However, the "technology flow" is not just unidirectional, from nonfinancial to financial services. Automated teller machines, which are currently increasing at an annual rate of 30 percent, have dramatically improved the public's receptivity to other forms of automated self-service. For example, the Avis Corporation has begun to automate auto rental check-ins. Self-service airline ticketing is also believed ready to make a comeback after a disappointing trial experiment in a couple of major airports in the late 1970s.[16]

HOW SHOULD MANAGEMENT INTEGRATE TECHNOLOGY WITH STRATEGY?

How can financial service managements best manage the strategic deployment of the new IS technologies?

Although the issue of technology policy planning was addressed previously, the choice of systems architectures poses an added set of problems. Managing technology *policy* is one issue. As we noted, it should be centralized to avoid excessive redundancy, incompatibility, and the resultant expense. Designing the systems architectures themselves is quite a different issue, however.

First, while there are some common maxims that apply to all firms in terms of how they can best go about planning their technology policy, there is no universal "best fit" in terms of how any given IS technology should be applied or which systems should be used. Much will depend on the specific strategic goals of the firm, which markets are being targeted, and the size and geographical reach of the firm, among numerous other important variables.

For very small financial service providers it may not pay at all to develop expensive architectures or elaborate corporate strategies. Such firms will be led by others to the technology "trough," perhaps by way of invitations to share regional ATM or point-of-sale networks, or in the form of licensing arrangements for proprietary software, and the like. Nonetheless, even for small firms, it will still be necessary to pay attention to industry trends so that the most suitable hardware and software can be purchased to serve the firm's specialized market niche or local geographical area. The better capitalized institutions will serve as industry pioneers that will develop and conduct the pilot tests of new innovations such as point-of-sale debit systems, home banking, and so on. Smaller institutions that cannot afford the risk will be on the sidelines waiting until the dust settles before they attempt to use an innovative new product.

The point bears repeating: There is no single electronic road leading to one Rome—to the architecture of Big Blue or Ma Bell. There are many roads leading to many Romes. Some of the expressways will be shared systems and will have "utility" type features. Indeed, one of the most important strategic impacts of IS technology in the payments transaction field is that it will probably push individual firms into collaborative investment and sharing of POS and automated clearing house "expressways." This would appear an inevitable trend because there is no economically feasible alternative, if the scale efficiencies are to be realized and retailers and others are to be signed up. Nor would this be an institutional novelty. The payments clearing function has long involved administrative collaboration between individual competitors.[17] As mentioned earlier, a 1983 survey of bank managements by the Bank Administration Institute projects that by 1990 fully 50 percent of all banks will join in shared regional or national ATM networks.[18] EFT utility regulation is already the law in one state. Iowa passed a statute requiring a shared POS and off-premise ATM network. Currently, over 900 financial institutions and 800,000 debit card holders participate. In some areas, networking has become a defensive strategy to meet the competitive threat posed by retailers. In Florida, the Publix supermarket chain has invested over $50 million to install proprietary POS terminals in its stores.[19] In response, a large number of Florida financial institutions established the "HONOR" network.

Resource or Strategy?

As already noted, technology is a strategic *resource*, not a business strategy. Systems people may alert line managers to the possible market opportunities of new IS developments, but it is corporate strategy that must dictate the shape of systems architectures. And this strategy will, ultimately, be shaped by market tests of survivability.

For example, a bank's decision to invest in a PC-based system for remote banking (also called "home banking" despite the fact that it may be done from work using office-based PCs), does not dictate the marketing strategy to be followed. Thus Chemical Bank decided to license its proprietary *Pronto* software to other banks and institutional users. It sees advantages to leveraged marketing of the software to other banks. Also, Chemical views its home banking system as an entrepreneurial opportunity to become a middleman packager of other information services beside just banking services.[20] By contrast, BankAmerica has chosen to limit its proprietary *HomeBanking* system to its own customer base.

Although systems hardware and software impose some constraints on the design and delivery of financial service products, the marketing options are also constrained by the technology's suitability to the various institutional clay and soils. Supermarkets apparently see advantages to having ATMs on their premises. Providing banking services on premise draws in customers and also reduces check volume. Oil retailers, by contrast, have shown more interest in point-of-sale debit systems. Oil retailers find POS more attractive for several reasons: It reduces the amount of cash that can be taken by armed robbers, reduces the float costs from credit cards, and increases operational efficiency because debit card purchasers are more likely to fill up their tanks.[21] And most oil retailers already have a large card-holder base to build from.

Strategically viewed, the payments system is like an ecosystem in that it provides differential advantages to the various media (cash, checks, and credit and debit cards), according to the type of retail or wholesale setting, size of transaction, whether payments can be "batched," and so on. In deploying technology as a strategic resource, FS managements must avoid the temptation to view the new IS technologies as templates having uniform applicability across the entire payments system spectrum. To try to force a specific delivery system into a niche where, under current technology, it will not find market acceptance, may foreclose future investment opportunities. Consumers might sour on a system application that, at a later date or under different circumstances, might well have worked.

Determining the right mix between a centralized versus decentralized infrastructure for systems architecture will also depend on the business strategy being pursued. Citibank, for example, finds advantage in adopting a systems architecture that is much more autonomous than the one being developed at BankAmerica Corporation. Citi has more data processing facilities ("distributive units") operating independently of one another around the country. This difference in technology deployment makes sense given Citi's strategic objective of going after a highly variegated nationwide retail and corporate market. Its systems control and management must be sufficiently decentralized to accommodate a geographically dispersed aggregation of market segments.

By contrast, BankAmerica is implementing more centralized architecture because it views its strategic priorities differently. It is targeting more selective market segments in those areas where it believes that centralized systems architectures will help build scale barriers to entry, especially in its high-volume California retail payments market and its offshore global network. (BankAmerica is pursuing both differentiated product niche and low-cost supplier strategies in its various strategic business units.)

But as noted earlier, though strategic policy decisions will determine the extent to which systems architectures are centralized, technological policy making should be centralized regardless of the strategic corporate-wide plan.

Another important characteristic of the strategic, as distinct from earlier tactical, applications of technology is that investment and resource decisions require a longer time horizon and a more entrepreneurial attitude among financial services managements. The push for market leadership will drive some firms to undertake experimental POS, home banking, telephone bill paying, and other projects. Many such investments could never be justified if management had its eyes on the impact to the balance sheet's bottom line three, four, or even 10 quarters ahead. Such investments are being made precisely because technology has become a strategic resource in which market penetration for the long haul is the objective. In some cases, experiments can be justified as a way of exploring the technical workability of various IS systems. This makes sense even if the economic incentive structures remain adverse to broader marketing applications—as is the case with many POS trials currently. But some financial services managements also view both their pilot programs and full-gauge marketing programs as being vital to their effort to gain and retain a lead over competitors in market share.

In the case of the new treasury management products, on-line transactions and information services will clearly be profitable for banks and may be vital to the survival of any bank seeking to keep a foothold in the middle corporate market.[22] However, household and individual remote banking "at home" by PCs is projected to grow to between only 5 and 11 percent of all U.S. households by 1990—and it is not expected to be profitable for many years. Yet knowledgeable observers believe that no fewer than 50 percent of all American banks will offer this product. The reason given is competitive pressure. Banks need to maintain a forward-looking image of being technological innovators, especially if they hope to attract the profitable upscale consumer market.[23]

Without trial and error, the templates of technology might never be tested and the bugs would not be worked out. Doubtless there were bankers 50 years ago who scoffed at the idea that most American households might one day follow commercial firms and switch from cash to check payments. ATMs are another case in point. ATM usage had a slow start at first. Usage rates began to climb only after the machines had become more reliable and user friendly. Currently 63 percent of all commercial banks and thrifts having $100 million and more in deposits offer ATM services to their customers.[24] Managements are seeking further boosts in ATM usage rates by applying new merchandising and marketing tools. Although ATM usage nationwide remains stuck at 30 to 35 percent, this is probably only half the market penetration that can eventually be expected. In a recent nationwide study, only 36 percent of those surveyed said they would definitely *not* use an ATM.[25]

Defensive investment to keep market options open in the event the technology does begin to pay bottom line dividends will require special care in designing the strategic game plan—for the simple reason that banks face tighter capital restraints and must pay more for their capital today. However, it is also reasonable to assume that some players will remain passive bystanders because of the high investment risk in relation to the revenue gains they can reasonably expect. By contrast, an aggressive technology policy posture will require investment capital beyond what many institutions can afford. Those banks that decide to become followers rather than pioneers in technology development may be making the optimal strategic decision in view of their asset strength, market reach, and other capabilities.[26]

TECHNOLOGY IS A TOOL

To repeat the point made earlier, business strategy will have the upper hand in systems applications because technology is a tool with many potential applications. For example, Security Pacific's decision to establish its information systems engineering division as an autonomous profit center is based on its goal of competing against other telecommunications vendors for the business of smaller financial institutions that cannot afford to develop their own systems.[27] There is nothing inherent in telecommunications technology, for example, that can decide which is the optimal strategy—whether a bank would do better to act as a "middleman" and sell access to one or more of its electronic highways to other institutions, as Security Pacific contemplates doing, or build its system network for the exclusive use of its own customers.

Although markets drive technology, economics ultimately drives markets. There are many who are skeptical about the extent to which EFT systems will effectively cut into the growth of checks. Demand account checking was the revolutionary new "software" of the 19th century, and it is easy to forget that at one time checks were the new labor savers. Check transfers posed less hazard of theft than currency shipments and they were highly flexible. One piece of paper could accommodate any dollar amount!

The "cashless society" was first heralded in the mid-1960s, but never quite arrived. Paper checks still account for 95 percent of all noncash transactions, although they account for less than 10 percent of the total dollar value of all payments transactions.

Yet the potential economic savings of the EFT systems are so obvious that electronic funds transfers will remain the central strategic anchor of the new IS technologies. EFT is the hub in the wheel of IS technology because the potential economic impact is so great. At the present time, check processing is estimated to cost banks in the neighborhood of $7 billion a year. Supermarkets handle approximately 3.6 billion checks annually at a cost of almost $2 billion dollars.[28] But besides the chilling cost of paper-based systems, the warming economic reality is that EFT can eventually reduce those costs once customers and markets accept the technology and the institutional barriers relating to pricing, the development of industry-wide formatting standards for networking, and so forth, are overcome. In a study prepared for the California Interlink POS system by Arthur Andersen, it was found that checks cost supermarkets 42.3 cents compared with just 11.5 cents for debit cards. For oil retailers, checks cost 73.2 cents, or 10 times the cost of debit card use (7 cents). Even cash costs more than debit cards![29] Moreover, in contrast to paper-based systems which have few economies of scale, EFT costs ratchet downwards as volume increases. This is the reality that will eventually deter the continued growth of paper-based transactions in favor of a shift towards electronic transfers. It is why payments and also, to a lesser extent, the new information service products will remain at the core of the strategic use of technology.

TECHNOLOGY, STRATEGY, AND CONNECTIVITY

From the standpoint of product markets, the strategic use of today's new IS technologies has implications for service that are at least as important as the potential implications for cost structures. This development can be summed up in a single word: "connectivity," which refers to the increased integration among data systems, customer accounts, product delivery and other services. It provides the ultimate in customer access to bank services anytime, anywhere. Just as the new technology is driving integrative managerial structures and systems architectures in a mixed format of centralized policy-making and decentralized applications, it is also revolutionizing the "marketing imagination" in financial service institutions.

In banking, the marketing of stand-alone products is giving way to integrated account management (or "relational" marketing as it is also called). The dual investment/transaction account that was first pioneered by the money market funds, then developed further into integrated or core accounts (combining credit, investment, transaction, and asset management products) will evolve even further. When combined with remote self-service banking by PCs, ATMs, and the like, it will enable customers to obtain access anytime, anywhere, with full "transaction mobility," to an increasingly broader range of services. Centralized customer information files (CIFs) are already being developed by some institutions to further the "connectivity revolution." Because of the dramatic reductions in information processing costs, technology has repersonalized and individualized financial services. The standardized stand-alone products are going out; individually "customerized" products are replacing them.

The higher levels of services integration enable further significant improvements. Some industry observers believe that by the mid-1990s individual customers will have access to integrated accounts of the kind now being offered to corporate treasurers. These accounts will include financial planning and analysis tools that enable the customers to explore sophisticated "what if" scenarios.[30] "Smart cards" with embedded chips containing customer account and other information would further extend the range of service options and communications alternatives. Just as bricks and mortar branching and the mass merchandising of bank services finally democratized banking in the first half of the twentieth century, microprocessors may finally democratize the expensive tax and financial planning services heretofore available only to upscale market segments.

Technology's Impact on the Customer

In whatever way financial services managements decide to use the new technologies to maximum strategic advantage—and their choice will depend, as discussed, on a variety of contingencies and different corporate goals—the strategic impact of technology on both retail and wholesale consumers of financial services is unmistakable. It has improved service while reducing cost. It is humanizing service even while reducing the labor content behind those services. And the labor that is being replaced by microprocessors and machines is mainly the drudgery of routine actions that had earlier interfered with personalized service to customers. With new levels of integration, the revolutionary new IS technologies will eventually put elite financial products previously available only to the affluent into the hands of all who need and want these new informational products. Indeed, as artificial intelligence technology and smart card appliances evolve, such access will be placed literally in the hands of bank customers.

The individualization of financial service represents the future from the customer's standpoint. From the standpoint of financial services managements, the new technologies have increasingly made it possible for each institution to pursue more distinctive and specialized market strategies.

Banks and other financial service providers will increasingly feel pressures to find a distinctive marketplace niche. Just as the standardized products of the era of heavy regulation have given way to a profusion of new financial services, business strategies will increasingly diverge as each provider seeks to exploit its comparative advantages. For example, some banks are specializing in providing wholesale service to other banks. Banc One in Ohio specializes in credit card processing for other institutions. As mentioned earlier, Security Pacific turned its systems engineering group into an independent profit center in the hope of becoming the low cost supplier of quality telecommunications services (electronic mail, PBX, etc.) to other banks. The Bank of Boston is pursuing a regional niche strategy as a "wholesale middleman" by providing switching services for the MONEC regional ATM network along with payroll processing for corporations.[31]

Indeed, the more specialized niche strategies characteristic of today's deregulated high-tech environment mean that many banks will find that their chief competitors are not banks but retailers and other nonbank institutions.

Just as there are many electronic highways that a firm can choose to travel, there are also numerous strategic business opportunities to choose from. Finding the right mix of systems architectures to match a given strategic design, and learning how to manage those systems competently to the end of achieving strategic business goals will without a doubt be the most important challenge for financial service managements through the remainder of the 1980s and well into the 1990s.

NOTES

1. Metzger, Robert O., Ian I. Mitroff and Susan E. Rau. "Challenging the Strategic Assumptions of the Banking Industry." *The Bankers Magazine* (July-August, 1984) pp. 29–34.
2. Wriston, Walter, "The Information Standard." *Euromoney* (October 1984) pp. 92–95.
3. Auerbach, Isaac. "The Business of Banks." *The Bankers Magazine* (September-October 1984) pp. 79–80.
4. Giroux, Gary A., and Peter S. Rose. "An Update of Bank Planning Systems: Results of a Nationwide Survey of Large U.S. Banks." *Journal of Bank Research* (Autumn 1984) pp. 27–31.
5. Shirrell, Rick D., "Microcomputers in Banking." *Magazine of Bank Administration* (October 1984) pp. 12–14; Lam, Chun H., and George H. Hemple. "Microcomputers in Bank Management: Actual Applications." *Journal of Retail Banking* (Winter 1984) pp. 8–13.
6. Weiss, Henry. "The Fastest Information Sources in Banking." *Computers in Banking* (September 1984) pp. 48–51.
7. Smith, Robert D., and Glenn N. Thomas. "Information Management in Banking." *The Magazine of Bank Administration* (March 1984); Hanley, Thomas H., Jeffrey L. Cohn, Carla A. D'Arista, and Neil A. Mitchell. *Electronic Banking: Yesterday, Today and Tomorrow*, New York: Salomon Brothers, Inc., 1984, p. 1.
8. Svigals, Jerome. "Electronic Banking: Every Manager's Business." *Computerworld* (October 29, 1984) ID/4.
9. *Effects of Information Technology on Financial Service Systems*, Washington, D.C.: U.S. Congress, Office of Technology Assessment, (September 1984), pp. 71–75.
10. This is advised by practically every writer on the subject of strategic technology use. Frohman,

Alan L. "Putting Technology into Strategic Planning." *California Management Review* (Winter 1985) p. 49. Also, Smith, Robert D. and Glenn N. Thomas. "Information Management in Banking." *The Magazine of Bank Administration* (March 1984) pp. 31–35.

11. "EFT Comes of Age: A Report to American Business on Electronic Payments." Bank of America, 1984, p. 5; Arthur Andersen & Co., and Bank Administration Institute, *New Dimensions in Banking: Managing the Strategic Position*, 1983, p. 23.
12. "Innovative Thinking Helps First Tennessee Bank Pave the Way for the Future." *The Magazine of Bank Administration* (February 1985) pp. 82–83.
13. Teweles, Gillian. "Chase's Automation Game Plan." *Computers in Banking* (December 1984) pp. 30–38.
14. As of February 12, 1986, these units assumed a *direct* reporting relationship to BASE.
15. Svigals, Jerome. *Planning for Future Market Events Using Data Processing Support*. New York: Macmillan and Co., Inc., 1983, pp. 3–33.
16. Zimmer, Linda Fenner. "ATMs." *Payments in the Financial Services Industry of the 1980's: Conference Proceedings of the Federal Reserve Bank of Atlanta*. Westport: Quorum Books, 1984, pp. 7–8.
17. Edwards, Raoul D. "Competition, Cooperation—And the Consequences of Error." *United States Banker* (August 1983), pp, 4–6.
18. Arthur Andersen & Co. and Bank Administration Institute, *New Dimensions in Banking: Managing the Strategic Position*, 1983, p. 24.
19. Meyers, Nancy. "Points of Confusion." *Computers in Banking* (September 1984), pp. 80–84.
20. Pomeroy, Lee. "Chemical Bank's Experience with Home Banking." *Economic Review* (July/August 1984) pp. 36–39.
21. Whitehead, David. "Firms Involved in ATM, POS, and Home Banking: A Survey." Atlanta Federal Reserve, Economic Review Board, 1984, p. 7, footnote of p. 124.
22. Willumstad, Robert B. "A Home Banking Case Study." *The Bankers Magazine* (November/December 1984) pp. 41–45.
23. Arthur Andersen & Co. and Bank Administration Institute, *New Dimensions in Banking*, 1983, p. 23.
24. *ATMs and Cash Dispensers: An Evaluation of Expansion Rates, Productivity Card Issuance and Shared Interchange*, A report of Trans Data Corporation, 1984, p. vii.
25. *The New Consumer Financial Services Market*, A report published by Payment Systems, Inc., Vol. II, 1984, p. 129.
26. Bank Administration Institute and Arthur Andersen & Co., *New Dimensions in Banking: Managing the Strategic Position*, 1983, p. 26.
27. Fioravante, Janice. "Security Pacific Automation Co. Off and Running." *Computers in Banking* (January 1985) pp. 20–26.
28. United States Office of Technology Assessment, 97th Congress, *Selected Electronic Funds Transfer Issues: Privacy, Security and Equity* (March 1982), p. 3; Van L. Taylor, David Jr., "Debit Cards." *Payments in the Financial Services Industry of the 1980's*, Conference Proceedings, Federal Reserve Bank of Atlanta, 1984, p. 13.
29. "EFT Comes of Age," p. 5.
30. Cox, Edwin B. "Integrated Financial Services." *Payments in the Financial Services Industry of the 1980's: Conference Proceedings*, Federal Reserve Bank of Atlanta (Westport, CT: Quorum Books) 1984, pp. 19–20.
31. Hanley, Thomas H., Jeffrey L. Cohn, Carla A. D'Arista, and Neil A. Mitchell, *Electronic Banking: Yesterday, Today and Tomorrow*. Salomon Brothers, Inc., (April 1984), p. 22; Fioravante, Janice. "Security Pacific Automation Co. Off and Running." *Computers in Banking* (January 1985) pp. 20–26.

19 Management of Technology into the Financial Services Organization

DAVID J. BLACKWELL

All major segments of the financial services industry have long been dependent on information as a fundamental ingredient of their product and service offerings. In most this dependence has become institutionalized to the point that it is taken for granted. Information-related activity has, however, tended to concentrate itself in the routine, operational side of the organization.

As the financial services industry evolves, information and the technology that is needed to optimize its utilization are becoming more pervasive in other facets of the business. This chapter will address some of the challenges that are faced in managing technology and information into the organization as a whole as well as within the technology function itself. The major premise is that the skills of the people involved will be key determinants in the success or failure of technology within the organization.

In fact, most activities in any enterprise are dependent on the quality of the people selected to manage them. It is essential that the right individual be selected to lead the technology function and to act as its representative in the top councils of the corporation. Without this relationship at the strategic level, the building of knowledge at the tactical and operating levels will be less apt to happen and much less productive even if it does.

The individual selected must be a happy blend of technologist, strategist, and general manager. He or she must have the same level of CEO confidence that is given to the chief financial officer, the chief counsel, and the heads of sales, operations, and product development.

This participation of a technically knowledgeable peer ("chief information officer") in the decision-making process will have the long-term effect of building an understanding of the potentials and pitfalls of the uses of technology by all members of senior management.

As including the technology arm in the top committees of major financial institutions has become more common, alumni of the technology area have moved into major general management roles in innovative financial institutions. Citibank is probably the best known example, but it is far from unique. Aetna, Equitable, Mellon, and BankAmerica are other cases in point.

It is both unrealistic and undesirable to suggest that all top executives should have full and complete knowledge of technology. What is required is *adequate* knowledge to be reasonably sure that the strategic direction of the company is being served well by technology. The CEO does not expect to be expert in each functional area of the corporation. The technical area is no exception. (The most unfortunate member of any policy group is that individual who represents the CEO's original area of expertise.) Even in the financial services industry, where technology has become deeply woven into the fabric of the organization, few CEOs have come out of this area. As a result, the CEO needs to have complete confidence in the individual who represents technology in his policy setting group. The participation of the chief information officer in the policy committee will also serve to educate all members of that august group, and help them in their own internal operations.

THE MANAGERS OF TECHNOLOGY

The information function in any organization can be broken into two major categories:

- Running systems previously developed
- Developing new systems or products

To draw an analogy with the manufacturing world, the first category would clearly be part of the "factory" while the second would be the "R&D" department. This first area of the industry has enjoyed the longest and most significant uses of information and technology. Now the R&D function is taking on increasing importance. Each area is worth a closer look.

Managing the "Factory"

Many of today's managers came into the business after the first wave of computerization. They gained their knowledge of the role of technology at the same time that they were gaining knowledge of the daily functioning of their bank, insurance company, brokerage, or other financial services institution. Consequently, they took for granted those activities that had already married information and technology in their area of assignment. In an insurance company, for example, premiums have been billed and collected, dividends have been calculated and paid, and policies issued by computer ever since computers first appeared on the scene. Managers involved in those functions have, of necessity, gained knowledge of what technology was doing for them—and to them.

Mainline processes have undergone myriad changes in the 25 or more years since they were first computerized. Those changes have also served to provide dynamic education to the users directly involved. This osmotic process of familiarization has been the biggest single force in providing knowledge about the capabilities of technology. Technology has been experienced principally, however, by those who have been directly assigned to one of the operational transaction functions in the "factory" that have been the primary targets of its application. In addition, the knowledge thus gained by those in operational management positions has tended to be limited to those technologies which have been installed in the past, or to modest enhancements of the same technologies that are already being utilized.

Expectation levels for those in this type of environment have tended to be limited to the kind of technological support already being experienced, or to levels that have been provided to their peers—peers either in their own organization or in similar organizations where personal contact is available.

Finally, many senior managers of organizations did not come into the industry through the part of the organization most likely to offer a chance to absorb technology through osmosis; others entered the industry before computerization became widespread; and still others moved through the lower levels of management (where exposure would occur) so long ago that what little knowledge they have absorbed is now obsolete. In sum, limited (or nonexistent) exposure to technology has left many managers unprepared for radical technological innovation.

For example, many of those responsible for branch banking in other banks were caught flatfooted and overinvested in bricks and mortar when Citibank introduced ATMs. While it is true that those with vision often end up in the leadership roles associated with innovations, one would have to guess that those competitors with a grounding in technology reacted faster and smarter to Citibank than those without such knowledge.

Yet many managers are placed in positions where it is critical for them to understand the potentials of technology in making decisions about essential changes to their operations. How, then, can an organization assure itself that its operational managers have adequate knowledge and skills to recognize potentials and to make value-added decisions?

Before answering how to transfer this knowledge, or at least how to assure that those who already have the knowledge are appropriately placed, it is useful to provide an historical perspective on the management research and development efforts within the industry. For there is today a whole new set of demands put on managers involved in the R&D function.

Managing Product/Service Development

In the good old days, the life cycle of products in the financial services industry was relatively long. In that environment, the decision maker had much less motivation to understand what the technological requirements were for a new offering. Lead-time demands were less urgent, and the technology content of a new product was lower. The decision maker could safely delegate any knowledge of technology to one of his teams.

The pressures of shortened life cycles and increased technological content have forced anyone who wants to stay with the market to remain alert to both the potentials and the limitations of technology. Most managers on the marketing as well as the technology sides of the business have had to become increasingly knowledgeable.

The universal life insurance product offers a good example of the advantages of staying alert in the product development area. Those who first developed universal life understood the state of the art in technology well enough to realize that the types of calculations that had once been so cumbersome could now be done on a dynamic basis throughout a policy's lifetime. The developers apparently realized (as the bankers did when daily interest calculations emerged) that they could create a competitive edge in a product, an edge that would be worth the slightly higher cost of administration. They were willing to trade off those slightly higher costs against the sales potential of breaking apart the risk and the investment portions of a life insurance policy.

The universal life example emphasizes the close relationship between those who understand the changes in technology and those who are responsible for the strategic directions of any financial services institution. When technology permits the exploitation of a new product or service offering, maximum advantage is usually gained by timeliness and the proper juxtaposition of idea and technology.

Technology has also helped blur the differences between the offerings of banks, brokers, insurance companies, and other segments. As a result, the problem of getting the attention of nontechnologists for long enough to educate them has been greatly diminished. When market share is being attacked by a competing product, and that product has been made possible by technology, alert managers will want to spend time understanding how to react. These days, it is hard to imagine a banker who lacks a reasonable understanding of ATMs, a broker who does not appreciate the cost and complexity of building a system for cash management accounts, or an insurance company CEO who has not had an extensive briefing on why his old systems will not handle universal/variable life policies.

It is also important to understand what can be done with technology to develop additional services that will offer a competitive advantage. One example of this is in insurance, where the claims service function has become the *product*, while heretofore it had only been an internal service function. (Larger buyers are now insisting on a product generically known as "administrative services only." All that the insurance company provides is a claims service on a fee basis.)

Technology has allowed new competitors to come into the market. In insurance, the example previously described, new organizations have emerged that have no skills in risk underwriting. They exist and prosper by providing just the improved claims service capability, a capability that is largely dependent on systems efficiency and cost.

In directing this technology function, the manager must understand the trade-offs between making and buying. The choice is particularly important when purchase of software from third parties is under consideration. ATM systems, policy administration systems, check reconciliation systems, and pension administration systems are just a few examples of the packaged software that is available to perform information-processing activities for basic new products or services.

For example, when the universal life product emerged, every insurance company was faced with two basic decisions: Did it want to offer the product? And if it did, what were the time pressures involved to get the product to the market place? In most companies it was agreed that the product had to be offered, and that it had to be offered quickly to avoid the external replacement of existing business by those who already had the product on the street.

Once these decisions were made, an insurance company was faced with the problem of producing the new product. Because the basic administrative processing was so different from that already existing for the traditional life product, the company was typically told by its information processing people that a long lead time was required, either to build a new administrative system or to change the old system to accommodate the new functions.

A third alternative was to go to an outside supplier, a software house, which offered a system expressly developed to process the new product. There were short-term advantages to this alternative: Product could be on the street in a relatively short time; loss of new business market share could be avoided; and replacement of existing business by competitors could be reduced.

At the same time, however, the company was buying into a longer-term set of conditions that were not nearly as attractive. The new system would not handle the old business, so the company usually ended up with two basic systems of administration. The new systems were apt to be rudimentary, and in some cases combined the worst of both worlds—high computer costs per policy and high clerical costs surrounding the systems. Furthermore, the two administrative systems were not designed to talk to each other, and the fancy systems for terminal transaction entry that had been developed at a cost of millions of dollars would not work with the new system. There was more than a reasonable chance that the company would be better off choosing to take its time and come out with a well thought-out universal life product that would fit the old system. Going this route would permit a return to the expense factors and service characteristics of the old system.

Obviously, had the managers in these insurance companies known more about technology, these compatibility and cost problems would have been avoided. Yet many managers with no prior contact to technology are routinely required to make decisions essential to their operations that presuppose their being conversant with systems mechanics and capabilities. How, then, can an organization assure itself that its operational managers have adequate knowledge and skills to recognize potentials and to make value-added decisions?

TRANSFERRING KNOWLEDGE

In many financial institutions today, the information services function represents one-quarter to one-sixth of the entire staff of the organization. Both the development and the "factory" sides of this function offer strong opportunities for learning skills and knowledge that can be valuable in future management assignments at all levels, both inside and outside the information services area.

Nothing matches hands-on experience for acquiring knowledge. This fact makes a strong argument for rotational assignments early in the potential manager's career. Rotational assignments are an excellent way of sensitizing the manager to both the threats and opportunities of technology, and to what he can reasonably expect from the information systems people when he turns to them as a user-manager asking for support.

What exactly are the skills and kinds of knowledge a manager needs? Specific technological facts are very apt to be obsolete in five years or less. Little advantage is gained investing time in precise technical information that has such a short life expectancy. Companies that initiate rotational programs in the hope of imparting specific information are likely to waste their time and effort. Rather, rotational experiences should provide a mindset and frame of reference for the manager's future that is totally independent of specifics.

But even the general mindset needs to be refreshed with periodic exposure to the latest technologies and opportunities. A one-shot rotation is not the panacea. Rather, rotation should be seen as the foundation for an ongoing awareness of what is happening. It should provide an impetus to set up structures that ensure that future refreshing takes place.

Consider some of the functions of a manager that are heavily influenced by his access to, and use of, information and his understanding of technology.

First, each manager can expect to be called on to establish *performance standards* for the activities under his or her control. What quickly becomes obvious in an industry as pervasively computerized as financial services is that the manager's own performance and the performance of his unit will be heavily dependent on the performance they receive from those providing information services. A manager who has no frame of reference to fall back on to establish probable or possible performance from suppliers is really without hope of establishing standards. In such circumstances, the best approach is to make clear where responsibility lies. Customers, whether inside or outside of the institution, will not be put off by the manager's explaining his reliance on the information services supplier.

A tour of duty in the "factory" will equip this manager with the contacts and the knowledge to negotiate the best possible results. Time spent in the development area of information services will help him recognize changes he should be seeking, and will provide the linguistic tools to describe needed changes in terms that the information systems professionals can understand.

A second managerial function influenced by information knowledge is *expense control and reduction*. Knowledge of technology is critical to both control and reduction. In an industry where so much of salary expense comes from the information services operation and where most of the non-"bricks-and-mortar" capital expenditure comes from technology equipment, it is important for the operational manager to understand the charges or allocations being submitted by information services. At the same time that the manager is learning to understand—and worry about—expenses incurred in the present use of technology, he should be learning enough to recognize how further applications can help accomplish *expense reduction*. Direct personal involvement in the rate-setting (or allocation) process will equip the manager to better judge proposed changes to the operation.

A third function common to every manager is supervision of *work flow*. It would be a pleasure to report that workflow information is readily available from the technologists. In many organizations, however, this may not be the case. The 30-year history of computerization has trained many systems people to be specialists on what happens inside the technology, without instilling an appreciation for how computerization affects the operation. It is here that a fuller transfer of knowledge is needed. Some of the better information services organizations are equipped to provide work flow analysis to their counterparts on the line. All information services organizations should be providing them.

Transfer of Knowledge to Senior Managers

Because any financial services corporation has substantial investments in its information services organization, it is appropriate, even essential, that senior corporate or product line management make the best possible allocation of the information services resources to help accomplish the strategic and operational goals of the organization. The most significant opportunity to do this comes at the point in the strategic and operational planning cycle when corporate resources are allocated.

Data-processing steering committees have not in the past been active in strategic planning by senior managers. Many of these committee assignments were relegated to middle or lower-level management, even though in financial services organizations a very high percentage of strategic and financial plans depended on the application of technology for their success or failure. If corporate plans are constrained by a shortage of information systems resources, it is not logical to relegate the solution of the problem to some lower-level committee. This would be just as unthinkable as relegating the decision on a capital shortage problem to a second or third level of management. Therefore, it has become highly desirable that data-processing steering committee activities be merged into the deliberations of the highest policy committee in the organization, whether this is called the management committee, the policy committee, or the office of the president.

In an organization where the CEO is assisted by some group (e.g., a management committee) in his determination of corporate strategic direction, decisions must be made about the allocation and application of resources. Strategic and tactical plans have to be judged and approved by this committee, and technical knowledge is essential here. The policy committee should expect to deal with the quantity and quality of information systems resources required, and with the allocation of those resources to the various segments of the organization. The committee should first understand the technological objectives and likelihoods of success of the various projects that are being funded. It should then weigh their costs in time, attention, and money against the strategic objectives that the projects support. Where the committee style of management is not used, it is appropriate for the CEO to use the chief information officer as an active advisor to assist him in his review and approval of his subordinates' strategic and tactical plans.

Within the subdivisions of the company, be they product lines or functional areas, similar resource allocation activities should take place. It is crucial here too that the head of the unit take an active role. In each case the ranking information officer should be a participant, if not a partner, in the deliberations.

THE MANAGEMENT OF INFORMATION

The transfer of knowledge about technology is clearly not enough. The related issue is how to manage the information that technology provides. If one breaks all systems, somewhat simplistically, into three elements—*input, processing*, and *output*—it can be seen that *output* is the element that preoccupies most users.

Printed reports produced as part of the overall systems development process have always been the primary vehicle for circulating information gathered by the system. Regrettably, most systems indiscriminately have spread too much information to be useful to management. Because systems typically have acquired information as part of exhaustive and meticulous transaction processing, the comparatively few revealing outputs have generally been embedded in inconsequential detail that is cumbersome to use. Or worse, the meaningful data are unobtainable.

As a result, management use of the information has often been limited to manually prepared analyses done by those closest to the raw data. Blurred communication through layers of organization meant that managers suffered from reports that did not really provide what was wanted.

In recent years, two major classes of technology developments have created real opportunities for the handling and use of information. The first class comprises developments that have occurred outside the organization itself. Service organizations are increasingly gathering information which is particularly useful to the financial services industry, providing instant access to market changes and trades. These services are already being used by most of the industry. In addition, research data has become electronically available. Commercially available information banks provide access to demographic and other information critical to market analysis and product development. All this fully current data can be received through the umbilical cord that links a central data bank and a terminal. Also, balance information and funds transfer capabilities have not only speeded up the daily transaction activity, but have also provided a ready basis for decision making in cash management. In many cases the availability of information is well known to those performing day-to-day processing, but is not well known to those layers of management who could use the information in the decision-making process.

The second class of developments relates to new software that allows raw data to be analyzed for management purposes. Some of these advancements blossomed as by-products of improved processes for creating routine systems applications. For example, "fourth generation languages," which speed the process of administrative systems development, are often based on new ways of establishing data bases, data libraries (and the dictionaries needed to reference them), and usually have simplified query languages to search for that data. These tools, used until now primarily to accelerate the development process, may offer even greater potential for transferring information now in the province of the professional information-processing person to those who need it for management purposes.

A welcome possibility exists that many reports routinely prepared as an output of transaction systems may be eliminated. Currently, many of these reports are prepared in anticipation that someone will ask for an obscure piece of information otherwise buried in the stack of print-outs. Estimates as to what portion of the three-stage input/processing/output effort is consumed as output range from 30 to 50 percent. If one imagines how much of this activity could be eliminated by improvements in information handling, the opportunities for expense and time reduction are, indeed, exciting. Unfortunately, these same visions were held out prematurely by overly zealous hardware salespeople during the early days of database management systems. Although a qualitative leap has now been made, it is important that the advances be communicated to management throughout the organization.

The new capabilities are far from being installed universally, however. For this reason, it is timely for managements to ask their information professionals about the status of implementation and plans for further change. The benefits cannot start to flow until middle and upper management understand the potentials and limits of this new facility.

Use of Microprocessor Workstations

Another element in the management of information is microprocessor workstations, which are playing a dramatically expanded role. Granted, the promise of technology was dramatically oversold in the late 1960s and early 1970s. It is not that most of what was touted did not eventually happen. It did. But in almost every case, it lagged behind users' expectations by years. These expectations had been fanned into white heat by vendors and by naive technologists, neither of whom understood the basic problems of the business or the basic techniques by which businesses are managed. These same excessive expectations need to be avoided as powerful new technologies emerge.

It is critical for all levels of management to understand the capabilities of microprocessors. They offer managers new tools for acquiring information useful in decision making, as well as the means for shortening lines of communication. But less positively, there are still many things they cannot do. A small microcomputer may help Charlie Chaplin to manage a bakery, but it will not serve the basic administrative needs of an organization with hundreds of thousands, even millions, of accounts. However, when intelligently implemented in a major organization, microcomputers will find their place as one more piece in the complex mosaic of hardware and software that is used to provide information and support to the enterprise.

Micros have created an interesting conflict. In many organizations the central technology personnel, who by this time know the mainline business well and should be able to advise best about the choices that are emerging, often feel threatened by this invasion of their domain. The users (or potential users), on the other hand, may see the new technology as a safety valve to get around the shortage imposed by the corporation on the central resources. It is essential that top managers recognize the possibility of this basic conflict, so that they can work with the chief information officer until assured that the situation is not counterproductive to the organization.

Early in the chapter it was emphasized that organizations need a top information manager who retains the confidence of the CEO. This person is responsible for assuring the CEO that the inherent conflict is being dealt with in a manner that will actualize the potential of the microprocessor technology.

MANAGING THE TECHNOLOGY RESOURCE

Technology can help not only its end users but its technicians as well. Thus, one very constructive thing that top management can do is to encourage use of new technology by the central technology resource itself. With the cost of computer hardware coming down 12 to 15 percent per year and the cost of staff rising 8 to 10 percent per year, it also makes sense to make sure that the hardware dollars in support of the information professional are being spent at the appropriate level. A microcomputer workstation for each systems professional could address both the conflict mentioned above and the subject of systems professional productivity. For example, if every traditional systems developer's workstation was a personal computer, choices between micro solutions and traditional solutions to systems problems could be made at the level where it would do the most good. Moreover, what the information professional might otherwise view as a competitive threat could be turned into an asset for him as his ability to support and educate the rest of the organization expanded. This possibility is no longer merely theoretical. There is also a growing body of evidence that microcomputers will enhance the productivity of information professionals by 10 to 15 percent.

A second opportunity for applying technology to the information systems function itself lies in the area of programming development languages. Virtually all the major information systems areas in the financial services industry have developed their systems in the last 20 years in a computer language called COBOL. COBOL's language, and the techniques surrounding it, have become embedded in almost all major systems. Meanwhile, the technology surrounding these systems has changed four or five times in the same 20-year period. In effect, the shoemaker's child is still wearing the same shoes he first put on 20 years ago.

There is a growing body of knowledge indicating that fourth-generation programming languages, data bases, and dictionaries can be applied to 40 to 60 percent of the average development workload. These fourth-generation systems are not particularly effective on those portions of the system that must remain in a batch environment, but they can enable productive gains in both the development and operation of the interactive portions. In spite of this potential, though, most development organizations are still reliant on traditional COBOL techniques for systems development.

Of course, it takes time and money (not to mention delay in critical projects) to outfit the shoemaker's child in new shoes. Without understanding and support from top management the changes will never occur. And yet by most reckonings, the new approaches offer a 30- to 40-percent productivity improvement in the systems development process.

The need for speed in introducing products has put many organizations into a reactive mode. Demand for resources has tended, therefore, to focus on optimization of currently used technology—the registered rep's need for quicker, better data on securities; the optimization of ATMs; the enhancement of computerized insurance sales illustrations. Even organizations that once led the introduction of technology for strategic purposes have tended to reduce their concentration on developing totally new technology. Often, in fact, they have become so involved in optimizing technology that is already in place that they have reduced or entirely eliminated the staff assigned to investigate new technology.

It is important for top managers to recognize this phenomenon and insist that their technology groups invest some effort in research and development into new technology. Further, top management should recognize and expect that the R&D mode will inevitably produce some failures. Otherwise it is not reaching out at all. Managements have become so accustomed to 100 percent success rates on projects that many of us are not prepared to invest in pursuits that realistically are judged highly successful when they experience only a 50 percent hit rate. Citibank's development of the ATM was cited earlier as a classic example of how technology can be critical to the direction of a major corporation. Examination of the trash cans at Citibank would undoubtedly find other projects that once seemed to hold equal promise. And that is as it should be in an aggressive R&D environment.

A mechanism should be established to make sure that newly acquired R&D knowledge is matched to the strategic needs of the corporation. This need appears particularly urgent when one considers how profoundly technology is affecting the creation of new products and services. Among the better publicized technologies that are already spawning product and service offerings are "expert systems," voice recognition, smart cards, video-text, and portable personal computers. Responsibility to keep the organization abreast of technology is not limited to R&D. It is incumbent on all layers of management to set up a mechanism that systematically searches the emerging technology and communicates its findings to those charged with product and service development.

CONCLUSION

The young people coming to financial services firms from our better educational institutions will be used to and will therefore expect the availability of computing power to help them in whatever they are doing. Many universities are already requiring that a personal computer be purchased by each entering student. It is already hard to imagine the college student who is not at least partially computer literate.

We should not, however, jump to the conclusion that the influx of computer-literate college graduates will eventually eliminate the knowledge gap that separates systems professionals from their users. Many new employees who know how to use a computer will elect not to. With a five-year cycle for technological obsolescence, many other employees who have once been fluent in systems will need their working knowledge refreshed.

It will, however, be important for all managers to understand the potential and the limits of what to expect. This means that serious, though not necessarily formal, education is in order. This education will come through the same process of osmosis described earlier for today's operational manager. Information handling, as it affects the top manager, will change slowly. The technological potential will be there long before it is widely used. So, as the potential is slowly realized, the top manager will go through a learning curve so gradual that he will hardly realize it is happening. The true technologist may be impatient with this process, but that is the nature of change.

There is no quick fix for getting knowledge about technology to those not directly involved. Most knowledge will be acquired gradually over time. Senior management can, however, arrange organization and resource allocation reviews to speed its familiarization with technology use and put it in a position to enhance the organization's ability to take advantage of technological opportunities. Information handling and technology will steadily become more deeply woven into the fabric of the financial services industry, as indeed they will be in the fabric of daily life. The organizations that manage this change intelligently can find increasing competitive advantage in the judicious application of emerging technology.

20 Operations Management

RICHARD A. RIZZOLO

The past 10 years have shown a quiet yet dramatic change in the back offices of financial services companies throughout the world. The change has taken a function that once was considered the corporate graveyard to a place many now argue is the place to be. In fact, in regional and money center banks, operations executives are rising above their colleagues as technology and noncredit services continue to revolutionize the industry. The American Banking Association recently reported a growing list of high-echelon bankers who have risen to the top of their organizations after having spent at least a portion of their careers in charge of an operations department.[1] The list is quite impressive and includes, among others, John S. Reed of Citicorp, Robert I. Lipp of Chemical Bank, James G. Cairns, Jr. of Peoples National Bank, Seattle (and president of the ABA), Barry F. Sullivan of First Chicago, John J. Evans of Manufacturers Hanover, Arthur F. Ryan of Chase Manhattan, and Ian Arnof of First Commerce Corporation in New Orleans.

Today the operations manager is viewed as an integral member of the management team and usually works alongside marketing professionals, product development managers, and sales executives. But the rapid rise in status of the operations manager has come not without difficulty. One major problem is that in most financial services organizations, tailored training materials have not been available to the operations manager. Despite the attention, emphasis, and new strategic importance that management of operations is receiving, the operations manager can only find partial support from the volumes of management and accounting literature primarily written over the past 100 years to aid the manufacturer of goods.

There is no doubt that America's manufacturing experience can be of aid to the financial services operations manager; however, the translation of this accumulated knowledge into the realities of a service industry is neither complete nor straightforward. This chapter begins by discussing operations in financial services from an historical perspective, and then examines the limits of the manufacturing analogy. Next, the relationship between customer service and technology will be analyzed for signs of an emerging conceptual foundation useful to the financial services operations manager. Last, a "quality framework" will be presented to aid managers as they organize and direct financial services operations.

HISTORICAL VIEW

Ten years ago, the operations side of a financial services company was considered relatively unimportant, unexciting, and of minor strategic importance. This attitude existed for several reasons. Not the least of these was the comparative ease with which a bank, for example, could attract funds at low cost, invest them at a higher rate (without undue sacrifice of control), and derive a comfortable return. Moreover, banks had enjoyed an exclusive franchise over a primary financial service—the checking account. Operations was viewed solely as a back-office expense, and its impact on profitability was seen as related to the manager's ability to demonstrate cost containment. Not suprisingly, members of top management typically rose via a nonoperations career path, whether it was credit, financing, planning, or the like. Consequently, few executives had any first-hand experience with operations management—nor was such expertise perceived to be particularly important.

The lack of attention an operations division received was reflected in the quality of management time devoted to it. In the early 1970s MBAs generally avoided operations, viewing it as the least likely route to the chairman's office. The few who did pursue an operations career, on the theory that they would rise in meteoric fashion unhindered by significant competition, found few financial institutions which offered appropriate positions. Still fewer, if any, had training programs designed for operations managers. Most of the training programs that did exist specialized in credit analysis.

During the 1970s dramatic changes began to occur. Interest rate fluctuations became more frequent, margins became tougher to maintain, loan losses and nonperforming assets rose, and more and more large corporations issued commercial paper. At the same time, competition intensified, particularly following the passage of the Depository Institutions Deregulation and Monetary Control Act of 1980, which allowed the creation of negotiable orders of withdrawal (NOW) accounts at mutual savings banks, savings and loan associations, and credit unions nationwide. This legislation was followed by the government's neutralization of Regulation Q (interest rate ceilings), and private institutions' creation of the money market deposit account. These factors caused two fundamental changes in the way financial institutions were managed. First, increased competition and tighter margins forced institutions to place far more emphasis on cost containment and productivity, especially in their operations divisions. Second, the shift away from lending as a source of income created more emphasis on the fee-based services that are usually provided with operations support. These two changes have contributed to the rise in stature of the operations executive. They also have determined the characteristics that will distinguish a provider of financial services in the future: a sharp focus on its operational resources and technological capabilities.

Buyers of financial services have traditionally selected their providers on the basis of convenience, service specialization, and price. But today the notion of what these concepts mean to the customer is changing rapidly. For example, convenience is no longer simply determined by the service-delivery capabilities of the branch-office system. Similarly, checking accounts are no longer all the same, nor are they exclusively a service of commercial banks. Furthermore, price competition can only intensify after deregulation and the advent of regional and nationwide banking. Increasing competitive pressures in financial services mean that the creativity, expertise, and professionalism required of the operations manager are now several levels higher than they were just a few years ago, and are likely to increase geometrically in years to come.

In some ways, the challenges are greatest for traditional finance services firms. New competitors can take maximum advantage of new technology, systems design and delivery mechanisms, while established institutions must integrate these components into a service environment conceived decades ago and perfected over many years. But where can the operations manager go to seek support in meeting these challenges? This topic will be discussed next.

THE MANUFACTURING ANALOGY

It is currently estimated that as much as 70 percent of the total workforce in the United States is employed in the service sector.[2] It can be argued, moreover, that the service sector is actually much larger, as every business at every level involves some degree of service. Despite the significant shift of activity to the service sector, until recently most of the operations management literature has focused on the manufacturing or factory environment. Naturally, operations managers in the financial services industry, as elsewhere, draw upon this literature to find solutions to the complex problems they face. However, the fundamental differences between manufacturing a tangible good and providing an intangible service appears to limit the validity of the analogy. David Collier, perhaps generously, estimates that only 50 percent of the general body of management knowledge is transferable from good-producing firms to service firms.[3] The following example may suggest why this convertability factor is so low:

In a commercial bank, the first function typically centralized away from the branch office system is check processing. At larger banks, this function historically exhibited many of the characteristics of Frederick W. Taylor's factory environment, including a large "blue collar" work force; multiple work shifts; high-volume, short-interval work steps; multiple deadlines; and equipment that was heavy and expensive (at least for a nonmanufacturing company). All these ingredients were needed to handle the movement and processing of large inventories of paper in a timely manner. But unlike an item being "manufactured," a check being processed was being closely followed by the customer, who was in a good position to judge the timeliness and accuracy of the process. Industrial management techniques lent themselves quite readily to check processing and provided many of the tools needed to manage production flow, error control, productivity, work measurement, exception processing, scheduling, and quality assurance. However, most of these management tools provided internal production-oriented controls and measures that related neither easily nor directly to the customer. Nor did they speak to senior management needs, except perhaps on matters of cost. If the customer wanted to know why his statement was late or his deposit posted to the wrong account, he felt little comfort in the knowledge that his bank had a .005 error rate on a volume of two million checks in the sorting department that day, which was the most precise information the bank could provide him.

The shortcoming of the manufacturing analogy, moreover, goes beyond the way it was initially applied to operations management in a financial services company. David Collier has cataloged the major distinguishing characteristics between goods producers and service providers into nine categories, as follows:[4]

1. Service package versus physical product
2. Customer participation in the service delivery system
3. Time-dependent demand
4. Noninventoriable output
5. Service-worker skills
6. Proximity to customer/multisite management
7. No patents on services
8. Resilience to economic cycles
9. International transportability

Without going into each difference, readers can imagine what is becoming evident to operations managers: Financial services are sufficiently different from manufacturing operations that exclusive application of factory-based techniques would probably be unsuccessful in their environment. No doubt, much time and effort has been devoted to force-fitting manufacturing techniques to financial services functions. But at best, ignoring the differences will lead to confusing results in a business where recognition of success is elusive even under optimal conditions. At worst, opportunities to improve and enhance the service creatively will be missed completely, as Dan R. E. Thomas of the Harvard Business School has written:

> The predominant mental image about 'the way things work' in business is a product-based image. This image leads to a product-oriented language, and the language in turn constrains communication in such a way that one cannot develop really innovative approaches to managing the service business.[5]

The manufacturing analogy has also proved to be of limited value when traditional cost-accounting methods have been applied to financial services. This weak applicability should come as no surprise since a major objective of the accounting profession is to reflect "reality" accurately in their financial presentation; techniques and methods designed to reflect reality in the factory probably *should* be deficient in describing operations dissimilar to the factory's in several fundamental aspects.

Product profitability is the fundamental reason why management looks to cost information in a financial service activity. But here too, the methods and techniques in general use for costing manufactured products do not really apply to service products and can, in fact, produce incorrect or misleading product evaluations and rankings. At present, the empirical studies and academic work done in the area of service management have succeeded better at identifying the problems a service manager faces and the differences between his job and that of his factory counterpart. Research and theory have been less successful at describing solutions. "Knowing what you don't know" is, of course, a necessary first step in this direction. Moreover, a conceptual foundation for dealing with these issues is emerging and is the next topic for discussion.

CONCEPTUAL FOUNDATION FOR THE OPERATIONS MANAGER

It is more than coincidence that the explosion of activity in office automation and personal computers has been simultaneous with the intensifying focus on the management of service operations in general, and financial services in particular. In each case, dramatic developments in technology have afforded the front office worker and the service operations manager with communications and computer-related capabilities they never imagined they needed, or even wanted. A stellar example is the development of the memory chip, now the cornerstone for the industrialization of many office and personal service activities. Prior to the chip's invention, the biggest change in the office/service environment was probably the substitution of a photocopy machine for carbon paper. Now technology is on the verge of leaping to the next generation computer memory chip—the megabyte random-access memory. Each quarter-inch-square chip will hold over one million bits of data in integrated circuits one micron thick (a human hair is approximately 100 microns in diameter). Exhibit 20.1 suggests the new frontier these superchips would open.

Technology has created alternative ways that services can be accomplished by varying combinations of people and hardware. Likewise, it has enabled providers to deliver those services in many combinations of media, formats, and time frames. The key now becomes understanding what the service really is to the customer, and then determining how technology can enhance its execution and delivery.

The financial services applications of high-powered data processing of technology seem almost boundless. But no matter what applications actually take shape

Exhibit 20.1 Evolution of Memory Chips

Circuit	Size	Memory Capacity	Power Range	Applications
1980	4 microns	64k bits	Desktop microcomputer	Digital watches video games personal computers
1985	2 microns	256k bits	Minicomputer	Lap computers, engineering work stations, programmable appliances
1987	1 micron	1,024k bits	Mainframe computer	Pocket computers, electronic map-navigation, high-resolution TVs
1990	0.5 micron	4,096k bits	Supercomputer	Robots that can see, freeze-frame TVs, computers that can recognize and use natural languages
1995	.25 micron	16,384k bits	Ultracomputers	Star wars systems, personal robots, computers with human-like logic

Source: Business Week, June 10, 1985 p. 85.

and become accepted in the marketplace, they are all likely to have in common the ability of financial services companies and their clients to exchange information faster, more accurately, more conveniently, in greater quantities, and over a greater variety of media than ever before. These are the very characteristics upon which an efficient and effective marketplace thrives and within which only well-tuned, innovative companies will survive. While new forms and variations of investment and financing will always be designed and revised, financial services companies will increasingly be distinguished by how ably they meet the service operations challenge.

Understanding the Service

Any manager who attempts to define the services provided by his organization quickly discovers two difficulties:

1. No clear, concise body of language exists to assist him in his project.
2. So many financial services overlap or depend upon one another that it can be extremely difficult to determine where one service ends and another begins.

The first issue relates back to Thomas's observation that the "product-based image" constrains innovation in services. Many financial services firms nevertheless use product language to refer to the services they provide. What is a "product" to one institution may well be an entire collection of services to another, or simply an element of a service to a third. But the lack of any standard usage across financial services may not matter. What is important at the outset is that an institution communicate consistently within itself and establish common points of reference. Internal standardization is never an easy task, though. In all likelihood, a rational hierarchy of product families, groups, lines, and elements will not correspond neatly to organizational lines. Nevertheless, without an internally accepted language and structure, an organization stands virtually no chance of achieving full potential for its services/products, either taken individually or collectively.

The second issue, service overlaps, shares features with the first, and is usually further complicated by an institution's organizational structure. A demand deposit account (DDA), for instance, maintains a record of transactions and represents a store of value to the customer, who also has certain rights and privileges. Records of its transactions are maintained both in a checkbook and by the bank's DDA statement service. Interest may or may not be earned on its balance; it often can be assessed in several ways for information, either to move funds to other accounts or to receive currency or cash equivalents; and it is often linked to other financial services. This collection of DDA services crosses, or at least touches, several organizational lines within a bank, and is therefore a challenge to the application of product language. Among all of these service features the most expensive and labor-intensive aspect of the DDA service is the return of each check to the owner of the account.

As electronic transfers become faster, cheaper, and more reliable, the operations manager has to determine how critical the return of checks is to what Collier terms the "implicit benefits" of the service package:

> A service is a package of explicit and implicit benefits performed with a supporting facility and using facilitating goods. For example, an individual checkbook service has explicit benefits by documenting and monitoring cash inflows and outflows. The implicit benefits of this service package include a sense of security, privacy, flexibility, control, and hopefully, stability in the individual's financial well-being. The supporting facilities include the main and branch banks. The facilitating goods are used or consumed by the individual. In this case, the facilitating good is the paper and checkbook.[6]

In other words, is check return inextricable from "the service package" for DDAs, or can that service element be changed in any way to the benefit of bank and customer alike? Perhaps the return of checks is no longer needed to assure the customer that every check written against his account was authorized, prepared and processed as his ledger indicates, and endorsed by the proper payee. And does the customer still need checks to serve as legal proof of payment, if necessary, in the future? If the customer can now do without the check, the operations manager can look for less costly and perhaps more effective ways of delivering the implicit benefits of assurance and proof. Questions of the technological capability needed to support potential alterations in check processing, as well as the cooperation of banking authorities and the U.S. check clearing system, make arriving at a solution even more complicated. At the same time, the example illustrates the importance of understanding a service package. The financial services operations manager must not only understand what is done in the factory but more importantly what the customer is really buying if he is to be truly effective. Charles Revson, the founder of Revlon, said it well: "In the factory we make cosmetics, in the store we sell hope."

Assessment of the Delivery System

Services are created through the effective combination of labor, capital, technology, and information. In one sense, the ultimate consumer has no interest in how these factors are combined, so long as he is satisfied with the net result. To the financial services company, however, the issue is of critical importance: Variations in the mix of labor and capital can have dramatic economic impact on the firm. More subtly, however, and unique to the service industry, the service customer involves himself closely in the production process, greatly influences how the service is to be delivered, and ultimately judges its quality and value.

It is important, therefore, to understand the manner and extent to which the customer is involved in the service delivery equation before improvements and adaptation can be made. A high-customer-contact system is one in which the customer has repeated, sometimes prolonged, contact with the provider in the creation of the service. A low-contact system is characterized by infrequent interactions of brief duration. As one might suspect, the greater the level of contact and interaction, the greater the difficulty for management in controlling the process. In the high-contact system (such as exists with services only available at a bank branch) facility location, layout, product design, worker skills, capacity planning, and so on must be developed with consideration to the customer's attitudes, preferences, and convenience. In a low-contact system, such as DDA statement rendering, most of the production system has been entirely separated from the customer and made less sensitive to his attitudes. Consequently, sealing off the "technical core" in this way allows the design of the production process to be made more efficient.[7]

Gauging the degree of customer involvement in service production is a necessary step in operations design. The Customer Service Delivery Matrix shown in Exhibit 20.2 can therefore help an institution sense how involved its customers are in the operation of each of its services. At the same time, the matrix can indicate the degree of automation present to support the delivery process. Extent of customer contact is shown on the matrix's horizontal axis. Degree of automation needed in rendering the service is reflected on its vertical axis. Some services may be almost entirely people-based in their execution, while some may be almost totally equipment-based. Examples of the former are arranging for the financing of a car, home or business; an example of the latter is the transfer and maintenance of account balances.[8]

Because the combination of high levels of automation with low levels of customer involvement affords the operations manager the greatest control of the production process and quality control, it comes closest to fitting the manufacturing analogy. The reverse combination—high involvement, low automation—is closest to personalized service, as offered by one individual to another. Yet when customer involvement and automation are both low, the service manager must control a labor-intensive function and assure consistent levels of productivity and quality (albeit he is spared the complications of customer interface). High automation and high customer involvement, shown in the final quadrant of the matrix, require failsafe mechanisms to keep the necessary equipment up and running under the critical eye of the customer.

Careful examination of this service inventory matrix will not only help the service manager understand the relative concentrations of service capabilities existing in his own firm, but also will help him to assess competitive advantages and opportunities for increased management attention.

Exhibit 20.2 Customer Service Delivery Matrix

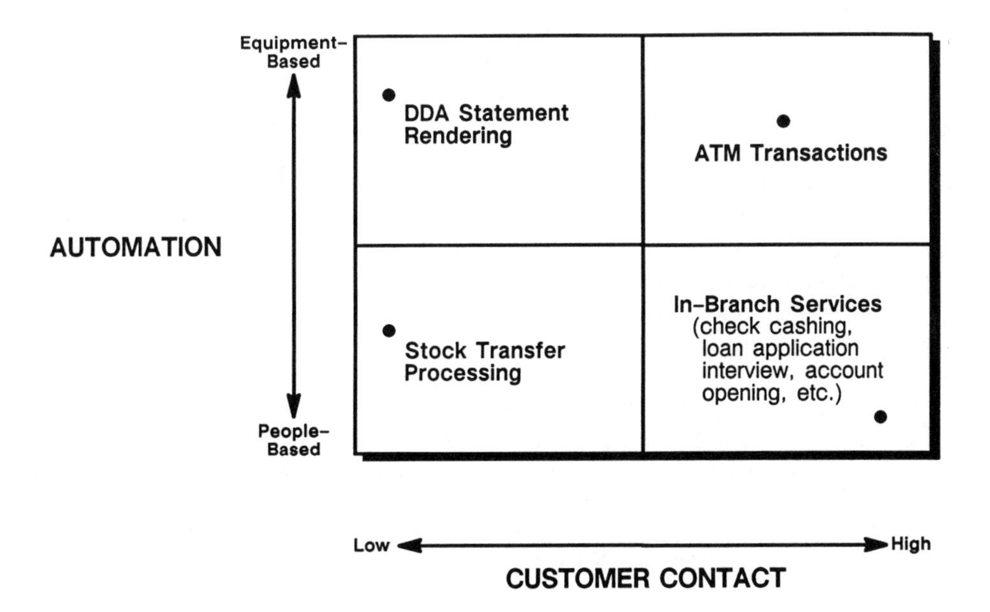

Opportunities for Innovation

The service operations manager, then, must not be satisfied with merely finding how new technology might be applied. He must also discover how a service might be better accepted, and rendered more convenient and more valuable to the customer, through the strategic introduction of technological enhancements. This discovery results from a better understanding of what the service really is and a clear evaluation of its delivery system.

One such strategic enhancement can be seen in the ATM endeavor. The technology for the cashless society has existed for some time and has been seriously discussed for almost 25 years. Yet automated teller machines have not eliminated branches and credit/debit cards have not even reduced, let alone eliminated, the volume of checks processed in the United States. Chemical Bank's Pronto home banking system is currently the strongest entry in a market that is developing more slowly than most observers predicted. Some suggest that the first wave of home banking users were those that, finding that they had no real use for their home computers, seized on home banking to finally justify their purchases. This is obviously a thin customer base. Videotex—PC-based access to phone directories, retailers, newspapers, and so on—will be a key element in broader expansion of the home banking service marketplace, although acceptance of Videotex has also been slow. The lesson seems to be that the spread of new technology depends on the attitudes of customers as well as providers. As Robert I. Lipp, president of Chemical Bank, has noted:

> Remember that our job is to deliver financial goods and services that are desired by the marketplace, and that technology can be a tremendous aid in the creation of these new or improved products. But don't kid yourself or get carried away with the glamour of technology—the fact that you and your operations division have the technology capacity to create a new product has virtually nothing to do with whether anybody is the slightest bit interested in buying it.[9]

Balancing the introduction of a new service against customer hesitation to use it is a delicate task. It was argued previously that blindly applying factory techniques to service operations will not lead to effective solutions; nevertheless, a service manager, like a product manufacturer, has to know what technologies and equipment-based systems can be utilized to accomplish his task long before public acceptance can be accurately estimated. One guiding principle can eliminate much unnecessary searching: The goal is to find carefully engineered solutions that leave to people only the truly human tasks.

In one sense, the challenge for innovative operations managers is to "industrialize" financial services. This concept attempts to take the best manufacturing techniques available and modify, tailor, or redesign them to work in the service operations environment. This challenge requires that the manager accept that:

1. It is not necessary or even desirable in many cases to encourage personal contact in the service environment.

2. Customers do not expect nor even prefer excessive personal contact and would rather select the occasions when contact is desirable.
3. Many customer segments are ready, willing, and able to play a greater role in the service creation process.

There are many examples of this approach in nonfinancial services industries. One of the oldest is the supermarket. Here the service manager allows his customers to enter his warehouse and assemble their own product—the items on a shopping list. Giving customers this freedom requires no special technology to implement and has been accepted by most experts as a definite improvement to the former system in which the customer was made to wait in several smaller shops for a store clerk to put his order together.

Theodore Levitt calls this the application of "soft technology" to the problem. The universal product code check-out system is an example of what he calls a "hard technology" application. This makes the entire operation a hybrid.[10]

Today self-service approaches to service are widespread. Three examples of soft-technology systems replacing individual employees in financial services are: prepackaged insurance programs, which replace the door-to-door salesman with mass mailings; mutual funds, which replace individual stock selection and portfolio management; and payroll deduction for automatic savings in various investment programs and automatic bill paying and automatic direct deposit of social security checks, which replace individual transaction processing. Three examples of hard-technology substitutes are: automated teller machines, which are now capable of executing most routine transactions that formerly required a bank teller; home banking computer terminals, which can move money between accounts, pay many bills, execute investment orders, and aid in financial planning, a task formerly requiring several financial service personnel; and automated credit card approval at point-of-sale, which greatly speeds the individual store-based credit approval process.

In addition, examples of hybrid technologies, combining features of hard and soft, can be cited: revolving credit card systems, which substitute one credit approval process for multiple transactions within a limit formerly requiring separate loan applications; automated teller assist machines, which count and dispense currency in order to expedite specialized customer requirements not handled by ATMs; and telephone-based information, loan application, and transaction execution systems, which assist customer service representatives. Successful implementation of these examples requires the creative homogenization of available technology with service objectives, and customer behavior modification and acceptance.

As technological improvements surge forward, new alternatives to existing services will become apparent to those looking for them. In addition, new services and delivery systems will be suggested by advances in computer and communications technology. Strategic thinkers are already studying the potential of "smart cards" capable of maintaining and updating large amounts of personal and financial data, as well as new digital-based systems for data security, personal recognition, and communications.

QUALITY FRAMEWORK

No matter what the service is, whether it is technology driven or supplied by human beings, the benefit provided to the customer will be most affected by the quality built into the service. Quality is implicit in the conceptual foundation which encourages the service manager to understand the service, evaluate its delivery system, and search for new opportunities to "industrialize" it. And it is the customer's view of what these elements can give that establishes the foundation from which all else is to be built.

Quality is elusive. Everyone recognizes it when he sees it, but few can really describe it well, let alone in terms that would be useful to an operations manager. To some people, quality in a car means horsepower, acceleration, cornering ability, speed, and handling, while to another group it stands for comfort, design, fit, interior craftsmanship, smooth ride, and range. In fact, members of each market segment may agree that the other's favorite car represents quality, but that its characteristics are not of sufficient value or utility to be of interest to them.

The pursuit of quality is even more difficult in financial services operations, where often no tangible product of any kind exists and measurements of achievement becomes subjective. Nevertheless, quality is the single most indispensible characteristic of every financial service. It is important, therefore, to establish a framework and a language to define, measure, maintain, and improve the quality of operations-based financial services.

The perception of quality in the marketplace is critical for any financial service; moreover, the array of elements that affects this perception is quite complex. Customers may consciously choose a relatively inexpensive financial service or option. But they seldom select one they perceive to be of inferior quality: At what price would customers buy a checking service if the accuracy of the monthly statement could not be relied upon with an extremely high level of confidence? Since the notion of quality is so important, dealing with it head-on during planning can be of tremendous benefit to the operations manager. The Quality Framework shown in Exhibit 20.3 suggests one format for describing, measuring, and evaluating service products in a financial services company. By utilizing a quality framework approach throughout the company, management can gain a consistent, organized view of what products are being offered, to whom, and with what level of quality.

Quality can be analyzed from two fundamental perspectives, level and content. In the outline in Exhibit 20.3, the product description and performance statement should describe the level of the service offered, while the service dimensions ought to describe its content. Thus, when measured on content, a four-star hotel and a budget hotel can both be of high quality, although each performs at a very

Exhibit 20.3 Quality Framework

Product Description	Simply, briefly represents the product/service and its market/customer segment	
Performance Statement	Describes performance, containing the essential service elements that are expected by (were promised to) the customer	
Service Dimensions		
Reliability	Frequency of error	**Measurable aspects of performance**
Timeliness	Delivery deadline	
Serviceability	Responsiveness	
Features	Enhancements to basic product	**Levels of evaluation**
Conformance	Consistent achievement of objectives	
Aesthetics	Packaging/presentation	
Perceived quality	Image	

Source: The Quality Framework was part of a study done by David A. Garvin, Assistant Professor of the Graduate School of Business Administration, Harvard University, and a Chemical Bank taskforce in 1984. Additional information can be found in "Product Quality: An Important Strategic Weapon." *Business Horizons* (May-June 1984) pp. 40–43, and "What Does 'Product Quality' Really Mean?" *Sloan Management Review*. (Fall 1984) pp. 25–43, both by David A. Garvin.

different level of service. Similarly, a bank may offer a custom-designed, personalized service in richly furnished, comfortable, and quiet surroundings to its best customers, while encouraging others to use an ATM in the corner. In both cases, the bank is offering an effective, useful, and appreciated service to a segmented group of customers. Determining the optimum level of performance at which a financial service should be offered is a matter dependent on corporate strategy, image, cost, market potential, and profitability. One thing is certain however: No matter what level is selected, achieving excellence in the content measures is essential to the success of every financial service.

The development of service dimensions in the second half of the framework is of key importance. The dimensions must be easily measurable and must relate to the delivery of the product in its final form as the customer sees it. Attention to both measurability and customer satisfaction is essential. For example, the "factory" may specify the goal that the check-sorting unit deliver sorted checks to the statement preparation department in 24 hours; yet achievement of that goal is of no importance to the customer. The quality framework in this instance calls for specifying how long after the monthly cut-off date a customer will have access to his statement, and in what form the bank will provide it.

In many cases, customer satisfaction in the delivery of a financial service cannot be captured in an easily measured internal performance statistic. Creative application of proxy ratings and substitute measures may be necessary. Complaint tracking, customer surveys, statistical sampling, focus groups, and selected customer interviews are examples of tested techniques mainly used by marketing and public relations departments which can be readily applied to the quality framework for direct use by the operations manager. It is also important to note that no matter how many separate operations units or departments may coordinate in the delivery of a product, the manager must assume responsibility for monitoring compliance with the established quality dimensions. He must also coordinate across management lines both service enhancements and solutions to problems. This type of matrix management, which overlays organizational structure with objectives of total service delivery, can only work if given top management support, direction, and encouragement. Exhibits 20.4 and 20.5 illustrate how the quality framework can be applied to a financial noncredit product at a large money center bank.

Exhibit 20.4 Sample Application of Dimensions of Quality Retail Remittance Banking Services[a]

Production Description

The Retail Lock Box operation is a cash management service utilized by firms routinely receiving through the mail moderate dollar amount remittances which are characterized by one check and one invoice. Clearance of the checks is expedited, transaction data is captured, and reports are generated and delivered to the customer with the invoices and/or via various electronic media. Typically this service is in demand by saving banks and realty companies that manage rental mortgage or installment payments. The benefits to customers are automated updating of their accounts receivables file, reduced mail float, reduced check collection time, and lower processing costs.

Performance Statement

The ability to provide timely and accurate remittance processing and to reduce mail time are absolute necessities if a customer is to derive any benefit from this program.

Service Dimensions

Additionally, Lock Box must communicate to its customers deposit and remittance detail that enables them to take advantage of investment opportunities, and it must credit customers' accounts on a daily basis.

Reliability

Adjustments errors are not to exceed five per 100,000 items processed (internal goal).

Timeliness

On-time delivery of (delivery schedules vary by customer)

Tape transmission

Twix/Telex

Audio response

Branch delivery

Exhibit 20.4 Continued

Messenger delivery
Chemlink
Provide customers with same-day remittance processing of all items in time to meet the earliest Federal Reserve schedules
Communicate deposit, by pre-designated schedules which each customer sets for himself intermittently throughout the day

Serviceability

Resolve customer inquiries within 24 hours
Process ail dollar adjustments within 24 hours
Execute all photocopying requests processed within 24 hours
Facilitate reaching Customer Service
Maintain high level of courtesy/knowledge among customer service representatives

Conformance

All the above are must items which consistently require overtime in order to meet the essential requirements of Retail Lock Box Customers

Features

Image output
Customer-tailored processing
Audio response
Unique zip code
Pro-active Customer Service
- Customer orientation/brochures
- Customer surveys to identify customer needs and concerns
- Dedicated technical sales force
- Dedicated customer service representatives/by account

Aesthetics

New customer welcome package
Customer service reference manuals
Quality control slips
Periodic "releases" relating to customer concerns

Perceived Quality

Chemical Bank conducted survey: July 1984
89.46 of all rental customers rated the service of their Lock Box as good or excellent
Negative or positive perception also results from the efficiency of
- Account officers
- Sales representatives
- Service representatives
- Customer service representatives

[a] Based on April 1985 study of Chemical Bank's Lock Box services.

Exhibit 20.5 Chemical Bank Lock Box Delivery System Checklist

Service Dimensions	Services	Chemlink	Systems	Customer Service	Transportation	Lock Box
Reliability						
Adjustements per 100,000 items processed	X[a] N[b]	X Y[b]				X Y
Timeliness						
Tap transmission	X Y					X Y
Twix/telex						X Y
Audio response						X Y
Branch delivery					X Y	X Y
Messenger delivery					X Y	X Y
Chemlink		X Y				
Same-day processing	X Y			X Y		
Serviceability						
Resolve inquiries within 24 hours				X Y		
Process all dollar adjustments within 24 hours				X Y		
Photo requests within 24 hours				X Y		
Ease of reaching Customer Service				X N		
Courtesy of Customer Service				X N		

[a] X—Indicates responsibility for a deliverable.
[b] Y/N—Indicates the existence of a goal and report supporting a deliverable.

Application of this framework to any financial service operation will of necessity be an interactive one. Initial ideas of what constitutes a product, a family of products, a subproduct, a service package, or a service element will undoubtedly have to be reworked several times. The result, however, will be a standardized language and approach to dealing with the delivery of financial services to the marketplace. Along the way, discoveries will also be made of what services need redirection, revitalization, or perhaps elimination. As with any management tool, the quality framework is merely a methodology to organize difficult concepts into useful patterns with which thoughtful managers can address competitive challenges and technological opportunities.

NOTES

1. Heaney, Christopher K. "The Rise of the Operations Executive." *ABA Banking Journal* (June 1985).
2. Collier, David A. *Service Management*. Reston, VA: Reston Publishing, 1985, p. 3.
3. Collier, David A. *Ibid*, p. 15.
4. Collier, David A. *Ibid*, p. 4.
5. Thomas, Dan R. E. "Strategy Is Different in Services Businesses." *Harvard Business Review* (July-August 1978), pp. 158–165.
6. Collier, David A. *Service*, p. 5.
7. Chase, Richard B. "Where Does the Customer Fit in a Service Operation?" *Harvard Business Review* (November-December 1978).
8. Thomas, Dan R. E. "Strategy Is Different." p. 162.
9. Lipp, Robert I. "Products—Not Technology—Are What Counts." *American Business Banker*, Vol. CL, No. 119 (June 19, 1985), p. 4.
10. Levitt, Theodore. "The Industrialization of Service," *Harvard Business Review* (September-October 1976).

21 Productivity Management

IRA B. GREGERMAN

The labor and capital productivity within the finance and insurance industries has shown dismal performance between 1973 and 1983. As Exhibit 21.1 shows, the average annual growth rate for labor and capital productivity has trailed significantly behind the general business economy. In fact, the only industries that have consistently shown worse performance are mining and construction. This low productivity performance indicates that the output of goods and services of the finance and insurance industries have not made up for the added costs of labor and capital. During those 10 years, the level of capital investment per worker in the white collar service industries was about $2,000. Exhibit 21.2 shows that the service industries may be suffering from underinvestment in productivity-advancing systems and equipment—especially when compared to the two other major business sectors.

To understand the slow productivity growth associated with capital expenditures, it is interesting to note how this money was spent (see Exhibit 21.3). Most of the funds have gone to improving clerical productivity with electronic memory typewriters, faster copiers, and better word processors. The next major productivity advances will have to come from investments in the sales, management, and

Exhibit 21.1 Annual Growth of Labor and Capital Productivity (%)

	Finance/Insurance		General Business	
	1973–1979	1979–1983	1973–1979	1979–1983
Labor Productivity	–0.1	0.0	0.8	1.1
Capital Productivity	–5.0	–8.1	–0.4	–1.7
Combined Productivity	–1.1	–2.0	0.4	0.1

Source: American Productivity Center.

Exhibit 21.2 Effectiveness of Capital Investments per Worker: 1973–1983

Business Sector	Capital Investment	Productivity Improvement
Farming	$35,000	180%
Manufacturing	$25,000	90%
Service	$ 2,000	5%

Source: Arthur D. Little

Exhibit 21.3 Distribution of Capital Expenditures[a]: Service Sector

Job Classifications	Spending
Clerical	47%
Sales	14%
Management	17%
Other Professional	22%

Source: Arthur D. Little
[a] 1973–1983.

professional ranks. To make up for lost time, expenditures for these nonclerical jobs will have to more than double their current levels. However, with the rate that technology is advancing, and its unit costs declining, the next decade should show significant increases in the placement of productivity-improving technology—both hardware and software—in the hands of managers and professionals. More and more, companies are recognizing this promise and are making commensurate efforts. But they are doing substantially more as well, often undertaking formal company-wide efforts to improve both productivity and quality.

This chapter looks at productivity improvement as an effort to be approached systematically on a corporate-wide basis. The emphasis is on achieving a flexible and well-adjusted perspective. As such, the chapter does not deal in depth with particular techniques. Rather, the selection of a technique is seen to depend largely on the circumstances and structure of each organization, its business unit strategies, and its culture.

MEASURING PRODUCTIVITY

Productivity is simply the efficiency with which an organization converts resources into products or services. The distinction between a product and a service is usually clear. At a service station, a customer may buy gasoline, a product; have his caburetor adjusted, a service; or have new brakes installed, a combination of product (parts), and service (labor). In the financial services industry, the distinction is less clear. Banks offer checking accounts as products but check cashing as a service. A brokerage firm offers margin accounts as products and custody of securities as a service. While the word "productivity" usually implies products, the discussions that follow will extend its meaning to services as well.

Exhibit 21.4 shows the product/service relationship in simplified form for typical resources and products or services. The conversion process is far more complex and multidimensional than can be shown. But the important limitation of the figure is that it does not suggest how to measure the efficiency of conversion. Measurement can be done by establishing one or more ratios relating the value of individual products or services to the cost of the resources used to generate them—in other words, by relating output to input. Any change in the conversion process should alter the magnitude of these ratios, creating productivity improvements. Ratios that reflect all inputs and outputs are called "total productivity measures," as opposed to "partial productivity measures" that leave out some outputs or inputs. Generally speaking, one or more partial measures are employed to measure productivity improvements. Total productivity measures are rarely used.

Partial measures must be selected with care. Ideally, there should be a clear connection between the ratio and the behavior it measures. For example, when a general measure such as "assets per employee" or "earnings per employee" is used, an employee has no real guidance as to how to improve the ratio. However, replacing it with the more functionally oriented "transactions per hour" helps the employee take actions or make recommendations to improve productivity.

Knowing the measured value is insufficient, however. What counts is the trend in value over time. And because this trend is so important, consistency in measurement must weigh heavily, even at the sacrifice of improved accuracy. The reason is simple. Inconsistent collection and treatment of data can distort representation of the trend. If, for instance, the measurement in a current period can be accurately determined as 12.67, it makes little difference if that value has to be rounded to 13, because equivalent accuracy was not possible in prior periods.

Exhibit 21.4 The Productivity Process

Resources		*Products & Services*	
Facilities		Credit cards	Casualty policies
		Commercial loans	Life policies
Funds		Check processing	Benefit payments
	Conversion Process →	Trust accounts	Security trades
People		Trade settlements	Ira/Keogh accounts
		Insurance payments	Margin accounts
Equipment & software		Pension distributions	Annuity accounts

What is important is whether or not the 13 becomes a 14 in the next measurement period.

Two other cautions should be raised on the subject of measurement. One concerns inflation, the other the mixing of financial and "physical" (volume) data. To avoid misinterpreting a trend, deflated dollars should be used for financial measures, and the format of the numerator and denominator kept the same. Consistency in the format insures that fluctuations in the numerator and denominator over time will be subjected in much the same way to such driving forces as inflation, market pressures, the cost of funds, product design changes, new technologies, and related adjustments. Ideally, only volume data should be used. This is in order to avoid problems with inflation. However, if financial values must be used, indexing the ratio to a base year will minimize the effects of inflation. If not, one can use the GNP deflator, the Consumer or Producer Price Index, or another indicator that may be appropriate. The assumption is that the value of both the input and output keep pace with inflation at the same rate, an assumption which may not always hold true.

The following are some examples of measures currently being used in various financial services institutions. Not all of them heed the cautions, a decision which is a matter of choice.

- A large consumer finance company, attempting to reduce absenteeism, established a measure related to monthly attendance. Improvement was rewarded through merchandise gift certificates. In six months, absenteeism went from an average of 1000 down to 275 days per month.
- A large retail bank in the northwest used fee and service income, coupled with operating expenses, to measure branch performance. Each branch had the option of either raising the income, lowering expense, or both. The overall effect was to improve the income/expense ratio by more than 300 percent, for a net pretax gain of $2.4 million.
- A southern retail bank developed three measures for its branches. The measures were formulated to indicate performance in terms of quality, funds handled, and transactions processed. For example, quality is measured by the ratio of the amount of money over, or short, to the total funds handled.
- A Texas bank uses a corporate measure of earnings per total employee expenses.
- A third bank in the southwest tracks corporate performance with the ratio: (net interest income + noninterest income) divided by (total operating expenses).

IMPROVING PRODUCTIVITY

A broad range of techniques and programs have been used to improve productivity. Among them are work simplification and methods improvement, gain sharing and incentive systems, quality control and zero defects, operations research and value engineering, and office automation and the application of new computer technologies. All of these approaches have been used in the financial services industry with varying degrees of success. However, the most successful programs are positioned as part of an overall corporate strategy, rather than in isolation.

Cost reduction is not the only way to improve productivity. Just as valid are increases in the quantity of product delivered for the same amount of resources employed. Increasing the output, or decreasing the input, or any combination of the two, raises productivity. The following examples focus on raising output or lowering input:

Increasing Output. Reducing errors makes it possible to handle more work with the same resources. For example, lowering electronic funds transfer errors frees staff time and equipment capacity for the performance of revenue-producing transactions. Improving equipment maintenance procedures increases availability and, hence, potential production.

Reducing Input. Introducing automation technologies lowers the need for use of other resources. For example, optical character recognition (OCR) equipment process proxy vote cards with reduced input from labor and with reduced errors—errors after all being a form of waste input. Automated mail insertion equipment similarly reduces the cost of handling and processing settlement checks, account statements, or stock transaction confirmations; it also lowers postage costs. Returning to the example of equipment maintenance, proper condition of equipment can defer the need to acquire replacements, or for that matter, to maintain backup pieces for breakdown situations. Finally, it should be stressed that general cost-reduction programs can result in significant cost savings without necessarily decreasing product output.

Assessing Opportunities and Setting Goals for Productivity Improvement. A company's routine business statistics—that is, turnover and absentee rates, equipment utilization and downtime, production and backlog quantities and quality levels—are a good first place to look. Comparing recent figures to historical data for the industry, geographic area, or the organization itself can suggest how much improvement to set as a realistic goal. Here are two examples of savings created by a careful examination of statistics:

- One large bank found that its reject rate for check processing was over twice the average for banks of similar size. Analysis of the causes and costs indicated that the bank was spending over $150,000 per year more than it would have at an average reject rate.
- A midwestern brokerage house found that back-room costs and backlogs were increasing faster than could be expected from increased trading activity. An operations review showed that as the workload increased, employees from other departments were being asked to assist—usually on overtime. Since processing transaction tickets was supplemental to the regular job

functions, and was performed on overtime, the employees were not anxious to trim their extra income by processing the transactions quickly. Changes in job designs and addition of part-time employees to the processing department helped reduce overall costs $200,000 and improved backlog 27 percent.

Opportunities to improve productivity can be found in many places. Opportunities for operations-related improvements can be spotted by analysis of the technical, quality, and productivity levels of computer systems. They include procurement practices and policies; quality costs for error prevention, inspection, rework, and customer-identified errors; and the level of spending on new technologies. Opportunities from nonoperations areas might be made evident by review of policies and procedures, benefits, organizational structure, employee training, advancement opportunities, and wage scales. Of course, isolating statistical aberrations is only step one. Step two is understanding the causes of the problem. Step three is developing a remedy, and step four is implementing it successfully.

THE COST OF PRODUCTIVITY IMPROVEMENT

Substantial resources are needed to initiate a productivity improvement effort capable of encompassing a large division, let alone the whole organization. Some rough indications of the magnitude were researched by the author from 1980 to 1983. Data on the number of people involved in the start-up of a productivity program in over 75 large and medium-size organizations, including 10 banks and insurance companies, was collected and analyzed. The results were translated into graph form to serve as a guide in estimating the number of full-time equivalent personnel needed to implement a company-wide productivity improvement strategy (see Exhibit 21.5). The graph can be used as follows:

STEP 1. Determine either the company's "gross revenue per employee" or its "net interest income plus fee income per employee." The choice depends on the nature of the business. For example, this illustration will assume a gross revenue per employee of $200,000.

STEP 2. Find this value on the horizontal scale and mark a vertical line until it intersects both diagonal lines marked "high" and "low."

STEP 3. At both points of intersection, draw a horizontal line across to the vertical scale ("full-time personnel factor"). The intersects corresponding to $200,000 per employee are 0.0035 and 0.0053.

STEP 4. Calculate the estimated manpower requirements. Multiply the figures found in Step 3 by the number of employees in the company or business unit. If the company in the example employs 3500 people, the number of employees needed to implement the strategy effectively would be between 12 and 18

Exhibit 21.5 Estimating Personnel for Start-Up

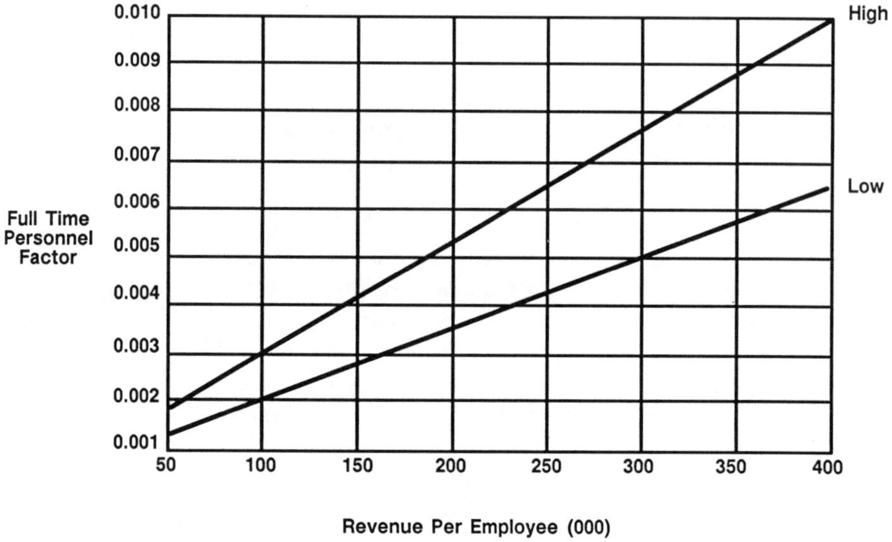

Full Time Personnel Factor
0.010
0.009
0.008
0.007
0.006
0.005
0.004
0.003
0.002
0.001
High
Low
50 100 150 200 250 300 350 400
Revenue Per Employee (000)

(rounded down to the nearest full person). Assuming an average wage, including fringes, of $20,000, the commitment in labor would require expenditures in the neighborhood of $300,000 in the first year.

MANAGING THE PRODUCTIVITY EFFORT

Organization

According to a 1983 study by Gray-Judson Inc., 62 percent of the productivity start-up programs that met with disappointing or minimal success had failed to organize on a company-wide basis. It seems that these programs are most likely to fulfill their goals when given total executive management support and commitment. Two contrasting stories corroborate this view. When a major bank in the Northeast initiated its program, the CEO conducted meetings for all employees during the kickoff—to dramatic effect. Employee feedback showed a high level of credence in and identification with the program's objectives. Not so successful, however, was another organization's use of videotapes of the chief executive. A better idea might have been to supplement the CEO's taped message with a live presentation by another senior manager.

Too many programs flounder because their supporters underestimate the amount of time and effort needed to implement and carry them out. Generally, the larger and more dispersed the operation, the greater the number of people needed simply to make the program work from day to day. In addition, the more emphasis that is placed on short-term goals over the strategic objectives, the greater the number of people needed. Painstaking organization is required to guide, support, and fund the effort.

Roles for directing this organization can take a number of shapes. Some institutions rely on a chief productivity officer (CPO), others use steering committees composed of representatives from business lines and staff units, and still others opt for a combination. The need for a chief productivity officer has been the subject of much controversy. However, the existence of a CPO position does dispel such problems as: Who will manage the effort? Who will see that the philosophy is spread to the whole organization? Who will ensure that the latest techniques are employed? And who will protect the gains already achieved? Also an important consideration is that some structures need to be permanent, whereas others are best left temporary. The optimal configuration depends on many factors, not the least of which is corporate culture. Adapting, as opposed to adopting, techniques to fit that culture will go a long way to insuring a good fit and successful effort.

Exhibit 21.6 shows the makeup of a steering committee for an insurance company. Its functions are multidimensional; it must facilitate interorganizational communication, sustain program visibility, maintain middle-management involvement and support, ease the way for technique implementation, open doors for the CPO, blend line and staff perspectives, and ensure that productivity efforts support corporate goals (see Exhibit 21.7).

One company structured its committee into two parts—a permanent membership part consisting of five top-level managers, and a rotating membership made up of three middle managers serving staggered one-year terms. This mix provided the committee with stability as well as a communications link to lower levels of the organization, while giving middle management an opportunity to guide the effort.

Such involvement is essential, as a productivity program based on edicts is bound to fail. Memos, posters, bulletin board pronouncements, and other paper-

Exhibit 21.6 Typical Steering Committee for an Insurance Company

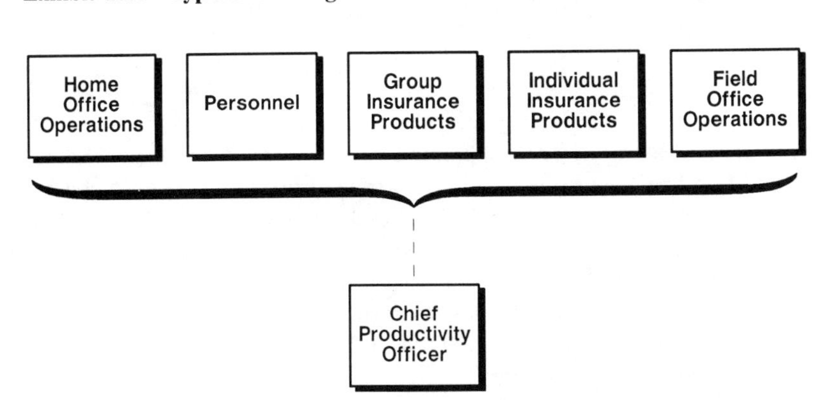

Exhibit 21.7 Six Phases of a Productivity Management Process Model

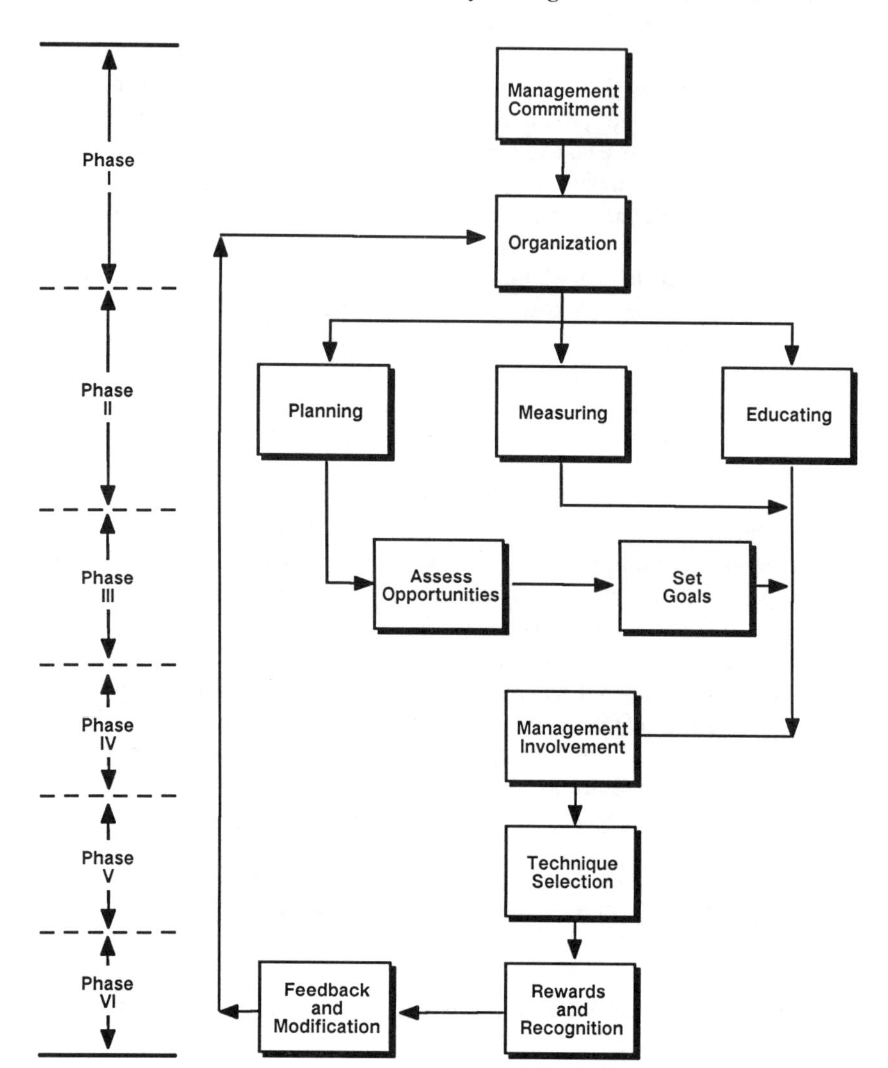

based communications yield disappointing results when used alone. Middle managers and first-line supervisors must support the effort. Winning their commitment is best accomplished by involving them early in the planning of the program, demonstrating how the program will benefit them, and clearly presenting the objectives of the activity. Attention to these three issues—involvement, benefits, and objectives—determines the level of supervisory and middle management support a program obtains. Because this is a multiplicative relationship, each variable can be extremely influential:

$$\text{Support} = \text{Involvement} \times \text{Benefits} \times \text{Objectives}$$

As the equation implies, if any of these factors is of negligible magnitude, the probability that the necessary support will be elicited from supervisors and middle managers is very small. In some cases it could be zero—even negative, if supervisors actively resist change.

The chief advantage of early involvement is the sense of ownership and commitment it breeds. But participating managers are also sensitive to the culture reigning in the organization's lower levels. Appreciation of individuals' "what's in it for me?" concerns is important in deciding which techniques will have the greatest chance of success. And clear understanding of objectives allows middle managers to evaluate conflicting interests and demands on their time.

Because employees often confuse productivity improvement with reductions in staff, their fears can stall the program and must be put to rest. Management first of all needs to emphasize the benefits of productivity improvement: more competitive posture for the institution, enhanced job security, improved quality of working life, improved promotional opportunities, and so on. In extreme cases, it may be necessary to deal with employees' concerns about job security by guaranteeing that terminations or salary reductions will not result from program improvements if job performance is satisfactory. Two caveats must be voiced, however: (1) some employees may have to be assigned to different jobs; and (2) jobs cannot be guaranteed during a business downturn.

Efforts to counter these fears and develop positive employee involvement most often rely on group problem solving. Group techniques have proved highly successful: return on investment for employee involvement programs has averaged about 6/1, with some returns reported as high as 20/1. Group approaches do well because the employees are working on problems directly related to their jobs and they are receiving a high level of peer recognition for doing so. Normally no financial incentives are provided. In fact, surveys have found that incentives are one of the least important factors used. The chief danger associated with employee involvement may be that management will rush to jump on the bandwagon and fabricate additional activities. Then involvement becomes a solution in search of a problem.

Care must be taken to avoid fostering the impression that employee involvement is just one more program that will not live up to its publicity and will eventually fade from prominence. Such has often been the case, for example with Mogenson's concept of "work simplification" and Odiorne's *Management by Objectives* in the 1950s, with the *Managerial Grid* of Blake and Mouton and *Transactional Analysis* by Berne in the 1960s, and now with the latest—the quality circle, a Japanese practice imported to the United States. Tomorrow's panaceas promise to be artificial intelligence, expert systems, and robotics. Will these technologies prove better or more long-lived than those of the past, or will they too become casualties? Time will tell. But when they do become available, careful selection and applications will be needed.

Maintaining Momentum

Productivity improvement is a dynamic and iterative process. Periodic review of progress against goals will inevitably yield alterations to the original design. These must be fed back to senior management for consideration and implementation. The mechanism to accomplish these goals is usually a formal reporting system. Out of necessity, its content and format will depend on the program and techniques selected.

Some form of reward and recognition should be provided to outstanding individual and group participants to encourage ongoing interest in and support for the program. Rewards can take three forms: cash, noncash financial compensation, and merchandise. Cash rewards are the payment of monies proportional to contribution to the program. Their main disadvantage is a tendency to blend with other income, giving them a short-lived impact on the recipient. Noncash financial awards—perhaps in the form of extra time off, company-paid dinners, theater tickets, or travel—have deeper and longer lasting influence. Merchandise awards have been found to have the greatest and longest beneficial effect. If the recipient gets to choose the award, the effect is magnified, for the simple reason that the merchandise is something the individual wants, and its permanent visibility or repeated use by the award-winner continually reinforces the program and builds loyalty to the company.

Recognition also comes in many forms. The most common include stories or announcements in company communications media and the public awarding of plaques, warm-up jackets, coffee mugs, and so on. The more thoughtful the award the better: One manufacturing company in northern Minnesota allows the employee with the best productivity improvement idea for the month a privileged parking spot closest to the main entrance. Wintertime recipients are especially grateful.

If executive management has not established a strategic philosophy at the start of the effort, now is the time to do so. Executed in concert with other strategic planning functions, productivity improvement can be integrated into the day-to-day operations of the company. However, infusing a productivity sensibility into the culture is difficult midway through the process. It is far easier to establish this orientation from the beginning.

Displaying a strategic commitment to productivity is vital to future achievements. Vehicles for displaying management's conviction include annual reports and articles in internal corporate communications relating the productivity achievements of employees. At the same time, long-range plans should spell out productivity objectives. Above all, repetitive reinforcement of the commitment is needed. Some approaches that have been used successfully are discussed as follows:

Productivity Measures. Many organizations have found that productivity measures maintain interest and provide motivation, especially when tied to an incentive system.

Incentive Systems. Incentives are important to maintaining interest and progress, particularly when the rewards are directly linked to the efforts of individuals or groups. One organization in the Detroit area ties achievement of productivity improvement goals to job performance evaluations and bonus calculations. A provider of health care insurance rewards its employees through certificates which can be accumulated and traded for merchandise.

Employee Involvement. An effective method of insuring continuity and commitment to improving productivity is through employee involvement. Involvement can take the form of team building, quality circles, suggestion systems, work simplification, or a number of other techniques instituted either singularly or in combination. Many companies have found that the strong positive feelings generated by an initial program are an excellent foundation on which to build future activities. By contrast, a large Southeastern bank that had failed to capitalize on this positive environment found its program fragmented and lacking wide support. From then on, new attempts at productivity improvement had to be sold individually to management, whose interest diminished daily. To avoid this lack of continuity, comprehensiveness must be made an integral part of the original plan.

Training and Development. Developing a productivity consciousness from the start of a program and reinforcing it in the future is important to maintaining momentum. All techniques for improving productivity require some degree of training, and it is a good idea to exploit training sessions to the fullest, either by attaching relevant activities to a core productivity program, or by incorporating productivity into a broader training session. Some companies, for instance, have built productivity training into their management training, new employee orientation, special skill development programs, and professional development programs.

A few companies outside the financial services community have created in-house "productivity colleges" and corporate-wide round tables or forums. The "college" provides a training program tailored to the specific needs and culture of the company, and help managers start productivity programs in their own business units. In addition, it can help strengthen communications between peer group managers and provide a platform for sharing ideas. Usually meeting on a regular schedule, the round table is informal, confined to a few participants, and narrowly focused. However, this format also provides opportunities to exchange information and generate peer group support as well as recognition.

CONCLUSION

The successful design and implementation of a company-wide productivity improvement strategy relies on five key factors:

1. Visible senior management support and commitment
2. A strategic perspective focused on long-term achievements

3. A select team of employees organized to implement and manage the improvement strategy
4. Development of broad middle management and employee involvement
5. A productivity measurement system able to track program performance

BIBLIOGRAPHY

Berne, Eric L. *Transactional Analysis*. New York: Grove Press, 1961.

Blake, Robert R. and Jane S. Mouton. *The Managerial Grid: Key Orientations for Achieving Production through People*. Houston: Gulf + Western, 1964.

Odiorne, George S. *Management by Objectives; a System of Managerial Leadership*. New York: Pitman, 1965.

SECTION 5 MANAGING STRATEGIC CHANGE

Probably no subject provokes more anxiety in organizations than does strategic change. If anxieties are to be allayed, people at all levels need to understand what the change will mean for them. All too frequently, executives fail to appreciate the need for a carefully reasoned change program, and therefore miss some of the key factors required to make it work. The ensuing unsuccessful attempts to implement programs are disappointing but not surprising. Although corporate leaders have worked hard throughout their careers to attain positions from which they can set the direction for their firms, many have limited experience in leading and managing major strategic change. Some believe that if they simply announce their intentions and make a few organizational adjustments, the change will happen. Others are uncertain how to proceed and in private moments of discouragement sometimes wonder just how realistic it is to strive for significant change in massive and strong-charactered organizations.

With these apprehensions in mind, it seems helpful to introduce this last section with a reassurance: Systematic ways of managing strategic change do exist. And the major ones will be described in the chapters that follow. From widely different perspectives—those of management process, human resources, and global business, as well as the strategic planner's and the CEO's—these chapters furnish practical guidelines for ensuring that the changes determined by top management have the greatest chance of being fully realized.

The authors themselves are all "plan neutral." That is, they approach their subjects without preconceptions about which strategic plans are or are not valuable. Instead, the focus of interest is on how to get things done, regardless of what firms have decided to do.

One distinction is worth making in advance. The strategic planning process is continuous and to a great extent low-key, whereas major strategic change is discontinuous and often dramatic. Corporations cannot afford to attempt disruptive alterations on a continual basis. Constant shifts in direction would send the corporation lurching about the business landscape only to collapse exhausted, disoriented, and worse off than before.

Because virtually all companies recognize the dangers of too-frequent change, a senior executive can expect to be personally involved in managing strategic changes perhaps two or three times in his career, seldom more. The same can be said for his peers. This means that any time a corporation sets out to accomplish strategic change, its leadership will be asked to move the firm toward objectives that the management collectively may never have imagined, let alone undertaken to meet.

If a dearth of practical experience in managing strategic change is common in business as a whole, it is nearly universal within the financial services industry. Within a few years, however, this management gap will have been all but eliminated, as pressures to make significant changes in business become irresistible. The era stretching from May Day 1975 to roughly 1990 will undoubtedly prove to be the single greatest period of restructuring in financial services that America has seen during this century. Indeed, it seems unlikely that anyone managing today, even at the most junior levels, will ever again be caught up in perturbations as unsettling as those we have lived through in the last five years. Under such circumstances, leadership clearly needs vision. But that is not enough. Vision must be translated into widespread commitment and unified action. This section provides guidelines for doing just that.

The first chapter in this section, by Stanley Davis and Robert Gogel, draws attention to the need for corporate organization structures to be aligned with current, rather than past, strategies, and for both strategy and organization structure to be designed with a clear idea of the corporation's existing culture, which often requires subtle manipulation and a great deal of time to reshape. Stan, a former Research Professor at Boston University's School of Management, has written extensively on the interrelations between corporate culture, organization, and strategy. Bob, a Vice-President with the MAC Group, has concentrated his financial services consulting practice on strategic assignments with cultural ramifications.

In Chapter 23, William White concentrates on the process of strategic planning as it applies across the financial services industry. In addition to being a practicing executive at the National Bank of Washington, Bill has authored a book on strategic planning.

Chapter 24 examines the challenges of converting domestic and semi-independent multinational businesses into highly interconnected global corporations, despite conditions that can vary considerably from one national market to another. The author, Alan Platow, a Senior Vice-President at CIGNA Corporation, illustrates his discussion with an account of the processes by which his firm effectively globalized itself within the space of just two years, an arduous feat to say the least. Platow's perspective is deepened by 15 years of international experience.

Next, Robert Beck examines the implications of change for the corporation's human resources, and suggests how closer attention to management development, training, compensation, and related matters can help create the unity and commitment needed for the implementation of strategy. Bob is particularly well-qualified to discuss this topic, being executive Vice-President of human resources at BankAmerica, and a former director of benefits and personnel services at IBM.

Last, in Chapter 26, Bob Gogel speaks to the problems of instilling commitment and creating unity. Bob encourages CEOs to explicitly use a six-point agenda in managing major strategic change.

The underlying message of this section, then, is that the management of strategic change cannot rely on magic. Rather, it depends on systematic and consistent approaches.

22 Managing Reorganization During the Transition

STANLEY M. DAVIS
ROBERT N. GOGEL

Revolution within an industry almost always forces companies in that industry to make profound adjustments to their organizations. These adjustments usually take the form of new strategies and modified organization structures, as well as new people and systems.

The financial services industry has been no different. Turbulence makes everyone feel a need for some kind of change. Over the last decade, most financial services firms have experienced at least one strategic review, management change, or restructuring. Yet in an alarming number of these institutions, the perception is that little has indeed changed—that the firm is not really progressing. Although it is difficult to pinpoint the causes of this malaise, the feeling still exists that when all is said and done, only the "boxes" have moved—the organization remains the same.

Part of the reason is that the most conservative solutions are tried first, usually for the most virtuous of reasons: the desire to avoid hurting people. There is an understandable tendency among managements to build new structures or modify existing ones around current players, without recognizing that some of the people may also need to be changed. Financial institutions have been especially prone to this myopia. Only later, when it is realized that the strategy is not working, does management make the tough decisions necessary to genuinely realign the organization and displace individuals. Unfortunately, the delay can be costly for both the individual and the strategy.

The problem is that many financial institutions view structure from a remedial point of view. In these cases, the focus is usually on how to change the way the organization is divided. The question, "What can we do to fix our current organization?" is asked, and the "boxes" are moved around with the hope that the reorganization will work. It often doesn't.

Instead, management would be wise to start by deciding what needs to be put in place today to ready the firm for tomorrow. Management's approach should include an analysis of both the required organizing dimensions and the nature of the relationships required by the strategy. The critical point is this: Because it will take a number of years to adjust to any new organization, the company needs to define a structure that fits its future—not its past or even necessarily its present. No time should be wasted fine-tuning an organization that was designed for a strategy that was itself developed five years ago.

But how can a reorganization be made to work? That is the focus of this chapter. Two basic steps are involved. The first is determining which structure is most appropriate to the future, as opposed to past, strategy. The second is putting that structure in place. Both steps are essential to successfully managing structural changes during the transition period that the financial services industry is experiencing.

SELECTING THE MOST EFFECTIVE ORGANIZATIONAL STRUCTURE

Structure, stated simply, is the sum of the interrelationships of the parts within a whole. The whole, for the purposes of this chapter, is the financial institution itself. How the whole is divided into parts, and how the parts are made to function in concert, are the two concerns of organizational structure.

Dividing the Whole into Parts

Financial institutions are organized no differently than other businesses. There is no one best way to organize, nor are there an infinite number. There are a limited number of choices in structural design, and that number is four. A business can structure itself around the things that it does, the things that it makes or provides, the places in which it does these things, and/or the people and other organizations for which it does them. In other words, it can structure itself around functions, products or services, geography, and/or markets. Which structure, then, is most appropriate for any given financial institution?

In part, the choice of an organizing dimension will depend on the general economic environment in which the company finds itself. In pre-industrial times, for example, the supply of raw materials and resources was a dominant concern, and larger goods-producing organizations were structured functionally. In the industrial period, the functional focus moved downstream. The core function was production, and the dominant structure became the product-division organization. This downstream movement has continued into the post-industrial or "service-economy" era. Geographic distribution and delivery, through technology-based communication networks, have become key ingredients. Marketing has become a core function, and market segmentation has become the basis for dividing the structural whole into its constituents.

This evolution from a functional to a marketing-based structure has also been evident in financial services. Thus, many financial services institutions still display elements of several structuring dimensions. Traditionally, for example, a functional structure was common. In banks there often were (and still are) a credit function and a loan function, the credit function being charged with analysis and review of the contracts generated by the loan function. Credit was most often a "staff" job, while lending was most often a "line" position. Within and between these two functions, there was what many institutions call "operations"; the information and clearing function.

This functional structure was adequate, given that product proliferation was relatively unknown for many institutions. Institutions specialized along functional lines in support of a limited number of products. Individuals progressed insofar as they were good functional managers; an employee would be promoted based on his or her success as a "credit person" or "investment person." But as the environment has become deregulated and competition has increased, the functional structure has become largely inadequate to respond to varied customer demands and the complexities of resource management.

In response to these changes, many financial institutions have developed a product orientation as their primary structuring dimension. However, a product/service structure is only appropriate if the markets being served are relatively homogeneous in their needs. In banking, many institutions organized themselves around business loan products, mortgage products, deposit products, consumer loan products, and so on. Similarly, insurance companies organized themselves along product lines such as property and casualty, life, and reinsurance. Eventually, however, product-line structures also proved inadequate in many cases, as customers became more sophisticated and began seeking higher levels of integration among products.

Many financial institutions, finding that geography was a natural design dimension, implicitly designed their structures according to this dimension. Every bank branch, brokerage office, or insurance agent represents a discrete geographic location. But geography alone has not proved fully adequate either. Like product organization, it does not take into account the multiple needs of customers.

For this reason, more and more financial institutions are using markets as their primary organizing dimension. A market-based structure becomes dominant when product delivery is largely standardized, when competition loses its local quality, and when basic products (passbook savings accounts, whole life insurance, full-service stock brokerage) reflect less and less fully the needs of most customers.

The fundamental market division in financial services is between wholesale and retail customers; that is, between corporate client and individual consumer. Differentiating between corporate, government, and financial institutions is a common way of segmenting the wholesale market. Within the corporate area, units are often structured around global clients, large domestic firms, the middle market, and the small-firm market segments. Parallel structures exist within the government and financial institutions markets. Within retail, common market segments used include mass market, high net worth, and small business. Highly detailed segmentation criteria have been developed to subsegment each of these markets and provide the basis for structuring around them.

How the Parts Relate to the Whole

So far, we have described structuring around one dimension of a business. What if, as is often the case, more than one dimension is critical? Many structures in financial institutions today are hybrids—that is, they contain elements from one or more of the structural models described earlier. For example, a brokerage firm may use the functional model to handle typical staff functions across the firm, such as human resources and accounting, while using the market model for interfacing with its various customer groups.

The arrangement which management selects should be that which most effectively serves the organization's strategy. If geography is paramount, then the market segments may be identified within each geographic unit. If market units are the basic dimension, then within each market group the subunits may be based on geographic distinctions. To complete the structure, management then must factor in product/service specialists and integrate the remaining functional units into the organization.

Traditional, hierarchical structures are not always the most effective alternatives in composite organizations. Who, after all, is to be first among equals? Sometimes the compartmentalizing of structural dimensions must yield to a form that allows decisions and actions to be coordinated on more than one dimension. This is the world of matrix management.[1] Exhibit 22.1 illustrates the difference between traditional hierarchical structure and matrix structure.

The matrix structure, although relatively easy to design, is not easy to implement. It is a particularly difficult structure to use because it means that managers

Exhibit 22.1 Contrasting Organizational Structures

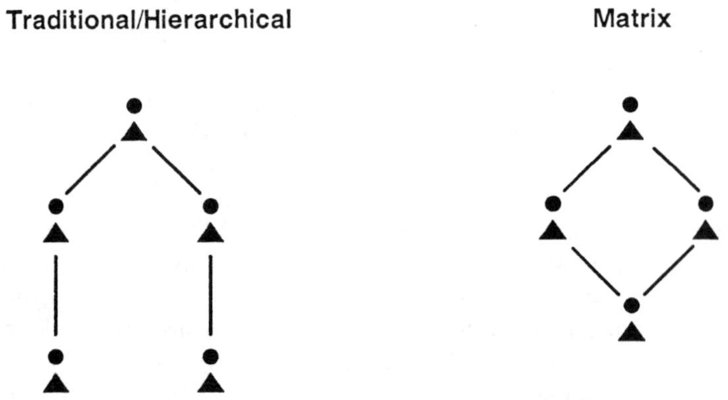

Traditional/Hierarchical

Matrix

will have two bosses. The habits learned under the traditional single chain of command system are hard to break. Managers must continually negotiate conflicts and maintain an institutional perspective at the middle levels of the organization.

In certain circumstances, however, the matrix structure is the best choice. If the willingness to communicate and resolve conflict does exist, a matrix allows decisions to be made lower in the organization where information originates and knowledge exists. Such willingness must be developed by continued training and reward, not dictated by management policy.

Few financial services firms have adopted full-scale matrix structures. Such an organization would interlock individuals who would otherwise have trouble meshing geography, market, and product specialty. Matrixing in financial services can most clearly be seen in dealings between product or functional specialists and the relationship manager. The relationship manager is not so much supervising these specialists as making direct demands on their output. By selectively recombining this output, in effect, he or she coordinates between the entire institution and its individual clients. It is precisely this need for coordination that makes a matrix structure so difficult to use, particularly in organizations where people are not accustomed to complex communication. However, if this structure is used effectively, it can improve the quality of decisions because representatives of the dimensions critical to strategic success will participate.

Citibank introduced matrix organization into its international business in order to focus on both geography and the global corporation market segment. This change, which was made in the early 1970s and which increased the priority given to large international organizations, enabled Citibank to have a better understanding of the worldwide financial needs and activities of global corporations than the chief financial officers of these corporations themselves had. Matrix was a strategic weapon in gaining a competitive advantage with this important segment of the international market. Despite these purported advantages, however, it abandons the matrix in the late 1970s because too many problems fell through the cracks; no one had picked up responsibility on major problems they had already exploded.

All the models described earlier are hierarchical in some way or other. Each implies a boss-subordinate relationship. This is true even of matrix managements. The difference among the models relates primarily to the focus of their activities, whether on function, product, geography, or markets. And while these dimensions will continue to play a key role in structuring financial institutions, what is likely to change is the fundamental nature of the hierarchical relationships within the business—how the parts of the whole relate to one another. In the future, one way these relationships are likely to be redefined is in terms of networking.

Networking means hooking together people who are geographically or hierarchically separated, so that they can communicate quickly and directly. The technological developments of computer networking have allowed communication across geographic space. The same developments can improve communication across "organizational space" as well. Managers will no longer depend on the hierarchy for information flow, but will have almost instant access to information throughout the organization network.

In a typical hierarchy within a bank, for example, approval of a particular credit typically flows up the chain of command and then all the way back down again. This chain of command often gets overwhelmed and causes blockages. Information technology, which allows decision makers in various parts of an organization to communicate with each other simultaneously, could significantly shorten the time needed for credit approval.

Although some financial institutions are beginning to understand networking, hierarchical relationships are deeply ingrained in the culture of most. Consequently, traditional structures are likely to dominate the industry for the next decade. This inertia is unfortunate, since those institutions which are able to redefine the relationships within an organization will undoubtedly gain a competitive advantage.

PUTTING STRUCTURAL CHANGES INTO PRACTICE

Choosing a structure is never easy, but it is almost always easier than putting the structure in place. There is a mistaken belief that a new structure is up and running the day it is announced. Not so. Organizational implementation usually requires a herculean effort, and a great deal of time. Because substantive results are rarely possible overnight, management must be doubly sure that employees and outside observers understand the anticipated time frame of the change. They must also be certain that real, not merely nominal, changes occur.

If change efforts are not coordinated, members of the organization will be sent signals that lead to confusion and ambiguity at a time when clear goals are needed. For example, when a functional organization needs to become market oriented, and responsibility for managing newly acquired businesses is put in the hands of the present functional heads, the old structure simply will be inadequate for the new strategy.

Rather, a new structure needs to be given months, and sometimes years, to take root and establish itself as viable within the organization because people's beliefs—and patterns of behavior—tend to be particularly intractable. Financial institutions that are able to manage the cultural aspects of a reorganization will likely be more successful than those that manage only the reorganization's structural aspects. The same is true for firms like Sears, which needs to diffuse its dominant retailing culture into its financial services subsidiaries such as Dean Witter.

Because bringing organization structures through the transition period of the 1980s will require great adeptness at managing culture, we now examine what culture is exactly, and why it exercises such a powerful influence.

Corporate Culture

All corporations, like families, ethnic groups, and nation states, have their own cultures. And it seems to be true that the best-run companies have distinct characters that set them apart from their competitors. Amex, Citibank, and Merrill Lynch all have well-developed corporate cultures that are often alluded to in the business press. Well-run institutions apparently have distinctive cultures that are somehow responsible for their ability to create, implement, and maintain their leadership positions.

Industries, too, have their own cultures and folklore. The cultures are generally set in the early periods of the industries' existence, just as the structures described in the first part of this chapter can be seen as an outgrowth of economic evolution. Many financial institutions, for example, have had "conservative cultures." This was due to the risk/reward tradeoffs that the industry faced. Recently, though, the competitive environment has changed; the tradeoffs have shifted, and the industry has had to reassess its position. Now it is trying to become less risk-averse. But just as structures lag behind strategies, so do cultures. When that happens, the lagging culture can either support or subvert reorganization. What follows describes how a culture's two major kinds of beliefs—guiding beliefs and daily beliefs—interact with attempts to reorganize for strategic reasons.[2]

Guiding Beliefs: The Basis of Corporate Strategy. Guiding beliefs are the principles by which top management wants to drive the business. They are the aspirations on which the company is built, the foundation and philosophical bedrock of the institution. Guiding beliefs express the long-range goals that should direct the choice and content of specific strategies. "Excellence in everything we do"; "Marketing is a way of life, not a tool"; "We will be first and foremost using new technologies," are all examples of corporate guiding beliefs that some financial services firms have begun to adopt.

The choice of guiding beliefs can also have a major impact on the choice of structures. For instance, with a guiding belief that propels the organization into using new technologies, the organization will likely make networking the basis for developing relationships within the organization. For another example, with a guiding belief that "marketing is a way of life," marketing is unlikely to be cast as a staff function. Rather, it will be defined as an integral part of every one of the business's activities. This was the case when the CEO of a major eastern bank decided that marketing was too important to be left to corporate staff. He disbanded the large marketing department and dispersed staff members into the line divisions.

Daily Beliefs: Key to Implementing Strategy. In contrast to guiding beliefs, daily beliefs shape day-to-day decisions and influence individual behavior on the job. They are the survival rules ("how the game is played") for individuals in their everyday worklife. While guiding beliefs are the principles for formulating strategy or structure, daily beliefs are the key elements in their implementation. Daily beliefs are the convictions that facilitate or constrain action. Daily beliefs that affect a reorganization's success might include such rules as "Ignore the changes—work around the new structure," or "Wait six months before making any decisions." Even though they are unwritten, such rules nevertheless can hinder the attainment of a reorganization's objectives.

What Is and What Ought to Be: The Gap Between Daily and Guiding Beliefs. It is important that daily beliefs develop from and lend support to guiding beliefs. One financial institution may, for example, have a guiding belief that every employee should have the opportunity to develop to his or her maximum potential. Ideally, the daily beliefs might then stress honest and regular feedback, meaningful performance evaluation, promotion from within, and excellent management development programs. In some instances, however, daily beliefs conflict with guiding beliefs. The following experience of a new worker illustrates the problem:

> A young trainee's initiation into a financial institution began with an extensive orientation program delivered by top management. For a full week she listened as each manager in turn proclaimed the lofty ideals and values of the company. The trainee heard all about rewards for high performers, open lines of communication to senior executives, and how "the customer was king." These were the institution's guiding beliefs.
>
> After orientation, the trainee went out to lunch with some of her friends who had been hired a year earlier. These already jaded veterans gave her the scoop about the way things really were. Here's a synopsis of their conversation on the daily beliefs:
>
> "First, don't put yourself out too much—there's little difference between compensation for highfliers and compensation for mediocre performers. Second, don't even try to go around your boss to speak to a top executive; that's taboo and grounds for finding yourself mysteriously assigned to a branch located in the far suburbs. Third, that stuff about the 'customer is king' is baloney. Just sell your quota, regardless of whether the customer needs the product or not."

Who is the trainee most likely to believe, management or her peers? Experience suggests that whenever there is a gap between the two sets of beliefs, daily beliefs are likely to have greater influence on trainees' behavior, regardless of what is heard during any orientation.

When daily beliefs reflect guiding beliefs, they facilitate implementation of the chosen strategy. Where there is a large gap between guiding beliefs and daily beliefs, however, cynicism develops. People come to believe that the espoused values of the company are "nothing but PR." Their behavior conforms to the conventional wisdom expressed in daily beliefs rather than the goals of the guiding beliefs. Employees tend to dismiss the longer range guiding beliefs as a smokescreen. In companies where such a gap exists, the daily beliefs will block progress toward the strategic goals expressed by the guiding beliefs.

Once cynicism has set in, it is hard to convince people to take guiding beliefs seriously. Experience tells them it is safer to maintain the status quo. Under these circumstances, the difficulties of effecting strategic change through reorganization are compounded by strong, although sometimes subtle, resistance.

ENSURING SUCCESSFUL REORGANIZATIONS

Many financial institutions have attempted several major structural changes over the past decade. But because daily beliefs do not change automatically with a change in structure, cynicism has spread. And when a reorganization fails, additional changes cannot be expected to have much impact. What, then, can be done to minimize the resistance?

The first priority in planning a reorganization is to imagine what kind of structure will be desired in the future. The planner then works backwards: What changes in the organizing dimensions and the nature of the relationships need to happen today consistent with the strategy's vision of the institution once its objectives are achieved? Explicitly addressing this question means the reorganization will be grounded in the future and not in the past.

The second step is to identify those aspects of the culture that are going to be particularly troublesome to the reorganization. In some instances, cultural barriers may be too strong to alter. When this is so, it is necessary to change the reorganization plan instead. Or alternatively, full-scale reorganization might be deferred. Perhaps the organization should pursue a new project or activity as if the new organization were already in place, giving individuals project-specific roles and responsibilities similar to those that might be assigned after a reorganization. With sufficient senior management attention to this pilot reorganization, the credibility needed to enact an eventual major change would be substantially increased.

The last element in ensuring a successful reorganization is perhaps obvious but needs to be reinforced. Reorganizations without changes in people and their reward systems are likely to fail. Reorganizations cannot and should not be considered as an abstraction divorced from the overall organizational paradigm that also includes people, systems, and culture.

The transition period for financial services is likely to continue over the next decade. Managing reorganization throughout this period is going to require a level of skill and leadership by senior executives that has rarely been demanded or tested so severely. One test will surely be to understand how the institution is divided and how its individual parts relate to one another. Understanding on this level will perhaps imply a more creative approach than the industry has used in the past.

How to manage imposing cultural obstacles will also merit thorough analysis and understanding. For many executives who have built their careers on such solid functional skills as deal-making, relationship management, or marketing, managing culture will seem a bafflingly elusive assignment. It is a skill that sounds far afield from the preoccupations of an investment banker, a commercial banker, or an insurance executive. But developing this skill faster and better than the competition is likely to be one of the decisive factors in making a reorganization work.

NOTES

1. Davis, Stanley M., and Paul R. Lawrence. *Matrix*, Reading, MA: Addison-Wesley, 1977.
2. Davis, Stanley M., *Managing Corporate Culture*, Cambridge: Ballinger, 1984.
3. Gogel, Robert N., Larry Benningson, and Howard Schwartz. "Guiding Beliefs and Daily Beliefs." MAC Group concept paper, 1985.

23 Strategic Management: Using and Choosing Management Processes

WILLIAM V. WHITE

Management processes are the tools which facilitate decision making and communication within an organization. The choice and use of the various management processes depends on the degree of change an organization must undergo. Obviously, the management of a major strategic change is a more difficult task than managing in a stable environment. And while managing in a stable environment can hardly be considered a science, management of change truly must be considered an art. Managers within the financial services industry are now faced with this challenge.

The first part of this chapter explores the basic uses of the major management processes: strategic planning, business planning, budgeting, measurement and control, and reward. Each process can play a different role depending on the needs within an organization and the degree of change required. The second part of the chapter deals with the key implementation requirement for management processes: good communication.

STRATEGIC PLANNING

The discipline of strategic planning, practiced for many years in American industry, is still relatively new to the U.S. financial services industry. Here, discipline has lagged behind other industries because the financial services environment, until the 1970s, was a stable and highly regulated one, where successful performance did not seem to require modern strategic planning techniques. Over the past two decades, however, changes in the environment, including market volatility, geography deregulation, product deregulation, and increased competition, have made strategic planning critical within the financial services industry.

Exhibit 23.1 The Strategic Planning Process

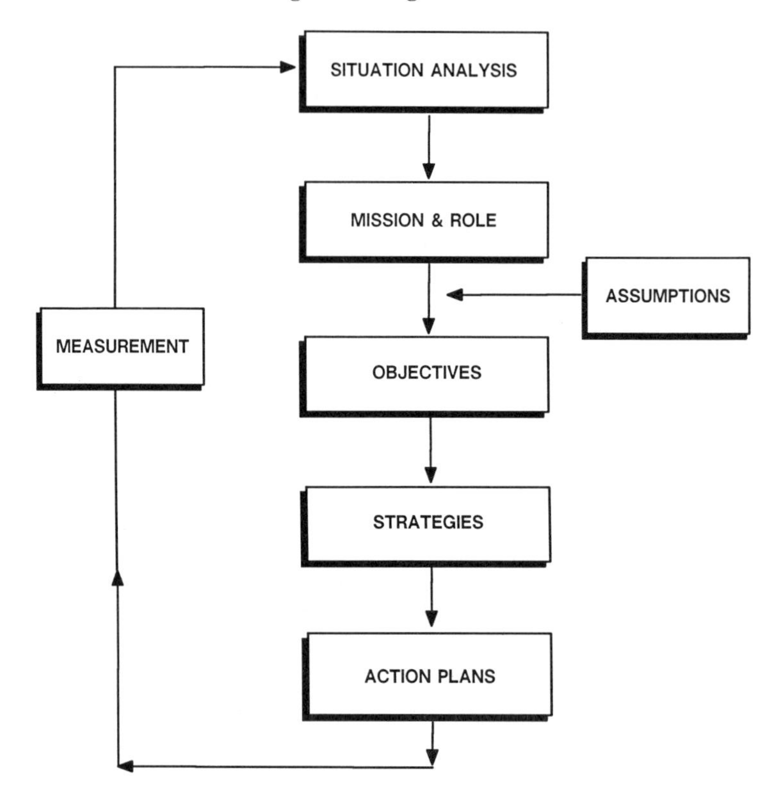

Strategic planning, in its simplest definition, is determining where a company is, where it wants to go, and how it will get there. Strategic planning develops a framework for current decisions that will produce a desired impact at some future time. The process for strategic planning may be displayed graphically as shown in Exhibit 23.1. Normally, the resulting strategic plan will contain the following elements:

Situation Analysis. Analysis examines the current position of the institution relative to markets, market share, lines of business, products and services, past performance, customer needs and preferences, customer loyalty, regulatory advantages and disadvantages, technological advantages and disadvantages, competitor characteristics, and the economic environment. This part of the plan is a comprehensive analysis of the institution's current position.

Assumptions. Explicitly defined, these concern the market, the economic environment, legal and regulatory matters, industry structure, technology, and other information which may impact the institution.

Mission. A broad definition of the business's role, the mission answers the question "Why does the institution exist?" The mission statement ought to be narrow enough to provide for an effective commitment of resources. It should also be broad enough that it need not change over several years to accommodate changes in the environment and the company's growth.

The following are representative mission statements from firms in various financial services segments. Each makes reference to the firm's purpose and chosen path to attaining that purpose. Each also identifies the firm's principal markets.

> *Diversified major bank holding company.* To provide a return to shareholders by serving the banking and financial needs of consumers, businesses, institutions, and governments, worldwide.
>
> *Institutional money market fund.* To earn a profit for equity investors by providing a family of money market funds for use by trust departments for investment of their customers' short-term cash.
>
> *Community mutual savings and loan association.* To provide customers of the association a full range of high-quality savings and investment services, and satisfy their finance needs by providing lending and mortgage banking services in the greater Columbia, South Carolina, area.
>
> *Discount brokerage company.* To provide a return to shareholders by offering low-priced investment transaction services, on both wholesale and retail bases.

Objectives. These are explicit statements of what an institution intends to accomplish within a given time frame. Objectives should be finite and measurable and should contain a specific date for accomplishment. They should be realistic and attainable, but at the same time represent a significant challenge or stretch for the institution.

Objectives usually evolve from tentative and preliminary ideas to more specific declarations of purpose. Normally included in the strategic plan would be financial objectives, other performance objectives, and qualitative objectives. Examples of objectives include:

> *Community bank.* Increase return on assets from 1.23 percent for 1985 to 1.40 percent by 1987. Correspondingly, achieve a 17.5 percent return on equity by 1988, and a 16 percent compound annual rate of increase in earnings.
>
> *Bank trust department.* By 1990, achieve an after-tax net income of 5 percent of trust revenue (with a full allocation of support costs and overhead, and excluding credit for deposit balances generated).
>
> *Credit life insurance company.* Increase credit life premium written by $275 million over the next three years. (See Exhibit 23.2.)

Strategies. These are directional statements, for either an entire institution or

Exhibit 23.2 Sample Credit Life Insurance Objective

	Premium Increase	Total Premium
	(in $ millions)	
1986	$ 75	$680
1987	90	770
1988	110	880

one of its business units, representing how the organization's objectives will be achieved. Strategies are developed from a number of alternatives, with the best one chosen. Strategy development is an iterative process that starts by asking, "What can we do?" and ends by answering "What we should do." Examples are:

Newly formed "boutique" bank. The general strategy is to segment the market by income and service-level requirements. The bank will specifically attract the high-net-worth, upper-bracket clientele that expects to be served by private bankers promptly and courteously in plush office surroundings. The bank will not have a teller line as such, and individual transactions will be conducted by the private banking staff using a "back-room" teller transaction facility. The bank will charge an annual retainer fee and require high minimum balances per client.

Mortgage banking subsidiary of a financial conglomerate. With excellent sources of investors, the company is limited only by the amount of product which can be generated for placement into the secondary market. The company will therefore maintain production offices in each of the top 20 U.S. residential housing markets. Primary marketing efforts will be conducted for the larger residential projects, and individual underwriting teams will be assigned to those projects with over 100 units.

Action Plans. These plans present detailed implementation steps which will aid in accomplishment of the objectives. Generally included in an action plan is a detailed description of the project, cost/benefit implications, risk implications, and an implementation plan giving time frame and responsibilities for accomplishment. Action plans are the most detailed and concrete element of a strategic plan.

Measurement. Parameters simply describe a methodology for determining progress against the strategic plan. Measurement may involve specific milestones and dates for accomplishment, or may merely specify a method for determining progress.

Strategic plans are relatively straightforward. Yet when committed to paper, they are at best snapshots of the organization's collective wisdom at a given time. As time passes, they need to be reviewed (as opposed to recreated) annually on a regular basis. Furthermore, while most institutions have undergone some kind of strategic planning within the past several years, much of this has degenerated into form-filling exercises. Information and sophisticated analyses have been developed—oftentimes in excruciating detail—yet the plan remains at the theoretical level. The challenge is to develop a plan which gives clear guidance to employees as to the practical actions they can undertake to help implement the strategy.

Business Planning

If the strategic plan is a vision for the future, the business plan is a detailed operating guideline for day-to-day management. Business planning often becomes a useful process to highlight within an institution that needs to develop some clear, short-term objectives and align resources behind specific projects. The business plan represents an important linkage between strategic vision and day-to-day operation. In simple language, it states what the management of the institution desires to accomplish for the next year, and provides a framework for a detailed profit plan which can then be developed. It can be as simple as the discussion of the following three elements:

Objectives. What will be accomplished next year? For most institutions, this will be expressed in terms of a balance sheet and income statement, along with any qualitative objectives.

Major Projects. What are the desired results for next year? How will they be accomplished?

Resources Required. What is necessary in the way of manpower, capital expenditures, external help, and major incremental expenditures?

There is basically no need to restate the role and mission, the strategy, and other elements of the institution's strategic plan which do not change. The business plan in its most effective form is short and simple. At the same time, however, it must be consistent with both the strategic direction and its short-term constraints/profitability objectives. The business plan must provide a detailed road map for a one-year period. It should also create a compatible framework for measurement of individual performance through the use of management-by-objectives (MBO) techniques and incentive compensation. In a complex multi-service institution, business plans should be prepared for each business unit or major organizational unit.

Profit Planning

Also simply known as the annual budget, this is one of the most detailed of the management processes. Each year, detailed estimates of balance sheet levels and income and expense items are projected from the business plan and included in the operating budget. Most companies use a pyramid approach, where budgeting occurs at relatively low organizational levels and results are summed to provide company results as a whole.

In most institutions, the operating budget is designed to provide a monthly measurement of results, and most systems are sophisticated enough to provide detailed variance and performance information. Most operating budgets are developed in an iterative process in the fall, with changes made progressively at each pass. In many cases, a plan for desired profitability is not attained during an early pass, calling for further effort to increase revenues or decrease expenses. In many cases, these changes in current-year efforts have strategic implications and should be carefully thought through relative to the strategic plan. It is most often in iterations of the profit plan that strategic direction may conflict with short-term profitability. The tradeoffs should be very carefully analyzed and informed decisions taken.

In many cases, the terms "profit plan" and "operating budget" are used interchangeably and are presented in an entirely numerical format with no narrative. When this is the case, a profit plan analysis is useful. This narrative explanation of expected changes in annual budgets should be examined in connection with the business plan to gain a picture of where the institution is going for the next year. A focus on profit planning becomes an obvious necessity when short-term profits are at risk or when a dramatic reallocation of resources is necessary. Effectively implemented, profit planning can become a way to galvanize an organization into action and develop a sense of urgency.

Control and Measurement

Success remains uncertain if there is no way to measure it. The financial services industry is changing fast enough that strategic plans should be reviewed annually. The review should not only measure progress against the attainment of strategic objectives, but should also test the current validity of assumptions made within the planning process. With change occurring at a rapid pace, it may be necessary to completely recast strategic plans; whether or not this is necessary can be determined from an annual review.

Business plans are normally formulated in the fall for the next calendar year. Since they tie directly to objectives and performance measurement for managers within a company, they should be reviewed at least quarterly. Probably the most successful type of review is a formal one led by the line manager responsible for the business plan. This type of review focuses on key accomplishments and major shortfalls. In addition, changes in the assumptions are discussed, and a fine-tuning of the plan may be desirable based on the results.

The operating budget provides monthly measurement of the earnings of the institution and, in most cases, detailed information concerning both historical trends and variances from the budget. A monthly review of the information is desirable, with the individual managers providing an explanation of major variations. Through a detailed examination of these variations, corrective action can be taken. Probably the most successful system is one in which staff support functions help to analyze the data as necessary, but line managers actually have the responsibility for identification and explanation of key positive or negative variances.

Using control systems to help manage change is a difficult challenge because, by definition, they come into play after the fact. However, control systems can play a major role in evaluating progress (or lack thereof) against strategic objectives. An obvious caution, however, is that the organization needs to ensure that control and measurement do not become the focus of managerial attention to the detriment of doing day-to-day business.

Reward Systems

Perhaps the area that can have the largest impact on the ability to implement strategic change is the reward system. In a growth or turn-around company, long-term rewards can effectively aid strategic change. In a more mature company, the focus tends to be on shorter-term rewards and incentives. In a company with a mature corporate culture, changes to the reward system are likely to be more difficult to make and their implications will be more sensitive.

The group component of incentive compensation programs is becoming more important. In general, today's management environment seems to be more participative. This is caused by an increasing complexity in the external environment and in the number of businesses operated by one management team. Also, a general movement is toward so-called Japanese management, which relies on participative decision making. Thus, while individual performance components are still important, the increasing importance of a group component is understandable, given a movement toward a team approach to management.

In any event, the reward system including incentive compensation remains a powerful mechanism to effect strategic change. While organizational structure should be dictated by strategy, the reward system should be driven by corporate objectives, both strategic and short-term.

The Management of Management Processes

As important as the outcomes of any of these processes is how the processes themselves are managed. The techniques used within the process are probably the most important variable in determining the overall success of the efforts.

The design of any planning process is a personalized effort for each institution. That design should take into account previous efforts within the institution and their success. For example, if the institution has little experience in planning, then a review of the planning activities of other companies will be helpful. Organizational responsibility must be defined, including the role of top management, the use of committees, management teams, or ad hoc working groups. The role of the board of directors within the planning process should be defined at an early stage, as well as that of the planning director or corporate planning department. The responsibilities of line managers for planning, and staff managers for support and review should also be defined at the outset. If a common format is to be used for all units involved in the planning process, this should be developed and communicated. The time horizon should be set, and the method for review and evaluation of the plan should be determined. Finally, a timetable for the planning process should be defined and communicated to all participants of the effort.

Several years ago, no common model for strategic planning was systematically used throughout the financial services industry. While there still may be no model, several commonly accepted beliefs have since emerged that guide efforts to run the process. These beliefs can also be extended to the other management processes as well.

Top management involvement and consensus is critical to the planning effort. The most successful companies appear to spend a great deal of time developing consensus at the top or with the executive management group on strategic change. Where top management of the company functions well together as a team, chances for success appear to increase.

Strategic plans should be prepared and implemented by line managers. The corporate planning function and staff support units should assist line managers with the efforts, and not "drive" the plans.

Consultants, if used for planning, should be facilitators of the planning process. Stated alternatively, management should plan, and consultants, if used at all, should be used to facilitate the process or to study specific questions relating to the business. Consultants should not be used for the broad development of strategic plans, although their help in specific strategy development may be appropriate.

A strategic mindset is a key ingredient in success. The ability to see things as they may be, rather than as they have been (i.e., the ability to think imaginatively) is a key success factor in the planning process. Innovation, entrepreneurship, and a highly inquisitive mind are all admirable characteristics. In addition, open debate and use of the corporate planner as a possible "devil's advocate" stimulate healthy thinking within the strategic planning process.

The risk of doing nothing is increasing. As the financial services industry changes, there appears to be an increased awareness that business as usual, however successful it may have been in the past, is not likely to achieve acceptable results in the future.

These beliefs suggest that effective management of management processes requires clear communications, the subject of the next section.

Communicating—Getting the Word Out

The very best management process, whether it be planning or rewarding, is doomed to stagnate if kept secret. The management of strategic change requires, in most cases, having individuals do their jobs differently. Much of the redirection can be achieved through adjustments in organizational structure and management focus. But the most successful companies have found that individual employee understanding of corporate direction is indispensable to improving performance. The question then becomes how to get the word out. To this question there is no simple answer.

Communication starts at the top. The board of directors, executive management, and top management of the company should actively discuss and review corporate strategy and plans. The management of strategic changes is not a once-a-year or once-a-quarter process, but a continuous reinforcement and communication of corporate plans and direction. The board should genuinely understand the various processes within the institution and not merely rubber-stamp corporate plans. Discussion at the board and top-management levels can be a useful tool in gaining understanding and acceptance of strategic direction.

The committee structure of the institution presents an ideal, and often overlooked, forum for communication of strategic plans. Committees are basically of two types—board-level committees and management-level committees. Board-level committees will generally include an executive committee, a salary and compensation committee, and an audit committee. In a bank, they will also include an asset/liability management committee, a loan committee, and a credit policy committee, among others. The presentation of strategic plans and business plans, or simply the discussion of general business strategy, can be useful in obtaining an understanding of what the institution seeks to achieve. Management-level committees are used for both decision making and dissemination of information. As such, they are especially useful in the communication process, providing an ideal forum for discussion of strategic plans and objectives.

A key link in the communication process is middle management of the institution. To these individuals, the business plan is an important element in communicating corporate strategy and bridging the gap with day-to-day operations. They need to be kept informed. In addition to the business plan, it is desirable to hold periodic meetings, with middle management to present and discuss changes in corporate mission, objectives, and strategy. Middle management is important in shaping the corporate culture and can clearly affect the success of strategic change. The more these managers accept and agree with corporate direction, the more likely the chances for successful implementation.

Below middle management lies a large number of managers, supervisors, and employees. In a financial services organization, these employees have the bulk of customer contact responsibility, and virtually all of the customer service responsibility. In a decentralized, geographically disbursed organization, the job of reaching these employees is even more difficult. Training programs can clarify corporate direction and help with strategic change for this employee base. In addition, internal newsletters, orientation programs, and periodic performance and strategy presentations will help to increase their understanding of objectives and strategy. While all these tools can help, the primary responsibility for communication with these groups should be that of middle managers.

An interesting example of communication and its impact on effectiveness concerns a recent bank holding company's acquisition of another organization located across state lines. The purchasing institution is a large one, with dominant market share and a decentralized management structure. The company operates multiple lines of business and has management which by all standards is excellent. The acquired company, on the other hand, is smaller and less dominant in its markets. Its top management structure is centralized, with the management team acting as a cohesive group when making individual decisions that affect the company as a whole. The management team is accustomed to working closely together and operating in an environment where active discussion of issues is encouraged. Disagreements are explored and resolved as well as possible.

As the integration process unfolds, an interesting thing is happening. Management of the acquired institution is having a disproportionately large influence on the direction of the merged entity. In fact, because of the cohesive working relationship of the acquired company's management team, it can almost be said that this group is actually "running" the merged institution. While it is too early to tell the final outcome, there can be little doubt that managers from the acquired institution are outperforming managers of the dominant holding company. Considering the similarities of the two institutions, the differences in communication and cohesiveness of the management group appear to be responsible.

CONCLUSION

The management of strategic change is essential for success in today's financial institutions environment. With a large number of management techniques and processes available to an institution to effect its changes, the key becomes to use and choose the appropriate ones at the appropriate time. While success cannot be assured, the following guidelines should help:

Use the management processes to identify opportunities and demonstrate the need for strategic change. Key elements for success include the ability to develop a vision for the future, a logical thought process, the ability to think broadly, and a great deal of common sense. Do not let a process be driven by numbers, planning format, or short-term earnings considerations only. Cut through all that and think about the fundamentals of the business and how they will change.

Use existing management processes to implement change. Clearly, communication is the most important single factor in implementing strategic change. Make sure that the process is clear to everyone. All levels of employees need to understand the company's mission, strategy, objectives, and how these large-scale concepts will affect the way they perform their jobs.

Consider carefully the implications for each decision, and test decisions for consistency with both strategic plans and business plans. Day-to-day decision making may have strategic implications.

A one-year business plan is a key linkage between strategic plans and day-to-day operations, and thus represents an important part of the communication process for strategic change. Business plans should be well thought out and widely communicated within the organization after approval.

Consider flexibility a must. Financial services industry deregulation has caused an increasing amount of uncertainty and has clearly accelerated the pace of change for customers and institutions. Time horizons for strategic plans have been shortened and increased flexibility is a must for implementation of strategic change.

Foresight and unified corporate action can be effectively promoted through a systematic effort. Consequently, companies with effective management processes are those that are most likely to achieve favorable operating results over the next several years. Deliberate, coordinated processes can do much to obviate the need for remarks such as this one from the chief executive officer of a major financial institution to a recently appointed profit center manager: "Do something, even if it's wrong."

Although the institution's servicing delivery system needed changing, in an era of intense competition and growing customer sophistication, the problem demanded careful attention, not knee-jerk responses. Obviously the CEO was venting his feeling of frustration with the pace of change. But he was also undercutting his institution's management process and jeopardizing the fabric of his strategy.

Processes should be allowed to function smoothly. Then random, unreflective initiatives will be minimized, and so will the chances of doing something wrong.

24 Managing Global Operations

R. ALAN PLATOW

Strategic planning, business planning, budgeting, control, measurement, and reward systems are basic tools in managing any business toward its goals. In a global corporation, the difficulty of effectively applying management processes expands geometrically with the geographic span of a firm's operations. The importance of these processes also expands as a global spreads its bases of commerce into new territory.

This chapter focuses on the use of management processes as tools with which to manage and change global financial services corporations. It will concentrate on the role of management processes as levers to shift an enterprise's direction. The chapter begins by describing the evolution of firms from multinational to global organizations, and goes on to explore the role of management processes in effectively managing this evolution. It concludes with an in-depth look at the actual management processes used by one prominent global financial services organization, CIGNA Worldwide, the international division of CIGNA Corporation.

MAKING THE TRANSITION FROM MULTINATIONAL TO GLOBAL STATURE

A fundamental distinction needs to be made at the outset between multinational and global firms.

Simply defined, multinationals are federations of business units, each unit performing most key functions itself. More significantly, multinational business units often pursue their own individual strategies. In many cases, the business unit's strategy bears little similarity to that of its sister business units in the corporation. Other than ownership by the parent company, common threads between local units are usually rare.

A true global corporation, by contrast, does not perform every business function in each country. Instead, it locates functions in the country or countries where they can be performed most efficiently. For example, a global bank may have loan officers stationed in all of its localities to perform the sales function. But its worldwide research and product development functions are apt to be centralized at the flagship bank in, say, London or Hong Kong. Similarly, an insurance company may have a sales force in every country where it does business, but it will probably restrict the underwriting of certain lines to a single office, thus concentrating the underwriting expertise required to assume large risks. Thus, a global's local operations are unusually dependent on activities performed elsewhere around the world. This heightened dependence increases the need for planning processes that coordinate the activities of local entities.

A second defining characteristic of global corporations is aggressive redeployment of capital. It might be said that if a multinational is a holding company of international scope, then a global is an operating company of worldwide proportions. And as an operating company, it strives to redistribute funds around its system quickly in response to local opportunities. Well-constructed management processes allow incremental capital to be allocated effectively around the world in order to gain the highest available returns. Also, effective processes help individual country managers appreciate how their own operations fit within the whole and how their roles influence the execution of the firm's overall strategy.

Thirdly, globals are configured to serve the needs of global customers. This means, for one thing, that they must be capable of operating 24 hours a day around the world. It also means they must be able to assure that the quality they offer in one country will be consistent with the standards they observe in another. Global clients are thus assuming that centrally purchased products (e.g., loans, insurance) will reflect a consistent quality standard around the world.

Global Companies: Financial Services Versus Manufacturing

The financial services industry is well suited to globalization. To understand why this is so, it is helpful to compare the business of financial services with the business of manufacturing. Because financial services are quite distinct in their essentials, however, these comparisons can only be pushed to a certain point, and no further. Still, when looked at broadly, financial services and manufacturing exhibit three telling differences.

To begin with, a financial services firm's products are intangible, whereas a manufacturer's are tangible. Because they are not physically made, financial products are easily created, do not require shipment, and, with minimal local customization, are marketable in most countries of the world, assuming that regulatory constraints are met. Unlike a manufacturing concern, a financial services firm consequently needs to make only nominal investment in local plants or equipment; often the only true requirement is the hiring and training of competent local sales and operational staff.

However—and this is the second revealing contrast—the financial exposures taken on by a financial services firm operating around the world are enormous in comparison to those of most manufacturing firms. For example, it is instructive to imagine the difference between the situations of (1) a local country salesman in a global manufacturing firm, and (2) a local country loan officer in a global bank. The product the manufacturer's salesman represents has a cost structure that is well defined prior to the time of sale. For that reason, the salesman can accurately calculate his company's profit on a given transaction once he has taken into account the variables of shipping cost, foreign exchange hedges, collectability, and of course contract price. By the time the manufactured product is delivered, the unknowns have generally been eliminated.

The loan officer of a global bank, on the other hand, will not know whether a commercial loan was profitable until it matures, often far in the future. There are a number of reasons for this uncertainty. Fixed-rate loans extended in one country may be funded by variable rate deposits accepted in another; Swiss franc loans could be serviced by cash flow in Danish kroner, for example. In addition, the evaluation of a potential customer's ability to pay the loan back fully and on time renders the forecasting of product costs almost purely an art, at least in comparison to the calculations the manufacturer's representative makes. At the end of a loan period, banks have to get their "product" back from the buyer. Any shortfall has capital implications. Similarly, in global insurance firms, losses can have a serious impact on capital and profitability years after the premium (or profit element) is paid by the purchaser. The Latin American debt restructurings which have at times threatened the stability of international finance are quintessential examples of situations where initial profitability targets will never be attained.

The third major difference between global manufacturing and financial services firms involves the scale of risk of their normal business activities. The salesman may sell an order at the wrong price, but rarely would his miscalculation put the company's future on the line. But every time the loan officer makes a major loan he puts a proportionately large slice of the bank's capital at risk. Exposures to "salesman" errors like this occur every day in the financial services industry. The more global a financial services company becomes, then, the greater this exposure. To guard against this increased local exposure, global financial services firms are driven to centralize. Exposures are just too high to have it any other way.

Drive Towards Centralization

Centralization, as the term will be used here, refers primarily to decision making. In a centralized corporation, management is of the belief that certain classes of decisions are so critical to the vitality of the business that responsibility for them must be assumed by the home or headquarters office. This viewpoint is directly opposed to that of management in most multinationals, for whom a great deal of autonomy at the local level is highly desirable, as it maximizes responsiveness to customer needs, competitor moves, changing availability of materials, government regulations, and so on.

For many multinational companies, decentralized management and systems may well be the appropriate solution. International communication technology being what it is today, when headquarters needs to talk over an issue with a foreign subsidiary contact is usually a phone call away. In most instances, communication will be eased by the subsidiary's contact being an expatriate staff representative; that is, a person who shares a common cultural and language background with home office management, but who works largely with nationals of the country in which he is based.

For the genuinely global corporation, on the other hand, decentralization is virtually inconceivable. In globals, it will be remembered, many important functions are not performed at the local level. At the same time, the local organizations are expected to be able to serve customers that may be located in several countries. Therefore, they must be able to offer much the same products and services found in other countries where the customer is located. Since the scale of involvement in a country has to remain proportional to the scale of demand in that country if the operation is to be profitable, decentralization would be uneconomic for the smaller outposts of global organizations. Country managers everywhere would need fairly equivalent skills at their disposal. For example, global decentralization would mean that a five-person operation in a tiny Caribbean island needed as much competence to run a business independently as that possessed by a U.K. operation with 1800 employees and 20 expatriates on staff. Global decentralization would require that indigenous staff address business problems as they occur, correcting them or asking for assistance to correct them. Global decentralization would also require a large proportion of expatriate staff familiar with head office procedures, a mode of operation that is unaffordable and impractical. Finally, a globally decentralized financial services company would require that all field operations fully understand the strategic and year-to-year direction of the company. Taken together, these requirements are difficult to meet in a domestic company operating in 40 states—they are impossible to meet globally.

Major insurance brokers provide one example of the difficulty of successfully managing a growing decentralized global network. The old model of linking up with local firms by making them associates or partners has proven ineffective for many global brokers, straining business relationships between the broker and the local partners. The local interests generally prevailed, to the detriment of the firm's strategy. Today, most successful global brokers have centralized by taking ownership of their foreign offices, and are therefore able to assert the required level of global control.

The costs of centralization—generally recognized to be a decrease in local market autonomy and a dampened entrepreneurial spirit—are offset by the benefits of quickly capitalizing on global opportunities. These unique opportunities may, however, be detrimental to the short-term profits of an individual country operation. Without centralization, the truly global opportunities would rarely be seized on a genuinely global scale. That is because global opportunities are never uniformly attractive throughout the world. Usually there are several countries in which, for economic, regulatory, or cultural reasons, the so-called opportunity is actually costly. For example, managing pension funds might be highly profitable if it could be performed on a completely international scale with efficient, centralized, routine servicing. But tax laws on pensions in some nations might make global providers uncompetitive with national providers.

The disparities between local management skill levels, the difficulties of multi-country communication, and the high financial exposures commensurate with the financial services business demand that global firms be highly centralized. This centralized direction and control, however, must be translated into action at the field level in order to be effective. Mechanisms must be created to allow local opportunities to be exploited. Management processes cannot of themselves address or solve all the problems of global operations—but if in place and realistically utilized, the processes can create an environment that mitigates the problems and takes advantage of the opportunities.

MANAGEMENT PROCESSES IN GLOBAL CORPORATIONS

Companies, whether centralized or decentralized, domestic or global, experience a fairly predictable management process evolution. The typical company is born virtually processless; personal relationships between a few people, often relatives or friends, take care of everything. But in their infancy, companies grow to the point where it becomes necessary to install a budgeting system than can plan for and control expenses. Although many companies stop at this point, others advance to some level of business planning.

Business planning efforts allow firms to look ahead at business opportunities and plan how to use their strengths to take advantage of these opportunities. Business planning is typically focused narrowly, with semi-independent efforts being simultaneously undertaken to solve issues in loosely related geographic, product, or customer markets. At the next juncture in their maturity, firms develop a strategic planning process that looks across individual businesses for areas of corporate opportunity. Companies attaining this level of planning integration rely heavily on their reward and measurement systems to ensure that individual behavior supporting the firm's strategic direction is strongly motivated. In some firms management processes are used to shape, direct, control, and manage the business. In others (all too often) they become paper exercises.

Companies of international scope cannot afford to let their processes be carried out in token fashion. All face large problems in dealing with often over 100 different countries. Most of the issues are commercial, some are ethical. Local and accepted "customs" and "business practices" which differ from U.S. corporate values are simply a fact of life in the global environment. Companies constantly need to assess their tactical use of gifts and promotions in marketing. While financial service companies tend to employ less dramatic "sweeteners" than manufacturers use, this reality of global business must nevertheless be appreciated by the head office. This is but one aspect of the need to integrate local business practices with the corporate outlook. Management processes are essential to doing that, by maintaining integration on a systematic basis.

For global financial services firms, the ability to use these processes as management tools has a direct impact on a firm's chances of success. The processes are used as true line management tools to set, maintain, and monitor a coherent, profitable business direction. In this section, each process will be examined, as will the importance of the linkages that unite the processes.

Strategic Planning

Strategic planning in a global corporation determines overall direction, including the missions of the individual country entities. It establishes the "gospel." The overall direction must be clear enough so that the plan will leave in the minds of country managers two or three major philosophies to follow. For example, one strategic objective may be to serve all the financial needs of multinational corporations. Brief as that particular philosophy is, it will have profound implications for each unit's way of doing business. If the company is in the process of evolving from a multinational to a global, for some units the philosophy will require learning to sell unfamiliar products. For others it will mean discontinuing operations previously conducted locally. Often it means investing in more sophisticated communications equipment. Whatever the actual implications, "serving all the financial needs of multinational corporations" is plainly no simple matter.

Global strategic planning, consistent with the philosophy of centralized control, is the strict domain and responsibility of the global corporation's home office. The primary reason is that the regional or country level manager in, say, Southeast Asia frequently is not in a position to relate and communicate the opportunities or advantages of his operation to the general manager of, for example, the U.K. operation. Second, as will be discussed more fully later, corporate field-level reward systems often emphasize local performance. They do this for good reason. However, country-level managers who are largely compensated on local performance cannot be expected to assume the necessary corporate perspective if at times it requires them to divest corporate resources away from their own businesses to regions of higher potential.

If local managers are not to impede but to further the goals of the global corporation, they must be persuaded to accept those goals. Given that strategy development is a centralized process in a global concern, intelligent managers can be expected to greet corporate strategies with a healthy dose of skepticism. How, then, can their detachment be converted to commitment?

Heavily involving local managers with the strategic planning effort at first looks like a promising method. These managers, after all, are the very people who will implement the plans and be held responsible for the results. But although it sounds attractive, local involvement is largely impractical. For one thing, the logistical difficulties in a global corporation are considerable. Still, these can be surmounted. The real argument against local involvement in strategic planning is deeper: The insights brought forward by regional managers are almost invariably self-serving. While this observation admittedly reflects a home-office perspective, people who have been involved in the process will almost certainly agree. It is tough for managers, or anyone else, to look very far beyond the boundaries of their familiar territory.

Only one feasible alternative for creating buy-in is left: persuasive and clear communication of the strategy. Communication must be persuasive so that local managers will approach this responsibility with the necessary enthusiasm. Effective persuasion depends on providing a convincing rationale for the strategy, explaining its assumptions, and elaborating its implications in such a way that local managers will be able to see how their operation fits into the global's scheme and can help attain corporate objectives. Communication must be clear and in sufficient detail so that local managers will understand how to weave the strategy's implications into their business plans.

Communication is not the ideal way to gain support for strategies, it is simply the most pragmatic. Support obtained through communication is unlikely to be as whole-hearted as that which might be obtained by allowing everyone involved in implementation a chance to shape the strategy. That fact acknowledged, senior management can still win for a strategy more than enough backing among local management to make it work successfully. This thought will be explored further a little later, when the methods used by the author's company are examined as a case in point.

Business Planning

Business plans determine how the local operation is going to convert the strategic plan into action in its designated market. Business plans also identify and justify investment in unique local opportunities. In a sense, then, business planning brings strategic planning down to the local business level. When used as it should be, it provides the necessary link between seemingly remote corporate ideals and the all too pressing, concrete constraints of budgeting.

Headquarters staff cannot and should not monitor developments affecting business in each of dozens of countries. Local management is paid to do this. As will be seen in a moment, headquarters' role is to monitor and reinforce the themes of the strategic plan.

Real-Time Budgeting

The complexities of global management necessitate heavy reliance on numbers to track unit performance. Given the nature of the product and the slim profit margins available to most financial services firms, financials figures are critical when used as tracking and control mechanisms. In an insurance company, for example, changes in budget numbers do not affect the current year's earnings—adjustments usually do not show up on the bottom line until the following year.

Three major budget levers exist: price and quantity of policies, loss experience, and underwriting expenses incurred producing the business. Time is needed for each to effect change. Pricing changes, for instance, have little immediate impact on a company's financial condition. Instead, results only appear on the bottom line as new or revised policies become earned premiums. Loss experience does not show up until well after the policy has been issued. Underwriting expenses, because they are 70 to 75 percent people-related, are best dealt with gradually. Therefore, rarely do budget-related adjustments improve short-term profitability. Still, the budget process does provide a tool to ensure that strategic investment, or disinvestments, will actually be made.

Keeping Control

Tight operational control is a necessity in the global financial services arena. Entry barriers are low and exposures are high, a combination of factors that allows no room for slipshod procedures. Tight control can be maintained from two directions. One is monitoring from the top in a centralized fashion, as discussed earlier. This method is indispensable but it is also insufficient. The second method, careful design of management processes, must be utilized as well to convey strategic direction and induce field entities to follow the lead.

Since financial services lends itself well to globalization, growth temptations drive companies to expand beyond what they can control with their existing processes. These companies need to ensure that control mechanisms are in place before expanding to global scale. There are numerous unhappy stories of firms that "went global" before they had the internal ability to cope with the requirements of expansion.

It's tough to keep everything working together internationally. The secret, if there is one, is to hire and retain the best people available. Otherwise, maintaining control of a global financial services company is akin to slaying the mythological multiheaded hydra. Once one deadly head has been severed, two others sprout up in its place. Of course, even the tightest controls can be breached by creative people, as Pepsico recently discovered. Some of this gamesmanship can be mitigated by the movement of key country managers to different locations. Also, frequent visits to the field by headquarters managers help. Pepsico provides a good illustration of the difficulty of keeping control.

Although Pepsico's strategic planning had long been admired, its control processes apparently slipped several years ago. In 1982 the company learned that its carefully formulated strategic plans were based on fraudulent data that its units in Mexico and the Phillipines had reported to the home office. Financial staffers in these countries had made a series of profit-boosting accounting decisions with long-term ramifications damaging to the health of the entire corporation. To set its house in order again, senior management was obliged to record a 25 percent drop in profits for the year, despite the fact that sales had increased from the previous fiscal period. If Pepsico had not been a manufacturer but a bank, the consequences would have been far graver. Undoubtedly the survival of the global corporation would have been threatened, much as Continental Illinois was nearly brought down by inadequate lending controls two years later. In both cases, after-the-fact criticism is not the point. The point is that controlling far-flung businesses is extremely difficult, and absolutely essential—even more so in global financial services.

Rewarding Performance

As previously mentioned, local management rewards can become disincentives to maintaining a global perspective. If local management is rewarded based on business volume and substantial investment is required to gain that business volume, local management will fight for the investment resources. In fact, these resources may be better spent in another subsidiary—at least from the corporate perspective. This conflict in goals can sabotage the global firm's effectiveness.

Reward systems in global corporations must include components for both local performance and corporate performance. In addition, "off-line" measures can be instituted for special situations. If money is taken from Japan to be invested in Spain, for example, a special bonus might be paid to the Japanese manager if he meets goals despite the lost investment resources.

Literature on matching rewards to performance abounds—the key point to remember as the financial services firm becomes global is that management must continue to recheck to ensure that reward incentives reinforce the company's global strategy at the local level.

The Importance of Linkages

In the elusive, "perfect" global corporation, each management process is not only an excellent system in its own right, it is also explicitly and clearly linked to its sister processes. These linkages are of the utmost importance. If the activities of a global corporation are compared to the performance of a team of trapeze artists, it becomes apparent that ultimate skill lies in perfecting the organization's timing and coordination. Strategic planning orchestrates the routine of the "act," determining overall corporate direction as well as missions for individual businesses. The other processes follow the orchestration so that the performance will be executed with precision and without slips. Planning lays out how each business will work to accomplish its mission. Budgeting determines the resource requirements and sets up the basis for accountability. Control and measurement systems allow progress against plan to be tracked, and reward systems provide the right kinds of incentives.

MANAGEMENT PROCESSES AT CIGNA WORLDWIDE

CIGNA Worldwide, the international arm of CIGNA Corporation, provides a prime example of the global financial services company in the midst of rapid and dramatic change. The author's first-hand knowledge and experience with CIGNA's management processes make the company a natural focus for this discussion. CIGNA makes no claims to having found the ideal in its processes, and this appraisal will be candid. Still, the experience has taught management some valuable lessons about harnessing processes to help set in motion and control strategic shifts. These lessons should likewise prove valuable for executives grappling with similar issues in other global firms.

CIGNA's management processes have undergone two major trials over the past three years: the first in 1982, when CIGNA Corporation was created through the merger of Connecticut General and the Insurance Company of North America; and the second in 1984, when CIGNA acquired the American Foreign Insurance Association. In both cases, but particularly in the AFIA acquisition, management processes facilitated the smooth integration of these companies and have also been critical to ongoing operations. It is the AFIA experience which is of principal interest here.

AFIA Merger: Building The Global Corporation

In 1983 an in-depth internal analysis of CIGNA Corporation's global business was initiated. Various theoretical marketing and financial models were used to analyze growth patterns and trends. Product line profitability was analyzed; and growth and profit opportunities were evaluated by product, geographic area, and country. In addition, competitors and acquisition candidates were thoroughly scrutinized. It was an unsparing examination and confirmed the realities of CIGNA's international market position: It stood at a distant third in revenues, and had a less attractive product mix and a more limited country/license structure than the two leading global insurance carriers.

Next, a range of expansion scenarios was developed as a basis for selecting the strategic direction that would most enhance the global posture of CIGNA Worldwide. CIGNA was faced with the choice of either continuing as a small player or attempting to increase market share. With the decision to expand via acquisition, CIGNA's management process "trapeze act" began.

In moving from theoretical and strategic planning stages of the decision process, the realities of coordination, timing, resources, and management dedication played important roles in reaching final strategy decisions. It was clear that growth by acquisition was the only viable method of becoming a premier *global* provider of insurance services. Based on evaluation of the various options, CIGNA Corporation management made the bold and unexpected decision to acquire the second largest international carrier, AFIA. The AFIA acquisition immediately doubled the firm's international presence.

But how are two decentralized multinationals to be melded into a single, centralized global organization? The usual problems of incorporating two large and independent companies were just the beginning. Management now had to determine how best to integrate each company's diverse approaches to marketing, underwriting, financial reporting, and personnel policies, while maintaining profit and production performance, maintaining staff morale, implementing operational efficiencies, and dealing with the day-to-day annoyances of conducting business through an acquired subsidiary based 5000 miles away.

Not only did answers for these how-to questions have to be found, but the underlying flow of management in each organization had to be reversed. Collective strategy for all units had to be authoritatively transmitted from the top, when in the past both CIGNA and AFIA had allowed their local managers a great deal of autonomy. Difficulties were compounded by the fact that the acquirer was half the size of its acquisition. CIGNA Worldwide—with strong commitment and support from the parent corporation—undertook a brief but intense period of management process development to address these issues of organizational change.

Processes for the global firm were developed jointly by CIGNA and AFIA. When counterpart technical and management units from CIGNA and AFIA met for the first time to work out process issues, they used outside consultants and a technique called "storyboarding." Each group spent a week of long working days developing its own sets of management processes to shape the new consolidated unit. Once each organization's modus operandi had been reviewed by the group, the rest of the week focused on blending the best approaches from each organization into a new CIGNA Worldwide standard. Strategic plans, business plans, marketing position, technical issues, budgets, controls, and personnel measurement standards were all openly discussed. Conflicts in approaches were identified, and resolutions jointly defined. The resulting hybrid processes would govern and shape the direction of the new CIGNA Worldwide. At the end of two months, two previously independent business entities had created a combined global approach with supporting operational guidelines, cultural change goals, and management processes.

The two years following acquisition were not without duress. Some people found the intense stress and change not to their liking. Nor, understandably, were they entirely happy to see their business prerogatives clearly delimited. Prior to globalization they had operated subject only to mild restrictions. Now a manager in West Germany, for example, found himself instructed to cease issuing new casualty business once he reached a set policy amount. Previously he had been free to do business in whatever measure appeared opportune. Some managers chafed. While the friction that arose between the home office and some local units was an identified risk in the process, it points up an important fact: The transition from a small decentralized multinational to a large, centralized, global corporation is tough and demanding. Creating the necessary linkage between each new process can be a painful exercise fraught with conflicts in culture, values, and business goals. Figuring all the angles calls for time, but there is no time. Action must be taken quickly.

Action was taken quickly, and effectively, at CIGNA. Three years later, the unanimous feeling at CIGNA Worldwide is that there was *no better way* to mold AFIA and CIGNA than through the management processes chosen. But putting the initial strategy in place was just the first step. Ongoing processes of managing the worldwide operations had to be put in place as well. A clearer understanding

Exhibit 24.1 CIGNA Worldwide Global Management Process Timing

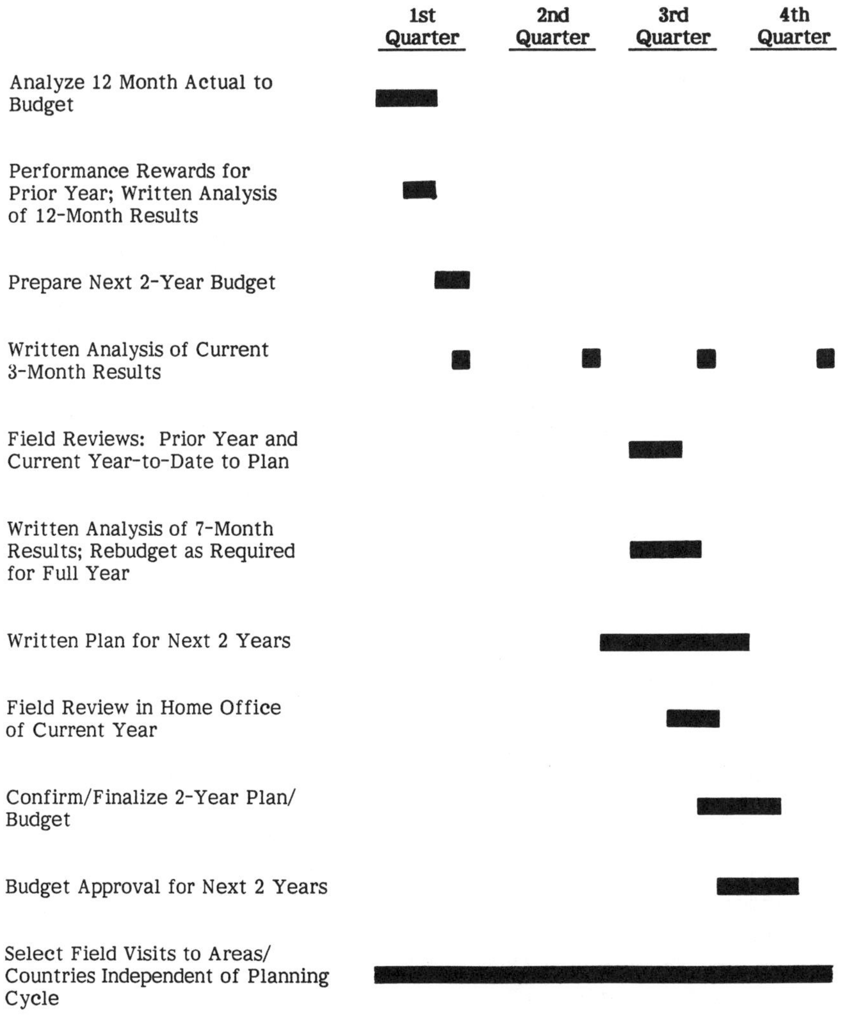

1st Quarter | 2nd Quarter | 3rd Quarter | 4th Quarter

Analyze 12 Month Actual to Budget

Performance Rewards for Prior Year; Written Analysis of 12-Month Results

Prepare Next 2-Year Budget

Written Analysis of Current 3-Month Results

Field Reviews: Prior Year and Current Year-to-Date to Plan

Written Analysis of 7-Month Results; Rebudget as Required for Full Year

Written Plan for Next 2 Years

Field Review in Home Office of Current Year

Confirm/Finalize 2-Year Plan/ Budget

Budget Approval for Next 2 Years

Select Field Visits to Areas/ Countries Independent of Planning Cycle

of management processes in general may emerge from a look at the outlines of CIGNA's processes in specific. To supplement the description of the various processes, Exhibit 24.1 illustrates their sequencing.

Strategic Planning

CIGNA Worldwide has accomplished a major shift in direction, from that of a multinational corporation focusing independently on each country to a global enterprise that effectively assesses and capitalizes upon global opportunities. The new, larger organization began to target the global needs of multinational corporations by presenting a coordinated, consistent approach to these customers. For the most part, this shift in strategy has worked well. Nonetheless, this has been a major undertaking. It is worth examining how the shift was accomplished by an insurance company recently composed of 85 "independent" country operations with substantially different cultures.

The CIGNA Worldwide strategic plan establishes only two or three core themes—no more. To keep the company's 6700 foreign-based employees moving in the same direction, it is imperative that the two or three key themes be communicated to and internalized by all field staff. Achieving corporate-wide singleness of purpose would be nearly impossible if strategic plans culminated in 100 pages of implications. From a strategic perspective, implications that go beyond the key themes are details and most appropriately end up as part of individual country business plans.

Communication begins with the commencement of the annual budgeting process. Senior home office and senior field staff meet to discuss new strategic directions for both CIGNA Worldwide and the parent corporation. Until this meeting, these directions have still not totally solidified. During the meeting, field managers' input is considered and consolidated. Global meetings are expensive, but the guts of business strategy cannot be expressed through position papers. What CIGNA buys in terms of personal interfacing and the resulting personal commitment of field personnel to the strategy is fully worth the meeting's costs and the efforts it requires.

The consolidated input is later taken under advisement by the home office. Input from local managers is regarded as just that—input. CIGNA's top management does not pretend that the corporation's strategic planning process is essentially democratic. Rather, senior executives fix the strategy, with due deference to the views of local managers. But CIGNA's strategic planners also recognize the dangers of becoming autocratic and unresponsive to signals from the outposts. For this reason, CIGNA management insists on the importance of selling the strategy it has chosen. The carrying wave they use to sell the strategy is justification—they emphasize why the strategy will work and what it will do for business, customers, and the people at CIGNA. Their preferred way to transmit the message is face to face. Talking up the strategy with local managers is at least half the reason behind CIGNA home office staff's heavy international traveling schedule.

Communication of strategy cannot be done once only or once every five years. When a plan is being modified or abandoned, the field must also be told what is happening as well as the reasons behind the change. Understandably, field staff can become discouraged if they have driven hard to reach a strategic goal that no longer rates with the head office.

By definition, long-term plans should not be totally redone each year. Partly for this reason, strategic planning is well suited to the use of outside consultants. Consultants who spend most of their professional time considering problems of strategy can provide insight and guidance to corporate executives for whom the planning process is a sometime affair. However, consultants should not create the plan on their own. A major purpose of the planning process is to stimulate management to broaden its thinking. If there is ever an opportune time to see possibilities beyond the familiar, this is it.

Budgeting and Business Planning

Budgeting, in direct contrast to strategic planning, is a 100 percent bottom-up exercise at CIGNA Worldwide. Beginning in March of each year, country managers reforecast the current year's financial outlook and prepare a budget for the next two years. Country budgets are reviewed with the area managers—about 20 countries to an area—and consolidated into area budgets. In addition, country managers prepare a business plan that supports the budget adjustments and forecasts.

At CIGNA Worldwide, then, budgeting drives business planning. Indeed, CIGNA Worldwide leapfrogs the business planning level to some extent. Business plans take the shape of a narrative which is submitted with the budget. This is not ideal. Ideally, business plans should be generated first, and budgets derived in turn. As a company, CIGNA Worldwide has not achieved this ideal level of management process sophistication. The risk is that the company may fail to see local opportunities that lie outside budgetary guidelines.

Meshing Budgets, Business Plans, and Strategy

Home office review follows area management review. In June and July, the home office planning staff spends three to five days at each area headquarters to review each country plan. This review concentrates on two major areas: compliance with strategic plan and fiscal reasonableness. The compliance test is the solid link between strategic planning and budgeting. How well do the country managers' planning documents reflect the theme set in the strategic plan? By far the most important element of these visits is the ability to add the strategic dimension to local plans.

Reasonableness in the country manager's business and financial plans is assessed by applying the home office's very different quantitative views. Does this comparison highlight areas for improvement or areas of unrealistic expectations? A generally stricter approach to productivity and spending in the business plan is also added before plans are finalized.

It should be noted that, consistent with CIGNA's bottom-up budgeting approach to business planning, home office staff regularly travel to the area business locations; not until the point of final presentation do the key country and area managers come to the home office. A clear benefit of these field visits is a gradual increase in sophistication of the field managers relative to business planning. Although slow, this method will eventually make business planning the driving force for budgeting, instead of vice versa. At the end of these field sessions, country and area managers are left with a series of questions or issues to address prior to the final plan presentation at the home office.

A recent situation CIGNA faced in Brazil serves to illustrate the value of these field visits: Forecasted insurance premium growth showed Brazil to be a major CIGNA growth country. Additionally, the local business budget looked extremely profitable. The recommendation to CIGNA by local Brazilian management was to expand further. And of course, the home office was sorely tempted. To a planning analyst at CIGNA Worldwide, the Brazilian operation's plan could only look phenomenal. But when staff made a field visit, the picture changed. What at first sight appeared lucrative was in fact fiscally shaky. Brazilian hyperinflation was camouflaging reality. Not only was CIGNA's local presence declining in real-dollar terms, but profitability was becoming elusive. If ratified without examination, the recommended Brazilian business direction would have been harmful to CIGNA's bottom line.

A second example demonstrates the continuing importance of bringing strategy to the field. CIGNA Worldwide is continuously facing the challenge of serving the needs of multinational corporate risk managers anxious for help in centralized management of their global insurance needs. Often this global approach is channeled through a corporation's own captive insurance company. Captives are designed to centralize risks as well as to produce corporate cost benefits. Assisting corporations in this global captive approach is very attractive business to CIGNA Worldwide. However, along with this "bread and butter" business, many multinational clients require their global insurer to write unattractive business, for example, local auto insurance. This means that the attractive local risk element is ceded to the captive multinational insurance company, while the local CIGNA Worldwide operation retains 100 percent of the auto coverages on its own books. Since the local auto business that remains generally has a negative impact on the country manager's financial performance, country managers are reluctant to write any aspect of captive business. Only through strong head-office controls, centralized solutions, some creative internal transfer pricing, field visits, and the establishment of a special captive unit, was CIGNA Worldwide able to overcome field bias and take advantage of this global opportunity.

If there is a point where CIGNA is weak in the top-down strategic planning effort, it is at the link where regional field managers communicate the themes to their subordinate country-level managers. Perhaps the reason that not every area management group does a proficient job at this is that they themselves have not bought totally into the strategic themes. Or perhaps they simply do not do a good job in communicating. Either way, the messages sometimes do not reach the country managers prior to the budgeting process. Recognizing the weaknesses of this link, corporate management reinforces the connection with home-office visitation to the field. If corporate strategy has not been translated into the plans, it will have to be explained, reaffirmed, and integrated into the local orientation by the end of these sessions.

In August the area managers and their staff finally come to the home office to present to senior CIGNA management the areas' business plans. These presentations cover the current year reforecast and the two-year budget. Following presentation, tactical business decisions are made—decisions that will affect the bottom line over the next year. Country by country, plan by plan, each area is reviewed for two days. Meetings get to the nitty gritty: "You have to get out of this line of business—the returns just are not there." "Why not invest more here? It looks like an opportunity." These are typical comments. Little by little the plans are reshaped into the working documents which will spell out accountabilities for field management.

Monitoring Performance

Each month, CIGNA operations generate more than 1000 pages of data reports on key product lines. Numbers quantify volume, claims, expenses, and much more. Performance is monitored from these reports by noting exceptions in month-to-month patterns.

Analyzing the financial performance of country businesses is fundamental to the performance review process. CIGNA Worldwide performance reviews are produced every three, seven, and 12 months, then shared each time with local management. Evaluations identify points at which a country is attaining, or not attaining, strategic objectives. Also monitored is the progress that key countries are making toward the production levels and the deliverables promised in their budgets and business plans.

In addition, home office staff travel in order to monitor and control performance. There is no substitute for sitting down with a country or area manager and reviewing not only his current results but also the backroom status of his business. Personal contact puts heightened demands on the headquarters staff, but it is a necessity that comes with being global.

Internal audit functions are also relied upon in evaluating the integrity of global entities. CIGNA Worldwide is no exception. The internal auditing force visits every one of the worldwide locations at least once a year to go through not only the books and documentation but also the business methods and procedures. Large or troublesome locations receive special attention.

Rewarding Performance

CIGNA Worldwide reinforces adherence to its management processes by rewarding good performers. Choosing the right inducements is never as straightforward as it sounds, and it is especially tricky for globals. Winning attractive business worldwide sometimes requires taking on unattractive business in another country. For instance, if CIGNA is trying to win the property/casualty business of a major automobile maker, it may be quite willing to conduct unprofitable business in a few, relatively insignificant local markets in order to spare the manufacturer the trouble of making special arrangements in those countries. Should the head office lock in this client, some local operations will unavoidably take a hit on earnings.

The reward system has to be designed to motivate performance that supports the corporation's interests in situations like this one, rather than being obstructive. Managers can be expected to absorb losses that can, from a corporate perspective, be viewed as costs. But they cannot be expected to do this if their paychecks will suffer. Sacrifices made at a local level have to be recognized for what they are, and adjustments made accordingly. Senior managements acknowledge this unhesitatingly, but they also tend to view the issue as a mop-up operation to be taken care of after the system is up and running. More often than not, the problem is forgotten and remains unsolved.

In the United States it is difficult enough to tie pay directly to performance. But in many other parts of the world, compensation is not the primary motivator it is here. In all countries financial remuneration is of course a positive factor, but in many cultures other aspects of a job are more meaningful. In the Far East, for example, the respect attached to a position and the senior status accorded to an individual holding a position for a long time are often just as valuable as money to employees. It is a trap to believe, as many global managements have, that Asians and others respond as quickly to monetary incentives as do Americans. They do not.

The difficulty inherent in this conflict has driven many global financial services companies to separate their multicountry business into a separate strategic business unit or division. An alternative, and the approach that CIGNA uses, relies on off-balance sheet calculations to make equitable adjustments. Systems need not be fancy or electronic, but they must allow for rewards to people who follow and implement the overall strategy. Adjustments are indispensable to maintaining credibility with country managers in the global business concept. Shouting globalization from the mountain tops, yet punishing managers that sign on to centralized direction (through bonus reductions), quickly leads to cynicism.

THE MANAGEMENT PROCESS OPPORTUNITY

The globalization of financial services has opened up myriad opportunities for financial services firms, as well as a Pandora's box of demons. Management processes are effective tools for addressing both the opportunities and the tribulations. Strategic planning, business planning, budgeting, measurement, control, and reward systems can be used together to translate global strategy into local market performance. They can help raise unique local market opportunities as well as take global opportunities to the local level.

At CIGNA Worldwide, management processes smoothed the integration of AFIA in building the global corporation from a multinational one, and today are used to manage the new company. CIGNA's experiences demonstrated the difficulty of using these processes. Change is never easy, but CIGNA'S experiences also show the power of the processes: This company has utterly changed direction, largely through smart use of management processes.

Rigorous self-examination is needed to discover whether a global firm is fully taking advantage of its processes. The cost of flaws is high. But the benefits are also extremely high when management processes are used judiciously to build and manage the global financial services corporation.

25 Strategic Management of Human Resources

ROBERT N. BECK

This chapter provides a comprehensive look at an often-neglected and sometimes maligned function: human resources. As shall be seen, it is becoming increasingly recognized that the management of people and their skills plays a major part in the overall direction of the financial services institution.

To demonstrate how the situation is changing, this chapter begins by examining the evolution of labor-related conditions in the twentieth century, and suggests how these conditions—regulatory, competitive, and technological—have acted to bring the human resource function to prominence. Next are presented the current philosophies of human resource management. Most pertinently, this section addresses the delicate balance that must be struck between human resource and line responsibilities. Following the historical and philosophical perspectives of human resources comes the heart of the chapter, an item-by-item look at systems and programs that enable financial services institutions to manage people strategically. These include: human resources planning, hiring, orientation, management development, succession planning, career development, employee development and training, compensation, and performance planning and objective setting. A discussion follows concerning how the success of these programs, and the performance of the people in them, needs to be measured. The chapter concludes with ideas on a side of human resources management that is surprisingly hard to do well—communications.

HISTORICAL PERSPECTIVE

The emergence of the human resource function as a professional organization that adds value to the bottom line is happening in the 1980s after many years of development. The historical underpinnings of the human resource function is one of administration. In the early 1900s, line management needed someone to hire employees as well as take care of people who were injured or became sick on the job. Employment departments were established and industrial nurses were hired. The 1930s saw the passage of labor legislation and some early benefit laws surrounding Social Security, hospitalization programs, and pension legislation. Human resource, or "personnel" departments grew in size.

From the 1940s to the 1960s, labor legislation exploded in such areas as civil rights and health and safety. Tax, accounting, and legal departments grew as a result, while the function of assessing impact and writing appropriate policies to deal with the increased legislation and legal exposures fell to the personnel staff. Despite this increasing visibility, the human resource function continued to play a primarily passive or responsive role. As a result, line management tended to see the personnel function as necessary overhead. Personnel was widely viewed as a unit to be dealt with after the decisions were made—a department whose task was to help implement.

The 1970s saw two major recessions, wage and price controls, and a movement away from increasing legislation. However, another factor was gaining prominence in the environment which would change the role of the human resource function. That factor, deregulation, created a market-driven environment in several major industries, including financial services. It also opened doors for international competitors operating in substantially different human and business environments. Pay scales and staffing configurations figured prominently in these differences. In response, line managements began to scrutinize labor costs and abandon the assumption that these costs were necessarily fixed. The importance of productivity and quality took on new dimensions. Top management began to take a personal interest in health care issues, training and management development, staffing strategies, recruiting processes, and compensation and benefits design. The amount of time being devoted to human resource issues increased, creating a high demand for the human resource staff. More and more, the human resource executive was being recognized as a member of the top management team that made the important decisions in many corporations.

Until 1982 banks had been heavily regulated. Their products, prices, and territories were established by government bodies, a fact which essentially guaranteed their profits. Because service industries like banking are heavily dependent on people, the need to change human resource policies and programs accelerated at a rapid rate. Historically banks were not leaders in pay (benefit plans tended to be very good, but actual cash compensation ranked among the lowest). At the junior levels of the organization, high turnover was commonplace. Managers were usually appointed based on their lending skills or customer relationships. Costs associated with human resources were ignored, or if they were given any attention it was to caution that costs be kept as low as possible. Many organizations had limited personnel staffs. As a result, personnel services were frequently vendored or purchased, often times directly by line management at lower levels in the organization.

The forceful entrance of new players into the financial services industry, the expansion of services by groups within the industry (e.g., the movement of savings and loans into traditional banking services), and the reduction of profit margins, have put a focus on obtaining greater efficiency. While many back-room operations and transactional services are being automated in banking, the increasing demand for more complex financial services is largely being delivered by people. This drive has in turn increased demand for scarce human resources, causing wages to escalate at a fast pace. Recognizing that the cost of hiring and developing good people is large, top management is demanding state-of-the-art human resource policies and programs to help meet business goals.

PHILOSOPHIES OF HUMAN RESOURCE MANAGEMENT

The distinction between line management and staff is blurring. Many of the "new" staff units can contribute directly to the bottom line through significant cost-avoidance, cost-savings, and productivity measures. Restructuring of pension and medical benefit plans can result in millions of dollars of savings with relatively little investment or risk. That savings is sometimes equivalent to a many-fold increase in sales, fees, or loans. In such an era, it is easy for aggressive human resource managers to assume a directive role.

This shift should not detract from the real purpose of the human resource function—to assist line management at all levels to achieve its goals. Excessive faith in the function's new-found importance can lead to difficult situations if the old adage of the "staff proposes and the line disposes" is not considered. One of the best ways human resources managers can keep a balanced perspective is to ensure line manager involvement in the design, development, implementation, and assessment processes. Strategic programs should be developed in concert with line managers and executed through them. Maintenance and "change" agendas should be publicly and privately embraced by the CEO and other appropriate levels of management. Accordingly, significant change agendas should start with the CEO and be communicated through his position.

Tactical programs can then be delegated to the human resource function. For example, the head of human resources, rather than the line manager, often makes announcements of policy/programs, such as changes in employee benefits or compensation (pay), and changes in staffing programs. This procedure creates the image of personnel, as opposed to line management, ownership. In good times this "front" role works fine, but in difficult times it can expose the human resource staff to attack by line managers who are "transparent" to tough decisions, and employees who want to question policy changes. If this happens, the "neutral" role of the human resource function to serve both managers and employees can be lost.

The structure of the human resource function, be it centralized or decentralized, will vary over time based on such factors as the life cycle of the organization, the external environment, and the quality of staff and management. Notably, for example, today's fast-paced financial services environment requires swift decisions in all aspects of the business. Consequently, the centralized human resource function that in many financial services institutions, especially banks, yielded handsome dividends through tight control, now tends toward slow decision making. Its former strengths, such as generating written standard procedures and removing human resource management from line managers, have become weaknesses in a world that rewards speed.

To work most effectively, then, the human resource function needs to develop policies that permit flexibility and depend on line management judgment. Its chief tools must be good communications programs, coaching, and management development. This approach is difficult for professionals who desire strong control and power. It also raises the risk that some policies will be enacted inequitably. However, in the long run rigid uniformity is generally more inequitable.

The new environment demands new skills and operating styles for human resource professionals. Notable among these are the needs for skill in integrating diverse people and activity, and an increased knowledge of the business. This situation creates something of a dilemma. On the one hand, human resource generalists become more valuable as advisors to line management, especially with increased legislation and court settlements on labor issues. Yet the increasingly technical nature of labor and tax laws demands high levels of specialization.

To resolve this dilemma and ensure functional excellence, a deliberate, planned, developmental process for the human resource function is required. Targeted entry-level hiring, coupled with planned rotational programs having select bridging points for specialist and generalist tracks, is vital. Rotational programs should incorporate seminars, forums, internal and external conferences, and education programs to complement direct experience on the job. Corporate human resource staffs will generally be comprised of a blend of seasoned generalists and specialists who have perhaps several years' experience in human resource areas beyond their specialty, as well as some divisional experience. The generalists would mainly assess business plans and external environments to permit design and development of policies and programs to achieve business goals. Implementation of measurements to assess effectiveness of policies is important to this process.

While line management is responsible for implementing change in the organization, the human resource manager becomes a key agent to facilitate the changes needed to meet business and environmental conditions. Customer demand for broader services from single institutions is leading many banks, savings and loans, and brokerage and insurance firms to expand into "supermarkets" of financial services. What results is often companies within companies. Standard policies—say, those designed for a retail or wholesale bank—have trouble meeting the more elaborate needs of these multidimensional organizations. Not surprisingly perhaps, human resource professionals have been criticized for resisting adaptation to what is demanded by these new organizations. For example, the growth of investment banking or mortgage banking within traditional retail or wholesale banks has led to conflicts centered around compensation schemes.

Clearly, altered conditions have to be addressed. Human resources must design tailored programs/policies that accommodate all units, while keeping the principles and values of the firm intact.

HIGH IMPACT SYSTEMS AND PROGRAMS FOR MANAGING PEOPLE STRATEGICALLY

Human Resource Planning

Due to the regulatory nature of their business, many financial institutions did limited operational and strategic planning and generally relied on budgets to manage the business. Human resources departments usually followed suit. In recent years, more planning and forecasting have been taking place at the top levels. But often the human resource function has not been made an integral part of the process. Lead times required for staffing and training may be critical to a plan's success, yet are often an afterthought to line management. What often happens is this: A line executive takes a business proposal to the top management committee, obtains approval, and only then notifies human resources of its intent to implement. As a result, the timely development of the staffing plans, position evaluation, incentive and pay plans, and training programs that would support his proposal are not developed, or are at best accomplished hastily, behind schedule, and at unnecessary expense. Execution of the business plan consequently suffers. If human resources is to help the line management achieve its goals, it must be involved in the process from the beginning, acting in partnership with line management and the chief financial officer's staff.

Lack of a long-established planning process—a commonplace in many industrial firms—tends to create two weaknesses in financial services institutions: a deficient or nonexistent management information system, and managers whose planning skills are underdeveloped and untested. The skills necessary to do environmental scanning, to forecast volumes/revenues based on different scenarios, and to assess their potential impact on human resource matters, is generally lacking. Worse, the absence of reliable historical data bases makes start-up difficult. In an industry characterized by high turnover, shortages of select skills, and rapidly changing requirements, the planning activity calls for even greater art.

After a long history of growth or stability, many financial institutions are now experiencing the need to reduce staff. With a long tradition of shunning layoffs, and influenced by a desire to maintain historical employee relations practices, many financial institutions are utilizing redeployment and attrition management to reduce or change the staffing patterns of the organization. The need to forecast when surpluses will arise in given skills, as well as when skills will be required under business plans, is critical. Financial institutions are among the leaders in this enlightened approach to human resource management.

Hiring

As markets evolve and financial institutions reconfigure to change strategic direction, new skills are demanded. Some can be developed through internal training programs. Others will have to be acquired through hires from outside the firm, and often outside the industry. The need for people experienced in data processing systems, management information systems, strategic planning, human resources, insurance, product management, marketing, real estate development, and so forth, will probably require a high level of hiring to build a core of competence. On that basis others can be trained. Since competition among firms for the limited supply of talent drives market prices up, human resource staffs must have a good knowledge of alternative sources to tap for qualified candidates. And to attract and keep the best people, they need appropriate skills and programs, including new career management and incentive pay schemes.

Human resources departments must also develop alternative forms of work scheduling that meet both business and personal needs. Expansion of service hours, round-the-clock availability, and reserve capacity to staff for peak loads are among the alternatives. More flexible approaches to part-time, peak-time, temporary staff, and innovative compensation practices are required to facilitate these changes. The solutions will have to take into account varied demand for financial services, multiple forms of work, and rapid changes occurring in the industry, as well as changes in labor law, such as employment at will.

The rapid hiring of many new people into the organization demands a well-planned orientation process that covers the first several years of employment. The need to have all employees understanding the company's values and strategies is vital to achieving success in a competitive industry, above all in one whose business is service. Although decentralized approaches permitting managers to conduct their own recruiting and orientation were adequate under a regulated environment, new conditions place a premium on quality of staff and a balanced mix of skills. Excellent selection techniques, something that most first-level and middle-level managers never had an opportunity to acquire, are indispensable. At the same time, many banks have for too long relied on search firms and agencies. Although this practice made possible a broad consideration of candidates, reliance developed into dependency. As a result, search firms, especially agencies, continually increased their fees. This inflated the cost of hiring, while robbing human resource staffs of the experience needed to do their own sourcing, and limiting their focus to career management.

Taking large numbers of experienced hires from multiple sources has drawbacks. For one thing, out-sourced people show a propensity to leave in a short period of time. The overall effect is a revolving door of agency people and inordinate recruiting costs. Another drawback results from the imported personnel's limited understanding of the corporation's culture and systems ("systems" here refers to how things get done in the organization, not just data processing). It has been suggested that a "tower of Babel" syndrome sets in when over a third of a management team enters the organization within a short period. Of course, when the team's bench is thin and growth is inhibited as a result of lack of management talent, external sourcing becomes a necessity.

Outside hiring's third pitfall is associated with the financial services industry's lack of a good mechanism for screening candidates who have been involved in defalcations, fraud or other "white collar" crimes. The desire to protect privacy is high, yet the exposure of electronic money transfer systems, credit card, home banking, and other devices, increases the risk of hiring people who may take advantage of the system. The human resource staff has to work up new reference checking and security approaches rather than relying on the FBI fingerprint system.

Once applicants have been hired, their power to manipulate operational systems for their own purposes must be controlled as well. Some firms have already begun to develop security zones or sectors within which individuals whose records are suspect do not work. More stringent measures may also evolve, like the governmental security clearance approach, where low-security employees are denied access to certain areas. From a personnel standpoint, this issue is delicate, with implications for promotions and costs of elaborate tracking systems.

Orientation

Whether they be experienced hires at the managerial level, or entry-level hires into such positions as teller, switchboard operator, or receptionist, all employees need proper orientation. This need is especially important in a rapidly changing service industry where customers are showing an increasing propensity to switch their business to competitors, an action so rare in the past that it was not considered a real threat to market share. Given this sensitivity in the market, the firm that invests in orientation programs which articulate, at least to some extent, the organization's mission, goals, values and strategies to all employees, will strengthen its distinctive competitive advantage.

Comprehensive orientation goes far beyond the first day or week on the job. Successful orientation programs involve a time-phased program over the course of the first six months to a year, and include group sessions as well as one-on-one meetings. Top management involvement and support is important. One-on-one meetings at the outset between the employee and the first- and second-line managers should establish what is expected, what is valued, and how things should be done. Knowing these cultural parameters will shorten the learning curve for new employees at all levels. Group sessions, often attended by the employee's spouse, generally cover general topics such as benefits, company history, products, and social programs (e.g., employee social, cultural, and recreational clubs if they exist). With experienced hires from out of town, the use of "host families" can be effective. In this program a host employee and spouse show the new family around and discuss matters of personal concern such as schools, medical services, recreation and entertainment opportunities, and shopping. The company provides reimbursement for reasonable expenses.

Management Development

The financial services industry has typically promoted to management positions individuals who have demonstrated proficiency in technical areas, especially lending/credit. However, the new environment calls for a readjustment of criteria, notably toward a higher level of general management skills as needed to direct and redirect increasingly diverse business or product lines and services. The lack of formalized on-the-job rotational developmental programs, integrated with external out-company development, has created a high demand for integral management development programs. On-the-job training requires monitoring programs for junior employees and needs assessment linked to rotational assignments. Off-the-job training ranges from in-company seminars to a formalized, required management development program for every manager.

One large firm has established what is called "change of role" training. When first promoted to manager, an employee is sent to a corporate management school. Subject matter is 100 percent internal to the company, operating effectively in the context of the corporation's mission, values, and strategies. Emphasis is placed on people management—the basics of "blocking and tackling," rather than on products and marketing plans. The corporation recognizes that when a person moves from a nonmanagement to a management position he is undertaking a fundamental change in role. To ensure proper management of the human resources for which that person is responsible, he should receive training within 90 days of appointment.

A second fundamental change of role occurs when a manager is promoted to a middle management position, one that requires the management of other managers. Without proper training soon after appointment, the middle manager will become frustrated, and will perform less effectively. Shortsightedly, many management development programs teach more of the same—material near-identical to that used in training programs for first-time managers. However, a most significant shift is occurring in the role of the middle manager. Those who step into this pivotal position must learn to act as coaches to other managers. They must become excellent communicators and interpreters of business goals, policies, and priorities. They must develop the ability to "walk around" and mix with employees at all levels, sense what is happening without infringing on the power of first-line managers, and stay in touch with the unit's customers, be they internal or external. This aspect of the job entails a downward focus.

Middle managers must also focus upward. This means communicating to higher-level management what programs, products, and policies are effective or not effective. Upward focus implies timely feedback on customer problems and needs as well as employee needs. It requires consolidation of input from lower-level units, with added value coming from the middle manager's broader perspective on possible tradeoffs and alternative outlooks. It assumes some familiarity with business strategy as this relates to implementation plans. Learning to get outside his own perspective, then, is the middle manager's greatest need. For this reason, it is the inculcation of downward and upward focuses that middle-management development programs most helpfully address.

One of the most effective approaches of the aforementioned training programs is the use of experienced line managers as instructors. Under this approach high-potential line managers are detached from their units for full-time assignments as instructors for one year. Although they are taught how to teach both content and skills by the human resource management development staff, the human resource people often resist the use of line-manager instructors, preferring instead to teach the courses themselves rather than designing and assessing programs. But the management development staff needs to overcome this understandable, if parochial, attitude. Measured studies show a high degree of effectiveness in changing managerial behavior when instructors have high credibility with their students. Moreover, teaching rotations are an excellent way to develop line managers.

The third change of role occurs when a middle manager moves into the executive ranks. At this level many financial institutions rely solely on external university-based programs. While these programs are good supplements, there is also a basic need to build an integrated top management team that understands the whole company, its strategies, and the trends of the environment in which it operates. In short, this level of development must shift up a notch the middle management perspective described above. Executives need to be made comfortable with policy formulation, strategic/competitive assessment, integration of operating and strategic planning, government and community relations (social responsibility), as well as new economic and political factors. They need help making the transformation from manager to leader.

This transformation is probably best effected through heavy use of external faculty, a high degree of discussion, and direct involvement in design and delivery by the corporation's very top management. The human resources function should act as the catalyst to provide the needed services, ensure that proper needs analysis is done at all levels, and direct measured follow-up as to effectiveness. Programs offered should be ongoing rather than occurring once every several years. In addition to broad corporate-wide programs, offerings tailored to the specialized managerial needs of managers in systems, branch, investment banking, and so on, can be offered when line managers express a need.

Succession Planning

The rapid increase in demand for different skills in the financial services industry has created a shortage of ready talent in some areas. Expansion of the competitive marketplace means that it will take several years before enough talent is attracted. Consequently, companies need to have a formalized succession planning process that starts at the top and goes throughout the managerial organization. Certainly there are times when a unique skill is needed and cannot be developed internally, for instance, when a bank expands into insurance. Still, the gradual development of lower-level people to fill higher-level positions has many advantages and minimizes the risks associated with outside hires. A formalized, publicized system will help attract and retain high-level performers. Just as important, it will ensure broader consideration of the organization's talent, permit the crossdivisionalization moves needed for developing general managers, provide better assurance that talent is ready when needed, and provide valuable input to internal and external development programs.

One way to start succession planning is to have the CEO and the top management team identify the positions, not the people, critical to the corporation's success. It is appointment to these posts that the team will want to control. Once identified, the positions should be slotted in some top-down groupings—for instance, A, B, C level or I, II, III—rather than by title or by the firm's position evaluation scheme. This independent grouping will create a focus on the skills required, regardless of what the marketplace compensates for the job. Additionally, having the top management team develop a common set of skills criteria means that a rational, predictive assessment system can be used. Without such a system, confusion is almost inevitable, as when companies ask about short- and long-term potential. Similarly, the phrases "senior management" or "high level" mean different things to different people, especially depending on their own level. Clear articulation of criteria permits evaluators to predict "A" potential or "B" potential with the expectation that their assessments will be interpreted correctly.

Once the identification and general assessment scheme is in place, some process needs to be implemented to look at incumbents and potential replacements. The process of filling out replacement planning tables, which are an aid in systematizing succession planning, should follow a consistent set of rules. One common tabular format ranks three or four candidates for each position and shows the estimated ready date for each: No candidate may appear as the first choice on more than one list. Another approach develops a pool, rather than separate tables, of candidates. This approach is used when several positions require similar skills, for example, when essentially interchangeable candidates are being considered for regional manager slots. In either case, high potential people will likely appear on numerous tables early in their careers. Their frequent appearance marks them as comers to upper level managers who might otherwise be unaware of their promise. A third approach stipulates that the top-ranked successor must be ready to take the job within six months, or sometimes 12. If no candidates meet this requirement, the top replacement positions should be left blank. A high proportion of blanks indicates that the bench is thin and that actions are needed right away. In this approach candidates should be ranked in order of readiness. While not required, identification of an emergency replacement is helpful. Normally not designated as the long-term replacement, this individual would possess the experience and availability to step in and quickly keep operations going while a permanent successor was found.

Cross-divisional development to build general managers with a broad view of the business is desirable. Cross-fertilization can be promoted by requiring that at least one candidate on each replacement planning table come from another division. By prompting executives across divisions or units to exchange candidates, the process alone serves as a healthy exercise in shifting management perspectives outward from their specialized concerns.

To make succession planning a living process rather than a "fill up the binders" exercise performed once a year, individual plans should be developed for each incumbent and successor candidate. Typical formats call for a brief description of current duties, biographical information, strengths and weaknesses or limitations (this area requires all managers to be frank if true development plans are to be implemented), and individual career aspirations including mobility and personal preference. Suggested next assignments and specific development plans with dates for completion are also important. On an individual level, the plans should be used by line managers for coaching sessions; on a group level, their analysis can suggest needs for internal and external development programs; and on a strategic level, summary analysis provides a solid indication of the capabilities of the organization, its depth of talent, its limitations, and its dependence on external sources.

To ensure that the program has optimum use as a human resource tool, key division and staff heads should be scheduled to review incumbents before the top management team. They should also use the occasion to discuss planned changes, developmental programs for key candidates, and assistance they needed to implement those plans. Because several hours should be allotted for each discussion/review, the process clearly must be regarded as a management priority. Some large firms' CEOs report that they spend more time on this single topic than any other, which reflects on the importance of succession planning to the success of the business.

Replication of this process at lower levels in the business will help ensure that a true feeder system is in place, and will also give junior-level executives the feeling that a career management process is working.

Career Development

A prominent reason for turnover is lack of career management. Employees with upward potential want a process that effectively matches company needs with individual aspirations. Job-hopping is bound to speed up as the industry expands. To minimize turnover within the organization, top management has to impress on middle-and lower-level managers their responsibility for hiring and developing qualified people and then making those people available to the rest of the company. Such directives must be supported both by a measurement system that tracks the movement of people, and by a reward system that encourages managers to initiate transfers. The tendency for managers to hold on to good people who can be important to their own success is natural, but detrimental. In the long run the organization loses.

Likewise, materials should be made available that help employees assess what skills, knowledge, and abilities (personal as well as technical) are required for various jobs and career paths. Since many jobs are changing in the financial services industry, a plan for periodic update is required to keep the information meaningful. For example, the expansion of investment banking products into traditional wholesale bank product offerings requires different considerations of what skills and career development programs are needed. The use of market segmentation (e.g., mass, upscale, and private) requires different considerations in the traditional retail market. For large firms, automated employee information profiles and job opening systems can be a great aid to career management. Smaller firms can purchase packaged programs or purchase a data service that offers these features as part of the payroll/human resource information system.

Employee Development/Training

Rapid change mandates significant increases in normal training budgets. Continual introduction of new products and services effectively makes employee training an ongoing process. To ensure effective utilization of available training resources, line management should be prodded to articulate its training needs in business plans, new product proposals, plans for change in ways of doing business, and any other substantial business developments. Human resources should translate these needs into appropriate programs, whether these be classroom, programmed instruction, video, or computer-based instruction.

Line managers should make subject matter experts available to the training design staff for the development of new materials. For example, experienced credit people should help design credit training materials; product developers should help design new product training. Further, where delivery of training includes classroom time, subject matter experts should be made available to provide actual instructions. Oftentimes these responsibilities are delegated to the training department, which lacks the on-the-job experience. Obviously, such shortcuts result in less effective training. Training design specialists should concentrate on course development and effectiveness assessment, not on delivery.

Small organizations will most likely have to purchase required training. However, purchase does not relieve line managers and human resources of the need to ensure the quality and effectiveness of the training. If the need for training in certain areas is continuous, a full comparison of the economies of making versus buying should be performed. If needs are sporadic, a buy decision is usually practical. Industry associations, such as the American Institute of Banking, have considerable experience and widespread delivery capability. Universities and for-profit training organizations are also a source.

The link to business planning and career path management makes the training function a key success factor in achieving business goals. Well-conceived needs assessments, both short and long range, for both individuals and company requirements, will provide a competitive edge in a dynamic marketplace.

Compensation

The undifferentiated approach to compensation traditionally used in banks is no longer effective. To attract, retain, and reward diverse financial services staff, new approaches to job evaluation are required—ones that ensure that organizations obtain a desirable mix of employee characteristics, including customer orientation and risk-taking. Pay-for-performance schemes have to be developed to motivate performance on these and other heretofore unrecognized dimensions, and to meet changing labor-market conditions.

For the general employee population, the merit-pay programs already well established in many industrial companies are adequate. Key to merit-based pay is a well-founded performance appraisal system that can measure significant differences between top and average performers. Correspondingly, managers should be provided with salary guides that allow them flexibility both in the percentage increases they award and in the timing of those increases. Appropriate merit differential targets should be established. For its part, human resources should provide middle management with periodic reports as to range of increases granted (both actual and annualized), actual salary differentials, and appraisal distributions.

In addition to comparing pay for performance by performance appraisal distribution, another helpful measure is to require managers to rank employees in similar groups. On a consolidated basis for like groups, human resources should furnish managers with data comparing compensation levels, increases granted (annualized), stock options, promotions, and so on. This practice will inject a measure of objectivity into the performance appraisal process.

Human resources should work closely with line management to determine what behavior is to be motivated and how it is to be rewarded. The "new world" of sales and incentive management takes a different approach than the pure salaried method. More than before, managers must know their employees well. They must have good awareness of individual skills, knowledge, and abilities, so that pragmatic goals and objectives can be set for each, especially where quotas are used for incentive payments. Marketing managers must also have a good knowledge of marketplace potential. Seasonal adjustments must be made. Marketing managers must also know the competition's products almost as well as their own in terms of price, features, and quality. Competing products will have impact on their products, sales potential, and hence on individual performance.

In designing compensation plans it is important for managers and human resource professionals to establish principles of design. Importantly, plans should attempt to determine the individual's power to influence outcomes for which he may or may not be compensated. Thus, choices as to whether a plan should have an earnings cap, whether it should enable deferrals (voluntary or involuntary), and what counts for benefit plan purposes, all need to be determined in the beginning. This is particularly necessary if individuals are ever to be charged back for business that turned "bad."

The modern financial services institution will have multiple salary structures in accordance with the variety of the labor markets from which personnel are drawn. An up-to-date job evaluation scheme, coupled with a salary survey process, will ensure that jobs are paid at competitive rates, and will provide a basis to answer employees' compensation questions. Few will have trouble recognizing that equal pay is not necessarily equitable pay, but all will want the differences explained.

Most new managers do not understand how salaries are set. But many compensation professionals have been reluctant to explain how salary programs are developed. As a result, inexperienced managers often lack conviction, which leads them to be "transparent" in answering employees' questions.

Like other human resources programs, compensation schemes should be considered line management's, and not the human resource department's, responsibility. To reinforce this policy, changes and implementation should be conducted through the line manager rather than the staff.

Performance Planning and Objective Setting

Performance planning and appraisal should be the process by which critical objectives and job behaviors are identified, set for the individuals, and the resources and steps needed to attain them documented. Performance planning/appraisal is one of the most fundamental processes that can be established to help management meet an institution's goals. Unfortunately, most managers dread the appraisal portion of the process. Worse, they tend to approach it retrospectively, and hence emphasize its judgmental aspects. Little attention is given to the establishment of concrete, measurable goals. Still less is reserved for periodic reviews. This is unfortunate, as frequent adjustments may be needed if the corporation is to meet its operational and strategic goals. By contrast, when proper time is devoted to planning performance goals, and when communication between the employee and the manager is good, the employee will clearly know what is expected, what his priorities should be, and what factors he should utilize to influence outcomes.

Well written goals also provide the manager with a frame of reference to coach the employee during the appraisal cycle. Managers often wait until the end of the performance period to provide constructive feedback and praise, and this is sometimes too late. Furthermore, many managers at the middle levels and above do not want to review performance planning and appraisals from others. The inconsistency here is obvious; if high expectations are to be demanded and rewarded, the process must be used at all levels.

In the past, the use of management by objectives (MBOs) did much to make expectations concrete and trackable. Unfortunately, the MBO process has often been misused or misunderstood. The chief mistake has been tying achievement of objectives to pay. Not surprisingly, managers often preferred to set targets low enough to ensure they could be met. In today's dynamic environment it is difficult to predict exactly what will happen 12 months in advance, and employees should not be forced to do so. Instead, an employee should be encouraged to establish "stretch" goals. Stretch goals acknowledge uncertainty, recognizing the variables and assumptions that underlie them. Through periodic coaching sessions, the manager and the employee can assess the "correctness" of these goals and make small adjustments based on factors outside the employee's control, such as changes in market forces, the economic environment, legislation, and so on. Additionally, new items may need to be added that could not be accounted for or were altogether unknown at the time the original goals were set.

Most firm-wide performance appraisal processes concentrate on the "bottom line." They ignore "people" objectives and fail to consider how managers achieve their goals. Conversely, a good performance plan contains explicit human resource or "people management" objectives in such areas as staffing, rewards, communications, equal opportunity and affirmative action, employee development, and employee relations. Only when a manager is made to understand that these are key objectives that affect his or her performance rating and pay are the objectives likely to be accomplished. Otherwise, managers will follow their natural inclination to restrict their attention to technical matters which were the basis for their previous successes.

A strictly bottom-line orientation can lead to behaviors that are counterproductive for the organization. Most disturbingly, it encourages a "results at all costs" attitude similar to that arising from misapplication of MBOs. True, a bottom-line focus quickly lets the individual know how he or she is doing. But it provides no frame of reference for periodically considering what the employee should stop doing, start doing, or what impact the individual is having on other employees. At times, it also begs the question of whose bottom line really counts. With customer demand driving an increasing interdependence among units in a financial services business, there will be many times when one unit must make a tradeoff for the sake of another.

The appraisal process should be an ongoing one with heavy emphasis on counseling—concerning good performance and bad performance alike. Praise at regular intervals is reinforcing and motivating to an employee who is achieving high levels of performance. The coaching portion is a major aspect of improving performance and helping the employee be successful. It is also a way to address the need for additional training—both on the job and off. The key is to use past performance primarily as a platform for focusing on the future. Coaching reduces the employee's tendency to become defensive, and permits a mutual concentration on improvement. It also reduces the manager's uneasiness about confronting the employee in a negative way, an attitude which inhibits frank and honest appraisal.

As with training on compensation practices, all new managers should receive a considerable amount of performance-appraisal training. Training should include role playing, and deal with writing performance standards, coaching, conducting performance appraisals, and managing unsatisfactory performers. Since the manager's subordinates' accomplishments are key to the manager's own future, a training program should occur very early in the manager's new assignment. Such training boosts the manager's confidence, creates an excellent opportunity for him to get to know his people, and sets the tone and standards for what to expect. Employees equally need some information on how the system works and why it is important to their future.

There is a natural tendency for managers to complain about the design of the forms used, the rating scales, and other aspects of appraisal tools. These complaints are understandable, but misdirected. Their emphasis must be on the process, not the administrative procedures.

The simple fact that a performance appraisal system is administered through many line managers means there will be differences in interpretation and execution. Use of many different approaches would therefore cause confusion among employees and managers alike. A common administrative system, on the other hand, permits a common "language" across managerial groups when dealing with staffing matters. Likewise, it enables common training programs and facilitates human resource audits/assessments across business units. A common system also gives a better chance of employees' perceiving the process as fair and equitable.

A change in a performance appraisal system should only occur when the current system becomes ineffective. For one thing, managers do not like to change their habits, and for another, employees often are apprehensive about such change. Major changes or minor "fine-tuning" changes should both be accompanied with excellent, well-conceived, field-tested communications.

The key success factor for an appraisal system is top management support, especially through role models. The CEO needs to establish the desired tone for appraisals through his own reviews of direct reports. Even well-designed systems can be unintentionally undercut by high-placed managers whose personal styles do not match the system's norms.

MEASURING PROGRESS

For many years, measuring the progress or the effectiveness of the programs and policies implemented by the human resource function was resisted. At times, the measurements were distinctly of interest to line management, who normally had to provide input to the measurement process. At other times, the human resource function itself resisted measurement, either because it lacked the needed analytic skills or because it feared that results would not reveal much value-added.

Measurements range from limited evaluations such as those used in training programs, to opinion surveys of overall employee satisfaction. Several of these are covered as follows to give thoughts and perspective, not to be comprehensive. It is assumed that the standard measurements for such routine staff work as compensation and benefit surveys are being done.

Employee Opinion Surveys

Use of employee opinion surveys has been growing as a management tool since the mid-1960s. The development and administration of surveys is a science and does require expertise either from within the firm or from a consulting organization that has expertise in this specific field. Not only how a question is asked, but the placement of the question in the survey can affect the outcome.

In deciding to use employee opinion surveys as a measurement tool, top management must agree on who the client is and what process is to be used to manage the data. Over the years, the experience of leading companies indicates that while the primary client for the survey process is top management, the emphasis should be on helping first-line managers. In other words, although top management gives the political and financial backing to sponsor the use of the surveys, first-line managers are the real beneficiaries. Thus, the majority of questions should be answerable in an action-planning way by a first-line manager, without his having to be continually "transparent" (e.g., "I'll tell the employees," or "I'll tell headquarters").

The most successful survey processes start with top management determining what broad subjects they want addressed, usually key success factors as they relate to human resources. The topics should address the company's strategies, goals, values, top management, pay practices, career opportunities, job satisfaction, utilization, training, and so on. Once the survey has been designed, it should be tested on various groups of employees. Next, the population needs to be identified. To ensure proper effectiveness as a change tool, the smallest discrete management unit that can be coded and yet give employees assurance of anonymity should be used. Usually groups of five to seven or more are safe. Managers need to be trained in the survey process, their role in it, how to interpret their data, and how to feed it back to employees in a department meeting setting that is non-threatening, but frank and open.

As managers complete their action plans they should send them up the line, with each level of management not only consolidating the material of managers under them, but adding value to the action plans in their capacity as coaches. To increase effectiveness and follow-through, action plans should be added to the managers' own performance objectives and ultimately to their performance appraisals. One company has adopted the approach that the top division manager will write personal letters commending the managers who rank in the top 10 percent in overall morale index ratings. The executive also writes to the bottom 10 percent reflecting personal concern with the low rating, and expressing confidence that it will improve in the next survey. While this method can be threatening, it reflects the serious nature of management's concern for human resource issues.

A number of companies also have the results of each division presented to the top management committee of the business by the division head. The fact that the management committee is usually made up of peers adds a bit of competition to the process, but also develops a broader, shared understanding for morale issues across the company by top management. Later, support for changes in human resource programs, policies, and practices will develop more easily since the need is better understood.

After one to four meetings to discuss high and low points and develop action plans to improve the work environment before the next survey, a manager should take the results up the line to the next level. Upper levels of management should not be allowed to see individual data until it is brought from the bottom up. For a large business unit such as a division, some companies use a gross summary form covering six to 12 key items to stimulate upper management's curiosity. One firm calls this a "flash report," a name that signals its chief usefulness is as a status rather than an action-oriented report. This bottoms-up, action-oriented approach makes what could be a threatening process for lower-level management a positive tool for letting the manager and the company know how things are going at that time. Employees who see management interest—and most important, action—know that management does care and values their opinions. Where employees have formed inappropriate opinions, it permits management to clear up misunderstandings.

A key factor in such a process is ensuring management support and employee awareness and understanding at all levels. The process must be built on trust and confidence. The process is also not one to be done once every several years. An established time schedule should be known by all participants (e.g., every 12, 18, or 24 months). Timely feedback of the results, such as four to six weeks after the survey is taken, will help underline its importance. Each company will need to decide whether the survey will be taken at the work site or at home. Experience indicates that it is much more effective for nonexempts to complete the survey during working hours, whereas many professionals (exempt employees) prefer the leisure of their home or a trip to complete the survey. In any event, the offer to give work time alone shows that management deems feedback important.

While division managers should be permitted to add some professionally written and tested questions, a common set of core questions should be used by all units in order to permit comparisons across business units. Some companies have formed a group to exchange data and agree to ask the exact same questions at about the same time each year. Special surveys can be used to assess the interest, awareness, or satisfaction in specific items such as flexible benefits and smoking policies.

Although surveys can be helpful, caution must be exercised to prevent the means from becoming the end. When too much importance is placed on survey results, especially in a manager's pay/performance rating, attempts may be made to manipulate employees in order to improve results. Keeping the emphasis on the survey as a first-line manager's tool lessens this possibility. A technique practiced by one large company is to ask managers to predict morale results before the survey is taken. This practice has raised comfort levels and produced a high level of manager commitment to addressing survey findings; the tool and the results thus become managers', and they want the data back as quickly as possible.

Business Results

To be most effective, human resource measures have to be linked with business results. A recent survey by a large independent business association of about 500 human resource executives indicated that one of the most important needs for the future was to link business planning with human resource planning. Respondents also said that no one made the link well. It will take some time for the line managers and the human resource professionals to build into the system the tools necessary and obtain the level of experience needed to make the connections with a sufficient degree of accuracy. However, some firms are making good progress.

First, they are making human resource planning an integral part of the planning cycle of the business. This puts pressure on the human resource people to learn more about the business, so that they can ask line managers the right questions and help determine the impact of change from a human resource perspective: If, for instance, the firm is going into a new business, product, or service, what kind of skills will be needed? Does the organization have them now? Where are they? What kind of training is required? Are job descriptions/evaluations ready? Do people need some type of incentive pay? What is the labor market for these skills? These are typical of questions that must be asked. A more difficult situation arises when a change of business will result in staff reductions or the divestiture of a business unit. Plans must be ready to deal with the effects of unemployment compensation rates, changes in image in the business and recruiting marketplaces, possible third-party actions, and other adverse effects, including what happens to the people directly involved.

Second, integrating human resources into business planning increases the need for human resource professionals to do environmental scanning and to translate findings into probable impact on the business. Assessment demands a broad knowledge of risk analysis, trends in compensation schemes, employment levels, labor legislation, third-party strategies, short- and long-range workforce trends, and changes in working patterns. Linking these factors perceptively to the firm's current and future business strategies can be difficult for human resource professionals, but it also makes their jobs more rewarding and enables them to provide greater value-added service to the firm.

Human resources should assist line managers at all levels in assessing the negative impact of short-run decisions. If a line manager significantly increases profit in one year, but does so either through inappropriate reductions in the salary program, by understaffing (assuming understaffing caused excessive overtime or higher turnover, for example), or by lowering the quality of hires (in order to lower starting salaries), then human resources must report these explanations to higher management on a timely basis. This is necessary both to minimize inappropriate behavior and to ensure that bottom-line rewards are not given for such behavior. Equally, good management practices should not go unrewarded. Among such practices are quality hiring, continuous development of good people for the whole organization, proper recognition of top performers, creation of good morale, minimization of turnover and grievances, and drive for equal opportunity and affirmative action. By contrast, after naming its branch manager of the year, one company discovered from a group of minority employees that the manager's branch had failed an equal opportunity audit by the government. That firm now requires the human resources executive to input to all division management performance appraisals/assessments.

COMMUNICATIONS CHANNELS

Internal Channels

The fast pace of change in the financial services industry, especially after a long period of relatively little change, has created fears, doubts and interest in what is happening in the firm. The media interest has added an additional demand to the internal channels. Too often employees can hear or read about something happening in their company from the media before they hear it from their own management. Studies show that employees prefer to hear news from their own managers. Noncommunication not only creates resentment and fears, it also makes lower-level managers look foolish when they are not told either. If managers are not generally aware of what is going on in the company, they are seen as powerless, a characterization that spills over into their effectiveness.

Each firm needs to establish an inventory of the various communications channels, and then to audit their effectiveness. Many companies have been surprised to find that many managers never received either the videos or the brochures/newsletters that were prepared for them. Both written and verbal channels need to be considered. Management newsletters, forums, management development programs, video reports, and so on should be tailored to managers' needs. Where practical, using the first-line manager as the primary conduit for information is desirable. Personnel research studies show that the satisfaction of employees receiving good communication from managers can be as much as 100 percent higher than the satisfaction of employees who rate communication low. Studies comparing like business units also show that high and low morale groups exist, even where all the traditional items, such as pay, benefits, and career opportunity, are the same. The difference is in management practices—communications being the biggest factor.

Every opportunity should be used to send messages. "Brown bag" lunches, quarter-century club dinners, company picnics, retiree clubs, skip-level interviews, house organs, and video reports all carry a human resource message. While to a gratifying extent employees are genuinely interested in hearing the business discussed in these forums, their real interest is in the human resource matters that apply to them.

Most financial institutions do not have third-party organizations representing their work force. Consequently, these companies need to have in place alternative channels to the normal chain of command. Besides opinion surveys, these might include suggestion plans, quality circles, skip-level interviews, and open-door or anonymous-letter channels that permit quick, fair investigation of employees' concerns. The true test of the value of these channels is whether employees trust and use them. Any large organization will have problems, which will either surface through internal channels or external outlets. On the face of it, solving the problem through internal channels may seem costly. But once problems are made external, they tend to become more severe, and the dialog confrontational. Resolution consequently becomes expensive. The price paid in a few messy cases handled through outside channels can therefore be higher than the cost of ongoing positive programs for all employees.

The key to the success of internal channels is top management support and involvement. Active participation in all channels by all levels of management will enable the firm to meet or exceed its goals, make more rapid changes to respond to the marketplace, and keep employee morale at a higher level, resulting in better customer relations.

External Channels

Because of the rapid changes taking place in the labor market, it is essential that the human resource function play an active role externally. In addition to active participation in professional societies, a participation in business coalitions or consortiums at international, federal, state, and local levels is important. Topics of pay (e.g., comparable worth, overtime, prevailing wages), benefits (e.g., pension legislation, medical costs, and regulations), staffing (e.g., hiring, business closure regulations/legislation), terminations (e.g., employment at will, benefits continuation), health and safety (e.g., visual display terminal use, rest breaks, smoking policies, and medical exams), all require a concerted effort by an industry group or multi-industry activity to influence proposed legislation to ensure workability.

New initiatives to solve social problems speak directly to the communities in which the firm does business. Participating in business groups on health to make the health care system more effective for all who use it, helping in the development of day-care facilities, and sponsoring the formation of hospice and home care, for example, all communicate to the community the values of the corporation. In addition to affecting customer attitudes, corporate social action also affects employees' attitudes about their company as a place to work.

Communications Planning

Most firms underestimate the need for a specific communications strategy on a planned basis at the beginning of each business year. Consequently, communication is often "event driven." Since events are problems in many cases, the substance of these messages is often negative. Positive news is equally often left unsaid. A specific communications plan for the year, organized by audience (employees, managers, community, government, educational institutions, and the media), should be made. The funds to support the effort should be budgeted. Where practical, a follow-up measurement as to the effectiveness of the communications should be part of the plan.

CONCLUSION

The critical success factor for a service business is its people. How they are hired, motivated, rewarded, developed, and terminated can have a significant impact on the bottom line. For these reasons, CEOs will continue to put increasing demands on the human resource function for playing a major role in the business process.

26 The CEO's Change Agenda

ROBERT N. GOGEL

> I've spent the last two years pushing this company in a new direction. I just can't get anything to happen. I don't know which way to turn next.
>
> —CEO of an insurance company

Rapid changes across many fronts—technology, the economic environment, government regulation, international markets—are forcing financial services institutions to make fundamental changes in the way they compete. Often they must transform a wide range of operations areas and the way those operations interrelate. Yet when senior managers try to maneuver their organization through that kind of change, they frequently collide with entrenched organizational routine. Their comments, like that of the CEO quoted previously, reflect their frustration:

> My organization is like a bowl of mush. When I reach in and try to take hold of something, the harder I squeeze, the more slips through my fingers.

> I feel like I'm the engineer of a long train roaring down the tracks. I don't know whether I'm in control, or all those cars are just pushing me along. It's really frightening.

While the obstacles to strategic change are formidable, the rewards for surmounting them are great. A financial services institution gains a powerful competitive edge when top management effects strategic change more quickly and at lower cost than the competition. The experience of one CEO is illustrative.

In 1980, after decades of steady growth, a leading financial services firm experienced declining financial performance. Senior management realized that a

---

The author wishes to acknowledge the support and contributions of Larry Bennigson and Howard Schwartz, both Senior Vice-Presidents with the MAC Group, in preparing this chapter.

fundamental change in strategy was essential. A new CEO was appointed and charged with reestablishing the firm's competitive position.

The new CEO believed that the firm's future success demanded a more consolidated, market-focused organization. He drew together his top reports to develop a clear, new vision statement. He and his senior team then communicated this vision throughout the organization. The new strategic focus would, the CEO emphasized, provide significant opportunity for the current management group. But he also stressed that managers would have to alter their values. Their orientation had to shift from individualism, complacency, and products, to "cooperation, competitiveness, and customers." To tighten control, the CEO established new performance measures. For example, he introduced monthly progress reviews against the new plan. To encourage consolidation, he changed the reward system for top managers to emphasize firm-wide performance. Within the first year, grass-roots activity in support of customer service had increased markedly. People were excited about the opportunities for initiative. Cooperation replaced a "fiefdom" mentality. The firm subsequently enjoyed consecutive quarterly earnings increases, while expanding its market share.

Unfortunately, success stories like this are rare. More often, the efforts of top management are marked by a series of false starts and a failure to meet financial goals. And while recent literature has touted the need for financial services institutions to become more adaptable, it has offered little advice about *how* to achieve such a change.

THE DEMANDS OF STRATEGIC CHANGE

Senior executives increasingly face the need for a new kind of change—more pervasive, comprehensive, and sharply divergent from the behavior and values of the past. Many also sense the need for management methods that can stimulate the creativity essential to success in today's marketplace. Lacking apparent alternatives, top management usually resorts to traditional techniques: They alter structure, modify some systems, and move a few key people.

Manipulating those "hard" systems is, however, not enough. When people must radically change their beliefs and behavior, there must be more than mere obedience to orders and an automatic response to measurement systems. A commitment to a new vision of the firm becomes essential. Employees must internalize new values that will motivate new behavior. To elicit the changes necessary for success, top management must also alter "soft" systems—including beliefs about the firm and its future, and the style of key managers. The unique challenge for senior managers today is to alter "soft" and "hard" systems simultaneously, while ensuring that they complement and reinforce one another.

How *do* some senior managers achieve strategic change that is effective, comprehensive, and enduring, when others use substantial human and material resources without gaining lasting change? Three years of detailed research on a broad range of financial services institutions, and 10 years of experience working with senior executives, indicate that certain activities are key.

The result of this study by the MAC Group was a "change agenda," a guide for senior managers undertaking strategic change. This chapter presents the agenda, while concentrating on the particular challenges of strategic change for CEOs. The lessons drawn are equally valuable, however, for all senior managers heading up a major change effort. Following the agenda can help top management focus energy on critical issues, win broad support for the new strategy, and establish enduring change.

The change agenda is most valuable for confronting the kind of fundamental and comprehensive challenge that may come only once or twice in a senior executive's career. Yet when it does come, the response must be decisive. How well or poorly the executive handles strategic change, which may take but a few years, can outshine—or eclipse—a long and distinguished career.

AN AGENDA FOR SUCCESSFUL STRATEGIC CHANGE

The MAC Group found that senior managers are most successful when they focus their energy on six change agenda items:

- Build knowledge
- Develop a shared vision
- Determine the desired changes in values
- Translate new values into concrete behavior
- Reorient power to support new values and behavior
- Harness high-impact management systems

These items are interdependent. Change efforts that manifest all six items are most likely to establish lasting alterations throughout the organization. Efforts that are missing one or more items seem to run into trouble. Where the missing items have been added, the pace of change has accelerated and its costs have been contained.

Leading Strategic Change

In addition, the MAC Group discovered that accomplishment depends not only on *what* top management does, but *how* it does it. Successful senior executives lead the change, as well as manage it. They use all the tangible and intangible power available to win broad commitment to the new direction. They know the symbolic impact of their actions, and systematically send implicit and explicit messages that further the change process.

When the senior person does not provide active leadership of the change effort, a number of problems are likely to surface. In many cases, ambitious players attempt to step into the leadership role, each operating from his own parochial perspective. The result is political in-fighting, as interest groups try to promote their own views of the best strategy for the institution. Without cohesive leadership, a credible vision of a new strategy is unlikely to emerge—and even a redirection of investment tends to be misinterpreted. As a result, employees consider the changes they experience as arbitrary and disruptive; confusion and insecurity grow. People react by trying to block new ideas in order to sustain the status quo. Those at lower levels retain old values and try to subvert or obstruct "new direction" programs. Often there is an exodus of good people.

Most senior executives realize that strong leadership is essential to prevent that kind of misunderstanding and resistance. Yet the conditions under which they must lead seem unfamiliar and confusing. Many important goals appear to be mutually exclusive. Although they want to develop creativity and broad commitment to the new strategy, they worry about losing control over the change process. While they feel a certain level of secrecy is necessary to avoid tipping off the competition, they also want to develop understanding and acceptance of the new direction throughout the firm.

In fact, no single approach will resolve all the dilemmas associated with strategic change. Every major change effort requires a process that fits the particular needs of the organization. The change agenda, while not marking a course, does provide a map of the territory. It identifies the activities of those who set useful priorities, avoid pitfalls, and institutionalize new behavior and values.

THE ROLE OF THE CHANGE AGENDA

The change agenda items represent activities that are essential to the success of any strategic change effort. The two cases that follow illustrate the way these six items interact to determine the outcome of a strategic change program. The cases demonstrate the importance of addressing *all* of the items. In one large regional bank, initial change efforts were marked by confusion and increasing skepticism. Only after top management incorporated "missing" items into the change program did real changes in behavior match espoused new values. The bank then began moving toward its new strategic goals. In the other example, that of a national brokerage firm, the CEO operated very differently. He appeared to address many of the change agenda items, at least in part. But his approach promoted conditions that were very different from those suggested by the change agenda. As a result, the change effort was mired in resistance and confusion. Serious losses were sustained in both financial and human terms before the CEO recognized the need to revise his approach to the change program.

Case I: Vision and Values without Power and Systems

In the mid-1970s, a large regional bank began growing extensively in the national and international markets. A new CEO with a strong record in corporate banking was brought in. Shortly after his appointment, the CEO concluded that the bank needed an explicit strategy to respond to the new challenges of deregulation, increasing competition, technological innovation, and the projected growth in the corporate and international market.

The CEO decided to make the formulation of a new strategy highly visible early in the process. He hired a planner and gave him strong, visible support. The planner led top management through a lengthy process of strategy development. Committees of top managers were formed to analyze the bank's position in each of its major markets. They developed recommendations about strategic direction, priorities, the definition of the businesses, and the direction of investment. A steering committee, headed by the CEO, utilized the working committee reports to develop a strategy, a statement expressing a new vision of the bank's future, and a set of objectives.

While developing its mission statement, the steering committee realized that the proposed goals would require a fundamental change in the bank's culture. The committee addressed the idea of cultural change explicitly, and held a series of meetings to define a new management style. One goal of the new strategy was to accelerate the bank's penetration into the corporate and international markets. The committee realized that this objective called for new values. The bank would have to develop more profit-oriented attitudes and a more "go-getting" approach. It would need more cooperation and collaboration across organizational lines, greater risk-taking and innovation, and a more analytical approach to decision making. Steering committee members were also careful to emphasize that many traditional values would be maintained. They wanted, for example, to retain the commitment to being a strong local bank, while expanding into national and international markets.

A statement describing the mission, objectives, and new managerial style was distributed throughout the bank. In addition, the CEO discussed the new vision of the bank's future in external and internal publications and personal appearances. The bank was also restructured. A corporate banking division was created to develop and serve the national and international markets. The rest of the bank was reorganized to establish divisions for various functions and geographic regions. There were, however, no changes in personnel at the top of the organization. There was no sizable reallocation of resources. The bank neither got out of, nor markedly raised its commitment to, any of its businesses. Essentially, it operated as it had in the past, although in a significantly altered organization.

During the next few years, the bank floundered. Despite verbal commitment to the new vision, values, and behavior, little change actually occurred. In part, managers hesitated because they were not sure how to go about doing what was being asked of them. Managers at the second and third levels down were not convinced that the CEO really meant what he said. When they looked around, they could see no one else acting according to the new principles—not even top management. Moreover, when they looked down, they saw potential massive resistance to the new style. The CEO and his top people had difficulty getting the businesses to provide the information necessary to reallocate resources. Investment continued to go into the businesses headed by officers with the most informal power, without justification of fact-based analysis. Product development lagged. Furthermore, although current products were technologically competitive, they were not selling at reasonable prices and clearly were not going to be profitable.

The CEO realized that the change process had stalled. He initiated a review to determine the obstacles to change. The review revealed that several key structures and systems discouraged new behavior. Yet resistance to the redistribution of power blocked resolution of those problems. Managers closely guarded their turf. Management at all levels, including the CEO, hesitated to shift power away from loyal staff.

After the points of resistance were identified, the CEO moved to resolve them. In a significant step, he altered the top management decision-making process to make it more consistent with the new values. That change was crucial because top management decision-making was an important high-impact system that strongly affected decision-making at other levels. The decision-making style at the top had been essentially one-on-one. Discussion was unstructured and unscheduled. Because people did not know in advance what issues would be considered, they were unable to line up staff to do analysis.

To transform that decision-making approach into a more orderly and fact-based process, the CEO established new senior management committees. Each committee had an identified purpose and a staff that supported the flow of decisions and published a decision calendar. The new decision-making process then served as a model for other levels of management. Other structures were also targeted for change. To be more customer-driven, for example, the bank had to strengthen its marketing capability. The CEO established a new marketing function powerful enough to drive the development of marketing skills. To give the function muscle, he recruited a forceful marketing executive from another bank and gave the executive ready and visible access to the CEO's office.

The change program included new values emphasizing a more profit-oriented, ambitious managerial approach. To support those values, the CEO established a new reporting system at the business unit level. Among the most significant of the new reports was a margin report reaching down three levels into the organization. The margin reports were used to identify profit contributions by each of the major businesses. The reports institutionalized the belief that profitability should guide decision making. Even more importantly, they were used as a high-impact system to significantly affect resource allocation.

In the most striking instance of power reallocation, the CEO forced top managers to reevaluate the new vision itself. Entry into the international market had been a central feature of the vision. The margin reports clearly revealed that such a goal was unreasonable. The CEO decided to reduce the international market division drastically. He closed several overseas locations and cut staffing in the remaining division offices. When he announced the departure of the division head, he made it clear that the bank's interests would prevail over division attempts to protect turf.

Various mechanisms were developed to encourage and support risk-taking and innovation. One of the most important was a quarterly review process. It began at the top between the CEO and the division heads. Within each division, a regular review process was established down to the individual business level. The reviews were specifically designed to encourage initiative and independent decision-making at lower levels. More open communication was encouraged throughout the business. A series of regular meetings between various levels was instituted. A new periodical for loan officers was introduced, and all communications systems were overhauled. The CEO also established a new product management system to drive product development. The new system bridged the gap between the marketing sector and the computer operations staff who design new products and maintain old ones. It provided open lines of communication between the two groups, bringing them together to set annual sales, profit, cost, and performance objectives for major products.

The reallocation of power, and creation or reorganization of high-impact systems, gave force to the values articulated by the vision statement. Without the vision, the changes in structure and systems would have been confusing and alienating. In conjunction with the new values, the structural changes helped move people in the direction the CEO desired. The CEO's leadership infused the new values with legitimacy. At the same time, the changes in structure and systems strengthened his influence by making his messages credible.

Three years after the structural changes were introduced, their effects were evident. The bank had achieved a considerably higher level of earnings, becoming competitive with its peer group. It made major acquisitions to fill in the markets it wanted to enter and added new capabilities that corresponded to the vision. Improvements in service and new product introduction helped to expand its customer base and market share. At the end of the third year, there was a strong sense of optimism throughout the bank.

Case II: Power and Systems without Shared Vision and Values

In the mid-1970s, a new CEO was appointed to head up a major brokerage company. Although the firm was developing globally and becoming increasingly technology-driven, it moved in slow, incremental steps. The CEO had grown up with the company, and knew its inner workings, its established values, its management style—and disapproved of most of them. While the company had kept pace with the economy, the CEO was convinced that it had the potential to be a high flier. He found its moderate pace and performance unacceptable. What he valued were new, higher growth opportunities, ideally in high-technology fields and services. He set out to change the direction of the firm. Having spent most of his professional life in the organization, he knew its strong beliefs about the proper way to manage. He felt, in fact, that the beliefs about proper management were so dominant they outweighed the impetus to make money. Those who lived by the existing beliefs were, in his view, emphasizing the wrong things. He considered the old culture an albatross, obstructing the transformation he had in mind. During his years with the company, the CEO had developed a new vision of its potential. Drawn from his own experience and beliefs, the new vision was strong, clear, and coherent. It emphasized rapid growth, innovation, and an entrepreneurial, risk-taking style. The CEO rejected the entire body of old beliefs, which had stressed methodical planning, short-term performance, and a stable growth rate. He developed the vision alone, then sought to communicate it single-handedly. An astute and skilled communicator, the CEO bypassed his top management and went directly to more than three dozen managers of strategic business units. He carried the message of the new vision, using the symbolic power of his office with flair and conviction. His speeches to training classes and management conferences, for example, were published in-house and distributed throughout the firm. He personally visited the top team within each business to conduct one-on-one issue-oriented reviews of the businesses. He was careful to ensure that his messages and actions consistently reinforced the same themes. He spent time with those who best promoted his vision, and developed "heroes" who represented the new values. He selected people whose skills supported the new visions to be speakers at management forums, and used them as models in his own speeches. He made clear the criteria he was using to judge people, and gave tangible and intangible rewards to those who met his criteria. He became personally involved in the design of management training systems to ensure that they developed skills and commitment consonant with the new vision.

He established new reporting systems to encourage people to be more strategically focused. One system, for example, tied manager compensation levels to performance against strategic objectives, as well as day-to-day operating objectives. He complemented the systems by giving highly visible recognition to people who represented the new vision. He also made sure the systems promoted those people. He made explicit changes in the power structure. He eliminated staff positions that seemed to interfere with the momentum he wanted to build. The entire planning staff, for example, was signficantly reduced and a zero-based planning effort was instituted. Those who led businesses that represented the new direction, such as high-technology shops, received greater power. Risk-takers and innovators were given greater freedom to try new ideas.

Clearly, this CEO addressed many of the six change agenda items. Yet his approach to some and partial neglect of others sabotaged his efforts. Although he communicated the vision and instituted new systems, in doing so he ignored most of his top staff. He imposed his own vision rather than developing a *shared* vision. As a result, he alienated many people needed to help implement the new strategy. Although he knew the power of the old beliefs, he tried to eliminate the entire set, rather than to reinterpret and use them selectively. In his speeches, and in meetings with managers, he insisted that only the new beliefs were of value.

His wholesale dismissal of the old belief system created needless resistance. Furthermore, the new vision did not match reality for the older businesses in the company's portfolio. These businesses felt excluded by the CEO's message. The CEO seemed, in fact, to devalue all the mature businesses. Managers who were part of those businesses failed to see any place for themselves in the "new" fast-moving corporation. When they tried to translate the CEO's message, they saw themselves, like the old culture, dismissed entirely.

The CEO was skilled in winning most people over to the new values. Unfortunately, however, he bypassed the management levels that could translate the values into concrete behavior up and down the line. His personal visits inspired top management in many of the businesses. Yet there was no ongoing support to help them translate inspiration into action. Employees who had ready access to the CEO were best able to translate the vision into behavior. But they were the very people who already represented the new vision. Those who had the most difficulty matching up to the vision also had the greatest difficulty reaching the CEO. No other resources were available to help them translate the vision into day-to-day reality.

Although the new high-impact systems were quite powerful, many affected only a small number of "heroes" directly. New measurement systems were undermined as bypassed managers dug in their heels and retained old ways of doing things. Project approval systems, controlled by middle management, choked off the flow of proposals from those responding to the CEO's call for new ideas. Similarly, the new strategic tracking system was administered by managers who had not bought into the CEO's vision. As a result, the system actually intensified the problem it was meant to ameliorate. The managers followed the firm's traditional values ("make your numbers") and emphasized the financial measures in the system. By doing so they reinforced lower level management focus on short-term performance. People became confused, wondering how they were supposed to put into action the high-flying concepts the CEO expressed.

During the following year, the costs of the change effort mounted. Valuable people left the firm. Morale was low. There was declining respect for the CEO's "heroes," who were increasingly perceived as yes-men. Innovative products languished as key product development people grew more averse to risks. The firm seemed to be drawing away from the CEO, a movement he himself could sense. He began to recognize the need to change his approach.

The CEO's response was belated perhaps, but the situation was not irrecoverable. He encouraged critical assessment of the change effort. During the year that followed, he moved to respond to the criticism that emerged. To build a widely shared vision, he included goals appropriate to the core businesses, as well as the fast-moving ones. He emphasized teamwork and an integrated approach to achieving new goals. He selected outstanding performers in the traditional businesses to be conference speakers. In his own speeches, he used models who interpreted the new values successfully within the context of the core businesses. He abandoned his "Lone Ranger" approach, and involved his top management group in promoting the new strategy. With them, he developed new systems to advance the new goals. He reaffirmed their worth with symbolic actions, personal visits, and public recognition for their efforts. He also gave them more tangible power, assigning them an important role in generating innovative products. In addition, the CEO worked with the managers of each business to design new measurement systems. The resulting systems both encouraged behavior consistent with the new values, and were appropriate to the business. He increased the power of R&D and marketing in every business. He also established regular channels for these functions to report constraints and new opportunities.

By the end of the second year, distinct improvement was evident. Morale rose as people in all businesses again felt that they were valued by the company. There was less turnover and more optimism. Training programs, tailored to individual businesses, provided more motivated and appropriately skilled people for each business. People throughout the company better understood the CEO's goals, and felt their contributions mattered. Although the firm continues to repair damage from the earlier period, the change effort is visibly—and measurably—more successful.

ELEMENTS OF THE CHANGE AGENDA

In the previous section, two cases showed how the agenda items work together to determine the outcome of a strategic change program. This section discusses the six items of the change agenda separately, but it is important to keep in mind that in reality they are interdependent. (See Exhibit 26.1 for an outline of specific activities associated with each agenda item.)

Build Knowledge

Most CEOs understand that a sound knowledge base is crucial to any major change effort. Those who employ the knowledge-building process most effectively use it to achieve two goals. One aim is to develop accurate knowledge about the firm and its competitive environment. The second is to build "ownership" of the new strategy.

The first task is often done in the context of strategic planning. Experience, experimentation, rigorous data gathering, and analysis provide a thorough understanding of the company's industry, market, competition, and economics. The speed with which these conditions are shifting makes it important to explore new developments that may affect the firm. That information stimulates ideas about attractive strategies for the future.

A well-run knowledge-building process also clarifies the firm's distinctive competencies and behaviors that both shape and limit strategic choices. MAC Group research indicates that the most overlooked area in understanding a firm's capabilities is the firm's culture—the values and beliefs that people in the organization share about the way things should be done. It is a dangerous omission. The institution's culture colors the way people in the firm—including the CEO if he

Exhibit 26.1 Key CEO Activities

Build knowledge.	Develop knowledge about competitive environment. Gain insight into objective and cultural characteristics of the company. Build "ownership" through participation in knowledge building.
Develop a shared vision.	Demonstrate commitment to the new vision through words and actions. Build a team that can carry the vision throughout the company.
Determine the desired changes in values and beliefs.	Identify values and beliefs that appear to conflict with desired change. Reinterpret old values and beliefs so that they support the new vision. Change the values and beliefs that inevitably conflict with the new vision.
Translate new values into concrete behavior.	Establish mechanisms to help people translate new values in the context of their own jobs. Establish feedback mechanisms so managers can evaluate their own decisions. Create models of new management decision-making and behavior.
Reorient power to support new values and behavior.	Determine who will resist and who will support the change, and why. Make the change real by shifting power toward people whose skills, beliefs, and/or functions support the new direction. Link power reorientation explicity to the new values.
Harness high-impact management systems.	Determine the most influential management systems. Alter high-impact systems to support the new strategy. Create high-impact systems that focus managers' attention on strategic change issues.

shares the culture—perceive "objective" facts. Those values and beliefs are reality to members of a firm's culture, providing familiar guideposts for their behavior. When employees say, "we are service quality leaders," or "we keep our interest margins slim," for example, they are voicing cultural values that guide day-to-day decisions and drive the company's operations. Four key areas provide insight into the institution's culture: (1) the major eras of the firm's history, as marked off by key events, successes, and failures; (2) dominant leadership styles; (3) the firm's traditional success factors that drive the behavior and beliefs of the old culture; and (4) current systems and procedures that reinforce those success factors.

Because financial services institutions are facing radically new conditions, it is critical that top management understand how the firm's culture influences their own and their employees' views. If they do not, they are likely to find that "nothing fails like success." Past success factors continue to guide values and behavior, even when external conditions call for change. New strategies that diverge sharply from those considered correct are likely to be rejected, even when they fit external conditions. Furthermore, when a change in strategy threatens embedded cultural values, people become confused, and often angry and defensive. The CEO who understands his firm's culture can assess how his employees are likely to respond to different kinds of change.

Skillful CEOs also use the knowledge-building process to build "ownership" among those who have to make the new strategy work. The CEO may, for example, enlist a balance of back-office and marketing people in the knowledge-building process so that he can tap their expertise and elicit their commitment. CEOs who engage others in knowledge-building early in the process of change are better able to avoid political struggles, high costs, and lost time. Converting knowledge into action is as important as managing the knowledge-building process effectively. Unfortunately, top management in many financial services institutions loses sight of this fact. The change process then becomes bogged down at the knowledge-building stage. By paying attention to all six items of the change agenda, CEOs can avoid that kind of "analysis paralysis."

Develop a Shared Vision

A broadly based awareness of a new business vision is essential to successful strategic change. The vision defines the firm's strategy in terms of how it will position itself against the competition, how it will grow, how it will manage, and what benefits will be involved in being part of its future. Such a broadly shared vision gives direction to people, answers compelling questions about the future, and explains the actions of management.

For most CEOs, promoting a new vision calls for skills outside their ordinary repertoire. Yet developing a shared vision does not require flamboyant showmanship. It does demand keen awareness of the symbolic power of the CEO's words and actions. Whether the new vision is his own product or is developed with many other people, the CEO must demonstrate his commitment to the vision. He does so by sending many tangible and intangible messages that are at once varied and in harmony with one another.

CEOs who understand the importance of a shared vision often forge a team that will carry the vision throughout the organization. Building a team at the top is particularly difficult in large financial services institutions where top management responsibilities are delegated among several executives. Yet it is precisely within such firms that teamwork and commitment to the new vision at the top appear to be most important.

Developing a shared vision may seem to be a straightforward task, but several pitfalls jeopardize this important goal. The CEO and his team must promote the vision among very different constituencies, including employees, customers, vendors, stockholders, and regulatory authorities. The response to change within and among those groups will vary greatly. Within the firm, people may resist the new vision for a number of reasons. They may lack information or believe that the strategy is unsound. They may fear personal loss, lack confidence that they will be able to change, or be skeptical about the likelihood of real change. CEOs are most successful when they confront resistance with appropriate tools. Where there is inadequate or incorrect information, for example, a CEO can draw people into the knowledge-building process so that they understand the rationale for change. In so doing, the CEO enlists the support of, and avoids conflicts with, the key people needed to implement the change.

The CEO also has to make the vision credible, and convince others that they *can* change because they *must*. In the effort to convince others, however, the CEO faces many tests of his commitment. One test lies in the extent to which the CEO's personal activities and expressed views are matched by the way the firm spends its money, and the structure of power and rewards. A credibility gap occurs when top management preaches about change but does not back it up with a redirection of investment and other tangible actions. CEOs avoid that pitfall by ensuring that the signals related to all change agenda items are pulling in the same direction. Inevitably, however, there will be some people who continue to resist the vision because they—correctly or incorrectly—fear personal loss associated with the change. Redistribution of power will be necessary to deal with that resistance.

Determine the Desired Changes in Beliefs

A new strategy requires new behavior of many people in the organization. Because beliefs strongly influence behavior, simply providing rational, analytical arguments for change—and even changing measurement systems and organization structure—is not enough. The culture must be tailored to support the new vision. In many financial services institutions, change is derailed because the CEO ignores traditional beliefs or deals with them indirectly. The culture is then like an invisible, impenetrable shield protecting old behavior.

A large insurance company, for example, traditionally valued being on the cutting edge of technology. Market conditions convinced top management of the need to shift to a more market-oriented appproach. They transferred responsibility for generating and evaluating new product proposals from a central operations group to marketing people in the divisions. The intent of the new decision-making system was subverted, however, by the old culture. The marketing groups, imbued with the old value of being a technological leader, tried to identify the most sophisticated products rather than those with the widest market appeal. Furthermore, since technical evaluation was not their forte, they chose products lacking both market *and* technological competitiveness. The company suffered serious losses before top management recognized the problem.

CEOs can handle these intangible forces most successfully by identifying the beliefs most likely to obstruct the change process. Beliefs that make up the firm's culture are usually deeply held, however, and are not easily changed. CEOs are most effective when they *use* the power of those beliefs rather than fighting them. They can do so by retaining and reinterpreting the old beliefs that support the new vision. They show that behavior must change in order to live up to traditional values in a changing world. They move to replace only the beliefs that inevitably conflict with the new vision. Top management of one bank faced widespread resistance, for example, when they began to emphasize advanced technology and consolidation. Employees felt they were undermining traditional commitment to serving "the little man." When the CEO carried the explicit message that technology and the efficiencies of consolidation were necessary *in order* to serve the little man, much of the resistance melted away.

One effective way to spread new values is to build a team of key opinion-leaders who can communicate the new values in their own part of the organization. The team leaders must receive enough information to understand the role of the new beliefs, and enough power to back up their commitment to the new values.

Translate Values into Concrete Behavior

The new vision and values indicate the kinds of behavior that are desirable. Obviously the CEO, more than anyone else, must demonstrate these values in his own behavior. In addition, people need help in understanding what the new values mean for their own behavior.

There are several techniques that successful CEOs use to send the message down into the organization in concrete terms. Regular problem-solving meetings are one effective tool. Such meetings identify what new behavior is necessary, the obstacles to developing that behavior, and the way to overcome the obstacles. Initial meetings between the CEO and his top people create a team that can translate the new values into action. Key managers then hold similar working sessions with their own top people to explain the values in terms of particular responsibilities.

Other useful techniques include training programs to help people understand the kinds of behavior that support the new values. Top management can use internal communications to send very explicit messages about what the new values mean for particular jobs. Feedback mechanisms help key managers assess how well their actions and decisions are promoting the new vision. Brief, periodic surveys of progress against selected performance measures, for example, are a useful guide for managers. Management can use such processes to carry the message about the new direction, translate it into specific behavior, and answer questions about what the new values mean for particular jobs. In some cases, the CEO may bypass several levels of management to spread the word about a new vision. CEOs who do so successfully, however, also build informed and committed management at each level who will translate the message into on-the-job reality. One CEO, for example, spent time with managers at all levels of the organization during the early stages of the change process. He then provided highly visible rewards for the managers of pilot change efforts at each level.

If the CEO does not clearly link new values to specific behavior, people may accept the new values in principle, but may still ask, "How do the new values apply to *me*?" One CEO exemplified the mistakes that can be made when he carried the message single-handedly throughout the organization. He failed to enlist middle levels of management that could translate the message into action. Although most people in the firm seemed to accept the new vision and values, few knew what they were supposed to do to help achieve the new goals. Confusion replaced optimism, and the change effort ultimately ran aground.

Reorient Power to Support New Values and Behavior

CEOs convince people that the change is real when they allocate power selectively and consistently to support new values and behavior. Effective CEOs usually face up to issues of power redistribution directly. They shift power toward people whose skills, values, or functions support the new direction. Power reorientation is a critical issue, because extensive changes in power without a clear rationale can be detrimental. When people observe broad power shifts without understanding the intent, they question their own value to the company. The resulting low morale can sink the change effort. It is crucial for the CEO to identify the precise kinds of power changes he wants and phase them in carefully.

At upper levels of the organization, CEOs tend to consider power in terms of individuals. They delegate power to people who are highly respected and will provide leadership in achieving change. CEOs may also reach down into the organization or bring in outsiders in order to place their own people in leadership positions. This tactic must be used with discretion, however. If large numbers of people are brought into the firm, developing a shared new vision and values becomes more time-consuming and difficult.

Bypassing the normal succession process also sends a loud signal to the organization. If it is clearly linked to new values, it is a powerful incentive to support the new direction. If it is not, it is often misinterpreted in ways that can seriously damage the change process. CEOs who reorient power most skillfully use the symbolic force of their action to invest implicit power in the "their people." They use many techniques, including spending time with those they want to empower, using them as examples to be emulated, and giving exposure to their "model" behavior. Most CEOs restructure their organizations during periods of strategic change. Yet many do not recognize that by altering structure they are altering power. CEOs who understand the ramifications for power alter structure in ways that strengthen the new direction. For example, to emphasize marketing, a CEO might create customer groups where none had existed before. In some cases, the structure must change before a new strategy can be developed. In one brokerage firm, for example, the structure discouraged the divisions from sharing information. The entire company had to be restructured around customer groups. Only then could top management get the information they needed to develop a new strategy. Power redistribution is often difficult because people do not like to deal explicitly with power issues. They are uneasy because power questions tend to become zero-sum games. There will always be relative winners and losers in any power shift. The CEO can, however, find ways to benefit from the talents of people who have in fact lost the battle. He may, for example, "promote" such individuals to positions with more formal prestige but with less power to inhibit the change process. This maneuver demands considerable finesse, however. If the failure to support the new direction is perceived as power-enhancing, it can undermine the change effort. CEOs who use this tactic successfully make it clear that the "promotion" is a symbolic acknowledgment of past and potential contributions, while it reduces actual power.

For many CEOs, reorienting power is difficult because they must take power away from managers who have been loyal to them. Too often, the CEO postpones a strategic change because it will hurt a company loyalist. The ability of a top manager to deal directly with these issues strongly affects his success in implementing a change program. The way power is reallocated is a strong signal about the CEO's commitment to the change effort.

Harness High-Impact Management Systems

All management systems affect behavior in some way and must eventually be fine-tuned to support a new strategic direction. In every financial services institution, however, some systems are more influential than others. These high-impact systems help determine the speed and success of the change effort. It is dangerous for a CEO to expect behavior to change before high-impact systems are revised to support the new direction. CEOs who get the change program moving quickly and with sustained momentum find out early which management systems have the strongest impact on behavior. They use those systems to steer the behavior of their people.

High-impact systems can take many forms. In some financial services institutions the expense or head-count budget is the control mechanism that affects managers most strongly. In others, managers are most concerned with the number and size of the capital projects they get approved. But in all companies, at least one of the resource allocation systems will be a key high-impact system. Compensation systems are often important high-impact systems that influence the perspective and behavior of managers. CEOs can also make a regular management activity into a high-impact system. For example, a CEO may use the agenda of regular executive group meetings to deal forcefully with the issues raised by the new strategy. It is not always easy for top management to identify the company's high-impact systems. Over time, these management processes seem to blend into the fabric of the organization. The primary motivating systems become all but invisible. The CEO may have to get input from line people directly affected by measurement and control systems, and from staff who are less directly affected, to pinpoint the most influential systems.

CONCLUSION

A turbulent business environment increasingly forces financial services institutions to alter their fundamental competitive strategies. The ability of top management to achieve strategic change has become a major determinant of competitive positions. Firms no longer have the luxury of spending several years, or decades, implementing strategic change. The firms that can bring about enduring change relatively quickly will establish strong competitive positions. Others will have difficulty overtaking them.

Senior executives of most financial services institutions, however, find that strategic change demands unfamiliar skills. They must *lead* the change effort, as well as manage it. They must exploit the symbolic power of their offices. Vision and values, once stable guides of behavior, must now themselves be altered. Obtaining employee commitment for the new vision and values is essential, especially as financial services institutions require greater individual creativity and initiative. Consequently, top management must ensure that both "soft" systems—vision and values—and "hard" systems—high impact systems and the power structure—reinforce each other. Like wind against the sails of a ship, shared vision and values billow out the systems and structure to impart movement. Senior managers who ignore these invisible forces will find it extremely difficult to reach their destination.

A senior executive can best meet the challenge of strategic change by employing a well-conceived approach for leading the change effort. Each strategic change program is, of course, unique. For the change effort to be successful, however, certain conditions are essential. The change agenda represents the activities that establish those requisite conditions. Although we have focused here on the CEO's use of the agenda, the agenda is equally valuable for all top managers who must lead a substantial change effort. The agenda helps to identify the major issues involved in achieving those conditions within a particular firm. It can also serve as a planning tool to ensure that the change program is sufficiently comprehensive and that the critical strengths and weaknesses of their organizations are accounted for. Senior managers who follow the agenda consider the objective, measurable features such as distribution of skills. They also seek to understand the intangible beliefs that drive behavior in the firm. They develop broad commitment to the new direction. They recognize the ways in which behavior must change, and they use tangible and intangible incentives to motivate such change. They identify potential points of resistance, and develop an approach that will bypass or overcome them. They determine whom to involve in different stages of the change effort. They utilize their formal and informal power to invest power in people who will advance the change effort, and neutralize those who would impede it. In sum, senior executives who carry out all the change agenda items succeed in orchestrating all of the tangible and intangible factors necessary to establish enduring strategic change.

Index